building
a better
future
for all

Building a Better Future for All:
Selected Speeches of United Nations Secretary-General Ban Ki-moon 2007-2012

Published by the United Nations
New York, New York 10017, United States of America

All queries on rights and licenses, including subsidiary rights,
should be addressed to:
United Nations Publications
300 East 42nd Street
New York, New York 10017
United States of America
e-mail: publications@un.org
website: un.org/publications

Requests to reproduce excerpts should be addressed to:
permissions@un.org

Paperback ISBN: 978-92-1-101271-2 | Sales No. E.13.I.1
Hard cover ISBN: 978-92-1-101274-3 | Sales No. 13.I.1 H
eISBN: 978-92-1-055995-9
United Nations Publication
Sales No. E.13.I.1

building
a better
future
for all

Selected Speeches of United Nations

Secretary-General **Ban Ki-moon**

2007-2012

Ban Ki-moon

BAN KI-MOON is the eighth Secretary-General of the United Nations. At the time of his election as Secretary-General, Mr. Ban was Minister of Foreign Affairs and Trade of the Republic of Korea. His thirty-seven years of service with the Ministry included postings in New Delhi, Washington D.C. and Vienna, and responsibility for a variety of portfolios, including Foreign Policy Adviser to the President, Chief National Security Adviser to the President, Deputy Minister for Policy Planning and Director-General of American Affairs.

Mr. Ban's ties to the United Nations date back to 1975, when he worked for the Foreign Ministry's United Nations Division. That work expanded over the years, with assignments that included service as Chairman of the Preparatory Commission for the Comprehensive Nuclear Test Ban Treaty Organization and Chef de Cabinet during the Republic of Korea's 2001-2002 presidency of the UN General Assembly.

Mr. Ban was born in the Republic of Korea on 13 June 1944. He received a bachelor's degree in international relations from Seoul National University in 1970. In 1985, he earned a master's degree in public administration from the Kennedy School of Government at Harvard University.

The Secretary-General speaks English, French and Korean. He and his wife, Madam Yoo (Ban) Soon-taek, whom he met in high school in 1962, have a son, two daughters and three grandchildren.

Mr. Ban took office on 1 January 2007. On 21 June 2011, he was unanimously re-elected by the General Assembly and will continue to serve as Secretary-General of the United Nations until 31 December 2016.

Introduction

One of the most important assets of any United Nations Secretary-General is the unique platform of the office itself. Its fundamental impartiality makes possible the exercise of good offices to defuse political tensions and promote the peaceful settlement of disputes. Its convening power allows for the bringing together of people and nations in common cause. Its perch atop the world's only universal organization gives the occupant uncommon visibility. The mix and frequency with which these and other tools are deployed is for each Secretary-General to define in the context of the times. But there is one constant: making maximum use of the so-called "bully pulpit".

Since taking office in 2007, I have delivered speeches in many settings: conference halls and conflict zones; parliaments, boardrooms and think tanks; clinics, classrooms and houses of worship. I have sought to engage the world's people about the urgent issues we face, and to rally support for the United Nations. In the process, I have learned a valuable lesson: listening is just as important as speaking. I may be the person standing at the lectern, but the concerns and hopes of people bring my role to life.

This collection of speeches aims to illuminate the work of the United Nations at a time of transition and test for the international community. The subjects range widely, but the goal is clear: peace for all, in the broadest sense of the word. I hope readers will enjoy this volume, gain a deeper understanding of our shared challenges and, most of all, join with us in promoting the values and work of our United Nations, the world's leading instrument of common progress.

BAN Ki-moon

Contents

Sustainable Development   135

Climate Change   179

Peace and Security   199

The Empowerment of Women and Youth   337

Glossary of abbreviations and acronyms   360

Credits   362

General Assembly

Address to the sixty-seventh General Assembly
A call to ambition

NEW YORK, 25 SEPTEMBER 2012

We gather annually in this great hall to look soberly, and without illusion, at the state of our world. This year, I am here to sound the alarm about our direction as a human family.

We can all see widespread insecurity and injustice, inequality and intolerance. I see governments wasting vast and precious funds on deadly weapons, while reducing investments in people. The severe and growing impacts of climate change are there before our eyes; yet too many people in power seem willfully blind to the threat.

This is a time of turmoil, transition and transformation – a time when time itself is not on our side. People want jobs and the prospect of a decent life. All too often, what they get instead is divisiveness, delay, and denial of their dreams and aspirations.

We need look no further than this room to see expressions of the thirst for progress. A large number of you are here for the first time – new leaders, installed by new voices, and expected to make decisive breaks with the past. Your people want to see results in real time, now, not the distant future.

The United Nations rightly faces the same scrutiny; the same impatience; the same demands for accountability. People do not look to this organisation to be simply a mirror reflecting back a divided world. People want progress and solutions today. They want ideas, your leadership and concrete hope for the future. Our duty is to respond to these frustrations and yearnings.

My action agenda highlights five imperatives, as I have set out in January this year: sustainable development, prevention, building a more secure world, helping countries in transition and empowering women and youth.

I take heart from important steps forward on some of these fronts. Extreme poverty has been cut in half since the year 2000. Democratic transitions are under way in the Arab world, Myanmar and many other countries. Africa's economic growth has become the fastest in the world. Asia and Latin America are making important advances.

Still, we must raise our levels of ambition. We need more from each and every one of you. And the world needs more from our United Nations.

Sustainable development is the key to our hopes for the future. It is my top priority as Secretary-General. Yet poverty and inequalities are still rampant. Our use of resources threatens the planet's limits. Ecosystems are reaching the breaking point. The world's best science tells us we must change course before it is too late.

Yesterday, the President of the World Bank and I announced that the Sustainable Energy for All initiative is ready to deliver tens of billions of dollars for energy access and efficiency. Tomorrow I will launch a new initiative – Education First. On Thursday we will announce major additional support for the Scaling Up Nutrition Movement. And over the past two years, the 260 partners in our Every Woman Every Child initiative have disbursed $10 billion in new money.

We are proving, on the ground, that well constructed partnerships can, and are, delivering results that none of us can deliver alone.

The deadline for the Millennium Development Goals is little more than three years away. We must intensify our efforts to eradicate extreme poverty. The economic crisis cannot be an excuse to default on your commitments to the basics that all people need.

Even if we achieve the MDGs, there is still a long way to go. The Rio+20 conference has pointed the way, including towards a set of sustainable development goals. These new goals and the post-2015 development agenda will guide our work for years to come. The MDGs sparked a remarkable global mobilization. These new frameworks must do the same, speaking to and inspiring people across the world.

Action on climate change remains a major piece of unfinished business. Last December, Member States agreed to reach a legally binding agreement by 2015. Now, you must make good on this promise. Time is running out on our ability to limit the rise in global temperature to two degrees centigrade.

Changing course will not be easy. But to see this as only a burden misses the bigger picture. Sustainability and the green economy offer compelling opportunities to promote jobs, growth, innovation and long-term stability. The future we want can be ours – if we act now.

J ust as there can be no peace without development, there can be no development without peace. I am profoundly concerned about continued violence in Afghanistan and in the Democratic Republic of the Congo. I urge Sudan and South Sudan to resolve all remaining post-secession issues. Somalia has made courageous advances and Libya has held its first free elections in half a century.

Gains must be nurtured and sustained. We must keep our focus on preventing conflicts before they erupt, and on settling disputes through peaceful means.

Myanmar's leaders have shown courage and determination in moving on the path of democracy and reconciliation. The country faces many challenges, from economic reform to the protection of ethnic minorities. As the Government and citizenry work together to meet these responsibilities, the international community and the United Nations must provide the strongest possible support.

The crisis in the Sahel is not getting sufficient attention and support. Poverty, fragility, drought and sectarian tensions are threats to stability across the region. Unconstitutional changes of government have taken place all too frequently. Extremism is on the rise. Arms are easy to obtain, while jobs are hard to find.

The international community needs a major concerted effort to address this alarming situation. Tomorrow, I will outline our ideas for an integrated strategy. Governments and organizations in the region, as well as international partners, will work out the details in the coming weeks. I urge you to engage and give your strong assistance.

The situation in the Sahel highlights the need to strengthen early warning for development. Sensors and seismographs across the world help us prepare for natural disasters. We must do more to detect the tremors of distress facing the poorest and most vulnerable.

We must also focus greater attention on food security and nutritional resilience. For millions of people, frequent shocks are the new norm. Food prices are increasingly volatile, provoking public anxiety, panic buying and civil disturbance. We need to bolster safety nets. We must ramp up investments in sustainable agriculture – particularly for smallholder farmers. Governments must not impose trade restrictions on grains or other agricultural products. This reduces food supplies and discourages farmers from growing more. Together, we can avoid the food crises we have seen in recent years and achieve our goal of Zero Hunger.

The situation in Syria grows worse by the day. The crisis is no longer limited to Syria; it is a regional calamity with global ramifications. This is a serious and growing threat to international peace and security, which requires Security Council action. I call on the international community – especially the members of the Security Council and countries in the region – to solidly and concretely support the efforts of Joint Special Representative Lakhdar Brahimi. We must stop the violence and flows of arms to both sides, and set in motion a Syrian-led transition as soon as possible.

Humanitarian needs are escalating, in and beyond Syria. The international community should not look the other way as violence spirals out of control. Brutal human rights abuses continue to be committed, mainly by the Government, but also by opposition groups. Such crimes must not go unpunished. There is no statute of limitations for such extreme violence. It is the duty of our generation to put an end to impunity for international crimes, in Syria and elsewhere. It is our duty to give tangible meaning to the responsibility to protect.

The winds of change in the Arab world and elsewhere will continue to blow. After decades of harsh occupation and humiliating restrictions in almost every aspect of their lives, the Palestinians must be able to realize their right to a viable state of their own. Israel must be able to live in peace and security, free from threats and rockets. The two-state solution is the only sustainable option. Yet the door may be closing, for good. The continued growth of Israeli settlements in the occupied Palestinian territory seriously undermines efforts toward peace. We must break this dangerous impasse.

I also reject both the language of delegitimisation and threats of potential military action by one state against another. Any such attacks would be devastating. The shrill war talk of recent weeks has been alarming and should remind us of the need for peaceful solutions and full respect for the UN Charter and international law. Leaders have a responsibility to use their voices to lower tensions instead of raising the temperature and volatility of the moment.

> **❝I am here to sound the alarm about our direction as a human family. This is a time of turmoil, transition and transformation – a time when time itself is not on our side.❞**

Building a more secure world also means pursuing our goal of a world free of nuclear weapons. As long as such weapons exist, we are all at risk. I look forward to a successful conference later this year on the establishment of a Middle East zone free of nuclear weapons and all other weapons of mass destruction. Iran must prove the solely peaceful intent of its programme. The Democratic People's Republic of Korea must move toward denuclearisation of the Korean peninsula. All relevant Security Council resolutions should be implemented in full and without delay.

We shall have neither peace nor development without respect for human rights and the rule of law; the empowerment of women; the protection of children; the treaties and declarations that have extended the umbrella of protection. They are our touchstones. Yesterday's high-level meeting on the rule of law sent a strong message about the importance of international law, justice and institutions within and among nations.

Over the past two weeks a disgraceful act of great insensitivity has led to justifiable offense and unjustifiable violence. Freedom of speech and assembly are fundamental. But neither of these freedoms is a license to incite or commit violence. Yet we live in a world where, too often, divisions are exploited for short-term political gain. Too many people are ready to take small flames of difference and turn them into a bonfire. Too many people are tolerant of intolerance. The moderate majority should not be a silent majority. It must empower itself, and say to bigots and extremists alike: "you do not speak for us". Responsible political and community leaders must step up at this time.

With so much at stake, the United Nations must continue to renew itself. We must deliver as one – across disciplines, structures and locations. We are building a global Secretariat to support our global presence. That means shared services, integrated approaches and innovative uses of technology.

Staff mobility is a crucial first step. This initiative is long overdue. We will be making a proposal in the weeks ahead, and we will need your support.

Let us work together for a streamlined budget process built on trust. Micromanagement serves no one – not Member States wanting quick results, and not us in the Secretariat who share your desire for excellence. As Secretary-General, I need space to manage in a dynamic environment.

Let us also prepare ourselves to harness the full power of partnerships across the range of issue areas. I will soon offer specific proposals for strengthening our partnership capacity. This will allow us to deliver more and better results, enhance accountability and improve coherence. Your support will be essential if we are to meet the many important mandates you give the United Nations.

A strengthened United Nations is a key enabler for all that we hope to achieve for the world's people. Let us prove that the UN can reform itself and keep pace.

I have always put people first, and challenges at the centre. We have worked together for solutions to the problems that matter to people by day – and that keep them up at night.

You, the world's leaders, hold in your hands the power of the state, the levers of government. Your people expect you to listen to their aspirations, and to unleash their energies and ideas. The world expects you to work with each other for the common good.

Nobody can do everything. But each of us, in our own way, can do something. Together, if we all uphold our responsibilities, we can meet today's tests, seize the opportunities of an era of dramatic change, and give new life to the principles and purposes of our founding Charter.

Address to the General Assembly
Five-Year Action Agenda:
The Future We Want

NEW YORK, 25 JANUARY 2012

Good morning and my warmest regards to you and for a happy new year. Last September I stood before you and outlined five imperatives for my second term; five key areas where we can, and must, make significant progress; five generational opportunities to creatively deliver on our core mission.

One: sustainable development.

Two: preventing conflicts and disasters, human rights abuses and development setbacks.

Three: building a safer and more secure world, which includes standing strong on fundamental principles of democracy and human rights.

Four: supporting nations in transition.

Five: working for women and young people.

Today I want to share with you an action agenda for the coming five years. A plan to make the most of the opportunities before us. A plan to help create a safer, more secure, more sustainable, more equitable future. A plan to build the future we want.

Today, I want to outline that plan in sufficient detail to capture the breadth and depth of our vision. The full Action Agenda will be distributed to you at this meeting, and will be available in all official languages later today. In the interests of transparency and information-sharing, we are also posting a link to that document on the UN Twitter account for the world to see.

The human and physical geography of our world is changing. New centres of economic dynamism are emerging. Technology continues to knit us more closely together. Yet, economic uncertainty and social inequity are widespread.

The global population has reached 7 billion people. In just five years, we will add another half billion people – all needing food, jobs, security and opportunity.

Environmental, economic and social indicators tell us that our current model of progress is unsustainable. Climate change is destroying our path to sustainability.

Ours is a world of looming challenges and increasingly limited resources. Sustainable development offers the best chance to adjust our course. That is why I placed this challenge at the top of the list. In this challenge, as in all others, we must pay special attention to the needs and priorities of Africa.

First, we are working on a final push to achieve the Millennium Development Goals.

There is a myth that development does not work. The facts show this is wrong. We have seen dramatic progress in a short time: more effective disease control. More children in primary education. Significant reductions in global poverty.

In the next five years, we will wipe out five of the world's major killers. We will end deaths from malaria, polio, new paediatric HIV infections and maternal and neonatal tetanus. And we will reduce measles mortality by 95 per cent.

We will also fully implement the global strategy on women's and children's health to save tens of millions of lives, including by providing reproductive health services.

We will also tackle extreme poverty and hunger. We will focus on inequalities, with particular emphasis on countries with special needs and those that have not achieved sufficient progress. We are preparing to unlock the potential of current and future generations by ending the hidden disgrace of stunting that affects more than 170 million children under five years of age. That is one child in every four.

We are also preparing to empower future generations by offering quality, relevant and universal education to meet the challenges of the 21st century.

Looking beyond 2015, we are working to forge consensus on a new generation of sustainable development goals that build on the MDGs – goals that will provide equitable economic and social progress that respects our planet's environmental boundaries. I will appoint a senior advisor to coordinate these efforts on my behalf.

Next Monday, President Halonen of Finland and President Zuma of South Africa will deliver the final report of my Global Sustainability Panel. Its recommendations can help to guide success at the Rio+20 conference.

We will mobilize the UN system to address the building blocks of sustainable development – from food and nutrition security to sustainable energy for all, from sustainable transportation and universal access to safe drinking water to adequate sanitation and the improved governance of our oceans.

But sustainable development will also depend on addressing climate change. At Durban last month, countries agreed on a timetable for a binding accord in which all nations would pledge to reduce emissions. We have a collective responsibility to deliver by 2015.

But Mother Nature will not wait while we negotiate. Over the next five years we must facilitate mitigation and adaptation action on the ground, including on Reducing Emissions from Deforestation and Forest Degradation Initiative. We must operationalize the Green Climate Fund and set public and private funds on a trajectory to reach the agreed $100 billion by 2020. I will also work with Member States to promote evidence-based policy. We need to act on the scientific facts.

Finally, I am announcing today that we will work with Member States to make Antarctica a World Nature Preserve.

It is well known that prevention is better and cheaper than cure. Focusing on preventing disasters and conflicts across all areas of our work – peace and security, promoting human rights and development – has the potential to save millions of lives and billions of dollars.

We know this from experience. It is time to prioritize prevention across the board.

On conflict, my agenda highlights early warning and action on conflict by mapping, linking, collecting and integrating information from across the international system. It emphasizes supporting national capacities for facilitating dialogue. And it specifies that UN good offices, mediation and rapid crisis response services must be made easily and swiftly available to Member States that need them.

We will also adopt a preventive approach to human rights.

The era of impunity is dead. We have entered a new age of accountability. We will extend the reach of the International Criminal Court and carve out a new dimension for the emerging doctrine of the responsibility to protect.

On natural disasters, we will work for risk reduction plans that address the growing challenges of climate change, environmental degradation, urbanization and population growth.

And we will place special emphasis on least developed and most vulnerable countries.

This brings me to the third agenda item: building a safer and more secure world by innovating and by building on our core business.

The role for our peacekeeping services continues to expand. We have come a long way from simply being ceasefire monitors. Today we are expected to keep, enforce and build peace.

Our operations build bridges – literally and among communities. We will build a new partnership for peacekeeping. This will entail even stronger collaboration with regional organizations and we will work to ensure that peacekeepers have all they need when they need it, to meet the demands of increasingly complex operations.

66 Waves of change are surging around us. If we navigate wisely, we can create a more secure and sustainable future for all. 99

Yet we will not create a safer and more secure world without building a more global, accountable and robust humanitarian system. To achieve this we will enhance collaboration among humanitarian organizations, particularly from the global south. We will strengthen community resilience and emergency response and establish a monitoring system to assess preparedness measures. And we will promote a global Declaration and Agenda on Humanitarian Aid Transparency and Effectiveness. We need to expand the Central Emergency Response Fund – which has worked extremely well – and identify additional sources of innovative financing for emergencies. Finally, I propose convening a first-of-its-kind World Humanitarian Summit to help share knowledge and establish common best practices.

We will also keep our sights firmly set on revitalizing the global disarmament and non-proliferation agenda. My message to the Conference on Disarmament is clear: get to work. We will also refocus our lens on nuclear safety and security, ranging from the threat of terrorism to the risk of environmental contamination from disasters such as we saw last year at Fukushima.

We will enhance coherence and scale up UN counter-terrorism efforts. Today, I propose creating a single UN counter-terrorism coordinator, by combining some of the existing functions. And we will address the heightened threat of organized crime, piracy and drug trafficking by mobilizing collective action and developing new tools and comprehensive regional and global strategies.

The fourth item on the action agenda is supporting nations in transition. Countries in transition from conflict are home to one-and-a-half billion people. They are seriously off-track on the MDGs. When events slip off the front page, when the cameras leave, the UN must be ready to maintain focus and attention. Countries in transition look to us – the United Nations – to help consolidate freedoms and opportunity.

We have a responsibility to help societies in transition. We also have the ability, based on vast experience. Now is the time to scale up our efforts, especially in areas where the UN's unique set of services is in particular demand – in peacebuilding, rule of law, electoral assistance, dispute resolution, anti-corruption, constitution-making and power-sharing arrangements and democratic practices. And we will support transition compacts with agreed strategic objectives and mutual accountability in fragile and conflict environments.

From sustainable development to a safer and more secure world, from prevention to transition, there is one essential cross-cutting element: empowering women and young people.

In too many countries, in too many communities, in too many households, women are still not recognized for what they can contribute. Five years ago, our work to change this was fragmented and inefficient. Today we have UN Women, consolidated and focused. We will deepen the UN campaign to end violence against women. We will enhance support for countries to adopt legislation that criminalizes violence against women and provides women with access to justice.

We will do even more to promote women's political participation worldwide, including a special focus on my seven-point action plan on women's participation in peacebuilding. We will encourage countries to adopt measures that guarantee women's equal access to political leadership that promote women's engagement in elections and that build the capacity of women to be effective leaders. And we will develop an action agenda for ensuring the full participation of women in social and economic recovery, so it does not pass them by.

We need to pull the UN system together, like never before, to support a new social contract of job-rich economic growth. Let us start with young people. Today we have the largest generation of young people the world has ever known. They are demanding their rights and a greater voice in economic and political life. We will do all we can to meet their needs and create opportunities.

We will deepen our youth focus and develop an action plan across the full range of UN programmes, including employment, entrepreneurship, political participation, human rights, education and reproductive health. And I will appoint a new Special Representative for youth to develop and implement our agenda and spearhead a UN youth volunteers programme.

These are the elements of my Five-Year Action Agenda. They are ambitious, but achievable.

Two forces will make all the difference.

First, the power of partnership initiatives such as Sustainable Energy for All, Every Woman Every Child, the Global Compact, Scale Up Nutrition and the Global Fund to Fight AIDS, Tuberculosis and Malaria are showing what is possible. We will harness the full power of transformative partnership across the range of UN activities by creating a new UN Partnerships Facility. It will work with the private sector, civil society, philanthropists and academia to advance common goals, catalyze commitments and promote accountability. I will also appoint a Senior Advisor to coordinate system-wide partnership efforts.

Second, a stronger United Nations. I have seen our staff at work in all corners of the world, in the most difficult conditions, sometimes at considerable risk to their lives. I will extend the work of the Change Management Team and move towards a new compact with staff and Member States alike, a compact based on budgetary discipline and flexibility, a compact based on effective service to the world's people. We will continue to drive forward our policies on staff mobility – building a modern multifunctional workforce supported by a global Secretariat. And in this age of austerity, we will continue to do more with less.

Finally, I propose to launch a second generation of Delivering as One, which will focus on increased accountability and improved outcomes.

Waves of change are surging around us. If we navigate wisely, we can create a more secure and sustainable future for all. The United Nations is the ship to navigate these waters. We represent all peoples. We engage on all issues. We facilitate dialogue and establish the universal norms that bind us. We are the venue for partnership and action.

Now is our moment. Now is our time to create the future we want. Thank you very much for your leadership and commitment.

Address to the sixty-sixth General Assembly
We the Peoples

NEW YORK, 21 SEPTEMBER 2011

Late next month, a child will be born, the 7 billionth citizen of our planet Earth. Let us assume this child is a girl. Most likely she will be poor. She may or may not grow up to be healthy and strong. If she is especially lucky, she will be educated and go out into the world, full of hopes and dreams. Beyond that, we know only one thing with certainty: she will enter a world of vast and unpredictable change – environmental, economic, geopolitical, technological, demographic.

The world's population has tripled since the United Nations was created. And our numbers keep growing. So do the pressures on land, energy, food and water. The global economic crisis continues to shake businesses, governments and families around the world. Joblessness is rising. Social inequalities grow wider. Too many people live in fear.

The UN exists to serve those in whose name it was conceived: "We the peoples". During the past five years as UN Secretary-General, I have travelled the world to meet people where they live, to hear their hopes and fears.

Two weeks ago I visited Kiribati and the Solomon Islands. Villagers told me of their fear of climate change. Rising seas are washing into their homes. One day, they might be swept away entirely. A young girl named Tamauri mustered her courage to speak. "What will become of us," she asked. "What can the United Nations do for us?"

Today, I pose her question to all of you, distinguished Heads of State and Government and leaders of the world. What can we do? How can we help our people find greater peace, prosperity and justice in a world of crises?

As I reflect on my time in office during the last five years, I am full of passionate conviction, unshakable faith in the enduring importance of this noble United Nations. Today, I would like to share with you my perspective on the way ahead. As I see it, we have five imperatives – five generational opportunities to shape the world of tomorrow by the decisions we make today.

The first and greatest of these is sustainable development – the imperative of the 21st century. Saving our planet, lifting people out of poverty, advancing economic growth; these are one and the same fight. We must connect the dots between climate change, water scarcity, energy shortages, global health, food security and women's empowerment. Solutions to one problem must be solutions for all.

Rio+20 must succeed. We must make progress on climate change. We cannot burn our way to the future. We cannot pretend the danger does not exist, or dismiss it because it affects someone else.

Today, I call on you to reach a binding climate change agreement; an agreement with more ambitious national and global emissions targets. And we need action on the ground, now, on cutting emissions and on adaptation. Energy is key to our planet, to our way of life. That is why we have launched a pioneering new initiative, Sustainable Energy for All.

We must invest in people, particularly in education and women's and children's health. Development is not sustainable unless it is equitable and serves all people. We must intensify our efforts to achieve the Millennium Development Goals, and more. Today, I urge you to think even bigger and beyond the 2015 deadline. Let us develop a new generation of sustainable development goals to pick up where the MDGs leave off. Let us agree on the means to achieve them.

A second great opportunity: prevention. This year, the UN peacekeeping budget will total $8 billion. Consider the savings if we act before conflicts erupt by deploying political mediation missions, for example, rather than troops. We know how to do this. Our record proves it in Guinea, Kenya, Kyrgyzstan.

66 Young people are more than our future. They are also our present, both in numbers and how they drive political and social change. We must find new ways to create decent jobs and opportunities for them around the world. 99

To prevent violations of human rights, we must work for the rule of law and stand against impunity. We have carved out a new dimension for the Responsibility to Protect. We will continue. To prevent runaway damage from natural disasters, we must work for better disaster risk reduction and preparedness. And let us remember: development is ultimately the best prevention.

Today, I ask your support. Let us commit the resources required. Let us raise prevention from an abstract concept to a core operating principle across the spectrum of our work.

A third imperative: building a safer and more secure world, our core responsibility as the United Nations.

This year we were sorely tested. In Côte d'Ivoire, we stood firm for democracy and human rights. Working closely with our regional partners, we made a difference in the lives of millions of people.

In Afghanistan and Iraq, we will carry on our missions with determination and commitment to the people of these proud nations.

In Darfur, we continue to save lives and help keep peace under difficult conditions. Our success demands the cooperation and full support of the international community, the parties on the ground and the Sudanese Government.

In Sudan, the parties to the Comprehensive Peace Agreement must work together to prevent conflict and settle outstanding issues.

In the Middle East, we must break the stalemate. We have long agreed that Palestinians deserve a state. Israel needs security. Both want peace. We pledge our unrelenting efforts to help achieve that peace through a negotiated settlement.

We must be innovative in maximizing the unique force for good that is UN peacekeeping. We are pioneering new approaches. We have strengthened our field support and reconfigured the architecture of peacekeeping operations.

In places like the Democratic Republic of the Congo and Sierra Leone, we are building peace by advancing civil society, promoting the rule of law and creating institutions of honest and effective governance.

Today we are capable of more rapid and effective response than ever before, and we will continue.

We remain the world's first emergency responders in Pakistan, Haiti and beyond. It is essential that we continue to build on our most innovative and effective tool for humanitarian relief: the Central Emergency Response Fund, or CERF. Famine in Somalia continues to spread. I appeal to you: help save the children of the Horn of Africa.

As we learned in Fukushima and elsewhere, nuclear accidents do not respect national borders. We need global action. We need strong international safety standards to prevent future disasters. Let us keep pushing on disarmament and non-proliferation. Let us fulfil the dream – a world free of nuclear weapons.

The fourth big opportunity: supporting nations in transition. This year's dramatic events in North Africa and the Middle East inspired us. Let us help make the Arab Spring a true season of hope for all.

In Libya, we are deploying a new UN support mission to assist the Libyan authorities establish a new government and legal order, consistent with the aspirations of the Libyan people.

Syria is a special concern. For six months we have seen escalating violence and repression. The Government has repeatedly pledged to undertake reforms and listen to its people. It has not done so. The moment to act is now. The violence must stop.

Others also look to us. A country may be emerging from war. It may be moving from autocracy to democracy, from poverty to a new prosperity. The UN must help that country find the right path. That may involve support to restore justice or build back public services. It may mean helping to organize elections or write a constitution. Our challenge today is to cement this progress and apply the lessons learned. Nowhere is this challenge more clear than in our efforts to help South Sudan build a functioning state after decades of conflict.

Fifth and finally: we can dramatically advance our efforts in every sphere by working with, and working for, women and young people.

Women hold up more than half the sky and represent much of the world's unrealized potential. They are the educators. They raise the children. They hold families together and increasingly drive economies. They are natural leaders.

We need their full engagement: in government, business and civil society. And this year, for the first time, we have UN Women – our own unique and powerful engine for dynamic change.

I am especially pleased to see so many women at this year's General Assembly. I welcome, in particular, the next speaker, Brazilian President Dilma Rousseff, the first woman in UN history to open our General Debate.

We can be proud of how many women leaders we have at the United Nations. We will continue our policy of promoting women at all levels of the Organization.

And we will focus on the new generation. Young people are more than our future. They are also our present, both in numbers and how they drive political and social change. We must find new ways to create decent jobs and opportunities for them around the world.

> ❝ We must connect the dots between climate change, water scarcity, energy shortages, global health, food security and women's empowerment. Solutions to one problem must be solutions for all. ❞

These are extraordinary challenges. We cannot respond in ordinary ways. We need one thing above all else: solidarity. That begins with the obvious: without resources, we cannot deliver. Today, I ask governments that have traditionally borne the lion's share of the costs to not flag in their generosity. Budgets are tight. Yet we also know that investing through the UN is smart policy. Burden-sharing makes the load lighter. Scaling back is no answer.

To the rising powers among you, whose dynamism increasingly drives the global economy: with power comes responsibility. For all, I ask that you give what you can – expertise, peacekeepers, helicopters. Never underestimate the power of your leadership. Again and again, I have seen how the smallest nations make some of the largest contributions to our work.

Governments cannot do the job alone. To deliver for those in need, we must broaden our base and extend our reach. We must harness the full power of partnership across the Organization. Our successes against malaria show the way. We see the transformative power of partnership in our Every Woman Every Child initiative, with funding commitments of more than $40 billion – four times the annual UN budget. When we combine the UN's unparalleled convening authority and technical resources with the various strengths of governments, the private sector and civil society, we are a formidable force for good.

Finally, we must adapt to changing times. At this time of austerity, we must do more with less. We must invest the global taxpayers' money wisely, eliminate waste and avoid duplication by delivering as one. Accountability and transparency remain our watchwords. We are accountable to the Member States. Yet we cannot become more efficient without their strong and consistent support.

We need to streamline the budget process and help the UN to deliver at a cost no nation can match on its own. We must keep pushing to build a more modern and mobile workforce – a UN that is faster and more flexible, a UN that innovates and draws on the power of social media and new technologies, a UN that helps solve real-world problems in real-time.

Last but hardly least, let us do everything we can to protect our UN staff. We have lost so many lives; the UN has become too soft a target. Today, we remember with gratitude those who serve with such dedication in so many dangerous places.

Here in this great hall, the shrinking islands in the vast Pacific may seem far away. Yet I hear that young girl's plea as clearly as if she were next to me. Perhaps that is because, sixty years ago, I was that child. The United Nations is the answer, as it was then. Standing here today, I hear many millions of other young boys and girls asking for our help, looking for hope.

"We the peoples". Seven billion now look to us, the world's leaders. They need solutions. They demand leadership. They want us to act. To act with compassion, courage and conviction. To act in concert, nations united, at the United Nations. Let us carry on this journey together.

Remarks to the General Assembly upon re-election as Secretary-General

NEW YORK, 21 JUNE 2011

With your decision this afternoon – with your warm words – you do me a very great honour, beyond expression. Standing in this place, mindful of the immense legacy of my predecessors, I am humbled by your trust, and enlarged by our sense of common purpose.

This solemn occasion is special in another respect. On being sworn in, a few moments ago, I placed my hand on the UN Charter – not a copy, but the original signed in San Francisco. Our Founding Fathers deemed this document so precious that it was flown back to Washington, strapped to its own parachute. No such consideration was given to the poor diplomat accompanying it; he had to take his chances. We thank the U.S. National Archives for their generosity in lending it today, and for their care in preserving it.

The Charter of the United Nations is the animating spirit and soul of our great institution. For sixty-five years, this great Organization has carried the flame of human aspiration – "We the peoples." From the last of the great world wars, through the fall of the Berlin Wall and the end of apartheid. We have fed the hungry, delivered comfort to the sick and suffering, brought peace to those afflicted by war. One Organization, dedicated to human progress – the United Nations.

> 66 To lead, we must deliver results. Mere statistics will not do. We need results that people can see and touch; results that change lives, that make a difference. 99

We began our work together, four and a half years ago, with a call for a new multilateralism – a new spirit of collective action. We saw, in our daily work, how all the world's people look more and more to the United Nations. We knew then, and more so now, that we live in an era of integration and interconnection; a new era where no country can solve all challenges on its own, and where every country should be part of the solution.

That is the reality of the modern world. We can struggle with it, or we can lead. The role of the United Nations is to lead. Each of us here today shares that responsibility. It is why the UN matters in a different and deeper way than ever before. To lead, we must deliver results. Mere statistics will not do. We need results that people can see and touch; results that change lives, that make a difference.

Working together, with goodwill and mutual trust, we have laid a firm foundation for the future. When we began, climate change was an invisible issue. Today, we have placed it squarely on the global agenda. When we began, nuclear disarmament was frozen in time. Today, we see progress. We have advanced on global health, sustainable development and education. We are on track to eliminate deaths from malaria. With a final push, we can eradicate polio, just as we did smallpox long ago. We have shielded the poor and vulnerable against the greatest economic upheaval in generations. Amid devastating natural disasters, we were there, saving lives – in Haiti, Pakistan, Myanmar.

As never before, the UN is on the front lines protecting people and helping build the peace – in Sudan, the Democratic Republic of the Congo and Somalia; in Afghanistan, Iraq and the Middle East. We have stood firm for democracy, justice and human rights – in Côte d'Ivoire, North Africa and beyond. We have carved out new dimension for the Responsibility to Protect. We created UN Women to empower women everywhere. That includes the UN system itself.

And yet, we never forget how far we have to go. As we look to the future, we recognize the imperative for decisive and concerted action.

In economic hard times, we must stretch resources and do better with less. We must improve our ability to deliver as one.

❝ As Secretary-General, I will work as a harmonizer and bridge-builder – among Member States, within the United Nations system, and between the United Nations and a rich diversity of international partners. ❞

We must do more to connect the dots among the world's challenges, so that solutions to one global problem become solutions for all – on women's and children's health; green growth; more equitable social and economic development.

A clear time-frame lies ahead: the target date for the Millennium Development Goals in 2015, next year's Rio + 20 conference, the high-level meeting on nuclear safety in September.

In all this, our ultimate power is partnership. Our legacy, such as it may be, will be written in alliance – the leaders of the world, leading in common cause.

As in the past, I count on your support and even deeper partnership. By acting decisively to renew my mandate, you have given the gift of time: time to carry on the important work that, together, we have begun.

In the months to come, we will be reaching out for your views and ideas. Drawing on those discussions, I shall present our broader long-term vision at the next General Assembly in September.

My predecessor Dag Hammarskjold once said, "Never for the sake of 'peace and quiet' deny your own experience or conviction." Like my distinguished forebear, I take this lesson to heart.

It has been a great privilege to serve as your Secretary-General. That you should ask me to serve once again makes it all the greater. With gratitude for your support and encouragement, in full knowledge of the responsibilities, I am proud and humbled to accept.

As Secretary-General, I will work as a harmonizer and bridge-builder – among Member States, within the United Nations system, and between the United Nations and a rich diversity of international partners.

To quote the great philosopher Lao-tzu: "The way of heaven is to benefit others and not to injure. The way of the sage is to act but not compete."

Let us apply this enduring wisdom to our work today. Out of the competition of ideas, let us find unity in action. Honouring your trust, I pledge my full commitment, my full energy and resolve, to uphold the fundamental principles of our sacred Charter.

Together, let us do all we can to help this noble Organization better serve "we the peoples" of the world. Together, no challenge is too large. Together, nothing is impossible.

Address to the sixty-fifth General Assembly
Pulling together in testing times: securing a better future for all

NEW YORK, 23 SEPTEMBER 2010

We, the peoples of the United Nations, are bound by certain sacred duties and obligations. To care for the welfare of others. To resolve conflicts peacefully. To act in the world with empathy and understanding. To practice tolerance and mutual respect as a bedrock principle of civilization.

Today, we are being tested. Social inequalities are growing, among nations and within. Everywhere, people live in fear of losing jobs and incomes. Too many are caught in conflict; women and children are bearing the brunt. And we see a new politics at work: a politics of polarization. We hear the language of hate, false divisions between "them" and "us", those who insist on their way or no way.

Amid such uncertainty, so much confusion of purpose, we naturally seek a moral compass. At the United Nations, we find the proper path in community, global cause, fair decisions, mutual responsibility for a destiny we share.

This is the soul of global governance, the theme of this General Assembly. A collective stand, principled and pragmatic, against forces that would divide us. And that is why the United Nations remains the indispensable global institution for the 21st century.

As we gather today, in solidarity, let us recognize: this is a season for pulling together, for consolidating progress, for putting our shoulder to the wheel and delivering results. Real results, for people most in need, as only the United Nations can do.

Together, over the past three years, we embraced an ambitious agenda, framed by three overarching ideas for our time. A more prosperous world, free of the deepest poverty. A cleaner, greener and more sustainable world for our children. A safer world, free of nuclear weapons.

Those are the great challenges of our era. They are not dreams. They are opportunities, within our power to grasp.

Together, we have made progress. We will press ahead – with fresh thinking, fresh approaches, a strong sense of leadership and political will.

The Millennium Development Goals Summit showed our collective determination. World leaders came together with concrete national plans to meet the Millennium Development Goals by 2015. They agreed on a responsible and mutually accountable partnership, a partnership that will better the lives of billions of people within our generation.

Our challenge is to deliver on this promise, to turn hopes into realities. We must draw on lessons learned over the past decade: helping people to help themselves; investing resources where they have the greatest effect – smart investment in education, decent work, health, smallholder agriculture, infrastructure and green energy; the importance of putting women at the fore.

> 66 The great goals are within reach. We can achieve them by looking forward, pulling together, uniting our strength as a community of nations in the name of the larger good. 99

That is why, at the Summit, I welcomed the endorsement of our Global Strategy for Women and Children's Health. Backed by billions of dollars in new commitments from governments, business, NGOs and philanthropic organizations, this was a tangible expression of global solidarity. That is also why, last week, I named a dynamic new head of UN Women. In Michelle Bachelet, the former President of Chile, we found a global leader who can inspire millions of women and girls around the world. We must support her to the utmost. Because, by empowering women, we empower societies.

Three years ago, we called climate change the defining challenge of our era, and so it remains. Clearly, the road toward a comprehensive, binding agreement, in Cancun and beyond, will not be easy. And yet, we have made progress, and we can make more. This is a year to build on important areas of agreement – on financing for adaptation and mitigation, on technology transfer, on capacity-building and preventing deforestation.

In the longer term, we face the "50-50-50" challenge. By 2050, the world's population will grow by 50 percent. To keep climate change in check, we will need to cut greenhouse gas emissions by 50 percent by then.

The world looks to us for creative solutions. And that is why, on Sunday, we hosted the first meeting of our High-level Panel on Global Sustainability. I am confident that it will stimulate new thinking as we work toward Rio+20 in 2012.

On nuclear disarmament, as well, we see new momentum: A new START agreement, the Summit on Nuclear Security, a successful Non-Proliferation Treaty review conference. Our role is to keep pushing, to find a path to bring the Comprehensive Test Ban Treaty into force, to realize agreements on fissile materials and securing nuclear materials and facilities. Tomorrow, we are hosting a high level meeting to rejuvenate the Conference on Disarmament. I believe the next few years will be critical. Will we advance our work on non-proliferation and disarmament, or will we slide back? It is up to us.

As always, over the past year, we were there for those in urgent need: the people of Pakistan, coping with epic floods and the monumental task of reconstruction; the people of Haiti, where the work of rebuilding goes on, and where so many lost their lives, including 101 of our colleagues; the people of Somalia, Sudan, Niger, Gaza.

As always, we continue to work for peace and security. Three years ago, in partnership with the African Union, we deployed the first peacekeeping force in Darfur. During the coming year, the United Nations will be critical to keeping a larger peace as north and south Sudan decide their future. Tomorrow's High-Level Meeting on Sudan will help chart that path.

In the Democratic Republic of the Congo, we have adapted our mission to new and changing circumstances. We have worked closely with the African Union in Somalia. We have seen victories for preventive diplomacy, as well. In Iraq, we helped broker the compromises that kept this year's elections on track. In Guinea, we stand with regional partners in insisting on democracy. In Sierra Leone, we helped defuse confrontations and keep peace moving forward.

Quick-footed diplomacy helped contain the troubles in Kyrgyzstan. In Afghanistan, we carry on our work despite exceptionally difficult security and humanitarian conditions. We will seek to reduce tensions on the Korean Peninsula and encourage the Democratic People's Republic of Korea to return to the Six-Party Talks. On Iran, we continue to urge the government to engage constructively with the international community and comply fully with the relevant Security Council resolutions.

In the Middle East, we see encouraging movement toward a comprehensive peace. Working with the Quartet, we will do everything possible to help bring negotiations to a successful conclusion. I strongly discourage either side from any action that would hold back progress.

In all we do, human rights are at the core. There can be no peace without justice. The global community has worked hard and long to usher in a new age of accountability. In our modern era, let us send a clear message: No nation, large or small, can violate the rights of its citizens with impunity.

Let me close on a theme that has defined our work together: building a stronger UN for a better world. The renovation of our Secretariat is on track, on schedule, on budget. Organizational changes introduced over the past few years are bearing fruit. Among them: the New Horizons initiative to streamline peacekeeping operations. In consultation with the Member States and our staff, we will do all in our power to create a faster, more modern, flexible and effective UN workforce, to recruit the best talent of tomorrow.

Today and in the months ahead, we will speak of many things – important issues, affecting all humankind. Let us remember, in these difficult times: we are being tested. Let us remember: the many lives lost in service to our ideals. Let us remember: the world still looks to the United Nations for moral and political leadership.

The great goals are within reach. We can achieve them by looking forward, pulling together, uniting our strength as a community of nations, in the name of the larger good. Thank you very much, and I count on your leadership and commitment.

Address to the sixty-fourth General Assembly
Now is our time

NEW YORK, 23 SEPTEMBER 2009

We gather each and every September in a solemn rite. We come to reaffirm our founding Charter – our faith in fundamental principles of peace, justice, human rights and equal opportunity for all. We assess the state of the world, engage on the key issues of the day, lay out our vision for the way ahead.

This year the opening of the General Debate of the sixty-fourth session of the General Assembly asks us to rise to an exceptional moment. Amid many crises – food, energy, recession and pandemic flu, hitting all at once – the world looks to us for answers.

If ever there were a time to act in a spirit of renewed multilateralism, a moment to create a United Nations of genuine collective action, it is now.

Now is our time. A time to put the "united" back into the United Nations. United in purpose. United in action.

First – let us make this a year that we, united nations, rise to the greatest challenge we face as a human family: the threat of catastrophic climate change. Yesterday, one hundred heads of state and government set out the next steps toward Copenhagen. They recognized the need for an agreement all nations can embrace, in line with their capabilities and consistent with what science requires, grounded in green jobs and green growth, the lifeline of the 21st century. Our road to Copenhagen requires us to bridge our differences. I firmly believe we can.

Second – let this be the year that nations united to free our world of nuclear weapons. For too long, this great cause has lain dormant. That is why, last October, I proposed a five-point plan for putting disarmament back on the global agenda. And now, the international climate is changing. The Russian Federation and the United States have pledged to cut their nuclear arsenals. This coming May, at the United Nations Review Conference on the Nuclear Non-Proliferation Treaty, we have an opportunity to push for real progress.

Tomorrow's historic Security Council summit – chaired by the President of the United States, with us for the first time – offers a fresh start. With action now, we can get the ratifications to bring the Comprehensive Nuclear Test Ban Treaty into force. Together, let us make this the year we agreed to banish the bomb.

Third – in our fight against world poverty, let this be the year we focus on those left behind. Some speak of green shoots of recovery, but we see red flags of warning. Our recent report, "Voices of the Vulnerable," highlights a new crisis. The near-poor are becoming the new poor. An estimated 100 million people could fall below the poverty line this year. Markets may be bouncing back, but incomes and jobs are not.

People are angry. They believe the global economy is stacked against them. That is why we have put forward a Global Jobs Pact for balanced and sustainable growth. That is why we are creating a new Global Impact Vulnerability Alert System, giving us real-time data and analysis on the socio-economic picture around the world. We need to know who is being hurt, and where, so we can best respond.

> ❝ We of the United Nations are the voice of the voiceless, the defenders of the defenseless. If we are to offer genuine hope to the hopeless, if we are to truly turn the corner to economic recovery, then we must do so for all nations and for all people. So much is possible if we work together. Together, we are here to take risks, to assume the burden of responsibility, to rise to an exceptional moment, to make history. ❞

That is also why, next year at this time, we will convene a special summit on the Millennium Development Goals. With only five years to go, we must mount a final push toward 2015. Rightly, we put women and children at the fore. UNICEF reports a 28 percent decline in child mortality over the past two decades. We can hope for similar progress on maternal health and mortality.

The prevention of sexual violence against women must be a top priority. Let us agree: these acts are an abomination. Leaders of every nation are personally accountable when such crimes are committed within their borders. When women die in childbirth, when they are raped as a weapon of war and have nowhere to turn, we of the United Nations cannot look the other way. And that is why, just recently, you agreed to create a single agency to address women's issues. We have never been more empowered to empower women.

This Assembly also reaffirmed the responsibility to protect. In our modern era, no nation, large or small, can violate the human rights of its citizens with impunity. Where conflicts arise, justice and accountability should follow. That is why the work of the International Criminal Court is so vital. We look to the review conference in Kampala next May as an opportunity to strengthen its mandate.

We can achieve none of our noble goals without peace, security and justice. In Darfur, that means consolidating recent progress and delivering on our mandate. We will be 90 percent deployed by year's end. Yet we still lack critical assets, particularly transport and helicopters. Meanwhile, we must continue to work, urgently, for the broader stability of Sudan and the region and shore up the comprehensive peace with South Sudan.

Somalia continues to demand attention whether to support African peacekeepers and the government or international anti-piracy efforts.

We will continue to press for resettlement, reconciliation and accountability in Sri Lanka. We welcome the government's commitment to allow all displaced persons to return to their homes by the end of January – as reaffirmed last week to my envoy.

We will work hard for freedom and democracy in Myanmar. The release of some political prisoners last week falls short of what is needed. We call on Myanmar's friends and neighbors to do more, much more, in the best interests of Myanmar and its people. If next year's elections are to be accepted as credible and inclusive, all political prisoners must be released – including Daw Aung San Suu Kyi.

We worked to stop the bloodshed in Gaza. Yet people continue to suffer. Issues of justice and accountability need to be addressed. We must revive negotiations toward a two-state solution and a comprehensive peace in the Middle East. We support President Obama's efforts for a resumption of peace talks and will work with the Quartet to that end

In Afghanistan, we face a difficult environment. Recent elections revealed serious defects. Yet we should not forget the progress made – progress we can build on. We are committed to seeing the Afghans through their long night. We will stay with them. We pledge to stand, as well, with the people of Pakistan.

We have made significant progress in Timor Leste, Haiti , Sierra Leone and Nepal . We see quiet progress in Iraq and fresh opportunities in Cyprus. Now is the time to take stock and move forward.

Let me close by inviting you to look around you. By the end of this General Assembly, our Secretariat building will be empty. Our staff will have dispersed across the city. Our United Nations will be completely renovated. Our common ambition is to make this outward renovation the symbol of our inward renewal.

That is why we have placed such emphasis on building a stronger United Nations for a better world. We have made progress in Delivering as One UN. We have made strides in getting peacebuilding right, so that societies emerging from war do not slide back into conflict. We have sharpened our tools of mediation and diplomacy so that we can stop crises from escalating into broader and more costly tragedies. We created the Department of Field Support, and we are developing the New Horizons strategy to make peacekeeping more agile and effective.

In this, we need the strong support of Member States, just as we do to secure the safety of our brave staff serving in dangerous places, too many of whom have lost their lives in the causes we all serve.

This year, I have traveled from the ice rim of the Arctic to the steppes of Mongolia. I have seen, first-hand, the effects of climate change on our planet and its people.

In the Democratic Republic of the Congo, I met an eighteen-year-old girl raped by soldiers. Her hope for a new life is the United Nations.

At summits from Trinidad and Tobago to London to L' Aquila, I have spoken out on one point above all others.

We of the United Nations are the voice of the voiceless, the defenders of the defenseless. If we are to offer genuine hope to the hopeless, if we are to truly turn the corner to economic recovery, then we must do so for all nations and for all people. So much is possible if we work together. Together, we are here to take risks, to assume the burden of responsibility, to rise to an exceptional moment, to make history. This year, of all years, asks no less.

Because we are the United Nations. We are the best hope for humankind. And now is our time. Thank you very much for your leadership and commitment.

Address to the sixty-third General Assembly
A call to global leadership

NEW YORK, SEPTEMBER 23, 2008

Welcome to the opening of the general debate of the sixty-third session of the General Assembly.

It is customary for the Secretary-General, on this occasion, to assess the state of the world and to present our vision for the coming year. We all recognize the perils of our current passage.

We face a global financial crisis. A global energy crisis. A global food crisis. Trade talks have collapsed, yet again. We have seen new outbreaks of war and violence, new rhetoric of confrontation. Climate change ever more clearly threatens our planet.

We often say that global problems demand global solutions. And yet, today, we also face a crisis of a different sort. Like these others, it knows no borders. It affects all nations. It complicates all other problems. I refer, here, to a challenge of global leadership.

We are on the eve of a great transition. Our world has changed, more than we may realize. We see new centers of power and leadership in Asia, Latin America and across the newly developed world. The problems we face have grown more complex.

In this new world, our challenges are increasingly those of collaboration rather than confrontation. Nations can no longer protect their interests, or advance the well-being of their people, without the partnership of the rest.

Yet I worry. There is, today, a danger of losing sight of this new reality. I see a danger of nations looking more inward, rather than toward a shared future. I see a danger of retreating from the progress we have made, particularly in the realm of development and more equitably sharing the fruits of global growth.

This would be tragic. For at this time one thing is clear. We must do more, not less. We must do more to help our fellow human beings weather the gathering storm.

Yes, global growth has raised billions of people out of poverty. However, if you are among the world's poor, you have never felt poverty so sharply.

Yes, international law and justice have never been so widely embraced as on this sixtieth anniversary of the Universal Declaration of Human Rights. However, those living in nations where human rights are abused have never been so vulnerable.

Yes, most of us live in peace and security. However, we see deepening violence in many nations that can least afford it. Afghanistan, Somalia, The Democratic Republic of Congo, Iraq, Sudan, to name a few.

This is not right. This is not just. We can do something about it. And with strong global leadership, we will.

Let me speak about the three pillars of our work: human rights, peace and security, development.

To put it bluntly, we face a development emergency. Over the past year, we watched with alarm as the price of fuel, food and commodities rose sharply. Wealthy countries worry about recession, while the poorest of the poor can no longer afford to eat.

That is why, two days from now, we will hold a High-Level Event on the Millennium Development Goals. We must galvanize global awareness and global action, with a special focus on Africa. As you know, progress has been uneven. Pledges have not been fully honored. Yet we have achieved enough to know the goals are within reach.

At this High-Level Event, I will bring together a new coalition to meet this challenge – governments, NGOs, chief executives, faith groups and philanthropists. We know this approach will work. It already has with malaria – a disease that kills a child every thirty seconds. Since last year, I brought together a pioneering public-private partnership, with an agreed science-based strategy, funding and unified global management. On Thursday, I will announce new research showing it to be a striking success. We are nearing a time when we will eliminate deaths from malaria as one of the last great scourges of humankind. And now we will apply this new model of global partnership to other MDGs.

I will ask you to be bold and specific. I will ask you to say what you will do, and how you will do it – to help us get on track for success by 2015. And I call for us to follow up these new commitments at a formal summit on the MDGs, to be held in 2010. Let us renew our leadership, starting here today. Let this call to action be heard, far and wide. The world's poor deserve no less.

The United Nations is the champion of the most vulnerable. When disaster strikes, we act. We did so this year in Haiti and other Caribbean nations hit by hurricanes. We did so in Myanmar after Cyclone Nargis. There, the challenge now is to push for political progress, including credible steps on human rights and democracy. We did so in Southeast Asia affected by severe flooding, and in the Horn of Africa afflicted by drought, where 17 million need emergency help.

Since taking office, I have called for more strenuous action in Somalia. Must we wait – and see more children die in the sand? We at the United Nations are leaders. We at the UN duty-bound to do what compassion and human decency demand of us.

The global food crisis has not gone away. It may have faded from the daily headlines. But note this fact: last year at this time, rice cost $330 a ton. Today it is

$730. In a single year, the food staple that feeds half the world more than doubled in price. People who used to buy rice by the bag now do so by the handful. Those who ate two meals a day now get by on one.

The United Nations has led the world's response. Our UN Task Force on the Global Food Crisis set forth solutions. We focused on getting seeds and fertilizers into the hands of small farmers. We aim to create a new green revolution in Africa. But the truth is, we lack new resources. The international community has not matched words with deeds.

We are well aware of the many challenges to peace and security around the world. In nations such as Burundi and Sierra Leone, Liberia and Timor Leste, more than 100,000 UN peacekeepers are helping people turn from conflict to peace.

We should never underestimate the power of the UN's good offices, particularly in preventive diplomacy. We see the fruits in Nepal, Kenya and, we can hope, Zimbabwe. In Cyprus, there is a real chance to reunify this long-divided island. In Georgia, the UN can help bridge the tensions resulting from the recent conflict. In Côte d'Ivoire, we will help organize elections before year's end – a major stride toward recovery and democracy. In Darfur, we face a continuing challenge in meeting deployment deadlines. We still lack critical assets and personnel.

> ❝ I see a danger of nations looking more inward, rather than toward a shared future. I see a danger of retreating from the progress we have made, particularly in the realm of development and more equitably sharing the fruits of global growth. ❞

I would not be doing my job if I did not point out how dangerous it is to pretend that the United Nations can solve today's complex problems without the full backing of Member States. If not matched by resources, mandates are empty. The global financial crisis endangers all our work – financing for development, social spending in rich nations and poor, the Millennium Development Goals. If ever there were a call to collective action – a call for global leadership – it is now.

At the Doha Review Conference, later this year, we have an opportunity to address the critical issues of international economic cooperation and development. I urge all Members to engage, at the highest levels. We need to restore order to the international financial markets. We need a new understanding on business ethics and governance, with more compassion and less uncritical faith in the magic of markets. And we must think about how the world economic system should evolve to more fully reflect the changing realities of our time.

Other issues demand global leadership. I am thinking, here, of combating malaria and AIDS, and of reducing maternal and child mortality. I am thinking of global terrorism, and the enduring importance of disarmament and non-proliferation.

I note the progress in the six-party talks on the Korean Peninsula and urge that all agreements be implemented. And I call again on Iran to comply with Security Council resolutions and cooperate fully with the International Atomic Energy Agency.

Above all, I am thinking of human rights. It is essential to act upon the principle that justice is a pillar of peace, security and development. We must advance the Responsibility to Protect. We recognize that such issues are seldom black and white. We accept that politics can be complex and full of trade-offs. Yet we cannot let crimes against humanity go unpunished. We have it in our power to combat impunity. And therefore we must.

Finally, I am thinking of the defining issue of our era, climate change. Last December, in Bali, world leaders agreed on a road map toward 2012, which is as far as the Kyoto Protocol takes us.

We must regain our momentum. Our first test comes three months from now in Poznan, Poland. By then we need a shared vision of what a global climate change agreement might look like.

We have only fourteen months until Copenhagen. I urge the governments of Poland, Denmark, and all UN Member States, to demonstrate their leadership – their global leadership – on this truly existential issue.

In closing, let me briefly return to the theme of my address to you last year: a stronger UN for a better world. The foundation of all our work is accountability. The UN Secretariat is accountable to you, the Members. And that is why I push so strongly for UN reform. We need to change the UN culture. We need to become faster, more flexible and more effective, more modern.

In the coming weeks, I will ask you to support my proposals for a new human resources framework. We need to replace our current system of contracts and conditions of service. It is dysfunctional. It is demoralizing. It discourages mobility between UN departments and the field. It promotes stagnation, rather than creativity. It undercuts our most precious resource – the global, dedicated corps of international civil servants that is the backbone of the UN.

Whenever I travel, I go out of my way to meet these brave and committed men and women. They work in the most difficult circumstances, often at great personal sacrifice. I cannot fully express my admiration for them. The time has come to invest more in our staff. And that is why I am promoting mobility, matched with proper career training, as a way to create new professional opportunities and to inject new flexibility and dynamism into the Organization.

Finally, let us also remember: you, the Member States, are accountable to each other and to the Organization, as well. You cannot continue to pass resolutions mandating ambitious peace operations without the necessary troops, money and

materiel. We cannot send our brave UN staff around the world – twenty-five of whom died this year – without doing all we can to assure their security. We cannot reform this vital Organization without providing the required resources.

It takes leadership to honor our pledges and our promises in the face of fiscal constraints and political opposition. It takes leadership to commit our soldiers to a cause of peace in faraway places. It takes leadership to speak out for justice; to act on climate change despite powerful voices against you; to stand against protectionism and make trade concessions, even in our enlightened self-interest.

Yet, that is why we are here. We have before us a great opportunity. We have ample reason to be optimistic. Today's uncertainties will pass. The challenges before us are our creation. Therefore we can solve them, together. By acting wisely and responsibly, we will set the stage for a new era of global prosperity, more widely and equitably shared. I count on your leadership.

Address to the sixty-second General Assembly

A stronger UN for a better world

NEW YORK, 25 SEPTEMBER 2007

Welcome, all, to New York in this beautiful autumn season. It is a pleasure and an honor to be with you, at this opening of the general debate of our sixty-second General Assembly. I expect the year ahead to be among the most challenging in our history. And I am sure that, together, we can make it one of the most successful.

We are off to a strong start. During the past week, we hosted a high-level meeting of the Africa Steering Group on our Millennium Development Goals – a clear signal of an important priority. World leaders also met to discuss our way forward on the Middle East, Afghanistan, Darfur and Iraq. Yesterday we concluded a highly successful conference on climate change.

Our goal was to galvanize our efforts, to coordinate our work under one roof – this roof of our United Nations – so that we fight global warming together, as one. This, in itself, is a signal accomplishment. It is a model of how I hope we can work together in the future.

Looking to the coming year, and beyond, we can foresee a daunting array of challenges to come. They are problems that respect no borders – that no country, big or small, rich or poor, can resolve on its own. More than ever, we live in an era of collective action. Often it seems as though everybody wants the UN to do everything. We cannot deliver everything, of course. But that cannot be an excuse for doing nothing. Hence the theme of these remarks: a stronger United Nations for a better world.

Our changing world needs a stronger UN. We all understand the importance of a strong, robust, empowered Secretariat. My vision is an administration focused on results – efficient, directed, pragmatic and accountable, an administration representing excellence, integrity and pride in serving the global good.

To deliver on this vision, we must modernize ourselves. We need an internal climate change at the UN. We need to think freshly about how we do our work. Our main themes should be to simplify, rationalize and delegate. To deliver on the world's high expectations for us, we need to be faster, more flexible and mobile. We need to pay less attention to rhetoric, and more attention to results – to getting things done.

I place a very high priority on implementing the management reforms you have previously approved to promote greater transparency, accountability and efficiency. I welcome the progress we have made over the past nine months in streamlining our budget processes, crafting our Capital Master Plan and putting our financial house in order. I am especially grateful to the 102 governments that have paid their annual budget assessments in full.

Together, we successfully re-organized our peacekeeping operations, affecting more than 100,000 UN field personnel in eighteen multinational missions. I plan to continue the effort by strengthening the Department of Political Affairs. We must become more proactive in responding to crises. Well-planned and executed preventive diplomacy can save many lives and forestall many tragedies – a core Charter responsibility of our UN.

I will leave no stone unturned to end the tragedy in Darfur. The government of Sudan must live up to its pledge to join comprehensive peace talks and implement a ceasefire. We must also move forward with the agreement that ended the long-running civil war between north and south and prepare for elections in 2009. The crisis in Darfur grew from many causes. Any enduring solution must address all of them – security, politics, resources, water, humanitarian and development issues. There, as elsewhere, we must deal with root causes of conflict, however complex and entangled.

Peace in the Middle East is vital to the stability of the region and the world. We know what is required: an end to violence, an end to occupation, the creation of a Palestinian State at peace with itself and Israel, and a comprehensive regional peace between Israel and the Arab world. With renewed leadership from the Arab world and the United States, coupled with the efforts of Quartet Representative Tony Blair, the elements for a renewed push for peace are being brought together.

We also sincerely hope that the Lebanese people through national reconciliation will be able to restore political and social stability by electing their new president in accordance with their constitutional process.

Iraq has become the whole world's problem. With the new Security Council Resolution 1770, the UN has an important role in promoting political negotiation and national reconciliation, as well as in providing humanitarian assistance to the Iraqi people. But we recognize that the safety and security of UN staff is paramount.

In Afghanistan, we must work more effectively with our partners to deal with drug trafficking and the financing of terrorism.

We are closely following events in Myanmar. We again urge the authorities in Myanmar to exercise utmost restraint, to engage without delay in dialogue with all the relevant parties to the national reconciliation process on the issues of concern to the people of Myanmar. In this regard, my Special Advisor is expected to visit Myanmar very soon.

From my first day in office, I have stressed the importance of disarmament, as mandated most recently in the General Assembly's support for my proposal to establish an Office of Disarmament Affairs. We must reinvigorate our effort to stop the proliferation of weapons of mass destruction and related technology, and especially to prevent such material from falling into the hands of terrorists.

I am encouraged by recent progress on the Democratic People's Republic of Korea issue. I sincerely hope that the forthcoming inter-Korean Summit meeting will create a historic momentum, to bring peace, security, and eventually a peaceful reunification of the Korean Peninsula.

I am confident that we will reach a negotiated solution with the Islamic Republic of Iran. Our ultimate goal remains the complete elimination of weapons of mass destruction. If we fail, these weapons may one day eliminate us.

We at the UN must take the long view, in politics as in life. Even as we deal with the here and now, we must think about tomorrow.

Yesterday, I spoke about climate change as a defining issue of our time. We all agreed. Now is the time for action. Let us go to Bali and make a break-though. We also agreed that solutions to global warming cannot come at the expense of economic development – the second pillar of the UN's work. Issues of development and social equity cannot take a backseat to issues of peace and security.

" The Human Rights Council must live up to its responsibilities as the torchbearer for human rights consistently and equitably around the world. "

This year marks the midpoint for our Millennium Development Goals. We have had successes. Around the world, unprecedented numbers of people are lifting themselves out of poverty. Yet the rising tide of globalization has not lifted all boats.

We see this most acutely in Africa, home to most of what one World Bank economist calls the bottom billion of the world's poor. We must pay careful attention to these nations with special needs. We must heed the voices of the world's poorest peoples, who too often go unheard. That is why I convened the MDG Africa Steering group earlier this month, bringing together leaders of major multilateral development organizations. Our Millennium goals remain achievable – so long as we help the poorest nations break free of the traps that ensnare them.

Some of those traps relate to bad governance. Others to disease and poor health care. It is intolerable that HIV/AIDS continues as a modern-day scourge. It is intolerable that almost 10 million children die each year before their fifth birthday, mostly from such preventable diseases as malaria. It is a scar on the moral conscience of the world.

This is not to say we will do things that these countries should, and can, do for themselves. The Asian Miracle has shown that successful development owes much to smart choices and rigorous execution.

For our part, we must try to make our multilateral development programs more effective and coherent, to better integrate our efforts in health, education, agriculture and infrastructure so as to deliver better results.

For their part, donor nations must do more to deliver on their promises of aid, debt relief and market access. Open, fair and non-discriminatory trading and financial systems are critical to the future of every developing country, in Africa and elsewhere. That is why we must do our utmost to advance the Doha Development Agenda, with its emphasis on development and aid for trade.

The third pillar of the UN, human rights, is codified in the Universal Declaration of Human Rights, which marks its sixtieth anniversary in 2008. The Human Rights Council must live up to its responsibilities as the torchbearer for human rights consistently and equitably around the world. I will strive to translate the concept of our Responsibility to Protect from words to deeds, to ensure timely action so that populations do not face genocide, ethnic cleansing and crimes against humanity.

Our international tribunals continue their work, from Rwanda to Sierra Leone and, soon, Lebanon. The age of impunity is dead.

Meanwhile, the UN's brave and exceptionally committed humanitarian aid workers do their best to save lives. They help protect civilian populations from the depredations of armed militias, children from starvation, women from shameful violence. This year did not bring a natural disaster on the scale of the 2004 tsunami. But the intensity of floods, droughts and extreme weather, perhaps made worse by climate change, have brought pain and suffering to many millions. This, above all, is the UN's front-line. We stand up to help those who cannot help themselves.

I am humbled, often, by the scale of the challenges before us. So much is expected of us. Delivering on those hopes, faithfully and effectively, will require great effort and discipline.

Transforming the way the UN does business – shifting our focus to emphasize results rather than bureaucratic process – will take patience, perseverance and courage.

The pendulum of history is swinging in our favor. Multilateralism is back. An increasingly interdependent world recognizes that the challenges of tomorrow are best dealt with through the UN. Indeed, they can only be dealt with through the UN.

Remarks to the General Assembly on restructuring the Secretariat

NEW YORK, 5 FEBRUARY 2007

I am glad to be back at Headquarters, and grateful at this opportunity to meet with all of you for the first time in my capacity as Secretary-General.

First, I am delighted to introduce to all of you the Deputy Secretary-General, Dr. Asha-Rose Migiro. Many of you have been fortunate to meet her in her former capacity as Foreign Minister of Tanzania. Today, it is I who am fortunate to be able to call her my Deputy. I know she will bring to the task exceptional leadership, wisdom, and commitment.

I am grateful for this opportunity to share with you my views on a topic of deep significance to all of us – how we can collectively strengthen the work of our Organization in the area of peace and security.

Since I was appointed by the General Assembly last October, my team and I have held meetings on this subject with many of you in regional and other groupings, as well as individually. Today, it is time for me to speak to all of you, as I lay out my views.

As I have made clear since I took office, my objective as Secretary-General is to increase your trust and confidence in the United Nations. From the discussions I have had with you, I know you share this goal. And I am convinced that together, we can achieve it. We can build a stronger, more coherent and more effective United Nations.

For me, that means taking the first steps to make the Secretariat more efficient, more results-oriented and more accountable.

In recent weeks, I have worked together with Secretariat staff and Member States to identify current strengths and weaknesses. We have looked at ways to reinforce strengths, and remedy weaknesses.

Today, I will explain where I want to concentrate these first steps. They are two of the most fundamental areas of UN activity: peace operations and disarmament. Of course, these are but two of the many crucial areas of the UN's work for peace and security, but my consultations so far lead me to conclude that they are the most urgent.

Let me assure you: our informal dialogue on this subject to date has only been the first step in the process. I recognize that any proposals I make will have implications for the Secretariat as a whole. I myself will engage in consultations with Member States, and I will ask my senior managers to engage in consultations at expert level with a view to finalizing a set of proposals at the earliest possible date. I am sure you all agree with the benefits of moving forward with urgency.

UN peace operations represent a unique contribution to international peace and security. One cannot overestimate their global impact. No other multinational actor deploys the same number of military and civilian personnel. No bilateral partner engages in multiple field operations of such scope and complexity.

Its unique nature, and its proven record on the ground, have led you, the Member States, to place ever increasing demands on UN peacekeeping. The number of peace operations is at an all-time high, with almost 100,000 personnel in the field. The figure looks set to rise still further this year. Last year alone, we started negotiations for Memoranda of Understanding with more than one hundred troop contributing countries; transported more than 800,000 passengers and 160,000 metric tonnes of cargo by air; and operated more than 200 hospitals and clinics in the field.

Because of the surge in demand, and despite the diligent efforts of our colleagues in peacekeeping, our system is dramatically strained and over-stretched. This comes at a time when we can least afford it, as we plan and prepare for new peace operations in Darfur and elsewhere around the world.

How we strengthen the ability of the Secretariat to support peacekeeping is something in which we all have a stake. It is also a matter of life and death to millions of people who depend on us.

The challenges are manifold. We must ensure that we have several crucial elements in place: a responsive capacity to meet the needs of the field; an integrated approach; adequate management capability; effective and accountable use of your scarce resources.

In addressing these challenges, I have been mindful of the mandates you have given us, and your positive response to the reform process initiated within the Department of Peacekeeping Operations a year ago. That process was part of the ongoing effort to fully implement the recommendations of the Brahimi Report of 2000.

One of the key aims of this reform process – and a priority of mine – is fundamentally consolidating, strengthening and integrating the Secretariat's capacity for planning, managing and supporting all peace operations.

As you are aware, today, many of the crucial components of mission support are scattered across the Secretariat. For example, field personnel management and administration are the responsibility of field missions, as well as several Departments in Headquarters; a similar situation applies to procurement management. Financial management is likewise distributed across the Secretariat.

When responsibility and resources are dispersed in this way, accountability, authority and effectiveness are bound to suffer. Given the steeply growing demands placed on us, bringing these components together has become an imperative.

That is why I propose to consolidate the support functions of UN field personnel, procurement and financial management, into one single, dedicated Department of Field Support. I believe this will allow us to advance on three fronts: supporting all field operations more effectively, coherently and responsively; managing Member States' resources in a more efficient manner; and, most important, establishing a clear point of responsibility and accountability for field support.

This consolidation of support functions would allow a separate, concentrated Department of Peace Operations to focus on the work it needs to do: strategic as well as day-to-day direction and management of peacekeeping operations; new mission planning; development of policies and standards; and fostering partnerships with a broad range of UN and non-UN actors, including regional organizations.

This creation of two departments would not only improve structural capacity. It would also give to peace operations desperately needed additional senior posts. It would strengthen the heavily overburdened senior management team of today's Department of Peacekeeping Operations, which performs its task with outstanding commitment, but under relentless and unsustainable pressure.

> ❝ We are confronted with so many grave crises around the world. At home, we face the challenge of management reform. Both should proceed together. If we are to meet the demands placed upon us, we need to put our house in order. ❞

Taken together, these measures would bolster and improve the assistance that Headquarters provides to field missions and to field personnel contributed by you, our Member States. It would mean more and better policy guidance from a dedicated Department of Peace Operations; more responsive support from a Department of Field Support properly equipped to address mission support needs; and, in sum, a better way to ensure the safety and security of personnel as well as the success of our missions.

By increasing capacity and designating clear responsibilities, we can also strengthen training and maximize oversight – both of which are essential to ensuring the highest standards of conduct and discipline among UN peacekeeping personnel. I am, as you know, determined to ensure that we protect and uphold the sacred trust that needs to exist between us and the populations we serve, and implement our zero-tolerance policy on sexual abuse and exploitation.

Clearly, these proposals can succeed only if we maintain the principles of unity of command and integration of effort. We know, from our experience over the past decades, how essential both principles are – at headquarters and in the field – if we are to make full use of our diverse capabilities and resources.

In upholding these principles, it is essential that we seamlessly link peacekeeping policy, operations and support functions. Therefore, the Under-Secretary-General for the Department of Peace Operations will be responsible for ensuring unity of command of all peacekeeping decisions, while the Department of Field Support will report to, and receive direction from, the Under-Secretary-General of the Department of Peace Operations on all issues related to peacekeeping. To preserve unity of action and purpose in the field, and strengthen the chain of command with headquarters, heads of UN peacekeeping missions will report to me through the Department of Peace Operations. Existing reporting lines within field operations will remain intact. The overall authority of the Special Representatives of the Secretary-General in the field will remain the same. And existing command and control arrangements applicable to Force Commanders in the field will not change.

Day-to-day management of operations will require Department of Peace Operations and the Department of Field Support to work in an integrated manner at all levels. This can be facilitated by establishing integrated teams of representatives from both Departments, which would pool substantive expertise and support functions, under the direction of the Department of Peace Operations. Let me note that this concept of integrated teams, initiated as part of the peacekeeping reform effort, was specifically examined by the Office of Internal Oversight Services, in its forthcoming report on the Department of Peacekeeping Operations' management structures, because of its potential to improve management and oversight of UN peacekeeping operations.

I would, of course, ensure that the necessary checks and balances are maintained in overseeing the activities of the revised organizational structure. This would ensure that the policy direction set by the legislative bodies is implemented in a coherent and consistent manner across the Secretariat as a whole, with respect to human resources, procurement, information and communication technology and finance, including budgeting and funds management. To fulfil the Secretariat's responsibilities in these areas, a thorough and substantive review and amendment of existing formalized procedures and delegations of authority would be undertaken expeditiously with respect to both the Financial and Staff Regulations and Rules. The consolidation of support functions for field operations would not result in duplicative structures at Headquarters. Rather, it would lead to clearer lines of accountability, and a more effective and targeted utilization of resources. Within that context, I am determined to align responsibilities with authorities and necessary resources.

On general administrative and management issues which do not apply directly to UN peace operations, the Department of Field Support would work together with the Department of Management, under the guidance of the Deputy Secretary-General, to ensure system-wide coherence of management and administration practices.

Excellencies, what I have outlined goes directly to the question: what kind of peace operations do we want to see in the future? These reforms would enable us to meet the growing demands placed on us with strengthened capacity, consolidated support, and a system that is more effective, transparent and accountable.

Today, the world is facing acute challenges in the area of disarmament and non-proliferation. Amid heightened global anxiety about weapons of mass destruction, States have been unable to agree on the way forward. Failure and deadlock have characterized major fora and instruments, such as the 2005 Non-Proliferation Treaty Review Conference, the Conference and Disarmament and the Comprehensive Nuclear Test Ban Treaty – and the absence of any reference to disarmament in the 2005 World Summit Outcome Document.

This deeply alarming situation makes clear the need to revitalize the disarmament agenda, through a more focussed effort. I have listened to your views on how the urgent issues in the area of disarmament and non-proliferation affect all of us. Sustained and determined leadership at the highest level is required to address all these challenges. I am personally committed to making that happen. I therefore propose that the Department of Disarmament Affairs be constituted as an Office with a direct line to me, thus ensuring access and more frequent interaction.

With this reconfiguration, we would make disarmament an integral part of the policy decision-making process at the highest level. This would strengthen existing synergies across the field of peace and security, and, at the same time, would help us build more functional and effective cooperation with global and regional intergovernmental organizations.

The Office would be headed by a Special Representative of the Secretary-General or High Representative, so as to maximize the flexibility, agility and proximity to the Secretary-General required to facilitate ongoing and new disarmament and non-proliferation efforts.

A Special Representative or High Representative would be able to operate with more flexibility in establishing cooperation and conducting dialogue with governments and other interested actors, including in country-specific situations. He or she would also act as a facilitator in finding solutions to issues of concern.

Proximity to the Secretary-General would allow for a strengthened advocacy role in mobilizing political will to overcome the stalemate in disarmament and non-proliferation. The Special Representative or High Representative would also act as a catalyst with civil society organizations, which play a vital role in building and activating public opinion for disarmament.

The new Office would continue to implement existing mandates. But at the same time, we would re-energize our work for simultaneous action on both disarmament and non-proliferation. The two objectives are inextricably linked, and neither can advance without the other.

In this way, I intend to strengthen the functions of the new Office so that we can advance the priority issues before us:

Working for universal adherence to international disarmament and non-proliferation agreements, and their full and effective implementation by the States Parties;

Achieving more tailored dialogue, cooperation and assistance to Member States and sub-regions, in order to help States build capacity to counter weapons of mass destruction proliferation, as well as tackle the proliferation of small arms and light weapons.

Please rest assured that over the past few weeks, I have taken account of your concerns. Every one of you has the right to be listened to, whatever the size of your country or budget, whichever hemisphere you call home.

I have sought to adjust my proposals in accordance with your concerns. And by speaking to you today, I hope I have been able to answer a few more of them.

As for senior appointments, I will be moving forward to fill existing posts as soon as possible. Decisions about appointments for any new entities would be taken at a later date, and would be done through an open consultative process.

This Organization needs to act as one. We are confronted with so many grave crises around the world. At home, we face the challenge of management reform. Both should proceed together. If we are to meet the demands placed upon us, we need to put our house in order. There is no time to lose. I would be grateful for the General Assembly's approval of my proposals as soon as is practically possible.

Address to the General Assembly upon appointment as Secretary-General

NEW YORK, 13 OCTOBER 2006

I stand before you, deeply touched and inspired by your generous words of congratulations and encouragement. With boundless gratitude for the confidence placed in me by the Member States, and with an unswerving resolve to honor that trust, I humbly accept the appointment as the eighth Secretary-General of this great Organization, our United Nations. I wish to extend my deepest respect and appreciation to all the leaders and peoples of the Member States for their strong support.

I follow in a line of remarkable leaders. They had also faced this moment, each at a critical juncture in the Organization's history. Like myself today, they must have pondered what the years ahead would hold at the helm of this dynamic institution. Each made important and lasting contributions to our common enterprise in upholding humanity's deepest values and highest aspirations.

In particular, you, Mr. Annan, have astutely guided our Organization into the 21st century. You have defined an ambitious agenda that has made the UN truly indispensible to peace, prosperity and human dignity around the world. Our debt to your courage and vision is immeasurable. I resolve to build upon your legacy.

By completing the appointment of the next Secretary-General with such alacrity, you have opened an unprecedented opportunity. Never before has an incoming Secretary-General been given sufficient time to prepare. You have given me more than two months. I will use these weeks to consult widely on how best to proceed with our common agenda of reform and revitalization. I will listen attentively to your concerns, expectations and admonitions.

I am deeply honored to become the second Asian to lead the Organization, following Mr. U Thant who ably served the world four decades ago. It is quite fitting that you have now turned to Asia again for the next Secretary-General to guide the UN system through its seventh decade. Asia is dynamic and diverse, and Asia aspires to take on greater responsibilities for the world. Having come so far and rising still, the region is living and shaping the full range of achievements and challenges of our current times.

Asia is also a region where modesty is a virtue. But the modesty is about demeanor, not about vision and goals. It does not mean the lack of commitment or leadership. Rather, it is quiet determination in action to get things done without so much fanfare. This may be the key to Asia's success, and to the UN's future. Indeed, our Organization is modest in its means, but not in its values. We should be more modest in our words, but not in our performance. The true measure of success for the UN is not how much we promise, but how much we deliver for those who need us most. Given the enduring purposes and inspiring principles of our Organization, we need not shout its praises or preach its virtues. We simply need to live them every day: step by step, program by program, mandate by mandate.

The surge in demand for UN services attests not only to the UN's abiding relevance but also to its central place in advancing human dignity. The UN is needed now more than ever before. The UN's core mission in the previous century was to keep countries from fighting each other. In the new century, the defining mandate is to strengthen the inter-state system so that humanity may be better served amidst new challenges. From the Balkans to Africa, from Asia to the Middle East, we have witnessed the weakening or absence of effective governance leading to the ravaging of human rights and the abandonment of longstanding humanitarian principles. We need competent and responsible states to meet the needs of "we the peoples" for whom the UN was created. And the world's peoples will not be fully served unless peace, development and human rights, the three pillars of the UN, are advanced together with equal vigor.

The road that we must pave toward a world of peace, prosperity and dignity for all has many pitfalls. As Secretary-General, I will make the most of the authority invested in my office by the Charter and the mandate you give me. I will work diligently to materialize our responsibility to protect the most vulnerable members of humanity and for the peaceful resolution of threats to international security and regional stability.

In order to meet these growing mandates and expectations, we have engaged in the most sweeping reform effort in the history of the Organization. The very scope of the reform has taxed the attention and energies of both the delegations and the Secretariat. But we must stay the course. We need to muster the human, institutional and intellectual resources, and to organize them properly. We should do our part in meeting the Millennium Development Goals, the expanding peace operations, the threats posed by terrorism, weapons of mass destruction proliferation, HIV/AIDS and other pandemics, environmental degradation, and the imperatives of human rights.

Let us remember that we reform not to please others, but because we value what this Organization stands for. We reform because we believe in its future. To revitalize our common endeavor is to renew our faith not only in the UN's programs and purposes but also in each other. We should demand more of ourselves as well as of our Organization. To cut through the fog of mistrust is going to require more intensive dialogue. We cannot change everything at once. But if we choose wisely, and work together transparently, flexibly and honestly, progress in a few areas will lead to progress in many more. Only the Member States can revitalize this Organization. But I will always be there to assist and facilitate as needed.

As Secretary-General, I am resolved to manage my office openly and responsibly. I will seek to build consensus through a free exchange of ideas and critiques. Only through the candid, open testing of ideas and proposals can we identify better means of serving the peoples of the world.

I will work actively in reaching out to all stakeholders. In particular, in order to bring the United Nations closer to the people, I will widely engage civil society in dialogue. I will seek the support and input of humanitarian advocacy groups, businesses and other constituents of the global citizenry for the good of the Organization.

My tenure will be marked by ceaseless efforts to build bridges and close divides. Leadership of harmony, not division, and by example, not instruction, has served me well so far. I intend to stay the course as Secretary-General.

I will be fully accountable for the management of this institution. Member States set the mandates and provide the resources. If the resources are not sufficient for the task at hand, I will not be shy about saying so, but once we in the Secretariat have taken on a task, we must accept full responsibility for its achievement.

I am eager to join the ranks of the world's premier secretariat. I have deep respect and admiration for the able, dedicated, and courageous men and women who serve this Organization day in and day out, often in the face of danger and personal sacrifice. To them, I pledge my utmost support, dedication and solidarity.

Maintaining their proud heritage, while vigorously holding them to the highest standards of professionalism and integrity, will be a prime goal of my tenure. The aim of Secretariat reform is not to penalize but to reward, so that their talent and skill, experience and dedication may be fully mobilized and properly utilized. Rewarding hard work and excellence to boost morale, making everyone accountable for his/her own action or inaction, and pushing for greater gender balance, in particular at senior levels: these will be my guide, as I rally the Secretariat staff for our very best performance in serving the Organization. As your Secretary-General, I am far from perfect, and I will need the unsparing support, cooperation and trust from all represented here. But I pledge to serve you well, with all of my heart and to the best of my abilities. I will seek excellence with humility. I will lead by example. Promises should be made for the keeping. This has been my motto in life. I intend to stick to it, as I work with all stakeholders for a UN that delivers on its promises.

My heart is overflowing with gratitude toward my country and people who have sent me here to serve. It has been a long journey from my youth in war-torn and destitute Korea to this rostrum and these awesome responsibilities. I could make the journey because the UN was with my people in our darkest days. It gave us hope and sustenance, security and dignity. It showed us a better way. So I feel at home today, however many miles and years I have traveled.

66 The true measure of success for the UN is not how much we promise, but how much we deliver for those who need us most. 99

For the Korean people, the UN flag was and remains a beacon of better days to come. There are countless stories of that faith. One belongs to me. In 1956, when the Cold War was raging around the world, as a young boy of twelve, I was chosen to read out a public message, on behalf of my elementary school, addressed to the Secretary-General of the United Nations, Mr. Dag Hammarskjold. We urged him to help the people of a certain faraway European country in their fight for freedom and democracy. I hardly understood the deeper meaning of the message. But I knew that the UN was there for help in times of need.

Fifty years later, the world is a much more complex place, and there are many more actors to turn to. During those years, I have travelled many times around the world. I have been elated by the successes of the UN in making life better for countless people. I have also been pained by scenes of its failures. In too many places could I feel the dismay over inaction of the UN, or action that was too little or came too late. I am determined to dispel the disillusionment.

I earnestly hope that young boys and girls of today will grow up knowing that the UN is working hard to build a better future for them. As Secretary General, I will embrace their hopes and hear their appeals. I am an optimist, and I am full of hope about the future of our global Organization. Let us work together for a UN that can deliver more and better.

The United Nations in A Changing World

Address to the National Assembly of the Republic of Korea
Together, building the future we want

SEOUL, 30 OCTOBER 2012

I am deeply honoured to be the first United Nations Secretary-General to address the National Assembly of the Republic of Korea. Ordinarily, as Secretary-General, I should speak in one of the official languages of the United Nations. But as a Korean, speaking in the National Assembly of the Republic of Korea, I hope you will understand why I will speak today in my mother tongue.

As I look back at the long special relationship between Korea and the United Nations, I am especially pleased to stand at the beginning of my second term in this august chamber which represents all of the Korean people.

Korea and the United Nations have worked hand-in-hand for this country's spectacular development. The special relationship began in 1948. The United Nations sent an electoral supervisory mission to witness Korea's first democratic general elections – the first such deployment anywhere in the world.

Following the outbreak of the Korean War two years later, the United Nations came to the defence of Korea, becoming a beacon of hope for the Korean people. With the help of the United Nations, Korea overcame the tragedy of war and quickly began down the path of astonishing economic growth and deeper democracy. Today, Korea stands as an example, ever striving to represent the ideals and objectives of the United Nations.

Throughout my travels around the world, I share the experiences of Korea's economic development and democratization process. I am often amazed to see the strong interest among leaders around the world to learn from Korea's example.

Korea also is achieving great global success in culture, sports and the arts. As is clear with the recent rise of Psy's Gangnam Style, the Hallyu wave and Korean pop music, Korean culture is making its mark on the world. Korea also showed its potential in sports in the London Summer Olympics, which impressed the global sports community. This youthful, creative and dynamic Korea is rising as a new hope in the world.

Today I would like to talk about how Korea and the United Nations can work together to build the future we want, a more secure and prosperous world for all. I want to talk with you about this because I fully appreciate your crucial role as elected members of the National Assembly in representing the people and their aspirations.

Wherever I travel, I seek out leaders of the national assemblies. I address Parliaments. I do so because you are the institution that puts people first and this is what ties you and the United Nations together. Indeed our Charter begins with the words "we the peoples".

The world is facing great uncertainty and undergoing a turbulent transition. Around the globe, there is rising insecurity, inequality, injustice and intolerance. These issues cannot be addressed by one country or organization alone, regardless of its size or resources. These are global challenges that require more effective global engagement and global leadership.

The United Nations is increasingly called upon to play a greater role in renewing and strengthening multilateralism. The United Nations is the one and only global organization, with universal membership, and the largest operational presence around the world to advance our common values.

Our funding is under severe pressure because of the global economic crisis. At the same time, the worsening situation is also increasing demand for the United Nations to assist the most vulnerable. We must find a solution to address peace and security, development and social challenges.

Let us not forget that when the world came to help Korea, many said in their own countries, "We have budget pressures and problems at home. Why should we help those people so far away?" Despite such questions, the peoples of other nations came to Korea's assistance in the hour of need because they knew it was the right thing to do.

Earlier this year, I thought of the importance of that global solidarity when I set out key priorities for the next five years. With the close cooperation of Member States, we are working to implement my vision of reforming the United Nations and building partnerships to do more with less.

I am fully committed to making the United Nations a more transparent, effective and responsible organization. This will require the full commitment of the international community to work with the United Nations in the spirit of advancing and deepening good governance everywhere. I am also committed to strengthening early response and conflict prevention measures and enhancing preparedness to reduce the risks from natural disasters.

In an unstable world, we must intensify our efforts to stop the spread of weapons of mass destruction and conventional weapons. We must do all we can to enhance nuclear safety and prevent nuclear terrorism.

Allow me to address some burning issues of global concern that are at the front and centre of our work. The Arab Spring has brought historic change to Tunisia,

Egypt, Yemen, Libya and even Syria. The people's will is sacred. The events in the Arab world showed once again what happens when leaders fail to listen to their people.

There are many parallels with Korea's own difficult transition from authoritarianism to democracy. Many lessons from that experience can be shared with the international community. I have urged leaders in countries undergoing transition to put aside narrow differences, respond to people's genuine demands, and follow the trend of history.

I am appalled that the recent call to suspend the fighting in Syria was ignored and violated by both sides. Instead of the agreed upon halt, more than 450 Syrians were slaughtered during the most important Muslim holiday period. This should be unacceptable to Syrian leaders, opposition figures, and all humanity.

No matter the divisions on a political solution for Syria, surely we can all unite around the conviction that the killing must stop.

It is clear that the Syrian people need to see transition and real change in their country. Violence is not the way to promote that change or stop it. There is no military solution. I condemn both sides for continuing to use arms instead of dialogue and mediation. The Syrian people have suffered far too much.

Starting with the Syrian Government and the armed opposition, we all have a responsibility to end the bloodshed, now. The international community must work together to resolve this crisis. The members of the United Nations Security Council, who are responsible for ensuring international peace and security, must speak with one voice.

For the past five years, the United Nations has developed a new principle, the Responsibility to Protect, as an integral part of national sovereignty.

The principle of the Responsibility to Protect gives expression to a growing global conviction that it is immoral and unacceptable for States to commit or allow serious international crimes against their people — acts or threats of genocide, ethnic cleansing, war crimes or crimes against humanity or their incitement. Now it is increasingly evident that those committing these serious crimes will eventually be held accountable and that there will no longer be impunity for international crimes.

Last year, the responsibility to protect went through the reality test – and passed. The results were not perfect, but democracy was restored in Côte d'Ivoire, and lives were saved in Libya, where that country's people rose up against the dictatorship.

Over the last two decades, international criminal tribunals and courts have been established from the former Yugoslavia and Rwanda to Cambodia, Lebanon and Sierra Leone. The permanent International Criminal Court was also created. These institutions have become important foundations for international criminal justice. A number of Korean judges have played an important role.

The winds of change that started with the Arab Spring will continue to blow. They are unstoppable. I will continue to remind leaders, in Syria and beyond, of their responsibility to listen and respond to the will of the people.

The international community must make progress on the three pillars of United Nations engagement. First: sustainable development. Second: conflict prevention and resolution. And third: advancing human rights and democracy. Korea has unique lessons to share on all three pillars and can be an active catalyst in bringing the world together on these issues.

> **❝ I wish to see my mother country, Korea, stand tall and proud as an advanced nation by making a bigger contribution on the world stage and gaining ever more respect in the international community. The window of opportunity is wide open. ❞**

Korea evolved from a developing to a developed country within the span of a single generation, and successfully hosted the G-20 Summit. The international community is looking to Korea with high expectations.

I thank you with respect for rising from a beneficiary to a donor. I take this opportunity to ask you to continue by focusing on five key priorities.

First, Korea made a promise to increase overseas development assistance. I expect that promise to be faithfully implemented. Yes, this is a way to repay the assistance the country received in the past to help it become a respected member of the international community. But it has even greater significance.

Africa is one of Korea's largest recipients of development cooperation. But Africa is also one of the fastest growing regions in the world with rich resources. Korea's development assistance must be seen as far more than charity. It is an investment for the future.

Korea must establish an advanced system to improve aid effectiveness. I applaud the Development Alliance Korea, a public-private partnership launched last August to do just that. I commend the decision to increase assistance to 0.25 per cent of GDP by 2015 despite the difficult economic climate.

I would also like to ask you to keep going. A pledge of up to 0.7 per cent would truly mark Korea's commitment to being a stronger and more developed nation on the global stage. I ask you to present a clear path to the international community and continue to move in that direction. I hope that the National Assembly will play a leading role in ensuring that Korea reaches this goal.

Second, we look forward to Korea's proactive efforts to help the world achieve the Millennium Development Goals over the next three years by the deadline of 2015. The target year of 2015 is not an end, but a new beginning. I also look forward to Korea's active participation in helping to establish the post-2015 development agenda and the sustainable development goals.

We need much cooperation in laying these foundations. The National Assembly's United Nations-MDG Forum can play a key role. The extension of the Airline Solidarity Levy as the first agenda item of the newly elected 19th National Assembly is an important example of your global leadership.

Third, the United Nations is focusing on a number of sustainable development initiatives. Scaling Up Nutrition and the Zero Hunger Challenge aim to revolutionize the way the world tackles the problem of under-nutrition and hunger. I am proud of the fact that the Republic of Korea has achieved Zero Hunger, and has challenged others to do the same. As the host of last year's Fourth High Level Forum on Aid Effectiveness, Korea should strive to align its development assistance programme with the goals of enabling all people, everywhere, to enjoy their right to food and for all food systems to be sustainable.

Women's and children's health is at the heart of achieving the Millennium Development Goals. Our Every Woman, Every Child initiative has galvanized over 260 public and private partners to save 16 million lives by 2015. The Republic of Korea can help us to achieve this objective by following through on its commitment to universal health coverage by 2015, and by adopting an integrated approach to health care delivery.

We have also just launched a new initiative: Education First. When I visit other countries, I share how Korea's investments in education paid dividends for success. I also relate how Korean students once used textbooks with the help of the United Nations. Education First will help open school doors for all children, improve the quality of learning, and foster global citizenship. We expect Korea to play an active role in this effort.

And we are strengthening partnerships for sustainable energy for all. This initiative has three complementary objectives to be achieved by 2030. First, providing universal access to modern energy services for all. Second, doubling of the rate of improvement in energy efficiency. And third, doubling the share of renewable energy in the global energy mix.

The Government of Korea has demonstrated strong leadership and commitment in this area. I have personally witnessed and benefitted from the energy transformation that happened in this country in the past century. I call on the Republic of Korea to work with us and lead the way to transform the world's energy sector.

Climate change, in particular, is a clear and present danger. The international community must work together to meet their obligations to establish a legally binding treaty by 2015. We must never forget that we are stewards, borrowing this planet from the next generation. We must strive to preserve the planet so that the next generation can live free from the fear of extreme weather.

Korea's leadership in green growth is a future-oriented strategy that takes into account both the needs of climate change and economic growth.

I believe that Korea must reach its target emissions rate and can play a leading role in encouraging other countries to do the same. I congratulate the recent launch of the Global Green Growth Institute in Seoul last week as an international organization. I am also pleased and happy to congratulate Korea on being selected by the board of the Green Climate Fund as the host of its new secretariat.

This reflects the international community's expectations for the Republic of Korea. There is a global recognition of the country's experiences as an emerging economy, as well as its efforts to help lead cooperation with industrialized nations on climate change. I hope that the Government and people of Korea will play an active role and strengthen its cooperation in boosting climate change-related agreements, as well as managing the development of the Fund.

Fourth, the Korean experience of advancing democracy, peace and prosperity is an important resource upon which the world can draw for international peacekeeping efforts. Since joining the United Nations in 1991, the Republic of Korea has contributed to global peacekeeping with resources and troops.

Korea's peacekeeping forces in various missions around the world have received high praise from the international community for their expertise and skills, excellent discipline, and ability to connect with the local population as "bridge builders".

On behalf of the United Nations, I thank the National Assembly for approving peacekeeping deployments to Lebanon, Haiti and, most recently, South Sudan. I hope that more can be deployed: more Korean peacekeepers, more police, in particular female officers. I also applaud the adoption of the 2010 Peacekeeping Operations Law and the creation of stand-by troops. I look forward to the Republic of Korea's continued and growing engagement with United Nations peacekeeping operations.

On the 18th of this month, the Republic of Korea was elected as a non-permanent member of the United Nations Security Council. I congratulate you on this great achievement, which marks the second time that the country will serve on the Security Council since it became a member of the United Nations in 1991.

This reflects the recognition by the Member States of the contributions that the Republic of Korea has made to the United Nations. It also reflects the high expectations that the international community places on Korea's contributions to international peace and security as well as global development.

Now is a good opportunity to build on this reputation and solidify Korea as an important contributor to peace. I believe that Korea will be able to contribute effectively to conflict prevention measures and efforts to expand universal values and human rights.

As Secretary-General, I often meet with leaders that have human rights and corruption challenges. I share with them my honest assessment based on Korea's own experience, and my candid warnings of the failure to act. Again and again, leaders who initially resisted talking about such issues eventually opened their minds after hearing about the Korean experiences and possibilities for change. I feel that this is a tremendous source of Korea's soft power.

Fifth, Korea can contribute more to empower women and youth. While Korea's population is aging fast, the world's population is increasing in developing countries, with more than half under twenty-five years of age. Young people want decent work. This is a global challenge and we must work together to promote dignity and opportunity.

The rights of women must also be given the high priority they deserve. This is a top goal for me. I have been urging leaders around the world to do more to place women in high-level positions. At the United Nations, I have increased the number of women in senior United Nations positions. As a result of my appointments, the number of women at the senior-most positions at the United Nations has increased by more than 60 per cent. By opening up the doors of opportunity, more women are making a difference by serving as my special representatives in the field, leading troops in various peacekeeping missions around the globe.

Finally, more work must be done to protect the rights of minorities. That means social protection for people with disabilities, migrant workers, refugees and the growing number of multicultural families. I am pleased that the Korean Government has recently lifted travel restrictions on those who are HIV-positive.

We commend the broad support provided to accelerate resettlement and social assimilation of those Koreans who have moved from North to South, seeking freedom. We hope such support will be further advanced and that relevant countries will provide assistance based on universal human rights and humanitarian principles.

As a fellow Korean, I hope for an improvement in the situation on the Korean peninsula. I have an ardent desire for moving towards unification. I fervently hope that the new leadership of the Democratic People's Republic of Korea meets the international community's call for denuclearization on the Korean peninsula. I also hope that as a responsible member of the international community, the leadership continues to take full responsibility in improving the lives of its people. I take note of the remarks by Democratic People's Republic of Korea's Kim Jong Un, First Chairman of the National Defence Commission, in his first public address on 15 April. He stated that the he would go hand in hand with anyone who desires the country's reunification and the nation's peaceful prosperity and would make responsible and patient efforts towards that end.

Human dignity must be enhanced by implementing the recommendations of the United Nations' universal periodic review of human rights. I will spare no effort to help both the South and the North move towards eventual reunification and a Korean peninsula that is peaceful and free of nuclear weapons.

As Secretary-General, I am committed to doing my utmost to play any role in helping to advance peace on the Korean peninsula. That includes visiting the Democratic People's Republic of Korea under the right conditions.

Today, the United Nations is leading the effort to provide humanitarian assistance to the most vulnerable in the Democratic People's Republic of Korea. In particular, children are suffering from malnutrition and stunted growth – a very serious problem. The future of the Korean people demands that we urgently address this challenge.

The United Nations is best equipped to provide needed assistance to those in need without diversion. I hope that Korea will look at this problem with big hearts in the interest of the whole Korean people and that the National Assembly will take the lead.

Looking ahead for the future of the Korean people, I hope that the Korean peninsula can move from being the land of challenges to the land of opportunities.

It is essential that we have the cooperation of our regional partners. North-east Asia is a rising global centre. Its intra-regional trade and exchanges have risen dramatically. However, tensions rooted in past history still remain. We must increase bilateral cooperation based on an accurate understanding of history and dialogue to look forward and address such tensions peacefully and expand interaction in all areas.

In parallel, efforts to promote intra-regional economic integration and political cooperation should continue. There is much to learn from the efforts of others such as Europe, Africa and South America, where intra-regional integration and cooperation are increasing. Greater engagement will require strengthened multilateralism and Korea can serve as a bridge. Through this process, I hope Korea will play a leading role in shaping the new order in East Asia.

As Secretary-General, I travel often to some of the farthest reaches of the planet. More times than I can count, I have often come across young Korean women or men who have volunteered to serve the neediest. I feel very proud when I meet those Koreans who show their love for humanity in difficult and conflict-riddled situations.

I am saddened to think of the young volunteers who lost their lives in Sri Lanka, but I believe their giving spirit will serve as an inspiration for us all and will long be remembered.

I see Korea's bright future through those volunteers. Korea ranks as a world leader in providing volunteers around the globe. That passion for service has been well appreciated by the international community. It also provides a good model to the UN Volunteers. I am confident that the young generation of Korea will continue embracing the world, and become global citizens by trying to realize " Korea in the world" and "the world in Korea".

The future we want cannot be created alone. As I said in my second-term acceptance speech, together, nothing is impossible. I draw strength from the proverb: if you want to go fast, go alone. But if you want to go far, go together.

When I became the United Nations Secretary-General in 2006, I vowed to strive to make more success stories based on Korean values and experiences. I wish to see my mother country, Korea, stand tall and proud as an advanced nation by making a bigger contribution on the world stage and gaining ever more respect in the international community.

The window of opportunity is wide open. We can add a new chapter to the success story of Korea. Let us never forget that ending poverty, advancing democracy, protecting human rights, working to secure peace, is possible.

That is the story of Korea. And with your help, we can make it the story of the world. I am confident that Korea will become a stronger partner of the United Nations in our journey to realize the future we want: a safer and more prosperous world.

I would like to take this opportunity to thank the people of Korea who have supported me since my appointment as United Nations Secretary-General. Yesterday, I received the eleventh Seoul Peace Prize. I was very honoured to receive such a prestigious distinction. It is a tribute to the work of the United Nations. I will do my best to promote a better life for all humanity and world peace.

From day one as United Nations Secretary-General, I have worked to take the initiative and set an example every day. I will work even harder with passion and compassion to live up to your support and the expectations of the international community. I sincerely wish for a bright future for the Republic of Korea. I wish you and your families much health, happiness and blessings.

유엔과 한국: 함께 이루는 인류의 꿈

SEOUL, 30 OCTOBER 2012

존경하는 국민 여러분, 존경하는 강창희 국회의장님과 국회의원 여러분, 그리고 주한 외교단과 내외 귀빈 여러분,

저는 오늘 유엔 사무총장으로서 처음으로 대한민국 국회에서 연설할 수 있게 되어 무한한 영광으로 생각합니다.

한국과 유엔의 길고 특별한 인연을 생각할 때, 저의 두 번째 임기를 시작하면서 대한민국 민의의 전당인 이 자리에 서게 되어 더욱 감회가 깊습니다.

한국의 눈부신 발전은 유엔과 함께 이루어왔다고 해도 과언이 아닐 것입니다. 한국과 유엔의 특별한 관계는 1948년에 시작되었습니다. 한국 최초의 총선에 유엔이 사상 처음으로 선거감시단을 파견하였습니다. 2년 뒤 한국전 발발로 유엔이 한국을 수호하기 위해 오면서 유엔은 한국인에게 더욱 소중한 희망의 등대가 되었습니다.

유엔의 도움으로 한국은 전쟁의 참상을 극복하고 짧은 기간 동안 놀라운 경제발전을 이루고 성숙한 민주주의를 구현해내었습니다. 오늘날의 한국은 유엔이 추구하는 이상과 목표를 잘 대변하는 모범 사례입니다.

저는 세계 각국을 다닐 때마다 한국의 민주화와 경제개발 경험을 소개하고 있습니다. 세계 지도자들의 한국배우기 열풍이 얼마나 큰지 저 자신도 놀랄 때가 많습니다.

이제 한국은 문화, 스포츠, 예술에 이르기까지 다양한 분야에서 커다란 성공을 거두고 있습니다. 최근의 '강남스타일' 열풍이 보여주듯이 한류, 특히 K-pop을 통하여 한국은 세계 문화의 새로운 흐름을 주도하고 있습니다. 런던 올림픽에서 보여준 한국의 저력에도 세계 스포츠계가 놀랐습니다. 이처럼 젊고 창의적이며 역동적인 한국은 지구촌의 새로운 희망으로 떠오르고 있습니다.

존경하는 국회의장님과 국회의원 여러분,

저는 오늘 이 자리에서 인류가 꿈꾸는 더 안전하고 번영하는 세계의 미래를 향해, 한국과 유엔이 어떻게 함께 나아갈 수 있을지에 대해 말씀드리고자 합니다.

유엔 사무총장으로서 저는 국민의 뜻과 열망을 대변하는 국회의 중요성을 누구보나 잘 인식하고 있기 때문에 세계 어디를 방문하더라도 그 나라의 의회 지도자들과 대화를 가지고 있습니다. 의회는 국민을 가장 우선적으로 섬기는(put people first) 국가기관이며, 이러한 의회의 역할은 유엔 헌장의 정신(we, the peoples)과 일맥상통하기 때문입니다.

존경하는 국회의원과 내외 귀빈 여러분,

지금은 불확실성과 격변의 시대입니다. 전 세계 도처에서 불안정(insecurity)과 불평등(inequality), 부정의(injustice)와 불관용(intolerance)이 증가하고 있습니다.

이러한 문제는 어느 한 국가 또는 어느 한 조직의 노력만으로는 대처가 불가능합니다. 이러한 전 지구적 도전은 보다 효율적인 전 지구적 개입과 리더십을 요구하고 있습니다. 특히 유엔은 다자주의(multilateralism)를 새롭게 강화하는데 더 큰 역할을 할 것을 요구받고 있습니다.

유엔은 가장 보편적인 범세계적 기구로서, 인류의 공동가치를 실현하기 위해 전 세계 도처에 가장 광범위한 조직을 유지하고 있습니다. 그러나 세계 경제위기로 인해 유엔의 재정형편은 어려워지고 있습니다. 또한 상황의 악화로 세계의 취약계층을 도와야 하는 유엔의 활동수요는 증대되고 있습니다. 세계의 평화안보, 개발, 사회분야에서 늘어나는 수요를 다룰 수 있는 방안을 찾아야만 하는 상황입니다.

세계가 한국을 도와주었을 때, 외국의 많은 사람들이 "우리도 경제가 어렵고 국내에 많은 문제가 있는데 왜 멀리 있는 그들을 도와주어야 하느냐"는 의문을 제기했었던 사실을 잊으면 안됩니다. 그러한 의문에도 불구하고 그들은 올바른 일이라는 확신을 가지고 한국이 도움을 필요로 할 때 도와주었던 것입니다.

금년 초에 저는 이러한 세계적 연대의 중요성을 염두에 두고 향후 5년간 중점을 둘 우선순위 과제를 제시하였습니다. 이와 함께 유엔의 전면적인 개혁, 그리고 민간부문과의 파트너십 확대를 통해 "보다 작은 재원으로 보다 큰 성과를 거두기 위한(do more with less)" 노력을 회원국들과 협력하여 펼쳐나가고 있습니다.

저는 유엔이 보다 투명하고 효과적이면서 책임성 있는 조직이 될 수 있도록 노력하고 있습니다. 이에는 국제사회가 유엔과 더불어 세계적 "선정(good governance)" 을 펼쳐가겠다는 의지가 뒷받침되어야 합니다.

분쟁에 효과적으로 대처하기 위한 예방과 즉시 대응의 강화, 그리고 자연재해의 피해를 줄이기 위한 준비태세 제고에도 힘을 기울이고 있습니다.

불안한 국제 안보환경 속에서 대량살상무기와 재래식 무기의 감축, 비확산 노력도 배가해야 합니다. 핵안전을 제고하고 핵테러리즘을 차단하는 데에도 만전을 기해야 합니다.

내외 귀빈 여러분,

지금 이 순간에도 우리 모두의 가슴을 무겁게 누르고 있는 국제적 현안들이 있습니다. "아랍의 봄"은 튀니지, 이집트, 예멘, 리비아, 그리고 시리아에 이르기까지 거스를 수 없는 역사의 흐름이 되고 있습니다. 민심은 천심입니다. 각국의 지도자들이 국민의 여망에 귀를 기울이지 않을 때 어떤 결과가 오는지를 잘 보여주고 있습니다.

국민의 힘으로 어렵게 이룬 과거 한국의 민주화 경험에서 배울 교훈이 많습니다. 저는 과도기를 겪는 지도자들이 편협한 이익을 넘어 국민의 열망에 조속히 호응하여 역사의 대세에 따를 것을 촉구하고 있습니다.

시리아에서는 지금 이 순간에도 무고한 시민의 비극적 희생이 매일 계속되고 있습니다.

저는 최근 이루어진 휴전이 양측에 의해 무시되고 위반된 것에 대해 경악하고 있습니다. 휴전이 지켜지지 않은채 이슬람 사회에서 가장 중요한 휴일동안 450명 이상의 희생자가 발생하였습니다. 시리아 지도자와 반정부 단체들은 물론 모든 인류에게 이는 결코 용납될 수 없는 일입니다.

시리아 사태 해결을 위한 정치적 해법에 어떠한 이견이 있더라도 인명 살상이 반드시 중단되어야 한다는데 대해서는 이견이 있을 수 없습니다.

시리아 국민들은 자국이 보다 민주적인 사회로 전환되고 변화하기를 갈구하고 있습니다. 폭력은 이러한 변화를 촉진하거나 중단시키는 방법이 될 수 없습니다.

군사적 해법은 없습니다. 저는 대화와 중재 대신 무기에 의존하는 양측 모두를 규탄합니다.

시리아 국민들은 이미 너무나 많은 고통을 겪고 있습니다. 시리아에서 진행되고 있는 유혈사태를 즉시 중단시켜야 할 책임이 우리 모두에게 있으며, 그 책임은 시리아 정부와 무장 반군단체로부터 시작되어야만 합니다.

이러한 상황은 도저히 용납될 수 없습니다. 시리아 지도자들이 즉각적으로 폭력을 중지하고 대화를 통해 문제 해결에 나설 것을 저는 다시 한 번 촉구합니다. 국제사회 전

체가 합심해서 해결 방안을 찾아내야 합니다. 국제평화와 안전을 책임지는 유엔 안전보장이사국들이 단합된 목소리를 내는 것이 무엇보다 중요합니다.

유엔은 지난 5년간 "국민 보호 책임(Responsibility to Protect)" 원칙을 국가주권의 불가분의 책임으로 발전시켜왔습니다. 국민 보호 책임은 국가가 자국민들에게 심각한 국제범죄, 즉 대량살상, 인종청소, 전쟁범죄 또는 반인도적 범죄를 저지르는 것이 비도덕적이며 용납될 수 없다는 세계적 확신을 대변하고 있습니다. 이제 이러한 중대한 범죄를 저지른 인사는 결국 책임을 면할 수 없으며, 국제적 범죄는 더 이상 면책이 되지 않는다는 것이 더욱 분명해지고 있습니다. 작년에 국민 보호 책임 원칙이 시험을 받았으나 확고히 견지되었습니다. 완벽한 결과는 아니었지만 민주주의가 코트 디브와르에서 복구되었으며, 독재에 대한 민중봉기가 일어났던 리비아에서 많은 생명을 구하였습니다.

최근 이십년간 유고, 르완다, 캄보디아, 레바논, 시에라리온에서 특별법원이 세워졌습니다. 그리고 상설 국제형사재판소가 설립되었습니다. 이는 국제형사정의 실현에 중요한 제도적 진전입니다. 여기에서도 다수의 한국인 판사들이 크게 기여하고 있습니다.

아랍의 봄에서 시작된 변혁의 바람은 계속될 것입니다. 이 바람은 그 누구도 막지 못할 것입니다. 앞으로도 저는 시리아뿐만 아니라 다른 국가들의 지도자들에 대해서도 국민의 뜻에 부합하는 조치들을 취해야 할 것임을 지속적으로 촉구해 나가겠습니다.

존경하는 국민 여러분, 국회의원과 내외 귀빈 여러분,

국제사회는 유엔을 중심으로 지속 가능한 개발, 분쟁 예방과 대치, 그리고 인권과 민주주의의 확립 등 세 가지의 큰 과제를 추진해 오고 있습니다.

한국은 이 모두에서 성공한 세계에서 유례를 찾기 어려운 모범사례입니다. 따라서 한국은 국제사회의 역량을 결집시키는 촉매 역할(catalyst)을 능히 감당할 수 있습니다.

> 저는 조국 대한민국이 국제사회에서 보다 크게 기여하고, 보다 큰 존경을 얻어 선진강국으로 우뚝 서는 모습을 보고 싶습니다. 한국의 성공 이야기에 새로운 장을 추가할 수 있는 "기회의 창"이 대한민국에 활짝 열려있습니다

한국은 한 세대 만에 저개발국에서 선진국으로 진입하고, G-20 정상회의를 성공적으로 개최하였습니다. 한국의 개발경험 전수에 대한 국제사회의 기대는 실로 큽니다. 과거 "수혜자"이었던 한국이 이제 "기여자"로서 많은 일들을 해오고 있는 데 대하여 경

의와 감사의 뜻을 표합니다. 아울러 이 자리를 빌려 다음 5가지 사항에 대해 특별한 당부의 말씀을 드리고자 합니다.

첫째, 한국은 대외개발원조(ODA)의 확대를 공약했습니다. 이 공약을 충실히 이행해 주시기 바랍니다. 이는 과거의 도움에 대해 보답하고 한국이 존경 받는 국제사회의 일원으로 인식되는 첩경입니다. 하지만 그것보다 더 큰 의미가 있습니다.

아프리카는 한국의 중요한 개발원조대상중 하나입니다. 또한 아프리카는 자원의 보고이자 경제적으로 가장 빨리 성장하고 있는 지역이기도 합니다. 개도국에 대한 지원은 온정적 기부를 훨씬 넘어서는 것입니다. 미래에 대한 투자인 것입니다.

대외개발원조의 질적 효과를 개선하는 선진체제도 갖추어야 합니다. 이런 점에서 한국 정부가 지난 8월에 민관이 함께 하는 개발협력연대를 출범시킨 것을 매우 바람직하게 생각합니다.

어려운 국내외 경제환경 속에서도 대외개발원조를 2015년까지 국민총소득의 0.25%로 증액하겠다는 한국의 방침을 높이 평가합니다. 한국이 진정한 선진 강국으로 발돋움하기 위해서는 이에 그치지 않고 국제적 목표인 0.7%를 향해 계속 나아가야 한다고 생각합니다. 국제사회에 명확한 목표를 제시하고 이를 달성하기 위한 노력을 계속해 주시기를 당부합니다. 아울러 이러한 목표를 향해 나아가는 데 국회의 선도적인 역할을 희망합니다.

둘째, 새천년 개발목표(Millennium Development Goals: MDG)를 달성하기 위해 2015년까지 남은 3년간 한국의 적극적인 협력과 지원을 기대합니다. MDG 목표 년도인 2015년은 종착역이 아닌 새로운 출발점입니다. 2015년 이후의 개발 의제와 지속 가능 개발목표(Sustainable Development Goals)를 확립하는 과정에서 한국이 적극적으로 동참해줄 것을 아울러 기대합니다.

이러한 노력에는 많은 협력이 필요합니다. 국회 UN-MDG 포럼이 큰 역할을 해주실 것으로 믿습니다. 새롭게 선출된 제19대 국회가 제1호 안건으로 빈곤 퇴치 기여금 연장법안을 통과시킨 것은 국회의 세계적 지도력을 확인한 중요한 사례입니다.

셋째, 유엔은 지속가능한 개발을 위한 여러 가지 특별사업을 추진하고 있습니다.

우선 "영양 증진(SUN: Scaling Up Nutrition)"과 "기아 종식(Zero Hunger Challenge)" 사업입니다. 이 사업들은 영양실조와 기아문제를 다루는 방식을 혁명적으로 변화시키기 위한 것입니다. 저는 한국이 기아를 종식시킴으로써 다른 국가들이 따를 모범을 보인 것을 자랑스럽게 생각합니다. 작년 부산 개발원조 총회의 주최국으로서 한국은 모든 사람들의 식량권 (right to food) 향유 및 모든 식량체계에 지속 가능한 공급을 목표 달성하는데 대외개발원조가 부합되도록 노력해야 합니다.

모자보건은 새천년 개발목표 (MDG) 달성의 중심적 사안입니다. "모든 여성과 모든 아동 (Every Woman, Every Child)" 사업은 2015년까지 1600만 명의 생명을 구하기 위해 260여 민관 협력파트너들이 참여하고 있습니다. 한국은 2015년까지 전국민 의료보험 (Universal Health Coverage) 공약을 이행하고 의료보험 제공을 위한 통합적 접근법을 취함으로써 이 목표의 달성에 기여할 수 있습니다.

또한 우리는 "교육우선 (education first)" 사업도 출범시켰습니다.

저는 세계 각국을 방문할 때마다 한국의 교육투자가 어떻게 성공에 기여했는지를 설명합니다. 한국이 어려웠던 시절, 유엔의 도움으로 교과서를 받아서 공부한 경험에 대해서도 말해주고 있습니다. 한국의 성공사례에서 세계 많은 나라가 큰 교훈을 얻고 있습니다. "교육우선" 사업은 모든 아동들에게 학교의 문을 열고, 학습의 질을 개선함으로써 세계시민을 양성하는 것을 도와주게 될 것입니다. 한국이 이 분야에서 적극적인 역할을 할 것을 기대합니다.

우리는 "모든 사람을 위한 지속가능 에너지(sustainable energy for all)" 협력을 강화하고 있습니다. 이 사업은 2030년까지 세가지의 보완적인 목표를 추구하고 있습니다. 첫째, 현대적인 에너지 서비스에 대한 보편적 접근 보장; 둘째, 에너지 효율성을 두 배로 개선; 셋째, 세계적 에너지원에서 재생 에너지의 비율을 두 배로 증대하자는 것입니다.

한국정부는 이 분야에서 강한 지도력과 의지를 보여주었습니다. 저는 지난 세기에 한국에서 이루어졌던 에너지 변혁을 직접 시켜보고 그 혜택을 누렸습니다. 한국이 유엔과 함께 세계 에너지 분야의 변혁을 수도하기를 바랍니다.

내외 귀빈 여러분,

특히 기후변화는 명확하며 현존하는 위험입니다. 2015년까지 구속력 있는 온실가스 감축합의를 달성해야 하는 의무를 이행할 정치적 의지를 긴집에 나서야 합니다. 우리 세대는 다음 세대들로부터 이 지구(planet)를 빌려 쓰고 있다는 엄중한 사실을 잊지 말아야 합니다. 우리 세대는 다음 세대들이 극심한 기상이변이 공포 없이 살 수 있도록 지구를 잘 보존해야 하겠습니다.

한국이 주도하고 있는 녹색성장은 기후변화와 경제성장이라는 두 마리 토끼를 잡을 수 있는 미래지향적 전략입니다. 한국은 스스로 설정한 국가적인 온실가스 감축목표를 달성하고, 이를 통해 세계적 감축을 선도하는 역할까지 해낼 수 있을 것입니다. 이런 점에서 지난주 서울에서 세계 녹색성장연구소(GGGI)의 국제기구 출범식이 개최된 것과 녹색기후기금 (Green Climate Fund) 이사회가 사무국 소재지로 한국을 선정한 것을 매우 뜻 깊게 생각하며 축하합니다.

이는 한국에 대한 국제사회의 기대를 반영합니다. 선발개도국으로서의 경험을 바탕으로 기후변화에 대한 선진국들과의 협력을 잘 이끌어 낼 것이라는 기대가 반영된 것입니다. 앞으로 세계적인 기후변화 합의를 이끌어내고 이행 기금을 확보하는데 한국정부와 국민의 적극적 역할과 협력을 희망합니다.

넷째, 자유민주주의를 지키고 평화, 번영을 추구해 온 한국의 경험은 국제평화유지 기여에 소중한 자산입니다.

한국은 1991년 유엔 가입 이래 재정적 기여와 평화유지활동에 꾸준히 참여해 왔습니다. 모범적인 기강과 진정 어린 대민 봉사 활동으로 한국부대는 주어진 임무를 완수하고, 지역주민들과의 교량 역할도 훌륭히 수행하고 있습니다.

한국이 레바논과 아이티에 이어 최근 남부 수단에 평화유지군 파견을 결정해 주신데 대해서 유엔을 대표하여 감사드립니다. 앞으로 더 많은 평화유지군과 더불어 경찰 인력, 특히 여성 경찰관 파견도 적극 추진해 주시기를 희망합니다. 한국이 2010년 "PKO법"을 제정하고 상비부대를 창설한 것을 높게 평가하며, 앞으로 평화유지활동을 위한 협력들이 더욱 강화되어 나가기를 기대합니다.

지난 18일 한국은 유엔 안보리 이사국에 선출되었습니다. 96년에 이어 두 번째로 이사국으로 활동하게 된 것을 축하합니다. 이는 그간 한국의 유엔 기여에 대한 회원국들의 평가이자, 앞으로 국제 평화와 개발에 더 큰 기여를 바라는 희망을 반영한 결과입니다. 국제평화 기여국 이미지를 확고히 함으로써 한국의 국격 제고에 좋은 기회가 될 것으로 믿습니다. 한국이 보다 효과적인 분쟁예방 장치의 마련, 그리고 보편적 인권과 가치의 증진에 기여할 수 있을 것입니다.

저는 사무총장으로서 인권, 부패 등 문제를 안고 있는 국가의 지도자들과 대화할 때가 많습니다. 저는 이들에게 한국의 경험을 바탕으로 하여 솔직한 충고를 해줍니다. 지도자들이 처음에는 듣기 거북해 하지만 한국의 경험을 듣고 변화의 가능성에 마음을 여는 것을 보아 왔습니다. 이런 점이 한국이 갖고 있는 연성 국력(soft power)의 중요한 원천이라고 생각합니다.

다섯째, 한국이 여성과 젊은 세대의 권익신장에 더욱 힘써주시기를 기대합니다.

한국은 급속한 고령화 추세에 있지만, 세계 인구는 개발도상국에서 늘어나면서 지금 인류의 반 이상이 25세 이하입니다. 젊은 세대들이 행복한 삶을 누리기 위한 일자리가 필요합니다. 이 문제는 전 세계적인 도전이며, 기회균등과 인간의 존엄성을 확보하기 위해서도 시급히 대처해야 합니다.

저는 회원국 지도자들을 만날 때마다 고위직에 여성을 더 많이 배려해 줄 것을 강조하고 있습니다. 취임 직후부터, 유엔 고위직에 여성의 진출을 획기적으로 늘리기 위해서도 최선을 다해 왔습니다. 그 결과 지금은 최고위직인 사무차장급의 여성 비율이 이전보다 60% 이상 증가 되었습니다. 해외주둔 병력을 지휘하는 사무총장 특별대표의 문호 또한 여성들에게 대폭 개방하고 있습니다.

아울러 한국이 소수자 인권보호에도 지속적인 관심을 가져주시기를 당부합니다. 장애인과 외국인 근로자의 권익, 난민 보호와 늘어나는 다문화 가정을 향한 보다 적극적인 사회적 배려가 필요합니다. 최근 한국정부가 HIV양성자에 대한 여행제한을 철폐한 것은 매우 고무적인 조치로, 이를 높게 평가합니다.

북한에서 자유를 찾아 이주한 주민들의 한국 정착과 사회동화를 촉진하는 지원이 체계적으로 이루어지고 있는 것을 높이 평가하며, 더욱 진전되어 나가기를 기대합니다. 또한 관련국들은 이들을 보편적 인권과 인도적 고려에 입각하여 도와주시기를 희망합니다.

존경하는 국민 여러분, 국회의원과 내외 귀빈여러분,

한국 국민의 한 사람으로서 한반도 상황이 보다 안정되고 통일을 향해 나아가기를 바라는 저의 열망은 누구보다 큽니다. 북한의 새로운 지도부가 한반도 비핵화에 대한 국제사회의 요구에 조속히 부응하고 주민생활 개선에 앞장섬으로써 책임 있는 국제사회의 일원이 되기를 희망합니다. 이와 관련하여, 지난 4월 15일 김정은 국방위 제1위원장이 행한 첫 공개연설에서 "나라의 통일을 원하고 민족의 평화와 번영을 바라는 사람과 손잡고 나갈 것이며 인내심있는 노력을 기울일 것이다." 라고 언급한데 주목하고 있습니다. 유엔 국별 인권심사의 권고가 이행되어 인간의 보편적 존엄성이 확대되어야 합니다.

저는 남북이 궁극적으로는 통일, 그리고 핵으로부터 자유롭고, 평화로운 한반도를 향해 나아가는 데 어떠한 노력도 아끼지 않을 것입니다. 유엔 사무총장으로서 한반도 평화증진을 위해 필요한 모든 역할을 할 준비가 되어 있습니다. 여건이 갖춰지는 대로 북한 방문도 고려하고 있습니다.

유엔은 북한의 취약 주민을 돕는 인도적 지원을 계속해 오고 있습니다. 특히 북한 영유아들의 영양 결핍에 따른 발육부진은 심각한 문제입니다. 우리 민족의 미래를 위해서도 시급한 도움이 필요합니다.

유엔은 지원물품이 전용 없이 꼭 필요한 사람들에게 전달되도록 하는 최선의 제도적 장치를 갖추고 있습니다. 한국이 민족 전체의 이익을 보는 큰 마음으로 이 문제를 다루고, 국회가 선도적 역할을 해 주시기를 기대합니다.

저는 우리 민족의 미래를 내다보면서 한반도가 "도전의 땅" 에서 진정한 "기회의 땅" 으로 거듭나기를 소망합니다.

이에는 지역적 협력이 필수적입니다.

세계 중심축의 하나로 부상하고 있는 동북아는 역내교역과 교류가 획기적으로 증대되고 있습니다. 그러나 과거로부터의 갈등요인이 아직도 없어지지 않고 있습니다. 올바른 역사인식과 대화에 기초하여 미래를 내다보면서 갈등을 평화적으로 관리하고 다방면의 교류를 확대해 나가는 양자 간 협력이 증진되어야 합니다.

이와 함께 역내 경제적 통합과 정치적 협력을 증진하는 노력도 병행되어야 합니다. 유럽, 아프리카, 남미대륙에서 활발히 진행되고 있는 역내 통합과 협력의 가속화 추세에서 교훈을 얻을 수 있습니다. 이 과정에서 다자주의가 긴요하며, 한국이 교량역할을 할 수 있습니다. 이를 통해 한국이 새로운 동아시아의 질서 형성과정을 주도할 수 있기를 아울러 소망합니다.

내외 귀빈 여러분,

저는 사무총장으로서 세계 곳곳을 방문하면서 수많은 한국의 젊은이들이 봉사하는 모습을 보아 왔습니다. 험지와 분쟁지역을 마다하지 않고 인류애를 실천하는 한국인들을 만날 때마다 가슴 뿌듯했습니다. 그러나 얼마 전에 스리랑카에서 순직한 젊은 봉사단원들을 생각하면 너무도 가슴이 아픕니다. 이 분들의 진정한 봉사정신은 지구촌의 많은 사람들에게 귀감이 되고, 오래도록 기억될 것으로 믿습니다.

저는 이들 봉사자들을 통해 한국의 밝은 미래를 봅니다. 한국의 봉사단원들의 규모는 국력을 감안할 때 세계 최고 수준입니다. 한국인들의 순수한 열정과 따뜻한 봉사 정신은 국제사회에 감동을 주고 있으며, 유엔 봉사단(UN Volunteers)에게도 좋은 모델이 되고 있습니다.

한국의 젊은이들이 세계를 향해 꿈을 더욱 키워나가고, "세계속의 한국", "한국속의 세계"를 실현하는 세계 시민(global citizen)으로 성장해 나갈 것으로 확신합니다

존경하는 국민 여러분, 존경하는 국회의장님과 국회의원 여러분, 국무총리님과 국무위원 여러분, 그리고 주한 외교단과 내외 귀빈 여러분,

우리가 꿈꾸는 이상적인 세계는 어느 누구도 혼자 이룰 수 없습니다. 저는 작년 두 번째 임기의 취임연설에서 "함께 하면 불가능한 것은 없다(Together, nothing is impossible)."고 강조한 바 있습니다. 저는 늘 "빨리 가고 싶으면 혼자서 가라, 그러나 멀리 가고 싶으면 함께 가야 한다."는 금언을 마음에 새기고 있습니다.

저는 또한 6년 전 유엔 사무총장으로 취임하면서 한국적인 가치와 경험을 바탕으로 좋은 "성공 이야기"를 더 많이 만들어 나가겠다고 다짐한 바 있습니다.

저는 조국 대한민국이 국제사회에서 보다 크게 기여하고, 보다 큰 존경을 얻어 선진강국으로 우뚝 서는 모습을 보고 싶습니다. 한국의 성공 이야기에 새로운 장을 추가할 수 있는 "기회의 창"이 대한민국에 활짝 열려있습니다.

우리는 절대로 잊지 말아야 합니다. 빈곤 종식— 민주주의 실현— 인권 신장— 평화 증진— 이 모든 것이 불가능한 꿈이 아님을 말입니다.

바로 이것이 한국의 이야기입니다. 그리고 여러분들의 도움으로 우리는 이것을 세계의 이야기로 만들 수 있습니다.

유엔이 추구하는 꿈, "우리가 원하는 미래: 더 안전하고 더 살기 좋은 세상"을 만드는 여정에 대한민국이 유엔의 든든한 파트너가 되어 줄 것으로 확신합니다.

유엔 사무총장 취임 이래 저를 한결같이 성원해 주신 모든 국민 여러분께 이 자리를 빌려 다시 한 번 진심으로 감사드립니다. 어제는 제11회 서울평화상을 수상하였습니다. 권위 있는 서울평화상 수상은 개인적으로 큰 영광이며, 그간 유엔의 노력에 대한 평가라고 생각합니다. 인류복지와 세계평화 증진을 위해 변함없이 최선을 다하겠습니다.

저는 유엔 사무총장에 취임한 첫 날부터 솔선수범하며 일신 우일신 하는 자세로 지내왔습니다. 앞으로도 여러분들의 성원과 국제사회의 기대에 부응토록 혼신의 열정으로 더욱 열심히 하겠습니다.

대한민국의 앞날에 무궁한 영광이 깃들고, 국민 여러분께 행복이 가득하시기를 빕니다.

경청해 주셔서 감사합니다.

Address on receiving the Seoul Peace Prize

I t is an immense honour to be awarded the Seoul Peace Prize. I thank the custodians of the prize for this recognition. I know that through me, you are also paying tribute to the United Nations, our work for peace across the world, and the diverse and talented staff who bring the UN Charter to life.

I am also keenly aware that I am the first Korean to win this award. That makes this moment especially moving. I think back to all those who have helped and inspired me along the way, from my school teachers during a war-time childhood, to mentors at the foreign ministry. I offer my profound appreciation to those men and women, who are dedicated to public service and helped to instill that same spirit in me. This is their prize, too.

Not many countries establish a prize for peace. The Seoul Peace Prize has its roots in the 1988 Summer Olympics, when this country opened its doors to people and athletes from more than 160 countries. Korea did so in part because it believes in the power of sports for peace and development. Just this morning, I spoke at a forum on that very subject.

But hosting the Olympics was also Korea's way of saying thank you to the world for supporting the country's struggle and transformation. Decades earlier, as war raged across the Korean peninsula, the troops of many countries came to the country's defence, under the flag of the United Nations.

Some of those who gave their lives for Korea's freedom are buried on Korean soil – far from their homes, but close to the hearts of the Korean people. One year ago, I visited the burial ground in Busan – the world's only United Nations cemetery – to pay my respects for their sacrifice.

Koreans benefitted again from international assistance during the monumental post-war recovery effort. Into the country, through the ports of Busan and Incheon, came vast amounts of school books, grain, vaccines and other vital assistance.

Another import was less tangible but every bit as consequential: solidarity. Korea drew strength from knowing that the country was not alone.

Three months ago, I visited two other Olympic sites in the span of a single day. In the morning, I took a symbolic run in the Olympic stadium in Sarajevo, a one-time war-zone. That evening, I carried the torch for this year's Summer Games in London, a city that has also experienced the destruction of war and the horror of aerial bombardment.

Bosnia, the United Kingdom and Korea have all rebuilt and gained the path of peace. So many other people in war-ravaged lands around the world want to make that same journey. With the help of the United Nations, they can.

That sense of shared hope and renewal is, for me, the meaning of this award. As a son of Korea and as Secretary-General of the United Nations, I am therefore pleased to accept the Seoul Peace Prize and to speak to you, on this important occasion, about the pursuit of peace at a time of global transition.

The human family is at a critical juncture. The world is moving through a Great Transition.

This transition is economic, as the digital revolution advances and as new powers and groups emerge. Today's engines of growth are largely in the developing world. Korea itself hosted the G-20 Summit two years ago – the first to be held outside North America and Europe. The implications of this momentous shift – from West to East, and from North to the global South – are only beginning to unfold.

The Great Transition is also developmental, as we seek a more sustainable path. The social perils of rising inequality and joblessness are clear. And our ecological footprint is overstepping the earth's boundaries. We are using resources as if we had two planets, not one. There can be no Plan B because there is no planet B.

Politics are also on the move, awakened against oppression, corruption and misrule. People are increasingly – and rightly – demanding a greater role in shaping their own destiny. Dramatic transitions in the Arab world, Africa and elsewhere have brought new hope to many countries and to others that have suffered severe democratic deficits for too long. More quickly than anyone foresaw, we have established an age of accountability for international crimes and grave violations of human rights. Leaders must listen to their constituents and must respond to their needs and aspirations – or make way for those who will.

The United Nations, too, must deliver. The United Nations must help the world turn back the tide of rising insecurity, injustice, inequality and intolerance. Peace and security, development and human rights are indivisible. We will not enjoy one without the others. We must deliver peace in the fullest sense of the word.

The UN's work for global peace and security draws on many tools. UN peacekeeping operations are in great demand – a sign of persistent armed conflict, but also a vote of confidence in the way peacekeepers can help countries transform their prospects for the better. The UN's peacebuilding efforts are being strengthened to help fragile countries emerging from conflict avoid a relapse, as happens all too commonly. The United Nations is strengthening mediation, preventive diplomacy and all our means of resolving disputes peacefully. The Organization is also focusing greater attention on drug trafficking, transnational crime and terrorism – security threats that have grown in intensity, and which feed off each other in deadly ways.

At this ceremony dedicated to peace, I must make a special plea about the threat of nuclear weapons. Some say nuclear disarmament is utopian, premature, a dream. I say the illusion is that nuclear weapons provide security. Defence establishments agree: nuclear weapons are useless against today's threats, from crime to terror to disease. Security experts also acknowledge that the very existence of nuclear weapons is de-stabilizing, since others feel they must have them for deterrence and their own protection – and since terrorists may seek to obtain nuclear materials. There are also real risks to human health and the environment.

How, then, do we explain that in a post-Cold War world, amidst a global financial crisis, the nuclear weapon states seem intent on modernizing their arsenals for decades to come? And more broadly, how can we justify global military spending that last year was twice as much in a day as the UN spent on all its activities the whole year?

I continue to pursue wide-ranging initiatives to realize our dream of a world without nuclear weapons. My UN five-point plan focuses on preventing proliferation, strengthening the legal regime and ensuring nuclear safety and security – an effort that was given good momentum by the Nuclear Security Summit held in Seoul earlier this year. The world is over-armed, and peace is under-funded. We need to get our priorities right, and stop spending billions on weapons instead of people.

The UN's work for development is now focused on keeping the promise embodied in the Millennium Development Goals: maternal health, so that women do not perish in the course of giving life; nutrition, so that every infant gets the start in life they deserve; education, for the skills needed to thrive in the knowledge economy; sustainable energy, to power long-term prosperity; environmentally friendly development, to protect our one and only planet; the empowerment of the world's women and young people – in many ways the key to all our hopes.

The 2015 Millennium Development Goals deadline is fast approaching. We have made important gains, but the economic crisis has stalled progress and threatens big reversals. In too many countries, on too many targets, we are falling short. We must keep our promise to the world's poorest and most vulnerable people.

66 The human family is at a critical juncture. The world is moving through a Great Transition. 99

Even as the United Nations makes this push to achieve the MDGs, there is also a need to articulate a post-2015 development vision. That vision must be bold yet practical. It must have sustainability at its core. And it must reflect challenges that have come to the fore since the MDGs were first agreed. We must make this long-term investment in people and the planet on which we depend.

People are also at the heart of our efforts to mainstream human rights and other democratic values. We have made remarkable advances – a wide-ranging body of standards and laws; the fall of dictatorships and corrupt regimes; the conviction of a former head of state for war crimes; the emergence of a new norm: the responsibility to protect people from genocide and other grave crimes.

Yet we are still witness to appalling abuses and discrimination. We see extremists in northern Mali and Pakistan committing cruel acts in a hateful, twisted interpretation of religion. Women and girls around the world are still subjected to violence, servitude and early marriage. We see hospitals and places of worship, once considered safe havens in wartime, now coming under attack – a reversion to barbarism of another day. And we see bombings of densely populated Syrian cities by the regime. We must do better. The United Nations must do better.

Most immediately, we must do more to respond to the violence in Syria. The United Nations is doing its utmost to ease the humanitarian situation and to set in motion a political solution to the crisis. But the international community remains at odds over what to do even as needs and attacks and suffering all escalate. I call once again for the Security Council, the regional countries and all parties to live up to their obligations and promote a ceasefire.

More broadly, we must do better to fight impunity, in Syria and elsewhere. We must further support the groundbreaking work for justice carried out by the International Criminal Court. We must show we are truly committed to implementing the responsibility to protect in practice, not just refining what we mean by it in theory.

In response to extremism, we must promote tolerance, including through initiatives such as the UN Alliance of Civilizations – our effort to promote mutual respect and understanding, culture to culture, country to country, people to people.

My remarks here tonight would be incomplete without a few words on East Asia itself, and the role of the Republic of Korea.

East Asia has risen. It is a dynamic economic force, a contributor to UN peacekeeping, a major development donor, and a source of innovations and ideas that are shaping our future. The countries of the region are now each other's most important trading partners. Yet tensions from the past are still all too present.

Every country in the region has a paramount interest in stability. Where there are differences, these should be managed and resolved peacefully. Leaders have a responsibility to show restraint, and pursue solutions through dialogue and cooperation.

Let us draw lessons from other parts of the world where regional integration and cooperation are well advanced. Let us all, leaders and ordinary citizens alike, be forward-looking in thinking about how best to build a peaceful Asia that enjoys prosperity and human rights.

The situation on the Korean Peninsula is one of the most challenging in the world, with regional and global implications. I am ready to play my part to work towards a peaceful and denuclearized Korean Peninsula – including through my own personal engagement and visit to the Democratic People's Republic of Korea, under the right conditions. I also look forward to the day when the Democratic People's Republic of Korea moves to heed the call for denuclearization of the Korean Peninsula, and for improving the lives of its people through respect for universal values and human rights.

Rates of malnutrition and childhood stunting in the Democratic People's Republic of Korea are alarming. Donor assistance, however, is declining, risking cutbacks in food and nutrition assistance. This is an immediate problem as well as a matter affecting the future of the Korean people as a whole. The United Nations will continue to do its utmost to provide humanitarian assistance to those in need, especially children and other vulnerable people. Even as we strive for a better future on the Korean Peninsula, there is an urgent need to ease human suffering today.

Our world is shifting. Changes and wake-up calls arrive with the speed of a tweet, on the wings of the world wide web. The Republic of Korea has an important role to play as we try to find our footing in this new era. With its vibrant democracy and well-established rule of law, Korea can play a bridging role for countries undergoing political transitions. With its robust economy, Korea can contribute greatly to sustainable development, including by increasing aid commitments beyond the generous steps it has taken already. And with its election earlier this month to the United Nations Security Council, the Republic of Korea can help keep the peace.

Times of transition are times of profound opportunity. The decisions we make in this period will have an impact for generations to come. I believe the Great Transition is propelling the human family towards a future in which we will come to know and influence and interact with each other more intensely with every passing day. That gives me great hope, because the great transition is putting power into the hands of people as they seek to make the values enshrined in the UN charter real and meaningful in their own lives.

Justice, equality, human dignity. That is our shared destination. As we navigate our way, let our passion for peace and our compassion for each other be our polestar.

Remarks to the sixteenth Summit of the Movement of Non-Aligned Nations

TEHRAN, 30 AUGUST 2012

I thank our hosts for organizing this important Summit of the Non-Aligned Movement and I would like to pay tribute to Egypt as the outgoing chair of the last three years. I am grateful for the hospitality of the Government and people of the Islamic Republic of Iran. The recent earthquake saddened us all. The United Nations stands ready to assist in any way.

Last month, I visited the Brijuni Islands in Croatia in what was once Yugoslavia. Gamal Abdel Nasser, Jawaharlal Nehru and Josip Tito met there in 1956 to help define the Non-Aligned Movement in its early days. The leaders agreed that "Peace cannot be achieved through division but by working for collective security on a world scale and by expanding the region of freedom."

At that time, nations and people were speaking of freedom from superpower rivalries and colonial domination. But freedom has other meanings, as well. Today, we see an equally powerful yearning for freedom within nations – the freedom to participate, the freedom to make one's voice heard and the freedom to choose one's government.

Since the last Non-Aligned Movement Summit in Sharm-el-Sheikh in 2009, this part of the world has been at the epicentre. Tunisia. Egypt. Libya. Yemen and beyond. The Arab Spring was not imposed or exported. It did not arise from an external conflict or dispute between states. It came from within; from people. People who stood up for a better future. People who spoke out for universal value.

In some places this has brought transformation and new beginnings, but in others, we see suppression and frustration. That is why I have urged world leaders to listen seriously and sincerely. To listen to the appeals of people for justice, for human rights, for dignity.

Today, the Non-Aligned Movement represents nearly two out of three members of the United Nations. You contribute four out of five United Nations peacekeepers. I thank you for those tremendous contributions. As we look ahead together, we must build on our strong partnership.

You represent diverse societies joined by common goals. I urge you to unite as well to promote and protect the values embedded in the United Nations Charter and the Universal Declaration of Human Rights, including freedom of expression and freedom of association. For much of your membership, this internal effort should be the next frontier of action for your people.

Our organizations must keep pace in changing times. Long-held assumptions may need to change. In too many places, for example, military spending continues to dwarf investments in people. Climate change is a clear and present danger. Too many women are still denied opportunity. Non-Aligned Movement members include some of the world's youngest societies. We must guide these youth to a world that resolves problems through cooperation, not confrontation.

Yet tragically, too often, conflict has replaced dialogue. We see far too many political disputes within and between states in the Non-Aligned Movement. I am concerned, for example, with the failure of Sudan and South Sudan to finalize their borders and prevent further bloodshed. In the Democratic Republic of the Congo, the security situation and sexual violence against women remain a source of deep concern. We continue to closely follow the unrest in Mali that has profound implications for the region. I commend the African Union for its firm stand against unconstitutional changes of government.

66 Prevention of conflict starts at home: by strengthening democratic institutions, safeguarding human rights, ensuring popular participation and guaranteeing the rule of law. 99

I urge all Non-Aligned Movement members to work within the principles of the UN Charter to resolve disputes peacefully. But it is not sufficient to focus on lowering tensions between non-aligned countries, as important as that is. We must prevent conflict between all UN member states. And from this platform – as I have repeatedly stated around the world – I strongly reject threats by any member state to destroy another or outrageous attempts to deny historical facts, such as the Holocaust. Claiming that another UN Member State, Israel, does not have the right to exist, or describing it in racist terms, is not only utterly wrong but undermines the very principles we have all pledged to uphold.

Today the United Nations and the Non-Aligned Movement face the supreme challenge of answering people's aspirations. I see two paths for rising to this challenge: prevention to help deal with a society's political grievances; and sustainability to help address society's developmental challenges.

With your support, we are improving the capacity of the United Nations to respond early to conflicts. But prevention starts at home: by strengthening democratic institutions, safeguarding human rights, ensuring popular participation and guaranteeing the rule of law.

S yria is only the latest example of what happens when that truth is ignored. The crisis in Syria started with peaceful demonstrations that were met by ruthless force. Now, we face the grim risk of long-term civil war destroying Syria's rich tapestry of communities. Those who provide arms to either side in Syria are contributing to the misery. Further militarization is not the answer. The situation cannot be resolved with the blood and the bodies of more than 18,000 people and counting. There should be no more bullets and bombs.

I urge all parties in the strongest possible terms to stop the violence now. The Syrian government has the primary responsibility to resolve this crisis by genuinely listening to the people's voices. Our diplomatic efforts will be led by the Joint Special Representative of the United Nations and the League of Arab States, Mr. Lakhdar Brahimi. He will need the united support of the international community. And all who have influence must be part of the solution to this crisis and work in close cooperation with the Joint Special Representative.

> **" I urge you to promote and protect the values embedded in the UN Charter and the Universal Declaration of Human Rights, including freedom of expression and freedom of association. For much of your membership, this internal effort should be the next frontier of action for your people. "**

There is no threat to global peace and harmony more serious than nuclear proliferation. Assuming the leadership of the Non-Aligned Movement provides Iran with the opportunity to demonstrate that it can play a moderate and constructive role internationally. That includes responsible action on the nuclear programme, which is among the top concerns of the international community. This concern has been demonstrated in repeated Security Council resolutions, including under Chapter VII authority, calling for transparency and full cooperation with the International Atomic Energy Agency (IAEA).

For the sake of peace and security in this region and globally, I urge the Government of Iran to take the necessary measures to build international confidence in the exclusively peaceful nature of its nuclear programme. This can be done by fully complying with the relevant Security Council resolutions and thoroughly cooperating with the IAEA. I urge, also, constructive engagement with the P5+1 to quickly reach a diplomatic solution.

And I urge all the parties to stop provocative and inflammatory threats. A war of words can quickly spiral into a war of violence. Bluster can so easily become bloodshed.   Now is the time for all leaders to use their voices to lower, not raise, tensions.

Let me also note that efforts to create a Middle East zone free of nuclear weapons and all other weapons of mass destruction are under way. Let us remember that it was Iran itself, thirty-eight years ago, that proposed the establishment of a nuclear weapon-free zone in the Middle East. As Secretary-General, I am absolutely committed to achieving a world free of nuclear weapons and other weapons of mass destruction. I also share your desire to strengthen controls against the illicit arms trade. Let us keep working for these common goals.

There can be no talk of international or national security without focussing on sustainable development. We have made important progress in reducing poverty, yet inequality is rising. And last year, official development assistance decreased for the first time in years. We must intensify our work to meet the Millennium Development Goals and bolster resilience to environmental, economic and social shocks.

While staying focussed on what must be done now, we are also looking ahead – looking to define a post-2015 global development agenda that is both bold and practical. This includes follow-up to the Rio+20 Conference, where the international community agreed to establish universal Sustainable Development Goals (SDGs). We need your political leadership and the full engagement of the Non-Aligned Movement and the G-77 and China group.

In this period of profound transition, the Non-Aligned Movement continues to define its evolving identity and address changing notions of sovereignty in an age of interconnectedness. As you engage in that process, your role at the United Nations will remain crucial.

We must also keep working together for greater democratic governance in international decision-making. That includes strengthening the UN from within and working to ensure that global institutions and bodies – including the Security Council – accurately reflect the realities and dynamics of today's world.

The United Nations and the Non-Aligned Movement have a close history over fifty years. Guided by our shared principles of peace, justice and equality, let us work together to meet the pressing challenges of our time.

Remarks to the Atlantic Council

WASHINGTON, D.C., 7 MAY 2012

D r. Kissinger, thank you for that very kind introduction. The world has looked to your wisdom and experience for many decades now, and your contribution has been great. I thank you, Dr. Kissinger, for your very strong support for the United Nations and for myself as Secretary-General.

Ladies and Gentlemen, let me join in congratulating the other honorees this evening: Anne-Sophie Mutter, Paul Polman, enlisted men and women of the United States armed forces, and his Royal Highness Prince Harry. This is really distinguished company indeed.

Thank you, as well, for your warm welcome. And thank you to the board of the Atlantic Council, also your chairman, Senator Hagel, and President Frederick Kempe, for this extraordinary honour. I take it as an eloquent symbol of our partnership: the United States and the United Nations. And on behalf of all the staff and peacekeeping operations staff and I humbly accept this honour. Seldom, if ever, have our principles and shared purpose been more relevant. Seldom, if ever, has this partnership been more vital than at this moment.

We just celebrated and commended the enlisted men and women of the US armed forces. As the Secretary-General of the United Nations, my thoughts are with more than 120,000 UN peacekeeping operations staff – from more than 120 troop contributing countries – who work day and night under very difficult and dangerous circumstances for peace and stability around the world. They have my deepest admiration.

Our world is a rough place. Let us cast our eye across the geopolitical landscape. In Syria, the violence still continues. We are in a race against time to prevent full-scale civil war and death on a potentially massive scale. Tensions between Israel and Iran remain dangerous. North Korea recently launched another missile and appears to be contemplating another nuclear test, in defiance of the international community.

We see famine coming in the Sahel. Military coups in Mali and Guinea Bissau. Sudan and South Sudan on the brink of conflict that not long ago claimed two million lives. Add to this the crisis in the euro area. Climate change. The pressures of a growing population of seven billion on our increasingly fragile planet.

Almost everywhere we look, it seems, we see growing insecurity, growing injustice, growing social inequality. If I were to speak like an economist, I might say we have an over-supply of problems and a deficit of solutions. A deficit of leadership.

That partly reflects the great changes transforming our modern world. Power is shifting. The old order is breaking down, and we do not yet know the shape of the new.

Twenty years ago, at the end of the Cold War, the United States and its traditional allies could be counted on to lead the world through uncertainty and change. Today, that is much more difficult.

And yet, tonight, I want to say clearly: we need leadership and your leadership. In these times of deep uncertainty, during this era of change and transformation, we need the sort of leadership that has long distinguished this venerable Atlantic Council. A leadership dedicated to the common good; a global common good. A leadership of nations acting in concert as we have seen, in truly global stewardship. This is the leadership that created the United Nations and its founding Charter. And this is the leadership that will keep its principles alive and strong.

As you may know, I lived through the Korean War, as was eloquently introduced by Dr. Kissinger. The United Nations led by the United States helped us through that dark hour. They came to our rescue when Korea was on the brink of collapse. Forever after, the UN for me has been a beacon of hope, and it still is for billions of others around the world.

> ❝ If I were to speak like an economist, I might say we have an over-supply of problems and a deficit of solutions. A deficit of leadership. ❞

Whenever I see people looking to the United Nations, I am humbled, just thinking of what kind of support I can bring to them. Today, as then, I believe the United Nations can – and must – be the solution to the world's great challenges. Engagement through the UN is the way forward to share the costs and responsibilities of leadership, to uphold universal values, and to steer the world through this Great Transition.

That is why in January, as I began my second term, I set out a road map for my five year second term as Secretary-General. Five imperatives for collective global action; five generational opportunities to create the future we want:

- How to fight climate change and chart a new path of sustainable growth and development.
- How to prevent conflict and better respond to natural disasters and other humanitarian emergencies.
- How to create a more just, secure and equitable world grounded in universal human rights.
- How to support nations in transition for democracy, where many people, especially in the Arab world and North Africa, are struggling for their rights and for their legitimate aspirations for human dignity.
- How to give the world's women and young people greater voice and opportunity.

I will not go into these here. But let me say a few words about the common thread that weaves through all of them. That is the importance of putting people first: the role of justice and fundamental freedoms, and the essential quality of human dignity. This is what the United Nations and I as Secretary-General are trying to achieve. Putting people first.

During the past year, our collective values were severely tested. To a degree greater than we might realize, the international community responded with courage, decisiveness and unity.

When an incumbent president refused to stand down after having lost an election in Côte d'Ivoire; when he threatened his people with civil war in order to preserve his own power, illegal power, we stood firm for democracy and human rights. Today, Laurent Gbagbo is awaiting trial in the International Criminal Court in The Hague, and a legitimate president, Alassane Ouattara, is in office.

When Muammar Qaddafi of Libya threatened to kill his own people, we acted. In doing so, we gave force to a fundamental new principle – that is the Responsibility to Protect.

In each case, it is important to recognize that we acted, collectively, under an umbrella of legitimacy provided by the United Nations and regional organizations – the African Union, League of Arab States and others. General Brent Scowcroft, who has been such a strong leader of this Atlantic Council, said himself that this is the way of the future. I could not agree more.

Few events in modern memory have been more inspiring or more challenging than the Arab Spring. From the outset of this transition, transformation, the United Nations and I called on leaders to listen to their people, carefully and sincerely. To listen to what their challenges are, what their concerns are, what their aspirations are and to enter into an inclusive dialogue with them; to act before it was too late.

Now, we must help these nations in transition. That is one of my priorities. In Tunisia, Egypt, Libya and elsewhere, we are working for solutions that focus on people: building democratic institutions, helping to promote human rights, creating jobs and economic opportunity, especially for women and young people.

The challenge in Syria is especially difficult. The government continues to assault its people. Every day, unfortunately we see the most appalling images: troops firing in city centers, innocent civilians dying, even children. Security forces are arresting and torturing people with great brutality. Meanwhile, attacks by the opposition and other armed groups have escalated.

As of today, the United Nations has deployed fifty-nine UN monitors. And we will expedite this number. By Thursday this week we will have more than 130, and by May 15 we will have more than 230. We are accelerating to implement Security Council resolutions to deploy the full complement of 300 military supervisors and approximately one hundred civilians by the end of this month.

Our most immediate goal is to save human lives, to see the end of this violence. The presence of UN monitors has in some cases reduced the intensity of violence in Syria. But the situation is still very precarious and fragile. We also seek to create an opening for political engagement between the government and those seeking change.

Let me say clearly: this is a difficult mission at a difficult moment, a very dangerous mission. We know the security risks to our brave UN observers. We know that Syrian citizens could face punishment for even speaking with them. And we know the nature of the regime, which could well use the presence of the mission to prepare for further violence.

The efforts of our Joint Special Envoy, Kofi Annan, embody a hard-headed strategy to deal with these challenges. Once again, I call on the Syrian government to uphold its responsibilities under the six-point plan fully, without further delay.

As ever, strenuous partnership is indispensable: the UN and regional organizations such as the League of Arab States; the UN and nations represented here tonight. We cannot predict how this will end. But we do know that there can be no compromise on fundamental principles of justice and human rights, in Syria or elsewhere. No amount of force can squash people's aspirations to live in dignity and decency.

Twelve days ago, Charles Taylor, former President of Liberia, was found guilty by our special tribunal for Sierra Leone. Today I say: no leader, anywhere, anytime, should imagine that he or she enjoys impunity for crimes of atrocity. Those responsible for such acts – in Syria or elsewhere – must be held accountable by the international community.

I began these remarks with a call to action: a call for global collective leadership that puts people first. We need to create a more humane world, a world of real solutions for ordinary people. A world of greater justice, with more robust and proactive protection of human rights and fundamental freedoms, with greater security and equity for all. As I see it, justice and dignity are not abstractions. They are not mere aspirations. They are rights of people; they are the responsibilities of governments to deliver.

None of these ideas are alien to anyone here this evening. They are core American values; they are core trans-Atlantic values, increasingly widely shared around the world. Our challenge is to continue to spread these principles, this universal code all around the world. And that takes leadership, your leadership.

If I could leave you with one thought, it would be this: the Atlantic Council has always stood firm for justice and equal rights in larger freedom. Now is not the moment to lose heart or change course. And I thank you very much for this honour and thank you for your leadership and commitment. Let us work together to make this world better for all.

Remarks at the gravesite of Dag Hammarskjöld

UPPSALA, 12 OCTOBER 2011

I t is with deep emotion that I stand by the graveside of my predecessor to pay tribute to him fifty years after his death. I am honoured to do so before you, Mr. Mayor, and before distinguished members of Dag Hammarskjöld's family.

Over the past few weeks, I have been honoured to participate in various commemorations of the fiftieth anniversary of Hammarskjöld's untimely passing. There have been eloquent speeches, stimulating discussions and insightful analyses of his leadership, legacy and achievements.

Many statesmen, including the Prime Minister and Foreign Minister of Sweden, have described well the accomplishments that serve us to this day.

We have discussed how Dag Hammarskjöld was the architect of peacekeeping as we know it today. How he designed the first complex peace operations, including what we know now as peacemaking and peacebuilding. How he pioneered the concept of the Secretary-General working with the Security Council to overcome deadlock. How, as problem-solver and mediator, he created the practice of direct, personal and quiet diplomacy. How he championed the concept of action taken on the basis of conviction and principle. And more than anything else, how he defined the role of UN Secretary-General and set a standard for the rest of us to aspire to.

The anniversary of his death has given us a valuable chance to remember these accomplishments. Even more important, to share them with succeeding generations.

Today, in the stillness of this sanctuary, I have the chance to do something else, something which was also one of Hammarskjöld's strengths: to stand in peaceful contemplation. To reflect on what it means and what it takes to serve in the interest of the greater good.

As Hammarskjöld wrote in his personal reflections, published posthumously as *Markings,* "The more faithfully you listen to the voice within you, the better you hear what is sounding outside. And only he who listens can speak."

Today, we know that this voice within guided Hammarskjöld never to do what was expedient or popular, and always to do what he believed was right. For that, he stands out among the leaders of the past century.

Those close to Hammarskjöld said he saw himself as a servant as much as a leader, and for that reason, he was followed by many. For that equally, he stands out among the leaders of the past century.

This morning, as we stand in the ancient city of learning and enlightenment that shaped Dag Hammarskjöld from his earliest days, we are reminded of another profound characteristic of his: the love he had for his own country, its traditions and its ideals, which inspired him to work in service to the world.

And so today, I take the opportunity to pay tribute to the people of Sweden for their unwavering commitment to the United Nations, fifty years after Hammarskjöld's death. Your contributions to peacekeeping and the rule of law, to humanitarian efforts and human rights, to democracy and governance support, speak for a tradition of solidarity that is enshrined in the very identity of your nation.

Fifty years ago, Dag Hammarskjöld made the long and final journey home from Ndola, 5,000 miles way, to this resting place. A quarter of a million Swedes gathered for a torchlight procession along the route his coffin took. At Uppsala cathedral, 15,000 of his fellow Uppsalians came to say their farewells. At the end of the service, church bells tolled across Sweden. The country came to a halt for a moment of silence.

66 Dag Hammarskjöld defined the role of UN Secretary-General and set a standard for the rest of us. 99

Before I ask you to observe a minute of silence, I would like to introduce my personal reflection – a personal anecdote.

Without knowing that, one day, maybe fifty years later, I would become Secretary-General, when I was a sixth grader in elementary school in my country, in response to the democratic uprising in Hungary in 1956, as student chair I read out in front of all the school children a letter appealing to then-Secretary-General Dag Hammarskjöld, "Mr. Secretary-General, please help the people of Hungary so they can have freedom and democracy." I do not know whether he heard my appeal, but I am sure he acted; and today, people in Eastern Europe and Hungary are now enjoying freedom and democracy.

When I was elected, I was thinking what message I should send out to the world. And in my acceptance speech in 2006, as recorded in the General Assembly record, I introduced this personal experience and anecdote. And I said that while I served as Secretary-General, I hoped I would not receive this kind of appeal any more from young people around the world.

In reality, unfortunately, I am still receiving those kinds of appeals from many people, particularly about what we are observing in the Arab region, in North Africa and in many parts of the world where people are oppressed, where people do not have freedom of expression and freedom of assembly. I am speaking out again today and I will continue to do so to the leaders of those countries, to please listen sincerely and attentively to the voices and aspirations of the people.

We must all work together to uphold the fundamental principle of democracy so these people, and all people, men and women, countries big or small, rich or poor, can enjoy genuine freedom and people can live without fear. This is what we have to do, upholding the torch Dag Hammarskjöld has left for us. I am committed to that mission. And I am very much humbled to serve as one of his successors.

I would like to observe that moment of silence again today. Let us join together in tribute to this giant among men whose life was too short, but whose legacy is eternal.

Remarks to the annual reception of the Francophone Community

NEW YORK, 22 SEPTEMBER 2011

Good evening. It is a great pleasure to be with you, here in this beautiful building.

Foreign Minister Juppé, you hosted this event once before, I believe, in the 1990s. Let me offer you a warm welcome back.

This has been a dramatic year for the francophone world – a year of transformation, even revolution. The Arab Spring has touched francophone countries, with democratic transitions under way in Egypt and Tunisia. Your experience, your courage and your commitment to these ideals have never served us quite so well as in this remarkable year.

Therefore, I understand why you hold so dear part of this group's cherished *raison d'être* – ensuring multilingualism at the United Nations. *Raison d'être*: I begin to understand just how much the French language permeates our work at the United Nations, and mine especially.

❝ How could we conduct business at the UN without a démarche or a note verbale? I summon my aide de camp and confer with my Chef de Cabinet before meeting my senior advisers for a tour de table. French truly is the language of diplomacy. ❞

Allow me to speak briefly in English, so you can hear for yourself the extent to which French has "invaded" the English language territory:

After all, how could we conduct business at the UN without a *démarche* or a *note verbale*? And consider how I begin a typical day. For a quick *tour d'horizon* of the latest news, I turn to Le Monde and Radio France Internationale. I read about the risk of a *coup d'état*. I summon my *aide de camp*, and confer with my *Chef de Cabinet*, before meeting my senior advisers for a *tour de table*, in turn to be summarized in an *aide mémoire* on the issues and options. At moments of high consequence, Permanent Representatives, or perhaps *chargés d'affaires*, come by for a *tête-à-tête*. It's a safe bet that, before long, I will be *en route* to the region, my *lais-*

sez passer in my pocket, for some urgent *pourparlers* to avoid a *fait accompli* on the ground.

You see? French truly is the language of diplomacy. Now I know: many of you fear an invasion of English – "Franglais," some call it. But do not worry. In Korea, we suffer the same fate, with the "Konglish" - that is to say, the invasion of English into Korean.

But let us also recognize that English, too, is subject to counter-invasion. From *chic* to *savoir faire*, from *voilà* to *comme ci, comme ça*. Perhaps we need a new group at the United Nations: L'Anglophonie! Or maybe we should all just speak "Globish."

Let me close with a last word – in French, *bien sûr* – which seems appropriate at this moment in history: *renouveler*. Appropriate because of the spirit of renewal and the Arab Spring. And appropriate, more personally, with the renewal of my mandate as Secretary-General.

This is the fifth annual Francophone event I have attended, and I am very glad that, thanks to your support, I will be here for five more. There is just one problem: I may run out of French jokes!

But seriously, let me say that I look forward to working closely with Francophone countries across our UN agenda. Who knows? Perhaps one day I will follow the example of my predecessor, Boutros Boutros-Ghali, and become Secretary-General of la Francophonie. Do I consider this a *fait accompli*? My French still has some distance to go, of course, but I am working on it. In fact, it is becoming second nature to me – as it should be!

With that, *Vive la Francophonie!* Thank you and *merci.*

Allocution prononcée à la réception Francophone

NEW YORK, LE 22 SEPTEMBRE 2011

Bonsoir. Je suis très heureux d'être parmi vous dans ce superbe bâtiment. Monsieur Juppé, vous avez déjà été l'hôte de cette réception, dans les années 90 je crois. Je tiens à vous souhaiter une nouvelle fois la bienvenue.

Cette année a été riche en rebondissements pour le monde francophone; ce fut une année de transformation, et même de révolution. Le Printemps arabe a touché des pays francophones; l'Égypte et la Tunisie sont en train de se démocratiser. Votre expérience, votre courage et votre attachement à ces idéaux n'ont jamais été aussi utiles qu'en cette année extraordinaire.

Je comprends donc pourquoi vous tenez tant à une des raisons d'être de votre groupe : faire respecter le multilinguisme à l'ONU.

Raison d'être: je commence à comprendre combien le français imprègne le travail que nous faisons à l'ONU, et surtout le mien.

Permettez-moi de dire quelques mots en anglais pour que vous puissiez vous rendre compte vous-mêmes de l'ampleur de l'invasion de cette langue par le français:

Après tout, que peut-on accomplir à l'ONU sans une démarche ou une note verbale?

Et comment commencer la journée sans un rapide tour d'horizon de l'actualité, grâce au journal Le Monde et à Radio France Internationale? J'apprends qu'un coup d'état vient d'avoir lieu. J'appelle mon aide de camp; je parle à mon chef de cabinet, avant de retrouver mes conseillers pour un tour de table; dont la teneur sera résumée dans un aide-mémoire sur les questions qui se posent et les options possibles.

Quand les choses se corsent, des représentants permanents, ou peut-être des chargés d'affaires, viennent me voir pour un tête-à-tête. Il y a fort à parier que dans peu de temps, je serai en route pour la région, laissez-passer en poche, afin d'aller mener d'urgence des pourparlers visant à éviter un fait accompli.

Vous voyez? Le français est réellement la langue de la diplomatie. Je sais aussi que beaucoup d'entre vous craignent que le français ne soit envahi par l'anglais, et réduit à l'état de « franglais », comme on dit. Mais ne vous inquiétez pas. En Corée, nous subissons le même sort, avec le « konglish »; c'est-à-dire, l'invasion de l'anglais dans le coréen.

Mais il faut bien avouer que l'anglais subit une sérieuse contre-invasion. Avec des mots comme « chic », « savoir faire », ou encore « voilà », et « comme ci, comme ça ». Peut-être faudrait-il créer un nouveau groupe à l'ONU : l'Anglophonie! Ou peut-être devrions-nous tous parler « globish ».

Permettez-moi de conclure avec un mot qui me semble approprié à ce moment précis de l'histoire : renouveler. Approprié, parce qu'il correspond bien à l'esprit de renouveau qui règne actuellement et au Printemps arabe. Approprié aussi, sur un plan plus personnel, à cause du renouvellement de mon mandat.

C'est la cinquième réception annuelle francophone à laquelle j'assiste et, grâce à votre appui, je serai ici pour les cinq prochaines. J'en suis ravi. Il y a juste un problème: je risque de ne plus rien trouver de drôle à dire en français!

Blague à part, laissez-moi vous dire plus sérieusement que je compte bien continuer de collaborer étroitement avec les pays francophones dans tous les domaines d'action de l'Organisation. Qui sait? Peut-être qu'un jour je suivrai l'exemple de mon prédécesseur, Boutros Boutros-Ghali, et deviendrai Secrétaire général de l'Organisation internationale de la Francophonie! Est-ce que je peux considérer cela comme un fait accompli ? D'accord, j'ai encore des progrès à faire en français, bien sûr, mais j'y travaille.

En fait, parler français est en train de devenir pour moi une seconde nature, et qui va s'en plaindre? Sur ce, vive la francophonie, et merci beaucoup!

Remarks to the Pacific Island Forum

AUCKLAND, 7 SEPTEMBER 2011

I thank Prime Minister Key, the Government and people of New Zealand for hosting this important summit. This is an interactive dialogue and I want to leave time for a full exchange.

First of all, let me say how pleased I am to be the first United Nations Secretary-General to attend the Pacific Islands Forum. I know many of you feel that your region has been overlooked at times. I am aware that many of you are frustrated when statistics look broadly at the region, not at your individual achievements or situations. I share your conviction that your countries should not be seen as places with problems, but as islands of opportunity. That is why I am here. I am eager to take the Pacific Island Forum-UN partnership to a new level. Now is the time.

Together, we have sought to advance economic progress, social justice, good governance, regional security and the Millennium Development Goals. The United Nations wants to work more deeply with you to support your efforts to implement the Pacific Plan.

We are living in an era where no country – no matter how big – can solve problems alone. And every country – regardless of size – can be a part of the solution.

> 66 Together, we have sought to advance economic progress, social justice, good governance, regional security and the Millennium Development Goals. 99

I have seen the difference your countries have made again and again over the last four and a half years. And I am here to encourage even more during my second term.

As we look forward, my primary question to each of you is this: what more would you like the United Nations to do for your countries – and what more can you do to support the work of the United Nations?

As you know, I have just visited Kiribati and the Solomon Islands. Two words describe my travels throughout your region: vastness and vulnerability. I now have a much keener sense of the distance between – and, indeed, within – the countries of the Pacific. And I have a greater appreciation for the challenges you face.

I would like to highlight three areas where our strengthened cooperation will be especially important. Then I am eager to hear your views.

First, sustainable development. Our challenge is to connect the dots among all the relevant challenges – climate change, energy security, food security, water security, infectious and non-communicable diseases, gender empowerment, and more. All these issues are connected. We must look at them in a comprehensive, integrated way. Climate change highlights just why.

Your communities are on the front of the front lines of climate challenge. You are all aware of my strong personal commitment to a multilateral arrangement that is fair for all – especially those who are the least responsible for the problem, and the most vulnerable. In July, we broke new ground in the UN Security Council by discussing climate change as a matter of peace and security.

I regard it as essential, even more so after my visit. President Tong said: "Seeing is believing". I am a believer. I saw breached sea walls. Evacuated communities. No fresh water. A young boy told me: "I am afraid to sleep at night" because of the rising water. Parents told me how they stood guard fearing that their children might drown in their own homes when the tide came in.

> **" I share your conviction that your countries should not be seen as places with problems, but as islands of opportunity. "**

We need you to continue making your voices heard – later this month in New York, later this year in Durban, and throughout the process leading up to the Rio+20 conference next June.

Let me now turn to a second area: women's empowerment. The world simply cannot do without the contributions of the world's women and girls. The Pacific has some of the world's lowest levels of women's participation in elected positions. We need to demystify traditional perceptions that somehow women and politics do not go together.

The appointment of women to some senior government positions does not diminish the need for parliamentary participation as well. There are nine Parliaments in the world without a single female member. Five of those nine are in the countries of the Pacific. You can change this.

I know your governments are working in a number of creative ways to improve the situation. Papua New Guinea has an ambitious plan to reserve one seat per province for women. I heard across-the-board support for a similar initiative in the Solomon Islands.

Understanding the sensitivities in your countries, I welcome your views on the most effective ways to maximize the potential of women for your countries's future. The United Nations stands ready to help as well as in developing national action plans to counter the pronounced gender-based violence in the region

Let me now turn to a third area: regional peace and security issues. The Pacific should be proud of the return to peace and normalcy in Bougainville, although the situation remains fragile. The United Nations will continue to support peacebuilding and development efforts.

In the Solomon Islands, I saw first-hand the important work being done by the Regional Assistance Mission for the Solomon Islands, RAMSI. I commend the region for this important initiative.

However, in Fiji, the military Government has still not initiated an inclusive credible process that will return the country to civilian constitutional rule. The United Nations continues to advocate an opening up of political space so that this can happen.

I know that the question of nuclear testing is another key concern. I want to thank your Forum for actively supporting nuclear disarmament efforts, including through the creation of the South Pacific Nuclear Free Zone established by the Rarotonga Treaty. I also welcome your growing support for the Comprehensive Nuclear Test Ban Treaty, your leadership for high standards for the safe transport of radioactive materials, and your ongoing efforts to prevent the illicit trafficking in small arms and light weapons, which continues to pose a serious threat to peace and stability in the Pacific.

As the Maori proverb teaches us: *He waka eke noa*. We are all in this canoe together. That is the Pacific way, and it is the way we can succeed together in meeting the expectations of your people and the global public.

Remarks to the Parliament of Uruguay

MONTEVIDEO, 15 JUNE 2011

This is an extraordinary honour for me to address this august chamber of Parliament. I have been looking forward to this visit for a long time.

I know that there is no official religion in Uruguay. But I have been told that there are two distinct sects: Peñarol and Nacional! I take no sides. I am neutral. Mr. President of the Assembly, I know you have a favourite. For the others, good luck in tonight's game against Santos. But as last year's World Cup in South Africa made clear: when it comes to Uruguayan football, all the world is a believer.

There were two things about that World Cup. First: on the way to the semi-finals, Uruguay eliminated the Republic of Korea team, my home team. Let me assure you: all is forgiven – at least as far as I am concerned. Second: when it comes to team colours, the United Nations and Uruguay share the same banner. *La celeste*.

How fitting. Because whether it is on the football field, or the field of international relations, the people of Uruguay are making a difference through a single act: poniendose la celeste. We do it, together, again and again: as Uruguay's brave sons and daughters help the UN keep peace in some of the world's hardest places. As Uruguay serves as a model for United Nations reform in the field of development through Delivering as One. As Uruguay raises its voice for a world free of nuclear weapons.

Let there be no doubt: Uruguay may be small on the map, but it is large in influence around the world. Today, I want to talk about that special brand of Uruguayan leadership and your global example.

There is no better place for me to do that than before you, the elected representatives of the people of Uruguay, because you represent the will of your people – you are the true representatives reflecting the aspirations of the Uruguayan people.

You, as Parliamentarians, approve the budgets. You debate the legislation. You ask the difficult questions. You bring the change. You are giving modern life to the moving words of your nation's great founder, Jose Gervasio Artigas. *Mi autoridad emana de vosotros, y ella cesa ante vuestra presencia soberana.*

The Uruguayan Republican values are an example to the world. So, in truth, my message today comes down to just three words: *muchas gracias*, Uruguay.

We meet in this magnificent house of democracy, rich in history and tradition. This building is home to one of the oldest democracies in Latin America. Your political parties are some of the longest standing, not only in the region but throughout the world.

I know you have lived through a dark period of dictatorship and human rights abuses. You transformed your pain into progress, tolerance and solidarity. The United Nations stands with you on the side of human rights and democracy.

You are a founding member of the United Nations. You have a deep commitment to dialogue. You are leaders in multilateralism and international cooperation. In just a few days, Uruguay will assume the Presidency of the Human Rights Council, and there will be the first female President of this Human Rights Council, Ambassador Laura Dupuy Lasserre.

I have come to South America with a message of broader engagement and deeper partnership. Across this continent, your economies are growing, your democracies are deepening, and your global influence is rising. I have come to recognize that progress. To salute your economic, social and human rights achievements, and to highlight your role as a bridge between South and North, even as you advance toward closer South-South cooperation.

Uruguay scored highest in equality in the region and lowest in poverty. You are a middle-income country, but I know you have development challenges. I am also here to encourage your efforts to fight poverty and inequality, to tackle the legacy of past human rights violations, to advance the rule of law and social inclusion. But I know you would be the first to say: more must be done.

I am convinced that the United Nations can play a greater role in this region, just as the region can play an ever more important role in the UN. And these are momentous times, a time of big changes and bigger hopes. Transformations that we might not have imagined in our lifetime are happening in the blink of an eye. In the Middle East and North Africa, people are raising their voices in a once-in-a-generation moment for freedom and democracy and greater liberty and participatory democracy.

I remain deeply concerned about the situation in Syria. Once again, I urge President Bashar Al-Assad of Syria and his authorities: protect your people. Respect their rights. Listen to their voices: what are their aspirations, what are their challenges. Create the conditions for refugees to return. Implement meaningful reform now before it is too late.

Closer to home, your dynamism and diversity, your growing empowerment of women, and your commitment to regional integration are ushering in what some call the Latin American Decade. These forward-looking changes are rooted in our deepest held values: dignity and opportunity, equality and justice.

In a larger sense, we have entered an age of integration and interconnection. The great tests of our era – climate change, sustainable development, pandemic disease, international financial turbulence – are global challenges requiring global solutions. Not a single country or group of countries can resolve these issues. We need collective wisdom and we have to use all the resources possible among the international community.

Next year's Rio+20 conference will highlight those interconnections. For Uruguay, whose economy and well-being is so closely tied to its land and natural resources, this is particularly important.

This age of integration reveals two 21st century truths. First, on the one hand, this must be solved through all the countries in the world putting their resources and wisdom together. And second, every country, every individual, small or big, can make a lasting difference. This, too, is what Uruguay is showing the world.

Let us begin with peacekeeping. For more than sixty years, United Nations peacekeepers have sacrificed and served to monitor ceasefires, provide security, support communities and protect the most vulnerable. They have maintained peace and security in some of the most dangerous places. For millions of people, United Nations peacekeepers are their last, best chance.

Uruguay has taken part in this lifesaving work since 1951. Over the years, more than 25,000 Uruguayans have served in twenty-one different peacekeeping missions. Right now, more than 2,400 Uruguayans serve under the blue flag of the United Nations. Uruguay, a country with a small population, contributes more troops per capita than any other Member State in the world. You are first in the world. I thank you very much for that commitment.

Thousands of miles to the north, Uruguayan soldiers are deployed in the proud but long suffering nation of Haiti. Thousands of miles to the east, they serve in another troubled place: the Democratic Republic of the Congo.

Your constituents might ask you, why do our sons and daughters have to be there? Seemingly, you don't have any such natural interest. The answer I would give is very simple. Again and again, Uruguayan troops have made a difference: often, the difference between success and failure. You made the difference by defending innocent civilians in the besieged city of Goma. In Haiti and elsewhere, you protect people and communities wiped out by natural disaster.

Your soldiers are highly trained. They know how to operate in difficult and hostile terrain. They provide the helicopters, a rare and precious resource for us, and rush the injured to medical care and rescue the innocent from harm's way. They provide the conditions for civilians to return to daily life and support the transition from conflict to development. The security for children to play freely, for women to safely carry water, for men and women to take up productive activities to support their families.

I was deeply moved by the account of a little girl, an eleven-year old girl, in the Democratic Republic of the Congo who told a Uruguayan peacekeeper, "Thank you. Because of you, I can now walk to school without the constant fear of being raped."

Uruguayans have made great sacrifices in the name of the global good. They have shed their own blood in the name of global peace. Twenty-seven of your finest young people have paid the highest price for the cause of peace, security and human rights.

Uruguay's peacekeepers are your brave sons and daughters, but they are also the world's best and brightest. I want you to know how proud I am as Secretary-General of the United Nations of them. I want you to know how grateful I am to all of you, personally, and how much we value your extraordinary contribution. And I want you to know that I am committed to solving the payments issue. We are working hard – very hard – to find a solution. I will not relent.

> **❝ Uruguay may be small on the map, but it is large in influence around the world. Every day you show us that it is not the size of a country that counts, but its spirit. ❞**

Uruguay is also leading the way in building a more coherent, more effective, and more efficient United Nations for the 21st century. The UN has launched a revolution in the way we work, on the ground, every day. A revolution that we believe will allow us to operate more effectively and more efficiently, that will help us listen more closely to government and civil society and address real needs that will help us mobilize expertise across the UN system.

We call it Delivering as One – *Unidos en Accion*. We chose a handful of places to test this innovation. When it came to selecting one middle-income country in the world, Uruguay stepped up. For the last half decade, Uruguay has been a global testing ground for a renewed United Nations' approach in middle-income countries, one that shifts from project-based assistance to policy engagement on issues that are as relevant to high- and middle-income countries as they are to low-income ones.

Middle-income countries are still home to many poor people, often due to regional, gender, and ethnic inequalities. But you also have a wealth of experience to share with others, particularly on the decent work challenge. Here in Uruguay, you have not only achieved the Millennium Development Goals, you are aiming higher with a MDG-plus agenda and I thank you very much for that.

Our common program in Uruguay is designed to continue reducing inequalities and social exclusion, especially among women and children. To strengthen institutions. Promote sustainable development. Protect human rights.

I saw an important example today relating to prison reform. Once again, the UN family is bringing our collective experience to advance solutions to complex national problems. Thank you for your confidence in us.

Later this year, the world will come together to share experiences on delivering as one. They will meet here in Montevideo. I thank Uruguay for hosting this conference. And I thank you for leading the way.

Let me conclude with yet another instance of global leadership: your persistent work to achieve a world free of nuclear weapons. I am especially grateful for Uruguay's support for my five-point nuclear disarmament proposal. Your country's commitment is rock-solid at every level, from your membership in the Nuclear Non-proliferation Treaty, to the Comprehensive Nuclear-Test-Ban Treaty, to the Tlatelolco Treaty for the Prohibition of Nuclear Weapons in Latin America and the Caribbean.

Uruguay has also stood up against the illicit trade in small arms and light weapons and for the negotiation of an arms trade treaty. Your timely action in ratifying the Convention on Cluster Munitions helped it to enter into force last August. I salute again your leadership. Let us strengthen our partnership in this great common cause.

Let me close with a personal story. When I was a young boy, I was told by my teachers that if you dug down to the earth, you will reach a special place, a place called Uruguay. Uruguay and Korea, we realize that we are antipoles. From an early age, Uruguay was planted in my mind as a place of fascination and curiosity. I wanted to go there.

Now, as Secretary-General of the United Nations, rather than fascination and curiosity, I am here more to strengthen our partnership for world peace and security, development and human rights. It has taken sixty years, but I made it. I did not drill the hole, but because of the volcanic ash, I came by air, by road and by sea. Perhaps digging would have been quicker to reach Uruguay!

But I want you to know something that I have come to learn in my many years of international service. When it comes to helping to lead on the big issues of the day, you are a beacon of tolerance, inclusion, solidarity.

Many years ago, when Korea was attacked by North Koreans in the 1950s and thereafter, the United Nations was a beacon to all Koreans. Today I meet many people around the world, young people, who look to the United Nations as their beacon. In that regard, Uruguay, every day you show us that it is not the size of a country that counts, but its spirit. I feel that spirit here, now. I have seen the difference Uruguay has made around the world.

Perhaps on the map, you and I come from different parts of the world. *Pero tenemos algo en comun. Somos todos orientales, incluido yo! Que les vaya bien a todos y todas, y arriba nuestro color – la celeste! Muchas gracias.*

Remarks to roundtable at the Central Party School

BEIJING, 3 NOVEMBER 2010

I am delighted to meet with such an eminent group – the future leaders of China.

Let me begin with a statement of fundamental principle: I believe the UN Charter resonates almost perfectly with the concept of a "harmonious world" - a vision of peoples and nations united in addressing global challenges and striving for collective security and peace. It is grounded in the understanding that true peace is dependent on better understanding between nations and among communities, the realization of their economic and social development, and respect for human rights.

I know that many of you at the Party School in China have devoted much time and thought to global governance in our changing world. I look forward to hearing your insights. If you are agreeable, I would like to have a conversation, an exchange of views on how we see the world and how we see the way ahead for China and the UN, working together in these very challenging times.

As you know, I have been travelling widely this week Thailand, Cambodia, Vietnam and, here in China, Shanghai, Nanjing and now Beijing. I want to tell you how impressed I am. Every time I come to China, I see dramatic changes.

On Sunday, I took the new Huning High Speed Railroad to Nanjing – 300 kilometers in just over an hour. And this is not even your fastest train. I also visited Expo 2010 in Shanghai – the first such expo in a developing country. By any standard, it was an extraordinary success; a remarkable celebration of global diversity, highlighting China's new standing in the world.

Clearly, China is on the rise. Its transformation has been profound. Its influence is increasingly global. Its power is real. I believe this rise is beneficial to the world. That is what I would like to talk to you about today. For with China's rise, with this remarkable progress, come great expectations and great responsibilities.

We live in an era of global challenges – global crises that no nation can solve alone. We face the challenges of climate change, the threat of global terrorism, disruptions in our transportation, communications and information systems – as well as the more traditional threats of infectious diseases, the proliferation of weapons of mass destruction, civil wars and intra-state conflicts.

In today's globalized world, these threats are increasingly interconnected. They demand concerted, coordinated action. No country or region can do it alone. For the UN to effectively address these myriad challenges, we need closer cooperation among Member States, stronger collaboration with regional organizations, greater coordination with groups like the G-20 and with civil society. We also need better frameworks, rules and institutions for handling the many issues that transcend borders, as well as better coordination in their implementation.

In all this, we need China's full engagement. We need China's leadership. You in this room – China's best and brightest – will play your part. I am confident that you will do so with vigor, vision and full commitment to the common values that unite us.

> **❝ Achieving the shared goals of human rights around the world is more than an aspiration: it is a foundation of peace and harmony in our modern world. So too is respect for freedom of expression and the protection of its defenders. ❞**

I am referring, of course, to the shared values and principles of the UN Charter, as well as the body of international laws and agreements that are the foundation of our common quest for development, peace and security and human rights. The values embedded in the Universal Declaration of Human Rights are timeless and shared yet unrealized in far too much of the globe. We must continue to work together to make those rights real in people's lives.

That will take a global effort. China's voice and example are critical. In this respect, I welcome China's commitment to building a rule-of-law society and its notable advances in that ongoing journey. China is contributing very constructively across a range of UN issues. And I want you to know: I am determined to make this UN-China partnership even stronger. Let me touch, very briefly, on just a few issues that dominated my discussions with your leadership.

First, climate change. As I am sure you know, last year's conference in Copenhagen did not meet all expectations. That said, we did establish a firm foundation for progress. At the upcoming meeting in Cancun, and beyond, our challenge is to build on that progress. In this regard, I thanked your government for hosting the latest round of talks under the UN Framework Convention on Climate Change in Tianjin.

I am also confident that, with China's engagement, we can make further progress on important issues. Among them: financing for adaptation, technology cooperation and deforestation. As with any great multilateral effort, the important thing is not to lose momentum. China knows only too well the dangers of climate change. We have no more time to lose.

Second, the changing international situation. We devoted considerable discussion to the delicate situation in Sudan. With the coming referenda, scheduled for early January, we are at a critical moment. I asked your government's help in assisting the two sides find their away to a peaceful future, recognizing their shared interests. We also recognized that China has a strong interest in strengthening its role in UN peacekeeping and peacebuilding. In this regard, Sudan represents an important passage in our growing partnership. In addition to your diplomatic engagement, therefore, I also asked China's help on logistical issues of transport and technical support in the upcoming voting.

We spoke at length about next week's election in Myanmar. I see it as an important test. Will the vote perpetuate an untenable status quo? Or will it set the country on course toward a more open, democratic and inclusive political future? As a trusted neighbour and friend, China's role will be critical in helping the UN to help Myanmar find its way forward.

We also spoke about the situation on the Korean Peninsula. As I see it, there is great potential for China and the United Nations to work together to calm tensions, revive the Six-Party talks and gradually bring the Demoratic People's Republic of Korea into a more open, mutually cooperative relationship with the international community.

Lastly, economic development – the focus of the bulk of our discussions. You are well aware of our UN effort to realize the Millennium Development Goals. This has been one of my top priorities   day and night, night and day, since I took office four years ago.

The MDGs represent the world's blueprint for lifting hundreds of millions of people from poverty – to bring better education, health and social security to the poorest and most vulnerable people of the world. Ten years have passed since we set these goals. Five years remain to our target date for achieving them – 2015.

That is why, in September at the annual opening of the UN General Assembly, I convened a special MDG summit. Premier Wen came and renewed his commitment to advancing the goals. So did leaders of many other nations. China, of course, is well-positioned to meet all the goals. We can do so in many other nations, as well. But it will take a special effort.

We have learned many lessons over the past decade – what works, and what does not. With the right mix of policies, targeting the right needs and the right people, we can create a multiplier effect that dramatically accelerates social and economic progress.

One thing we need above all else. That is leadership: political will and committed leadership. As a global leader of the 21st century, China can help lead this campaign. China can help other countries lift themselves from poverty, much as China has raised its own people. Indeed, I see this as China's responsibility, commensurate with its new place in the world.

An opportunity to exercise such leadership will come at the G-20 summit in Seoul, beginning next week. The global financial crisis, adversely affecting so many poorer countries, has forced us to re-assess global institutions. We hear some countries speaking of resolving problems without full consultations; some even question the relevance of the United Nations. That is why the summit in Seoul is so important. For the first time, G-20 leaders have put development issues on the agenda. The danger, as in the past, is that these critical discussions will be over-shadowed by on-going debates over the financial crisis.

In my meetings with your leadership, I stressed the importance of speaking out forcefully on the needs of developing countries during this very difficult period. I see this as a necessary and vital element in China's vision of a "harmonious society."

No country can claim a perfect record. Everywhere, there is room for improvement. As we move forward, we recognize that achieving the shared goals of human rights around the world is more than an aspiration: it is a foundation of peace and harmony in our modern world. So too is respect for freedom of expression and the protection of its defenders.

In our modern world – this world where everything and everyone is inter-related – society is global. More than ever, it is a practical and moral imperative to help those who are less fortunate – to help in direct proportion to our abilities. I know that China still considers itself as a developing country, rightly. But China today is also much, much more than that – not unlike my own country, the Republic of Korea. That is why we count on China's leadership. The UN and China have many avenues for greater cooperation in enhancing global governance, based on shared and common values.

The UN is the world's preeminent international organization. The world needs a strong UN. But the UN can be strong only with the full support of its strongest members. I am very happy to share views with you, after meeting China's leadership. I can say that we are in full agreement. The way to address all the issues we have discussed is through a greater role and enhanced authority of the United Nations. I am confident that, together with China and the rest of the international community, we will make headway towards more harmonious global governance and a better world for all. Thank you. *Xie xie ni.*

Remarks to the European Parliament

STRASBOURG, 19 OCTOBER 2010

G ood afternoon, *buenas tardes, bonjour, gueta dag. Je suis très honoré d'adresser le Parlement Européen. Estoy muy feliz de estar en Estrasburgo.* It is a great honour to be here addressing the European parliament.

You have been sent to Strasbourg by your citizens to build a stronger Europe for the 21st century. I have come to Strasbourg because you are the democratic voice of the people of Europe, nearly half a billion strong.

You pass budgets, consider legislation and debate the issues with tremendous passion. You serve as a vital link between the global, the regional and the local. You are a powerful force of peace, stability and prosperity in your own neighbourhood. And you are playing a pivotal role in shaping policy that goes far beyond borders. Your responsibilities will only grow with the avenues opened by the Treaty of Lisbon. We welcome this progress.

The United Nations and the European Union are natural partners. We are making a real difference for people all around the world. Millions of poor girls and boys are in school, millions of young children are being immunized against deadly diseases, thousands of soldiers are keeping the peace from Lebanon to Central Africa to Cyprus and beyond, all as a result of our partnership and Europe's extraordinary generosity and leadership. That work must deepen and grow.

We are confronting many challenges, multiple crises. But something else is happening – a light bulb moment around the world. Country after country, leader after leader, is coming to recognize that the best way to address our challenges is by taking them on together, with the United Nations and all the members of the European Union. No nation, no group, no region can do it alone. If we share in the burden, we will share in the benefits. So, today, I would like to talk about solidarity. How, together, the European Union and the United Nations can address the real fears of real people.

Everywhere, we see currents of concern. Jobs are scarce. Tensions are high. People are hurting, angry and disillusioned. That has led to an erosion of trust in institutions, in leaders, and among neighbors. These are testing times, even in a prosperous region like Europe. I believe we can pass the test.

Together we have framed a vision for our work, a precise definition of the overarching challenges of our time. We have mobilized global support for common action. And let me be clear: we are beholden to the people, who rightly demand results. Now is not the time for simply delivering speeches; now is the time to implement those speeches and now is the time for delivering action. I would like to focus on three global challenges that we must address together.

First, tackling extreme poverty around the world; second, confronting climate change; and third, building a world free of nuclear weapons. Let me be specific.

First, the poverty challenge. Last month, world leaders gathered in New York for the most significant global development summit in a decade. There is good news: major progress in combating extreme poverty and hunger, in school enrolment and child health, in clean water and fighting malaria, tuberculosis and HIV.

Yet achievements are uneven. Obstacles stand in the way. Global trade talks have stagnated, locking in place harmful subsidies and an unfair regime that deny developing countries new opportunities. Rising prices are putting essential medicines out of reach of many of the neediest. Nearly one billion people go to bed hungry every night. And this year alone, an additional 64 million people will fall into extreme poverty.

All of this calls for a renewed push to achieve the goals by the deadline of 2015. At the recent MDG summit, that is precisely what we agreed. We will boost resources and accountability. I commend those members of the European Union that made strong commitments despite fiscal pressures. We can tighten belts without closing our eyes to common challenges.

I ask all of you to support the United Nations where action is urgently and especially needed. We must focus on employment-centred growth, on decent work. Investment in clean and renewable energy is crucial for jumpstarting jobs and innovation. Where people go hungry, we must help – help people help themselves. Thank you for your investment in the European Union Food Facility in the amount of one billion euros.

And we must put resources where they will have the greatest impact – in particular, the health and empowerment of women. Last month, we received $40 billion in pledges over the next five years for our Global Strategy for Women's and Children's Health. This is the most stubborn of the MDGs.

Some might say, go for the easy wins. But I do not believe in declaring victory that way. We must strive for the hardest to reach goals, the hardest to reach people, in the hardest to reach places. We can save the lives of more than 16 million women and children.

Our second great challenge is climate change. Here, too, Europe's vision and voice have been central. Scientists warn that the extreme weather we have witnessed in many countries could be the opening act on our future. We have seen raging fires in Russia. Epic floods in Pakistan. We must always be careful however about linking specific weather events to climate change. But neither should we avert our eyes from what is plain to see.

The message is clear: the more we delay, the more we will have to pay in competitiveness, in resources and in human lives. We must take action now to reduce climate risks, strengthen our resilience, and support developing countries in pursuing clean energy growth.

Copenhagen was not perfect, but it provided an important basis for moving forward. Since then, there has been progression of important implementation issues such as adaptation, technology cooperation, and steps to reduce deforestation. Movement has been slower on mitigation commitments, including long-term financing monitoring and verification and the future of the Kyoto Protocol.

At the upcoming UN climate change conference in Cancun, we must capture progress on those issues where there is consensus and on those issues still unresolved, and governments must agree on how they will move forward to resolve them. I call on all parties to show flexibility, solidarity, and muster the courage to compromise if needed. The health, security and prosperity of millions of people depend on it. There is no time to waste.

❝ For Europe, "winning the peace" was the narrative of the last century. The 21st-century European challenge is tolerance within. Europe cannot afford stereotyping that closes minds and breeds hatred. And the world cannot afford a Europe that does this. ❞

Most immediately, finance is crucial for building trust and spurring action. There is a wide gap of trust between the developing and developed world. The quickest way to bridge this gap is through providing financial support to those who do not have any capacities. I call upon all developed countries, including those represented in this Parliament, to provide their fair share of the $30 billion in fast-track financing pledged at Copenhagen for 2010-2012.

Many view this as a litmus test of industrialised countries' commitment to progress in the broader negotiations. We have to also generate $100 billion dollars annually by 2020. This was a promise by the developed world made in Copenhagen. My High-Level Advisory Group on Climate Change Financing has been working this year and they will come out with several options on how to generate $100 billion dollars annually by 2020.

Climate change is a crucial part of the broader agenda on sustainable development. That is why I recently established a new High Level Panel on Global Sustainability, co-chaired by President Halonen of Finland and President Zuma of South Africa. Their job will be to connect the many different dots which are interconnected to find the right path through the inter-linked economic, social and environmental challenges of the coming decades.

In all this, Europe's leadership – your leadership – will be essential. Europe has been a historic engine of growth and change. Now, when governments are not moving, when the train has hit the buffers in our talks on climate change or other issues, Europe can be the locomotive, driving it forward. You can push, you can pull, you can get the train back on track. You can keep us moving in the right direction.

We are also advancing together on building not only a cleaner world, but a safer one. This is our third global challenge that I wish to bring to you today. The goal of achieving a world free of nuclear weapons. That is a subject of great interest to the Members of this Parliament. I commend you for speaking out on disarmament issues, posing timely questions and urging new progress. Thank you for your resolution of April 2009, which supported total nuclear disarmament and cited the proposal for a Nuclear Weapons Convention.

Today, there is new momentum in fulfilling disarmament commitments. This progress will continue if, and only if, the voices of the people are fully reflected in national and regional issues. And if the half billion voices in the European Union speak out in harmony on this issue, joined by voices from other regions. I welcome support for my five-point proposal on nuclear disarmament and non-proliferation from many leaders, including the Inter-Parliamentary Union. We are working to eliminate other weapons of mass destruction, curb trade in small arms and light weapons and counter the risk that nuclear materials could fall into the hands of terrorists. Let us move beyond our over-armed and under-developed age to a more secure world for all.

❝ I have confidence in the European model and in the Europe that has come to represent an ideal, not a mere geography. An ideal of mutual respect, tolerance, and the power of collective action in the name of the global good. ❞

These are big challenges and great goals. Diverse issues with a common denominator: global solidarity. We rise or fall together. So we must guard against division: division around the world, division within societies, communities.

Almost seven years ago, my predecessor Kofi Annan stood before you. In his address, he made an impassioned call for Europe to seize the opportunities presented by immigration and to resist those who demonized these newcomers as "the other."

I wish I could report, today, that the situation in Europe has improved over the intervening years. But as a friend of Europe, I share profound concern. It is almost a cliché to say that the birth of the European Union ended centuries of war and brought lasting peace to the continent. Yet it remains a profound truth and a beacon of hope. Europe has served as an extraordinary engine of integration, weaving together nations and cultures into a whole that is far, far greater than the sum of its parts.

But for Europe, "winning the peace" was the narrative of the last century. The 21st century European challenge is tolerance within. Inclusion, building diverse communities, is as complex a task as the one Europe faced after the Second World War. None of this is easy. Migrants suffer disproportionately, whether from within Europe or beyond. Unemployment. Discrimination. Unequal opportunities in schools and the workplace.

And a dangerous trend is emerging. A new politics of polarization. Some play on people's fears. They seek to invoke liberal values for illiberal causes. They accuse immigrants of violating European values. Yet too often, it is the accusers who subvert these values, and thus the very idea of what it means to be a citizen of the European Union. Europe's darkest chapters have been written in language such as this.

Today, the primary targets are immigrants of the Muslim faith. Europe cannot afford stereotyping that closes minds and breeds hatred. And the world cannot afford a Europe that does this.

The vision is clear: a Europe built on human rights and humane values, a continent united by shared values, not divided by ethnic and religious differences. A Union where any child of parents of any background has an equal chance of success. A strong, cohesive and vibrant Europe for the 21st century.

I have confidence in the European model and in the Europe that has come to represent an ideal, not a mere geography. An ideal of mutual respect, tolerance, and the power of collective action in the name of the global good. In a word, solidarity. I feel it here. I see it in you.

As Albert Schweitzer, that great son of Alsace, reminded us: "The first step in the evolution of ethics is a sense of solidarity with other human beings." Let us continue that journey together.

Remarks to the Caribbean Community

It is a profound honour to be the first United Nations Secretary-General to address a CARICOM Summit. And it is good to do it here in Montego Bay. In 1947, the Montego Bay Conference generated the notion of a Caribbean regional movement, which led to the West Indies Federation and then to CARICOM itself.

We discussed many of these issues at the CARICOM Mini-Summit held at the United Nations last September. It is good to be here today to deepen our work in addressing complex and multiple challenges. The threat of climate change. The fallout of the global financial crisis. The security burden posed by organized crime.

And, of course, natural hazards. It is especially moving for me to be with all of you as we approach the six-month anniversary of the earthquake that devastated Haiti. Above all, I have come here to say thank you for your support and commitment. CARICOM countries, institutions and citizens demonstrated profound solidarity with your newest member. You made Haiti a priority and played a key role as an advocate for recovery. You have appointed a Special Representative for Haiti and created an office to oversee CARICOM's reconstruction efforts. Your engagement is central to ensuring sustained and long-term attention to Haiti's needs.

Haiti is also a priority for the United Nations and I thank and commend the leadership of President René Préval. Six months after the earthquake the Government and people of Haiti have accomplished much in collaboration with the international community. Thousands of survivors have received medical assistance. Emergency shelter has been distributed to more than 1.5 million people. Widespread hunger and disease have been averted. Children are back in school and commercial life is resuming.

Nonetheless, we have an enormous task ahead – especially with the onset of the hurricane season. Humanitarian needs will remain for many months to come. Recovery will take many years, and will require consistent effort by all Haiti's partners. Promises will not feed the people of Haiti – pledges alone will not shelter them. I am working to expedite the help that the people of Haiti need.

The upcoming November elections will also be fundamental for ensuring Haiti's democratic future. It is essential that they are transparent and credible. We are working with the Government of Haiti and international partners to support that process. I am grateful for CARICOM's support.

Let me now highlight three broader priority issues for the United Nations: economic and development concerns, security challenges and climate change.

First, the financial and economic crisis continues to take a heavy toll. Many Caribbean countries face declining revenue, weakened growth, reduced tourism and high levels of debt. You have made commendable progress towards the Millennium Development Goals. Yet, you are highly vulnerable to external shocks. I know you have discussed the need for a new economic model for development: debt relief for middle-income countries, special treatment in the global trading system, and dedicated credit for dealing with natural disasters.

I agree that the international community must collectively address the impact of the sustained economic crisis. As I said at the G-20 meeting in Toronto last week, the international community cannot abandon its commitment to the most vulnerable. In particular I advocated for investment in key areas where we can expect substantial and immediate returns: jobs, a green recovery, and health systems.

> 66 The Caribbean community has conveyed an important message to the world: the threat of climate change is urgent and growing. You have been pioneers in calling attention to the specific vulnerability of Small Island States. 99

I welcome the General Assembly decision sponsored by CARICOM to convene a high-level meeting in September 2011 on the prevention and control of non-communicable diseases. I also look forward to your participation in this September's high-level meeting on the Millennium Development Goals in New York. You have many valuable lessons to offer.

We simply must deliver results for the world's most vulnerable. Governments must agree in September on a concrete action plan that provides a clear road map to meet our collective targets and promise by 2015.

We must also do more to empower women. I am pleased to inform you that, just two days ago, we established the newest member of the United Nations' family. It is called the UN Entity for Gender Equality and the Empowerment of Women or UN Women – *ONU Femme*. This will boost our common effort to promote gender equality, expand opportunity and fight discrimination around the world.

My second point: the growing security threat posed by organized transnational crime and the proliferation of small arms and light weapons. Crime has a devastating impact on a country's social fabric. Of course, the challenge goes beyond borders. Our solutions must, too. CARICOM and the UN Office on Drugs and Crime have developed a joint action plan, and we are working to implement the Santo Domingo Pact and Managua Partnership. It is important to consider the problem of drug control and the prevention of crime and terrorism in a regional context and through the prism of development, human rights, the rule of law and security reform.

We must address security issues and social causes simultaneously. In this regard, I welcome the fact that the recently launched Caribbean Basin Security Initiative goes beyond traditional law enforcement approach, and I applaud CARICOM States on all your efforts to combat illicit trade in small arms and light weapons.

My third point concerns climate change. It impacts all our concerns: development, health, security. I commend CARICOM countries, once again, for your leadership in the lead-up to the Copenhagen climate talks and during the conference. The Caribbean community has conveyed an important message to the world: the threat of climate change is urgent and growing. You have been pioneers in calling attention to the specific vulnerability of Small Island States to climate change. Adaptation strategies to this very real threat will require sizeable and sustained investment.

The Copenhagen conference called on the international community to mobilize $30 billion a year between now and 2012 and $100 billion a year up to 2020 for mitigation and adaptation actions in developing countries.

I have recently appointed an Advisory Group on Climate Change Financing, co-chaired by Prime Minister Meles Zenawi of Ethiopia and Prime Minister Jens Stoltenberg of Norway, to push this forward. I thank President Bharrat Jagdeo, of the Republic of Guyana, for his contribution to the group, and look forward to welcoming him in New York in July for the next principals' meeting.

Caribbean nations were prominent in Copenhagen. I count once again on your strong voice as we continue our negotiations for the climate change conference in Mexico.

The Caribbean region is vital to the United Nations. Just as you are helping to advance our agenda, I would like to reiterate the commitment of the United Nations to your goals and aspirations. You can count on me to promote security, development and human rights.

I take strength from the immortal wisdom of a great son of Jamaica. I will "get up". I will "stand up". And I won't "give up the fight."

Address to the Global Compact Leaders Summit

NEW YORK, 24 JUNE 2010

Welcome to the third Global Compact Leaders Summit. A special welcome to you, Mayor Bloomberg – a great leader of a great host city, New York, a good friend of mine and a good friend of the United Nations. Thank you very much for your participation and your leadership. Like so many others here today, you are a true business visionary. Thank you for joining our effort to take the Global Compact to the next level.

Before I became Secretary-General of the United Nations, I saw the power of business up close. As minister for foreign affairs and trade of the Republic of Korea, I saw how smart investment can bring both profits and social advancement in all parts of the world. As a boy growing up in a war-torn country, Korea, I saw what business can do to help rebuild a country and transform an entire region.

Now as Secretary-General of the United Nations, I am delighted to have this opportunity to push the Global Compact forward to the next higher stage and equip it for its second decade. I am eager to work with business, with each of you, to generate the benefits we know are possible – the benefits I have seen first-hand.

In its first ten years, the Global Compact has become the world's largest and most ambitious initiative of its kind. Corporate sustainability is becoming a byword in companies across the world.

At first, the Compact was driven solely by morality. We asked businesses to do the right thing. Morality is still a driving force. But today, the business community is coming to understand that principles and profits are two sides of the same coin.

This realization could not be happening at a better time. Ours is an era of tectonic shifts in the global order. Wealth and economic power are shifting to emerging economies. Major economies continue to cope with the greatest economic and financial crises in most of our lifetimes. Business itself, in the aftermath of scandals and mismanagement, faces the need to build and renew trust.

The Global Compact can be just the vehicle we need to carry us forward to sustainable growth and to markets that bring profits and social advancement at the same time. I see four priorities ahead of us.

First is leadership. Leadership of everyone present this morning. It is incumbent on you, the participants and stakeholders in the Global Compact, to lead. You are at the forefront of globalization. You can and must play a central role in sustaining the openness on which development and prosperity depend. That means emphasizing sustainability across your operations and in your investment strategies. It means inspiring others into a race to the top. And it means thinking differently about how and where we invest; thinking differently about creating markets of the future and creating opportunities for growth.

At the G-20 Summit meeting this weekend, you are likely to hear leaders of the world stress the need for austerity and budget consolidation at a time of crisis. I will argue exactly the opposite: that we cannot afford not to invest in the developing world. We all know that is where the greatest need is; but that is also where some of the greatest dynamism is. Global economic growth requires investment in the developing world. With official development assistance under pressure, foreign direct investment is that much more important.

Second, we must heed the lessons of the financial crisis. Businesses must move away from their devotion to short-term profits, which distorts both accounting and daily operations. The private sector must go further in embracing long-term value creation. An ethical culture must be embedded into business practices. Distinctions between right and wrong cannot be ignored.

Third, we need business to support the Millennium Development Goals. This is a blueprint that world leaders adopted for the harmonious prosperity and the development of the world at a time of the 2000 Millennium - the new millennium. In our efforts to eradicate poverty, create jobs and control disease, ten years of experience has shown us what works and what doesn't work.

❝ Today, the business community is coming to understand that principles and profits are two sides of the same coin. ❞

Our challenge now is to again scale up our commitment. We have made that job easy for you at this Summit. Through a rigorous process of vetting and analysis, we have identified fifteen partnership opportunities – fifteen ways to move us toward the Millennium Development Goals. They cover a wide range: hunger, disease, green energy, protecting girls from violence. They include our Joint Action Plan for Women's and Children's Health. But here is what they share: each is ready to be scaled up now; and each has a powerful multiplier effect. Let us remember: investments in the developing world are investments in growth everywhere.

That brings me naturally to the fourth priority: embrace and adopt new strategies and tools for this new era. The Blueprint of Corporate Sustainability Leadership being launched at this Summit draws on a decade of experience and will be the cornerstone of our efforts as we move ahead. It contains fifty ways for companies to distinguish themselves.

My Special Representative on the issue of human rights and transnational corporations and other business enterprises, Professor John Ruggie, continues his efforts. We also have developed new frameworks for anti-corruption and environmental stewardship; new principles to guide business on women's empowerment, social investment and children's rights; a sustainability guide for supply chains, and guidelines for responsible practices in conflict areas.

These new resources, combined with the enduring power of the Compact's ten principles, can help you attain higher levels of performance across the sustainability agenda.

While I am asking you to take the lead, you will not be alone. To governments of the world, I say: renew your commitment to transparency and smart regulation. I also urge you to build up your capacities to work with the private sector. To investors, I say: embrace the Principles for Responsible Investment; and integrate environmental, social and corporate governance issues into financial decision-making. To the academic community: incorporate business ethics more fully into your core programmes, in keeping with the Principles for Responsible Management Education. To civil society leaders: continue your vital watchdog function while also seeking more partnerships with the private sector.

As for the United Nations itself: let me assure you that the United Nations is evolving to fulfil its side of the Compact bargain. Our mindset has changed as well. Ten years ago, only a small group of business leaders assembled here to launch this Global Compact initiative. Today, we have more than 8,000 participants. Today, we can set a new goal: 20,000 participants by 2020.

Our hope is to create a truly transformative movement. Our aim is to reach a tipping point towards a new era of sustainability. And our commitment is to do all this while maintaining the integrity of the initiative. Already, in the past two years, we have de-listed more than 1,300 companies for failing to communicate progress in implementing the Compact principles. The Compact may be a voluntary initiative, but that doesn't mean we lack teeth in policing it.

Let us carry forward the great momentum that you yourselves have been so instrumental in shaping – the momentum has already been generated. Let us all be architects of a brighter, more sustainable future. I look forward to continuing our work together on the path to that right and necessary destination. You can count on the United Nations, you can count on me and, likewise, I count on your leadership and commitment for a better future for all.

Remarks at memorial ceremony in honour of those killed in the Haiti earthquake

NEW YORK, 9 MARCH 2010

Dear colleagues, dear friends, above all, dear families of those to whom we sadly bid farewell: let us begin by thanking the families and friends who have traveled far to be with us. To those who could not be here, please know that our hearts are with you.

We are joined by duty stations around the world – the men and women of our proud United Nations. Among them are the members of our UN mission in Haiti, who have carried on despite their pain and hardship.

I thank Mr. Edmond Mulet and his courageous staff who are working tirelessly – day in, day out – in MINUSTAH, the UN Stabilization Mission in Haiti. I highly commend you and I am deeply grateful to all of you.

Today, we commemorate the single greatest loss the UN has suffered in its history. We remember 101 lives of consequence. We honor 101 unique paths that joined in Haiti to write the larger story of the United Nations.

These women and men were our own. They were family. They came to Haiti from all corners of the world, from all walks of life. Yet they shared a common conviction – a belief in a better future for the people of Haiti, and a common resolve to help them build it. Now those 101 paths come together one final time, here in this chamber, through us – families and friends, colleagues and loved ones.

The world knew them as trusted diplomats, dedicated humanitarians and conscientious professionals. They were doctors and drivers, police officers and policy advisers, soldiers and lawyers – each contributing to the mission, each in his or her own way.

To us they were even more. We knew them, very personally. We knew their smiles, their songs, their dreams. Now we cannot forget the last email, the last conversation, the last meal together, the last *au revoir*. Their words echo: "Don't worry about me. This is where I need to be."

At the United Nations, we do not simply share office space: we share a passion for a better world. So it is no surprise that many of these 101 paths criss-crossed the globe through the years. In Cambodia and the Democratic Republic of the Congo. Eritrea and East Timor. Kosovo and Sierra Leone. Whether they came to Haiti or came from Haiti, they knew that hope shines in even the darkest corners. And so they chased the flame. Wherever they went, they carried the light of hope. And as they fulfilled their mission in Haiti, they illuminated a profound truth: earthquakes are a force of nature, but people move the world.

Today, our hearts are heavy with a burden almost too difficult to bear. Yet perhaps like you, it is gratitude that I feel most of all. Gratitude to the international community for the spontaneous, whole-hearted and unstinting support in the face of this tragedy. Gratitude to the rescue teams, aid workers, governments and non-governmental organizations that rallied to our side, determined to help Haiti to recover and, in time, to build back better. Gratitude to the people of Haiti, for their strength, resilience and faith – the faith of human spirit, the spirit that burns in all of us today.

> 66 Earthquakes are a force of nature, but people move the world. Today, our hearts are heavy with a burden almost too difficult to bear. 99

I commend and appreciate the leadership of President René Préval and his Government and his people. Gratitude fills this chamber – profound thanks that our world and our lives were touched by the grace and nobility of these 101 UN heroes.

In life, we are measured by the company we keep. To those here today, let us know that this is our measure. This is the company we keep. To those we have lost, let us say: we will never forget you. We will carry on your work.

In a moment we will read out their names – the roll call of highest honor. Look at their pictures. Look into their eyes. Remember their smiles and their dreams. Together we stand in honor of the victims and in deepest sympathy for the bereaved. May I now ask you to rise and join me in a minute of silence.

Address to the
Global Insight Summit

JACKSON HOLE, 6 JUNE 2008

T hank you, Bill Rouhana, for those kind words and for your support of the
United Nations. I consider you a true friend of the UN family. Let me also
thank the organizers of the Jackson Hole Film Festival, especially Eben Dor-
ros and Todd Rankin. You and your team are showing great dedication in highlighting global issues.

I am very happy to be here at this first-ever Global Insight Summit. It is important to get outside one's natural habitat sometimes. If my life were a movie, instead of Indiana Jones and the Temple of Doom it would be Ban Ki-moon in the
Negotiating Room. Against this beautiful backdrop, the Teton mountain range, it
might seem odd to speak about the world's most forgotten peoples in the most forgotten places. But they are precisely who you care about.

By bringing together leaders from the creative community, concerned members of the public, and the United Nations, I believe we can highlight the plight of
children around the world and the role of the UN in helping them.

As UN Secretary-General, my work is naturally concentrated in the world of
diplomacy. The reality is most of the time I have a much smaller audience than the
average re-run of The Lone Ranger.

And it is true that we come from different cultures. It is not just that the UN
and Hollywood are world's apart – the West is another world altogether. Here you
have No Country for Old Men; I just meet old men from different countries.

The UN is the world's only truly universal organization, which today is facing
an unprecedented surge of demand. The world is asking the UN to do more – in
more spheres of activity, in more locations, in more challenging circumstances –
than at any point in the Organization's history.

The UN is where the action is, in some of the toughest hotspots on the planet. We have over one hundred and ten thousand peacekeepers deployed in twenty countries on four continents, providing security to millions affected by conflict.
Our agencies, like UNICEF, are saving millions of children in silent emergencies
that do not make headlines. Twice a minute, a child dies of malaria. We are trying
to deliver bed nets to protect them. Malnutrition is another stealth killer. So is the
lack of sanitation. We are doing all we can to stop these unnecessary deaths.

When cyclones hit, when wars erupt, when people flee their homes, the UN
rushes to the scene, helping more than 10 million refugees and 2 million displaced
people globally. Two weeks ago, I saw first-hand the damage caused by the cyclone
in Myanmar. As all of you know from the tornado that hit parts of Wyoming just

last month, such disasters have a devastating impact on everyone, whether rich or poor, young or old, educated or uneducated.

Two days ago, in Rome, I convened an emergency summit to address both the short-term and long-term solutions to the "silent tsunami" of rising food prices around the world. In that crisis, as in so many others, children are the most vulnerable of all populations. Yet they are often the most overlooked. The reality is that millions of children are exposed to such ills as armed conflict, poverty, and disease. They are deprived of their fundamental right to childhood and many grow up without ever knowing peace, love and good health – things that most of us in this room have been fortunate enough to be familiar with since a very young age.

As Secretary-General, I am personally committed to being a voice for the voiceless and an advocate for their needs to help ensure that every child on earth can grow up in a peaceful, prosperous and just world.

In a way, we are victims of our own success. The more we do well, the more demands are placed on us. We are grateful for this global vote of confidence, but it has to be backed up by the resources we need to do the job. Look at Darfur. We have been asked to mount our largest peacekeeping operation there, and we are up to the job – but we need troops. We need equipment. We need your support.

The UN has always worked with governments to achieve our goals. And we always will. But we need new strategic partners and we need fresh creative thinking. Governments cannot succeed alone – you in civil society have a powerful role as a force for change. And the creative community has a far reaching influence that can be harnessed for the greater good. The audience numbers in the billions. For better or worse, many people, when they think of Gandhi, picture Ben Kingsley. Many people had never heard about the role of gems in war until they saw Leonardo DiCaprio in Blood Diamond. One unknown Rwandan hero became legend when Don Cheadle portrayed him in Hotel Rwanda. Of course I could go on, but you know even better than I do how popular culture affects consciousness.

I am happy to say the United Nations already receives a great deal of support from individual celebrities. I will not name them because the list is too long, but these are Oscar winners, rap stars, singers, supermodels, athletes and others who want to make a difference. They use their fame to shine the spotlight on global problems and what the UN is doing to address them. A model talking about abuses against women. An actor speaking out about the importance of disarmament. An actress helping refugees in camps and letting the world know, just by being there, about their plight. You know who you are. These individuals, and others who do not work directly with the UN but still share our concerns, are making an immeasurable contribution to the success of our work.

But, ladies and gentlemen, I believe we can do more. Much more. This is why I have decided to launch a Creative Community Liaison Office at the UN, led by Susan Farkas, Chief of the Radio and Television Services at the UN, which we will build up to develop this relationship with the creative community. For the first time ever, the United Nations will have a dedicated capacity to partner with the creative community.

This is an obvious place to start. The creative community is working behind the scenes to recreate the drama that we face on a daily basis: war, rising sea levels, pandemics, natural disasters. Unfortunately, we have got it all. When a crisis hits, the UN stands ready to respond, ensuring security, promoting development and fighting for human rights.

You in the world of entertainment and new media have a unique power to connect the UN and people in every corner of the world. I can shout until I am hoarse or I can ask for a microphone. You have the microphone. I am asking you to join this effort to amplify the UN's message.

This Global Insight Summit can help forge new partnerships to spotlight critical issues and solve them together, as a global community. I hope this unique meeting will set creative ideas flowing and mobilize action. Then this Summit can be a building block towards dynamic partnerships to tackle the pressing issues faced in today's world, and ensure that every person can enjoy a full and peaceful life.

There are a number of UN experts here who are eager to work with you. The panels tomorrow will be confronting some of the toughest issues we face: children and armed conflict, and HIV/AIDS.

There is no way to accurately count the number of children who are being robbed of their childhood in wars, but we estimate that 300,000 child soldiers are fighting in three quarters of all conflicts in the world. Ishmael Beah, one of our UN advocates, lived through this nightmare. He is here and he can tell you first-hand how devastating this problem is.

66 **You in the world of entertainment and new media have a unique power to connect the UN and people in every corner of the world. I can shout until I am hoarse or I can ask for a microphone. You have the microphone.** 99

These children are often ripped from their homes, assaulted, abused, drugged and forced to become weapons of war. They are ostracized by their communities and have no hope of attending school. Many are stuck for years in militant groups that perpetuate a culture of violence. Girls and boys all over the globe are subjected to unimaginable abuse and are forced to commit atrocities they should not even know about, let alone participate in. We need to expose this exploitation and save the hundreds of thousands of children who are in grave danger right now.

At the United Nations, we carry out programmes called Disarmament, Demobilization and Reintegration which have helped to release thousands of children from militant groups. Our personnel work with these children to help them heal psychologically and learn skills to return to a normal life within their communities. In addition, the UN works on a daily basis to address the underlying issues that allow child exploitation to happen.

AIDS continues to be one of the leading causes of death worldwide, and children are particularly hard-hit. At last count, 2.1 million children under fifteen were living with HIV, and children comprise 15 percent of all new infections annually. In addition, over 15 million children under the age of eighteen have lost one or both parents to AIDS. Treatment, prevention and support should be available to all affected by this deadly epidemic, especially children.

But do not take my word for it. I hope you will attend the panels tomorrow. Not only will you benefit from having an interactive session with Ann Veneman, the head of UNICEF, Radhika Coomaraswamy, my Special Representative for Children and Armed Conflict and Deborah Landey, the Deputy Executive Director of UNAIDS; I think you will also be impressed by some people you may not have heard of. Mariatu Kamara is a survivor of the conflict in Sierra Leone where children were exploited as soldiers. Keren Gonzalez is a thirteen year old who has turned her own experience living with HIV/AIDS into a way to help other children and youth via family workshops and being an editor of a magazine for her community in Honduras. Princess Zulu is a Zambian woman who has brought her story of growing up as an HIV/AIDS orphan to the halls of Congress and even to the White House.

Awareness and understanding are powerful weapons against injustice, war and violence. I look to all of you here to join forces with the brave men and women of the United Nations and be a beacon of hope for those who are most in need. All of you have a voice – but more importantly, you can be a voice for the voiceless. Together we can be a powerful movement to find solutions for these problems. We can bring this real drama into the consciousness of the public and spur action.

Address to the Asia Society

NEW YORK, 6 NOVEMBER 2007

Thank you, Ambassador Hill, for your kind words. And thank you all for your very warm welcome. This room may be full of dignitaries, but it feels more like a homecoming.

Of course, the Waldorf was my home until recently. The Secretary-General's official residence has been undergoing a face-lift, and this was the family dining room. I am glad we now have down-sized.

Tonight, you are recognizing some remarkable individuals. May I salute Mr. Yoshio Taniguchi on the beautiful new Museum of Modern Art. Shahram Nazeri is a musical icon. I am delighted that he will be performing with the Rumi Ensemble this evening. I am pleased too that you are honouring Neville Isdell of Coca-Cola. I know him well from our work together on the UN Global Compact, promoting corporate responsibility worldwide. Congratulations to you all.

For my part, it is simply an honour to be here on this special occasion. The Asia Society was founded fifty-one years ago to promote greater understanding in America. Today, your Society is a truly global institution, gaining ever more prominence as Asia emerges on the world's stage. You have offices in Hong Kong, Shanghai, Mumbai and other world cities. It is only fitting now that you are opening a centre in Korea, and that my beloved Seoul takes its place among you.

When I decided to run for Secretary-General of the United Nations, I sought out the Asia Society to make my case. Now that I am back a year later, I can see many friends who helped. I will not embarrass them all. But I would like to acknowledge Ambassador Richard Holbrooke, who prepared me for the bruising that was to come.

We had barely finished shaking hands when, in his trademark fashion, he gave me a shot right between the eyes.

"Ban," he said, "what's Article 97?" Reluctantly, I admitted I had no clue. "Chief Administrative Officer," he informed me, pointing a finger, "You're the guy who's supposed to make the trains run, who reports to the General Assembly." And there I was, thinking about the general in the title of Secretary-General.

Thank you, Richard, for the cold shower. That was the beginning of a hard and long campaign, answering many such difficult questions. You helped me find the proper path. I thank you again for that, and look forward to our continuing work on HIV/AIDS.

The Asia Society enjoys unique standing in our new era. We may or may not be witnessing the dawn of the Asia-Pacific century. But no one can deny the importance of Asia's rise, nor the growing importance of institutions such as the Asia Society.

From my earliest days as a young diplomat, I knew this to be a place for dialogue – for discourse rather than declaration, engagement rather than confrontation. It is a place where reason and understanding trumps sound bites and easy political rhetoric.

As you know, this is my style as Secretary-General. I believe in the power of
diplomacy and engagement. When I was Foreign Minister, the Government of the
Republic of Korea advocated détente with the North.

When some in the world called for sanctions and punitive action, South Korea
pushed for dialogue. That requires listening, as well as speaking. It means sticking
to principles, but also attempting to understand the other side, however irrational
or intransigent it may sometimes appear.

I quote my friend Ambassador Hill, and his first principle of diplomacy: "When
something has happened, it has happened for a reason. You must do your best to
understand that reason."

As Secretary-General, I may not always deliver the pleasing sound bite. But you
can be sure that, behind the scenes, I am seeking to understand the situation from
all sides – and pushing hard for concrete results.

We are doing that now in Myanmar. As we speak, my Special Adviser, Ibrahim
Gambari, is back in Yangon. I met him this weekend in Istanbul to go over his brief.
That is to be the honest broker, the facilitator of a dialogue between Government
and opposition leaders, particularly Ms. Aung San Suu Kyi. I have said publicly to
the Security Council and I say again here: it is time for Myanmar's Government to
release all detained students and demonstrators, to engage with the opposition and
move towards a more democratic society. Above all, it is time for Myanmar to rejoin
the international community.

This brand of diplomacy is not easy. There is seldom applause, often no outward evidence of movement. It is a quiet, painstaking, behind-the-scenes slog. You
have to work the phones, cajole world leaders to do this or that. It is a symphony –
often not a very harmonious one – of small steps that you hope will lead to something greater.

You expect nothing. You can only keep trying, keep pushing. Maybe it works,
maybe not. Then you try some more, in a different way, aiming all the while for
some small progress that makes the next step possible.

We are at this point now in Darfur. No other issue has claimed more of my time
or attention. I have spent hundreds of behind-the-scenes hours working with various parties to the conflict – the Government of Sudan, rebel leaders, neighbouring
countries, partners of the African Union. Just this afternoon, I had a long and fruitful talk with Mr. Salva Kiir, the first Vice-President of Sudan.

Meanwhile, we are pushing ahead with one of the most complex peacekeeping operations in our history. We are sponsoring very difficult peace negotiations
in Libya. We are feeding and protecting hundreds of thousands of displaced people. And yet, all this is only the beginning. Beyond peacemaking and peacekeeping,

there is a third and underappreciated layer to the conflict: an immense crisis of resource management and economic development, starting with water.

A peace agreement in Darfur is possible. But it can last only if we address all the causes of the conflict, developmental as well as political.

We can hope to return more than 2 million refugees to their homes. We can safeguard villages and help rebuild. But what to do about the essential dilemma – the fact that there is no longer enough water or good land to go around?

66 As an Asian Secretary-General I hope to see an Asia that is both better integrated and more internationally engaged. 99

Today, these resource issues are at the core of the UN's political and development work. More and more, they have become central to our strategies of conflict resolution and conflict prevention.

That is why I am so pleased that Neville Isdell is being honoured tonight, in part for making water management and conservation Coca-Cola's number one issue. What Coca-Cola has pledged to do with its plants and operations, the international community needs to pursue on a much grander scale in Darfur. We must replenish Darfur's disappearing water and land resources. Our success can translate a peace agreement on paper into lasting peace on the ground. But, if we fail, we fool nobody but ourselves in proclaiming empty ceasefires and hollow treaties.

As an Asian Secretary-General addressing the Asia Society, I would like to close by sharing my views on Asia's role in the world today.

We Asians inhabit the world's largest continent. We are the world's biggest population and its fastest growing economy. We have a rich history and an ancient culture. Yet, in international affairs, our role is far less than it could be.

Asia's contribution to the United Nations, though significant, could be much greater. Its humanitarian assistance – I want to put this politely – is less than generous. We are the only continent where regional integration and common markets have not taken hold.

Latin Americans and North Americans dream of creating a free trade zone – a United States of the Americas. Europeans speak of building a United States of Europe. The African Union aspires to become a United States of Africa. Why no United States of Asia? Then we would have three new USAs!

Why is Asia different? There are many reasons. History, cultural diversity, unresolved territorial and political disputes, lack of multilateral experience and the predominance of one or two centres of power. But the main reason is that we have not tried.

Asia does not do itself justice. As an Asian Secretary-General I hope to see this change. I hope to see an Asia that is both better integrated and more internationally engaged.

I expect particularly great things of my fellow Koreans, a remarkable people who have come into their own – as the Asia Society recognizes with its new centre. I hope to see Korea assume more responsibilities in the world, commensurate with its growing economic clout – especially in the area of development, one of the three pillars of the UN Charter. Korea should be more generous in its official development assistance. Koreans need to step up, speak out and do more.

The time is ripe. For this we owe much to Ambassador Christopher Hill, a diplomat *par excellence*. He has done more than any other to make the six-party talks with North Korea a success.

Chris, your persistence and skilful negotiation have brought us close, I believe, to resolving this last legacy of the Cold War. As a Korean, you can imagine my happiness at the prospect, expressed in the General Assembly's recent resolution on Peace, Security and Reunification on the Korean Peninsula. A peaceful, nuclear-free, united peninsula is no longer a pipedream, thanks largely to your efforts.

We can only imagine how difficult a diplomatic challenge it was – coordinating all this within your own Government, let alone with North Korea. The fact that we are dealing with the most sensitive security issues, involving four big Powers, as well as the two parties directly concerned, proves that multilateralism can work in Asia as elsewhere in the world.

It is encouraging that North Korea has now begun to dismantle its nuclear facilities, true to its word. If and when this process successfully concludes, we can foresee transforming the six-party mechanism into a more permanent security framework for North-East Asia.

This is a promising beginning, for Korea and for the cause of peace and regional integration. Let us build on it.

Here I am, urging my fellow Asians to speak out – when I have spoken so long.

I am afraid I must leave for the airport. I have to catch a plane to Buenos Aires this evening – my first stop on an eco-fact-finding mission that will take me to Argentina, Brazil, Chile and Antarctica. I want to see for myself the toll that climate change is taking on the Amazon rainforest and the polar icecap. I want to see how these Governments are responding. Among the many global challenges we face, I consider global warming to be the most critical.

Once again, thank you Mrs. President and Chairman Holbrooke, ladies and gentlemen and friends.

Address to the United Nations Association of Sudan

KHARTOUM, 3 SEPTEMBER 2007

It is a very great pleasure to be with you today, here on my first trip to Khartoum as Secretary-General. I am happy to have a chance to address the UN Association in Sudan. And I am pleased to see so many students at this gathering, as well as representatives of civil society. The fact that I am meeting with you this evening, having only just stepped off my flight from Europe, testifies to the importance that I attach to this visit, and to this particular audience – you in this room. Ultimately, it is you who will carry forward the work of building a lasting peace in Sudan. It is you who will need to work, hard, to bring unity and prosperity to your beautiful country.

I have a special attachment to this land, Sudan, both personally and officially. Officially, Sudan has recently been at the centre of the UN's agenda for restoring peace and security in the region. Personally, this is the country where my daughter began her career as a young officer with UNICEF.

For all these reasons, I urge you to think of the United Nations – and me, personally – as your friend, always by your side. I urge you to do everything you can to advance our common cause – building a better Sudan, and a better world, for yourselves and for future generations.

Let me explain why I am here. For four long years – too many years – your country and fellow countrymen in Darfur have been torn by conflict. For too long the international community has stood by, as seemingly helpless witnesses to this tragedy.

That now is changing. As you all well know, in July the Security Council adopted a resolution authorizing the deployment of 26,000 multinational peacekeepers in Darfur, jointly run by the United Nations and the African Union. This unprecedented operation marks a new era in UN-African Union cooperation. It is one of the largest and most complex peacekeeping missions the UN has ever undertaken. It reflects the international community's commitment to contribute to bringing peace to your country.

I should also say that this agreement comes after many months of very difficult diplomacy. Much of it was invisible, conducted across time zones and in quiet meetings in many capitals of the world. We all must seize this historic opportunity.

That is the first reason why I have come to Sudan. I want to see for myself the plight of those we seek to help, and the conditions under which our peacekeepers in Darfur will operate. But most of all, I want to see the foundations of a lasting peace laid down. My goal is to lock in the progress we have made so far. To build on it so that this terrible trauma may one day end.

Yet there must be a peace to keep. Peacekeeping must be accompanied by a political solution. That is the second reason I am here. It is so very important that we keep moving ahead with the Darfur political process. Everyone agrees there can be no military solution. We need a ceasefire now. The violence must stop. I want to see us begin a new and conclusive round of peace negotiations as soon as possible. My aim is to keep up the momentum, to push the peace among the parties with a view toward issuing invitations to a full-fledged peace conference as soon as possible.

During my visit, I will meet with President Omar al-Bashir and many other senior leaders. I look forward to a frank and constructive and fruitful discussions. The goodwill and cooperation of your Government has been instrumental in the progress we have made so far. I will also meet with First Vice-President Salva Kiir in southern Sudan, as well as opposition representatives.

At the same time, we also need to push ahead on a broader initiative, underscored by my visit to Juba. That is the Comprehensive Peace Agreement between the north and the south. As you know well, this remains an essential – and rather fragile – cornerstone of peace across the whole of Sudan, well beyond Darfur.

The third reason for my visit involves humanitarian aid and development. Any real solution to Darfur's troubles involves something more – it requires sustained economic development and solutions that go to the root causes of the conflict. But we cannot effectively address development issues until there is a peaceful environment in Darfur and a political solution to the conflict.

Until then, the world's largest humanitarian operation, currently assisting more than 4.2 million people, must continue. I urge to you do your part to ensure an immediate end to violence and a rapid political solution.

Precisely what these development activities will entail is unclear. But we need to begin thinking about it, now. There must be money for new roads and communications, as well as health, education, sanitation and social reconstruction programmes. The International community needs to help organize these efforts, working with the Government of Sudan as well as the host of international aid agencies and NGOs working so heroically on the ground, in very difficult circumstances.

In your very kind invitation, you asked me to speak a bit about how I see the UN and its role in a changing world, particularly in this part of the world. Let me say, here, something about who I am. I am not a philosopher. I have never put much stock in grand rhetoric – dreams of the future, visions that promise more than can be delivered. I am a realist, a man of action. I believe in results, not rhetoric.

As I look out at the coming year, and beyond, I see a growing number of extraordinary challenges. Darfur and the crisis in Sudan are among my very top priorities. But there are many others. Iraq, where we are likely to be tasked with ever greater responsibilities. Climate change. Making development work in Africa, so that we can fully realize our Millennium Development Goals. The list goes on, from Somalia and the Middle East, to new crises and opportunities that the world will bring our way. It think it is fair to say that the demands to be placed upon us have never been greater in our sixty-two-year history, even as the resources available to us grow proportionally more scarce.

> 66 For too many years, your country and fellow countrymen in Darfur have been torn by conflict. For too long the international community has stood by, as seemingly helpless witnesses to this tragedy. 99

Where does Sudan stand in relation to the UN, and more broadly in the international community? You are the largest country in Africa, rich in natural resources. But there is a need to create conditions enabling more development. Fighting has claimed the lives of hundreds of thousands of people. Many more have become refugees and displaced persons, making Sudan among the world's trouble spots. This is regrettable, given the great potential of your country.

The UN has broad responsibilities, which can be thought of as three pillars: peace and security; economic and social development, as set forth in the UN Millennium Development Goals; and human rights. The UN has a direct responsibility to advance in all three of these areas. As for the first, that is why I am in Sudan.

With respect to the second, much has been done in advancing our MDGs in Sudan. In southern Sudan, for example, the number of children enrolled in school grew from 343,000 in 2005 to more than one million in 2007. We have vaccinated cattle, distributed food and vitamin supplements to children, drilled hundreds of new water wells, and helped rebuild roads. Still, much more needs to be done if Sudan is to be on track to meet the Millennium Development Goals.

As for human rights, we have only to look around us to see how far Sudan has to go in upholding human rights and protecting people from suffering. Justice is an important part of building and sustaining peace. A culture of impunity and a legacy of past crimes that go unaddressed can only erode the peace.

Let us now turn our thoughts to how we can work together, and how the UN can make a difference in your lives and help create a better future. As I said earlier, I am not a man of dreams and high rhetoric. I believe in solutions that are real solutions. And I know that there can be no solutions to Sudan's political problems without sustainable economic development.

I have mentioned some of the ways we are already helping, and what more we can do – from helping to provide better health care to promoting better agricultural techniques to encouraging small business development. But when it comes to providing root solutions to the country's problems, it begins with a core issue facing so many people in Sudan and elsewhere in this region.

You all know that the conflict in Darfur began, long ago, in part because of drought. When the rains failed, farmers and herders fell into competition for an increasingly scarce resource. The decisions of man to wage war over these precious natural resources further compounded other factors and challenges.

But the fact remains. Lack of water, and a scarcity of resources in general, has contributed to a steady worsening of Sudan's troubles. As part of the solution, the Government with international assistance will have to ensure that the people of Darfur have access to vital natural resources – water being chief among them. The UN stands ready to assist in this effort.

I realize this all sounds very practical and down-to-earth. It is. If you were hoping for high-minded declarations of global principles, I may have disappointed you. But that is the point. As Secretary-General, I would like to look only for results. Tangible action, solutions you can see and touch, measurable progress. After all, who can eat or drink only words?

I have discussed this matter with our European partners, as well as the world's aid and financial institutions. I am going to host an MDG Africa Steering Group meeting next week in New York. I promise you that I will pay as much attention to this as I have to matters of peace and security.

I am very happy to have been able to meet with you here. It has been a pleasure speaking with you. I look forward to seeing more of your beloved country. I count on your continued support. Thank you very much for your strong commitment to the United Nations, and for your help in our work – present and future. *Shoukran jazeelan.*

Address to the Korea Society

I t is truly a delight for my wife and me to be here. This is not like going out to dinner. This is like coming home.

In fact, it is my home. Let me welcome all of you to my residence. Owing to extensive renovation work at the official Secretary-General's residence at Sutton Place, I am still staying here at the Waldorf Astoria Hotel.

But on a less material note, let me say that for all the years I have been coming to New York, as Foreign Minister of Korea and before, the Korea Society has been a home away from home. And for all Koreans and friends of Korea, you provide a bridge between the United States and my country.

Since its foundation fifty years ago, the quality of the Korea Society's programmes has been invariably outstanding. Let me congratulate you warmly on this fiftieth anniversary.

But your achievements go even beyond that. You have made it your mission to work for better understanding of issues related to the entire Korean Peninsula. You have helped Washington and Pyongyang know each other better. You have made clear the need to improve relations through diplomacy and a clear grasp of each side's position.

And you have firmly established the Society as the authoritative forum for active discussion on issues concerning Northeast Asia as a whole. I hope you will work to further facilitate active dialogue in the region, so as to help lay the foundations for a peace framework – one which Northeast Asia has lacked, in contrast to other regions.

Ambassador Gregg, let me praise the exceptional leadership and vision you have demonstrated in making the Korea Society what it is today.

On a personal note, I would add that I have always benefitted from your guidance since the days when you were the United States Ambassador to Korea, and I was Director-General of the American Affairs Bureau at the Korean Foreign Ministry. I extend my sincere thanks to you.

And let me say how happy I am that you have been joined at the Society by another equally trusted friend of mine and of Korea, Ambassador Evans Revere. Together, you make up a dream team.

I offer my warm congratulations to the winners of this year's Van Fleet Award – Mr. and Mrs. Houghton and Doreen Freeman, and the Korea Foundation, represented by its President, Ambassador Yim Sung-joon.

I am grateful for this opportunity to take all of you on a quick tour of my agenda as Secretary-General of the United Nations. I have been in office for only four and a half months. I assure you, I feel more of a sense of responsibility than glory. In any event, whatever moment of glory there was has long since passed.

In some ways, the experience has been like that of riding a very fast horse and seeing the landscape flash by. Even with this very brief and rushed set of impressions, I have become profoundly moved by the professionalism, strong commitment and sense of ownership among UN staff, many of whom operate in very difficult situations, often in dangerous circumstances.

Since taking office, I have been committed to a range of pressing priorities, from alleviating suffering in Darfur and working for a durable peace in the Middle East to addressing climate change and strengthening the capacity of our Organization. The challenges fall into three broad categories – the geopolitical, those related to long-term vision and goals, and those of putting our house in order.

The most acute of these challenges is of course Darfur. Not only are innocent lives at stake, but also the authority of the Security Council, the image of the United Nations in the Arab world, and the credibility of the United Nations.

I have been working with the Government of Sudan, regional actors and the Security Council to put a credible force of the United Nations and the African Union on the ground. I am encouraged that the Government has accepted the second package of UN support to the African Union.

But the Government of Sudan will have to honour its commitment to the implementation of this crucial support, and cooperate with the African Union and UN as it is deployed. The package will also lay the groundwork for the eventual establishment of an African Union-UN hybrid peacekeeping operation, the planning of which is being finalized with the African Union.

> **❝ A peaceful and nuclear-free Peninsula will serve as a bridge connecting the whole region, with free trade and movement of people. Let us work together towards this bright future. ❞**

Enduring peace in Darfur, however, can only be achieved on the basis of a political solution. I have worked closely with the African Union's Chairperson Konaré and the Special Envoys of the UN and the African Union to accelerate the peace process and agree on a common strategy. We are currently finalizing a road map for the political process.

And yet, despite our joint efforts to reinvigorate the peace process and strengthen peacekeeping in Darfur, the violence continues. The toll it has taken on human lives is intolerable. Everything possible must be done to secure an immediate ceasefire and return to the path of dialogue.

The international community must also continue to provide support and focus on the implementation of the Comprehensive Peace Agreement, even as it exerts its full efforts to bring lasting peace to Darfur.

At the same time, the situation in the Middle East presents huge challenges. I am deeply committed to addressing the complex conflicts in this region, whether it is Iraq, Lebanon or, above all, the Arab-Israeli conflict. Over the past two months, I have visited the region three times.

In Iraq, violence continues to take an unbearable daily toll in civilian lives. We cannot leave Iraq to grapple with this on its own. The international community as a whole, and in particular Iraq's neighbours and regional countries, must work together to help the Iraqi people build a peaceful, unified and prosperous country.

Almost two weeks ago in Sharm El Sheikh, in the presence of more than seventy delegations, the international community launched the International Compact with Iraq. Under the Compact, the Government of Iraq has pledged to pursue a programme of economic, political, and security reforms, and to promote national reconciliation. In turn, the international community has agreed to help Iraq achieve those goals. A number of countries have made concrete commitments under the Compact – including specific financial pledges estimated at more than 30 billion dollars. I am encouraged by these developments, and intend to keep pressing for real follow-up.

Also high on our agenda in the region is the situation in Lebanon. Security Council resolution 1701 was crucial in bringing an end to the devastating war of last summer. The cessation of hostilities has held well, and the military and security situation in the UNIFIL area of operation is generally stable. I commend Korea's contribution in sending peacekeeping contingents to UNIFIL.

But as you are aware, Lebanon's political impasse continues, despite sustained regional and international efforts to encourage dialogue and compromise. There are two major issues at stake: the establishment of a Special Tribunal to try the perpetrators of the Hariri assassination and other related crimes, and an agreement on the formation of a national unity government.

Yesterday, Prime Minister Siniora of Lebanon asked me as a matter of urgency to place before the Security Council the request that the Special Tribunal be established without delay. Today, I conveyed this message to the members of the Security Council, who will now consider what action to take.

I am of the conviction that the Special Tribunal must be established to put an end to impunity for political assassinations. Continued uncertainty about the Tribunal could negatively affect Lebanon's stability.

Throughout the Middle East, and around the world, the Arab-Israeli conflict, with the question of Palestine at its core, remains an issue of profound concern. It is incumbent on all of us to encourage all positive developments, and to build on current opportunities.

I draw hope from some recent developments. The Quartet, bringing together the UN, the EU, the US and the Russian Federation, has been meeting more often than before, a demonstration of its commitment to find a way forward. The Arab League has underlined its commitment to peace with Israel by stressing the continued relevance of the Arab Peace Initiative. I will continue to encourage movement towards the shared goal of all parties for a just, lasting and comprehensive peace.

At this point, I would like to inject a note of optimism on a subject which I expect is uppermost on the minds of most of you here tonight – the Korean Peninsula. I remain convinced that by acting together, the international community can help achieve a secure, prosperous, and democratic Peninsula. I also believe that the Korean people's dream of a reunified Peninsula will come true. All of us should embrace the change coming to our part of the world. It is time to set aside the divisions of the Cold War, and focus on the future. I assure you that the United Nations, for which the Korean conflict has been of special significance, will be an active and constructive partner in this quest.

Right now, the nuclear issue remains the most pressing challenge on the Peninsula. As someone who has put his heart and soul into resolving this issue through diplomacy, I am heartened to see the multilateral negotiating process back on track.

Allow me to express my particular appreciation to Assistant Secretary of State Christopher Hill, who is with us tonight, and who personifies the best in American diplomacy. Ambassador Hill has vision, creativity, and a readiness to listen, learn and work with others towards common objectives. Ambassador Hill, I congratulate you, as well as your able co-negotiators from the other countries in the six-party talks, on the accord you reached in February on initial actions towards a denuclearized Peninsula. While we would all like the talks to move at a faster pace, we know that what is needed is considerable patience, perseverance and political will.

At this critical juncture, I want each participant in the six-party talks to know that the United Nations is their friend and collaborator. I am determined to explore every practical way, for myself as well as the United Nations system as a whole, to support, facilitate and contribute.

Of equal importance to me as Secretary-General is working for more UN assistance to those in most need in the Democratic People's Republic of Korea – especially vulnerable groups such as children, women and the elderly. I am determined, through dialogue and engagement with the Democratic People's Republic of Korea and other countries, to mobilize international support for both humanitarian and longer-term development needs in the North Korea, as well as work for goodwill and mutual understanding in the region.

Beyond a peaceful resolution of the nuclear issue with North Korea, we should aim to establish a peace mechanism, through transition from armistice to a permanent peace regimen.

Everybody stands to benefit from durable peace and prosperity in the Korean Peninsula. A peaceful and nuclear-free Peninsula will serve as a bridge connecting the whole region, with free trade and movement of people. Let us work together towards this bright future. The Korea Society has an invaluable role to play in that process.

Since taking office, I have also worked to strengthen the United Nations' ability to act on a number of global issues that go beyond any one nation or region.

Climate change is a quintessentially global challenge that cannot wait. It will be one of my top priorities, and at long last, it is rising on the international agenda as a whole. The recent report of the UN's Intergovernmental Panel on Climate Change emphasizes that the science on climate change is clear, that the warming of the climate system is unequivocal, and that this is happening because of human activities.

The United Nations has a unique role to play in addressing climate change, and I am committed to galvanizing action. Two weeks ago, I announced the appointment of three special envoys who will consult with Member States on how we might move forward both in reducing greenhouse gas emissions and in adapting to the impacts of climate change, which are already upon us.

In human rights too, we have an ambitious agenda. I intend to strengthen our mechanisms for the prevention of human rights violations, and to work for steps to make operational the concept of the responsibility to protect.

To address effectively any of the global challenges before us, we must make the UN system more coherent in the areas of peacekeeping, development, humanitarian affairs and the environment.

If we are to reach the Millennium Development Goals by the target date of 2015, it is essential that we be able to deliver as one. In this context, I hope that Korea, as a country that has produced the Secretary-General of the United Nations, will increase its Official Development Assistance so it plays its full part in the global efforts to reach the Goals.

I am also striving to change the working culture of the United Nations itself. Since taking office, my first priority has been to enhance accountability and transparency for senior managers.

I believe the quickest way to change any culture is to lead by example. On my first day in office, I submitted a financial disclosure statement for standard external review and then made it public.

I have sought to advance mobility by opening up positions in my office to applicants throughout the UN family.

I have asked senior managers to enter into a Compact with me, whereby they identify their priorities and goals in a measurable way. Their performance will be subject to annual review.

I have introduced a term limit and set a standard contract period of two years for senior officials. This is renewable, subject to a performance review. And I have asked senior officials to give up their so-called reversion options, under which they used to have the automatic right to revert to their previous level and stay in UN service, even after being relieved of their senior position.

For me to succeed as Secretary-General, the UN will need to work closely with many partners. The relationship with the United States – key to our creation, crucial throughout our history – will be indispensable to our future. I will need our partnership to be strong, deep, and broad – politically, morally, operationally and, not least, financially.

As the first Asian Secretary-General since U Thant, I am also committed to working for an expanded role for Asia in the international arena in the 21st century. This is a new and exciting challenge: to bring together the UN's universal values and the distinct culture of Asia, in a complementary and synergistic way. To bring more of Asia to the UN, and more of the UN to Asia.

In that mission, the Korea Society has an important part to play. I wish you a most auspicious fiftieth anniversary, and many happy productive years ahead.

Address to the African Union Summit

ADDIS ABABA, 29 JANUARY 2007

I am most moved and grateful for this warm welcome. Allow me to express my appreciation to the Chairperson of the Union, President Denis Sassou Nguesso, and the Chairperson of the Commission, Alpha Oumar Konare, for their leadership of this Union, and for their pledges of close cooperation with the United Nations and with me personally.

I am deeply honoured to address you today. After fifteen years of African leadership, the United Nations has a non-African at the helm. But like all human beings, I trace my roots to the cradle of humankind that is Africa, and I am proud of it.

Allow me, at the outset, to pay tribute to my predecessor, Kofi Annan – a great African and a great Secretary-General. He led the United Nations with courage and vision, and ushered it firmly into the 21st century. He helped create a new partnership between the United Nations and Africa. I resolve to build on that partnership. In that mission, and in all the work that lies ahead for the United Nations, I am heartened that I will have as my deputy an African woman with singular leadership qualities: Dr. Asha-Rose Migiro, whom all of you have known as Foreign Minister of Tanzania.

Excellencies, I owe many of you my gratitude for supporting my candidacy for the office of Secretary-General. It is only four weeks since I assumed this office, but I feel as if some of you have already become friends and allies. I look forward to forging strong bonds with all of you in the years ahead.

As I join all of you today, I see a vivid illustration of the unity of purpose that characterizes this continent when it is at its best. It was that unity of purpose that drove your countries' quest for independence. It was that unity of purpose that laid the foundations of your Union. It is that unity of purpose that is the key to Africa's progress in the years ahead.

Unity of purpose is also the foundation of Africa's partnership with the United Nations, as we take on the broad range of challenges we share.

We can see concrete examples of that unity of purpose in so much of our joint efforts, as expressed in the cooperation agreement between our two institutions, signed by my predecessor here in Addis last November.

Unity of purpose guides our collaboration for democracy, human rights and good governance, including through the New Partnership for Africa's Development.

It drives our collective efforts for peace and security, including the UN's commitment to developing the African Union capacity to plan, launch and manage peacekeeping operations.

The same applies to our efforts to build enduring peace in countries recovering from conflict. Two outstanding examples are Burundi and Sierra Leone, where, after the successful conclusion of peacekeeping mandates, the UN is working closely with these countries to help shape a better future, through the efforts of the United Nations Peacebuilding Commission. Last week, I allocated 35 million dollars from the Peacebuilding Fund to support critical peacebuilding priorities in Burundi. We will soon complete the process of allocating funds to Sierra Leone.

Two thirds of the blue helmets deployed in UN peacekeeping operations are in Africa. I have just come from the Democratic Republic of Congo, where I saw, at first hand, how unity of purpose has guided our common efforts there. Last year, the UN worked with the African Union and other partners to support the Congolese people in holding the first free elections in more than forty years. This endeavour was a remarkable peacekeeping achievement, and the largest electoral support engagement in UN history; but above all, it was testimony to the steadfast courage and determination of the Congolese people, as 70 per cent of the electorate turned out to cast their vote in a calm and peaceful ballot.

The story of Liberia, too, shines as an example of what can be achieved through our collective will for peace and security in Africa. Let us bring the same unity of purpose to bear on those intractable crises that bleed like open wounds on the face of the Continent. Let us bring it to bear on our efforts to bring peace to Somalia and Côte d'Ivoire.

Above all, let us bring it to bear on the tragedy of Darfur. We must open a new and different chapter in this story of broken hope. I pay tribute to the valiant job the African Union force has done in Darfur. But the toll of the crisis remains unacceptable; it is also holding back the potential of Sudan as a whole to develop as peaceful, prosperous and democratic nation – and that, in turn, could hold back the future of the entire sub-region.

Since taking office as Secretary-General, I have made Darfur my top priority. I will continue to do so regardless of the challenges ahead, and I look forward to productive discussions with many of you during this summit. The partnership between the African Union and the UN is of central importance to how we fare on this, the largest humanitarian crisis in the world. Together, we must work to end the violence and scorched-earth policies adopted by various parties, including militias, as well as the bombings which are still a terrifying feature of life in Darfur. We must address the regional dimensions of the crisis. Life-saving humanitarian work must be allowed to resume, and civil society in Darfur must have a voice in the peace process. And we must persuade non-signatories to join, while building consensus for the urgent deployment of a UN-AU force on the ground. I sincerely hope we can reach agreement on this vital issue during our discussions in the margins of this summit.

In many other parts of the continent, Africa has made remarkable progress in ending armed conflict. This is not only a matter of survival and security for those whose lives have been directly affected. It is also a condition for building better lives in the longer term for all people throughout Africa, and setting them firmly on the path of development. I know, from my own childhood in Korea, how war robs individuals of the chance of building a decent life, and whole societies of the chance to prosper – long beyond the boundaries of the war zone, long after the gunfire has been silenced. I have seen the hardship and hunger, the degradation and disease that come with prolonged warfare. Elderly women scavenging for scraps, toddlers weak from malnutrition and unsafe drinking water, buildings dilapidated, corn fields rotting, an infrastructure on its knees. This I witnessed as a young boy, and the images haunt me to this day.

But I also witnessed how, through unity of purpose, my country was able to transform itself from a traumatized nation with a non-existent economy, into a vibrant, productive society and a regional economic power. That unity of purpose brought together an unbeatable combination: the concerted and enduring assistance of the international community, and the courage and determination of the Korean people.

Let us bring the same unity of purpose to bear on development in Africa. Six months ago, when I spoke to this Union to present my candidacy for Secretary-General, I said that the success or failure of the United Nations in the coming years will be determined largely on this continent. I pledged to do my best to mobilize political will among world leaders, international financial institutions and other stakeholders, and work with African governments to reach the Millennium Development Goals. The Goals represent our common vision: a partnership between rich and poor countries for building a better future. I intend to hold to the promise I made to you. I owe it to you, and to the people of Africa.

❝ Unity of purpose is also the foundation of Africa's partnership with the United Nations, as we take on the broad range of challenges we share. ❞

Many of your countries have made remarkable progress towards reaching the Millennium Development Goals. Since the late 1990s, more than a dozen African nations have achieved average growth rates of above five per cent. Many low-income countries have lifted sizeable proportions of their citizens above the poverty line. Several are on course to meet the target of halving poverty by 2015. Around fifteen African countries have already achieved universal primary education, or are on track to do so. And most Southern African countries are on course to attain gender parity at the primary school level.

These advances are precious, and we must ensure we replicate and build on them. That means ensuring a true partnership for sharing science and technology, which is rightly one of the themes of this summit. And it means empowering women and girls, through education and through creative tools such as microfinance, which has proved its value, many times over, as a weapon to break the vicious circle of poverty.

If we are to make the target date of 2015, we have to see concerted action in 2007 – the mid-point in the work to reach the Millennium Development Goals. In the coming months, I will convene a working group on Africa and the Goals – a coalition of the willing bringing together key African stakeholders, as well as international organizations and donors. We will aim to meet by March to formulate an action plan supporting practical initiatives for accelerating progress in 2007 and 2008. We will work to ensure the plan is ready in time for the Group of Eight summit in June.

Let me be clear: on some of the specific goals, we face enormous challenges. Consider Goal Seven, that of ensuring environmental sustainability. You who are gathered here today know that the impact of climate change will fall disproportionately on some of Africa's poorest countries. UN figures show that 30 percent of Africa's coastal infrastructure could be inundated by rising sea levels linked to global warming. More than a quarter of species' habitats in Africa could be lost by 2085. And the livelihoods of tens of millions of people could be in jeopardy.

By making this issue one of the main themes of your summit, you are tackling, head on, what climate change will do to Africa. I say "will", for climate change and its impact are no longer a matter of speculation. You can be sure that the challenge of climate change – including in Africa – will be one of my priorities as Secretary-General.

The time has come for the rest of the world to assist African countries in adapting to the effects of a warming planet, while strengthening efforts to mitigate climate change. We must implement the adaptation plan of action adopted at last year's United Nations climate change conference in Nairobi. And through the Nairobi Framework launched at that meeting, we must increase African participation in the Clean Development Mechanism. This innovative mechanism, a product of the Kyoto Protocol, is mobilizing billions of dollars in private and public sector investment globally. I will further engage the private sector by promoting market-based solutions.

At the same time, the UN is pursuing joint initiatives with a number of African governments to factor climate change into national development plans. I promise to work with donor governments to ensure that all such initiatives get the full backing they need. And I will push for ambitious emission reduction commitments by industrialized countries, since their leadership in this fight will be crucial, as well as generous, well-targeted assistance to African countries on the front line of extreme droughts and floods.

An equal challenge is the pandemics that continue to ravage Africa. They take their worst social and economic toll on countries that can least afford it. They also pose threats to peace and stability, in the devastation they wreak on capacity and governance. AIDS, tuberculosis and malaria are responsible for nearly four million African deaths every year.

But at the same time, there is hope. On AIDS, we have seen advances in treatment. We have seen a steady increase in political commitment. We have seen new resources. And we have seen a range or promising new initiatives, such as AIDS Watch Africa, set up by the African Union, in collaboration with UNAIDS, to help chart a direction for AIDS policy and define universal access targets until 2010. Let us keep pushing for both treatment and prevention for all.

Let us also seize the opportunity for a breakthrough in the comprehensive control of malaria by 2010. I pledge to work together with you for that success.

How Africa fares in reaching the Millennium Development Goals is a matter of life and death for millions of Africans. It is also a test of the ability of the United Nations to carry out the mandate our membership has given us. It will be one of my priorities to ensure that we meet that test – and I will take steps to strengthen the Organization accordingly.

Through unity of purpose, I believe there is no limit to what we can achieve. The partnership between the African Union and the United Nations is strong, broad and deep. Let us work together in the years ahead to make it even stronger, broader and deeper.

I will conclude today by paying tribute to both our host country and the African Union, through the words of Tsegaye Gabre-Medhin. This Ethiopian poet laureate, who passed away last year, sums up the aspirations for Africa better than I ever could, for it is his words that make up the anthem of this Union. And so, as Gabre-Medhin unforgettably wrote, let us unite to give the best we have to Africa, the cradle of humankind. Let us make Africa the Tree of Life.

As long as I am Secretary-General, I will spare no effort to help make it so.

Remarks to the United Nations Correspondents Association

NEW YORK, 8 DECEMBER 2006

Thank you, Mr. UNCA President, for those kind words. I am excited to be here.

First, let me add my voice to yours in tribute to President Clinton – a true citizen of the world, and one of the world's greatest natural assets. Speaking after him is a bit like having to sing after Frank Sinatra. I am certainly glad the old rumours about his future plans proved false, as I would not have wished to compete against him as a candidate for UN Secretary-General!

Ladies and gentlemen of the media, since this is my first UNCA dinner, allow me to introduce myself. My name is Ban. Not James Ban. I am not code-named 007. But I will take office in 07. And I have had seven weeks of transition. I may not be shaken, but I am a little stirred. Stirred by the challenge ahead of me.

> **❝ In Korea, we have an expression: *Un Haeng Il Chi.* It means words should be matched by deeds. This will be my guiding motto. ❞**

You journalists have already given me other names. In Seoul, several of your colleagues called me Slippery Eel. Here in New York, some of you have dubbed me the Teflon Diplomat. These names may reflect different cultures, but they all point to one and the same thing: when I want to, I will elude you as masterfully as any secret agent.

Rest assured, however, that my actions will be anything but slippery. I am a man of action. In Korea, we have an expression: *Un Haeng Il Chi.* It means words should be matched by deeds. This will be my guiding motto.

The challenge I referred to at the outset is of a different kind. How can you succeed when you are succeeding Kofi Annan? His shoes are too big to fill. Secretary-General, not only have you led the United Nations with exceptional courage and imagination. Not only have you given the Organization new relevance to the lives of people around the world. You are also the most elegant Secretary-General in the history of the UN.

How to follow in that mould? Should I grow a well-trimmed goatee? Don safari suits when travelling in warmer climes? Acquire a set of black turtleneck sweaters for those weekend crises that require me to attend emergency meetings of the Security Council? I thought I had the answer: Secretary-General, I could hire the same team of tailors as you! I'm told you have even been known to use the same tailor as James Bond. But then, my team reminded me of my policy encouraging mobility for all staff – including tailors. We must embrace change – even when it comes to changing clothes. And so, ladies and gentlemen of the press, I will not even try to match the Secretary-General's always matching attire.

That said, I will try to build on his example of open, regular and constructive exchanges with the media. I very much I look forward to working with all of you. But press corps beware – there may be a few surprises for you! To borrow from a carol of the season, entitled Santa Claus is Coming to Town: I'm making a list, I'm checking it twice, I'm going to find out who's naughty or nice. Ban Ki-moon is coming to town. Have a splendid evening everybody, and see you soon.

Sustainable Development

Remarks at World Food Prize Ceremony

DES MOINES, IOWA, 18 OCTOBER 2012

I t is a pleasure to visit Des Moines, Iowa, the heartland of America. This great city and state figure prominently in the popular imagination – for your role in feeding the world, and for your unique part in the American presidential process. I am glad to see some of this for myself. It is an honour to be here for the awarding of the World Food Prize, the world's top recognition of achievement in the battle against hunger.

The United Nations is glad to join our voice to yours in paying tribute to a remarkable scientist, Dr. Daniel Hillel. His work has transcended boundaries to help millions of farmers grow more crop per drop of water in some of the driest places on earth.

Sadly, this year, Iowans themselves know what it is like to live without rain. The effects of the drought in the United States are reverberating around the globe. When corn and soybean yields decline in Iowa; when shrivelled stalks replace full silos; the world, too, feels the pain. Commodity markets churn with volatility. Prices spike up, and the ability of families to feed their children goes down. Iowa is that important. Iowa nourishes the world.

The current crisis, however, is different. We have learned important lessons. More countries have put safety nets in place. There has been less panic buying, and fewer trade restrictions. Nations are also investing more in agriculture, and strengthening international cooperation. So many people in this audience tonight are contributing to the response.

Her Royal Highness Princess Haya Bint Al Hussein, in her role as a UN Messenger of Peace, has lobbied hard to end hunger and poverty. Senators, representatives and other United States officials continue to make the Food for Peace programme a staple of your overseas aid – including as the top contributor to the World Food Programme. You are being true to the legacy of Dr. Norman Borlaug, who knew that with the right tools even the most marginalized people on earth can escape the curse of extreme hunger and poverty.

Last week, the three UN food agencies – the Food and Agriculture Organization, the World Food Programme and the International Fund for Agricultural Development – jointly released the latest State of Food Insecurity report. It found that 870 million people are under-nourished. Thanks to international efforts and better data, that number is lower than previous estimates. But it is still unconscionably high.

In our world of plenty, no one should live in hunger. No child should have his growth stunted by malnutrition. No child should have her opportunity for a better life curtailed even before she is born, because her mother was undernourished.

On my way here today, I had the pleasure of visiting the World Food Prize Hall of Laureates. The exhibit includes a quote from Dr. Borlaug: "Food is the moral right of all who are born into this world". I agree. This is a matter of fundamental human rights – the right to food.

It is a question of fairness: some of us live in great prosperity, but many more live on the margins. These disparities are growing and they are dangerous. It is also a question of access: access to the benefits of research and technology, and to land, finance, infrastructure and markets.

There has been important progress toward the Millennium Development Goal of reducing by half the proportion of people who suffer from hunger. I thank all those involved with the World Food Prize for generating some of the ideas that fed into the very creation of the Millennium Development Goals.

> 66 **The effects of the drought in the United States are reverberating around the globe. When corn and soybean yields decline in Iowa, when shrivelled stalks replace full silos, the world, too, feels the pain.** 99

As the 2015 deadline approaches, progress in improving food security has slowed or stalled in many regions. The food and financial crises have taken an especially heavy toll in sub-Saharan Africa. Nearly one in five children under age five in the developing world is underweight.

Yet we draw hope from contributions like those of this year's honouree. Imagine trying to coax crops out of the dry ground of the Middle East. Imagine knowing that the only sources of water are a seasonal trickle and the occasional downpour. Imagine knowing that your country's fate could be reduced to a simple equation: produce or perish.

Some might have sought more fertile ground elsewhere, or gone into an entirely different line of work. Not Daniel Hillel. He stared hard at these circumstances. Instead of waiting for a rainstorm, he had a brainstorm. His irrigation system made the Negev desert a source of sustenance for Israel. Today drip irrigation is making the desert bloom on six million hectares of arid land in more than thirty countries. The fifty-two nominations of Dr. Hillel for the prize included submissions from Egypt, Jordan and the United Arab Emirates. His achievement started as a technical innovation, but it has made a signal contribution to global harmony, stability and peace.

Today the bleak face of hunger is especially visible in the Sahel. The region is gripped by its third drought in a decade. Crime, terrorism and conflict are spreading, preying on countries mired in hunger, poverty and poor governance. There are reports of teenage girls being forced into early marriage by their families, who can no longer afford to feed their children. These so-called hunger brides offer heartbreaking testimony to the grim choices people make when food, jobs and resources are in short supply.

This is all the more disturbing because girls and women are societies' best chance to overcome hunger. Women are the stewards of household food security and health. Women produce much of the world's food, yet are often denied access to land, credit, research and education. This is why the United Nations, on October 15th – the International Day of Rural Women – announced a new joint initiative to work toward the economic empowerment of rural women.

The United Nations is also championing the Movement to Scale Up Nutrition, now active in thirty countries. Two of its leaders are in the audience tonight: Dr. Helene Gayle, President and Chief Executive Officer of CARE USA; and Ms. Ertharin Cousin, Executive Director of the World Food Programme. They are just some of the remarkable individuals involved in this effort – several of whom are speaking at the Borlaug Dialogue this week.

Earlier this year I launched the Zero Hunger Challenge, which is now the focus of our High-Level Task Force on Food Security. The Challenge requires action on five fronts: Ensuring access to food. Ending childhood stunting. Doubling the productivity and income of smallholder farmers. Building sustainable food systems that ensure food safety and protect the environment. And finally, reducing food waste. Iowans know better than anyone the hard work and sacrifice that go into producing our food. Waste, be it in field, factory or kitchen, is tragic.

These different initiatives share the same objective: ending hunger in our lifetime. Achieving this goal depends on forging partnerships that make a difference. It calls for harnessing the creativity of scientists and economists, including World Food Prize laureates. It requires developing new approaches and technologies to respond to climate change, water scarcity and desertification. It means strengthening resilience in the face of price and market shocks. It compels us to inspire new generations to take up the struggle. I am glad to note that the World Food Prize Global Youth Institute is such an active part of these annual proceedings.

Ending hunger also requires better global governance. As we gather here, more than 1,000 representatives of governments, civil society, the private sector and scientific community are meeting in Rome to continue strengthening the Committee on World Food Security so that it fulfils its vital task.

The world's hungry also need political leaders who prioritize access and nutrition. The World Food Prize recognized this with last year's award to former Presidents Lula of Brazil and Kufuor of Ghana. You also did so in 2008 with the award to former Senators George McGovern and Bob Dole. Our thoughts today are with Senator McGovern's family, as they gather round him in a hospice in South Dakota. We at the United Nations have tremendous admiration for his contributions to the battle against global hunger.

In more than five years as Secretary-General, I have seen the progress that is possible when leaders take an issue seriously. And in my own life, I have seen the transformation that can happen with solidarity from abroad and hard work at home.

I grew up hungry and poor, in a country devastated by war. With the generous assistance of the United Nations, Korea got itself on the path to recovery. Before long, our bellies were full. Our bodies were nourished. We regained our strength and set off on building a better future. We then started helping others to do the same.

Ending hunger and malnutrition can be done. It is the right thing to do, the smart thing to do, the necessary thing to do. It is what we must do. After all, the world has enough food to feed every woman, man and child. Thank you for your commitment to this cause. The United Nations looks forward to working even more closely with you to realize this great goal and banish the demon of hunger from our world.

Remarks to UN Conference on Sustainable Development (Rio+20)

RIO DE JANEIRO, 20 JUNE 2012

This is a historic day. A major step towards the future we want. President Rousseff, let us once again thank you for your leadership, and your election as President of this conference. You have taken on a profound challenge. For on this day, ladies and gentlemen, we gather in Rio de Janeiro to shape the future of humankind. Let us not mistake this for hyperbole, mere rhetoric. To the contrary, we are here to face an existential reality.

Twenty years ago, the Earth Summit put sustainable development on the global agenda. Yet let me be frank: our efforts have not lived up to the measure of the challenge. For too long, we have behaved as though we could indefinitely burn and consume our way to prosperity.

Today, we recognize that we can no longer do so. We recognize that the old model for economic development and social advancement is broken. Rio+20 has given us a unique chance to set it right, to create a new model, to set a new course that truly balances the imperatives of robust growth and economic development with the social and environmental dimensions of sustainable prosperity and human well-being.

President Rousseff, you have brought the world to Rio. To all the distinguished Heads of State and Government who have come such a long way to be here, I say thank you for your engagement at this all-important moment. To the thousands of representatives of civil society and business, I offer you a special welcome. We absolutely need your partnership. We cannot succeed without you. Together, we are here to join forces in a great global movement for change.

As we look around our world, what do we see now? Too much political strife. Grave economic troubles. Widening social inequalities. A planet increasingly under stress, from climate change to growing scarcities of life's vital resources – fresh water, clean air, affordable food, fuel and decent jobs.

Twenty years ago, there were five and a half billion people in the world. Now there are more than 7 billion. By 2030, we will need 50 percent more food, 45 percent more energy and 30 percent more water just to continue to live as we do today.

Beyond a shadow of doubt, we have entered a new era: a new geological epoch, even, where human activity is fundamentally altering the Earth's dynamics. Our global footprint has overstepped our planet's boundaries. The lives and well-being of all humankind – particularly the poorest and most vulnerable – are increasingly in jeopardy. That is why I have made sustainable development as my number one priority.

Achieving that goal demands one thing above all: that is leadership – and your leadership. And that is why we are here. We are here to build a global movement for change: Heads of State and Government, business leaders, all the major groups of civil society – we need to work together.

We have made history this week. You are about to agree an outcome document that can guide our efforts for sustainable development in years to come. But, we need to keep our eyes on the prize. We need to act with vision and commitment, commitment and vision in the largest sense. Let us not forget the scarcest resource of all: that is time. We are running out of time. We no longer have the luxury to defer difficult decisions. We have a common responsibility to act in common cause, to set aside narrow national interests in the name of the global public good and the betterment of all.

As I stand here with you today, I am full of hope: because we are here, together. Because we know what we must do, and we have shown the world that we can agree on what is important.

I commend all those who have come to Rio with commitments for change. These will be a significant legacy of this conference – billions of dollars worth of actions and investments that will have the power to transform lives across the globe.

> 66 Rio+20 has given us a unique chance to create a new model, to set a new course that truly balances the imperatives of robust growth and economic development with the social and environmental dimensions of sustainable prosperity and human well-being. 99

But this movement for change also needs a firm mandate, and you will provide it in the Rio+20 outcome document. I thank the two co-chairs for guiding the negotiations. The negotiations have been long, and they have been hard; very difficult. Yet we have made significant progress, especially in the final stages. I commend Foreign Minister Patriota of Brazil for his able diplomacy, and I particularly thank President Rousseff for her strong leadership.

I am pleased that Member States have agreed to launch and take ownership of a process to establish universal sustainable development goals, SDGs. These SDGs will build on our advances under the Millennium Development Goals, and they will be an integral part of the post-2015 development framework. As Secretary-General of the United Nations I will spare no effort to implement the mandate given by the

Member States to realize our vision of sustainable development goals that build on the success of the MDGs.

I commend clear decisions and strategies on jobs, food security, energy, water, oceans, transport and cities. And I am glad to see a clear emphasis on gender empowerment and quality education throughout the document. We must now decide on the institutions we need to guide us to economic, social and environmental well-being.

We have made significant progress. Now is the time to take the final big step. Let us follow up on Rio+20 with strong commitment and action. Now is the time for action. Let us not ask our children and grandchildren to convene a Rio+40 or Rio+60. Now is the time to rise above narrow national interests; to look beyond the vested interests of this group or that. It is time to act with broader and long-term vision. Here at Rio+20, we can seize the future we want. Let us not pass it by. Let us make our legacy a foundation that future generations can build on.

Like most of you in this chamber, I am more than my title; more than simply Secretary-General of the United Nations. I am also a father and a grandfather. And like you, I want a world where our children, our succeeding generations, can prosper and be happy, a world where all people can have a decent job and live with dignity, a world where everyone can breathe clean air, drink safe water and have enough to eat, where everyone can live, confident in tomorrow.

That is the future I want – that is the future you want, and we want. And together, we can take a giant step to that future: right here and right now. I count on your leadership.

Remarks to World Future Energy Summit

ABU DHABI, 16 JANUARY 2012

E nergy is central to everything we do – from powering our economies to achieving the Millennium Development Goals, from combating climate change to underpinning global security. It is the golden thread that connects economic growth, increased social equity and preserving the environment.

I understand the power of energy first-hand. It transformed my life, my own life, when I was a young boy in post-war Korea. A simple light bulb illuminated a whole new world of opportunity for me, enabling me to study day and night. This memory has stayed with me such a long time, throughout my life. I want the same opportunity for all young boys and girls around the world.

Widespread energy poverty still condemns billions to darkness, to ill health, to missed opportunities for education and prosperity. That is why I say, energy poverty must end. Development is not possible without energy. It is neither just nor sustainable that one person in five lacks access to modern electricity. It is not acceptable that three billion people – three billion people – have to rely on wood, coal, charcoal or animal waste for cooking and heating.

We need to turn on the lights for all households. To do that, we need to scale up successful examples of clean energy and energy-efficient technologies. We need innovation that can spread throughout the developing world, where energy demand is growing fastest. We need partnerships with the private sector, which is the global engine of growth and the primary source of new investments. And we need visionary leadership from you – all of you; from governments, from the private sector, from investors and from civil society.

When access to energy services is combined with strategies that enhance incomes, and that strengthen public infrastructure, we can expect substantial and rapid progress towards meeting the Millennium Development Goals. But, ending energy poverty is only one half of the energy equation. Sustainable development needs sustainable energy.

Our planet is over-heating. We need to turn down this global thermostat. The Intergovernmental Panel on Climate Change, IPCC, tells us, unequivocally, that greenhouse gas emissions must be reduced to half by 2050 to keep global temperature rise to below 2 degrees centigrade since pre-industrial times. According to the International Energy Agency, we are nearing the point of no return.

At Durban last month, countries agreed on a timetable for a binding accord in which all nations would pledge to reduce emissions. But we cannot postpone action on sustainable energy while the negotiations continue. Nor can we continue to allow energy poverty, this way, to jeopardize progress toward the MDGs.

That is why I established my Sustainable Energy for All Initiative. It brings all key stakeholders to the table. It seeks to generate the action we need now. I have established three objectives to reach by 2030. Ensuring universal access to modern energy services to all the people around the world. Doubling the rate in improvement of energy efficiency. And doubling the share of renewable energy in the global energy mix.

These objectives – described in my Vision Statement released last November – are ambitious but achievable. They are fully complementary. I have appointed a High-level Group from business, finance, government and civil society to spearhead action on the initiative. Our host, Dr. Sultan Ahmed Al Jaber, brings great energy of his own to this effort. I encourage you to engage with the Group. Bring us your best ideas and boldest commitments.

66 Energy is central to everything we do – from powering our economies to achieving the Millennium Development Goals, from combating climate change to underpinning global security. It is the golden thread. 99

The Group has created a framework for a robust action agenda that we will develop in consultation with all relevant stakeholders in time for the Rio+20 Conference on Sustainable Development. It proposes national and international action to expand energy access, promote efficiency standards and policies, and strengthen investment in renewables. We will launch a formidable coalition of interests with clear commitments in Rio. Rio is our generational opportunity to create the future we want. But Rio is not the end. It is but the beginning of a multi-year mission to achieve Sustainable Energy for All. I urge you all to contribute.

We are here to build a new energy future, a future that harnesses the power of technology and innovation in the service of people and the planet. Sustainable energy for all is within our reach. For those who may doubt, I say look no further than the phenomenal spread of mobile phone technology. It has touched every corner of the world and empowered billions of people – a direct result of innovation, investment and government support. We can create a similar paradigm with sustainable energy.

I am personally committed to sustainable energy for all, and to mobilizing the entire UN system behind it. But we cannot do it alone. We need your partnership, your support, your commitment, your leadership and your action. Together, we can create a cleaner, safer, more prosperous world for all.

Remarks to fourth High-level Forum on Aid Effectiveness

BUSAN, 30 NOVEMBER 2011

It is a great honour to meet you today. Good morning. *Annyong hashimnikka.* President Lee Myung-bak of the Republic of Korea, our thanks on behalf of the United Nations for hosting this important meeting. I would like to thank the citizens of Busan, this vibrant and dynamic city, for their warm hospitality. I also want to thank the Honorable Secretary-General of the OECD, Mr. Angel Gurría, for his leadership.

We have noted the OECD survey on aid effectiveness, conducted in preparation for this meeting. The results are sobering. It found that development aid has become more fragmented at a time when unity of effort is much more needed. We can, and must, do better now.

We meet at a critical time. Only four years remain before we hit the target of the Millennium Development Goals by 2015. Aid is everywhere under pressure. We continue to feel the bite of the global economic crisis. Many countries face growing budgetary constraints. Among the developed nations, there is pressure to cut official development assistance.

Our agenda today is clear. We are here to build on the foundations we laid in Paris, Accra, and Rome before that. We are here to ensure that aid reaches those most in need, most vulnerable people who we have to take care of, that this aid is flexible, accountable, and country-driven. With this in mind, I have four messages to deliver to all of you.

First, to the traditional donors, I say: do not let this economic crisis, do not let short-term austerity deflect you from your long-term commitment to the world's poorest people. Aid has helped to dramatically reduce child mortality. It has slowed the spread of HIV/AIDS. It has reduced poverty worldwide. Cutting aid will not balance your budgets. But it will hurt the poor, the most vulnerable people of the human family.

Some countries, such as the United Kingdom, despite this very difficult economic crisis, has boldly proved that it is possible to meet global commitments and domestic fiscal needs at the same time. I applaud the leadership of Prime Minister David Cameron. I call on all traditional donors to make that same choice.

Assistance is not charity. It is smart investment in security and prosperity. It is an engine of growth that creates jobs and expands markets.

Aid is especially important for countries in transition from conflict. No conflict-affected country has achieved even one of the Millennium Development Goals. That is why I am very encouraged that the g7+ core of conflict-affected countries has been working with OECD donors and the United Nations to develop a "new deal" for more effective engagement. This new deal is an opportunity to focus much-needed attention on peacebuilding and state building. I urge all to pursue this important work.

My second message to the countries that receive aid is equally urgent. To those aid-recipient countries, I say: set clear development priorities and strategies. Build up your planning capacity. Deliver on your policy commitments. Enhance transparency. Stamp out corruption, which undermines trust in governance and institutions. Put in place the regulatory frameworks and incentives that will generate private investment and entrepreneurship. And engage civil society, crucial partner on the ground.

> **❝ Aid has helped to dramatically reduce child mortality. It has slowed the spread of HIV/AIDS. It has reduced poverty worldwide. And cutting aid will not balance your budgets. It will hurt the poor, the most vulnerable people of the human family. ❞**

Let me turn now to the growing club of new and emerging donor countries. To you, I say: step up. Europe and the United States may be struggling, but in East and South Asia, in Latin America and even Africa, many economies are growing. Millions of people have been lifted from poverty. With such success comes responsibility. This is your chance to assume your new leadership.

I urge you to increase your role as donors, as our host Korea has done. I am very proud as a Korean that Korea has now become a donor country in the world from a poverty-stricken, war-devastated country. Support highly productive multilateral initiatives such as the Global Fund to Fight AIDS, Tuberculosis and Malaria, which is in dire need of increased financial support.

Work with the United Nations, alongside traditional donors, to assist the least developed countries, countries emerging from conflict, countries in transition. The United Nations' Delivering as One effort aligns the work of our funds and programmes – and our peacekeeping and political support – with country priorities. It offers a coherent, country-level platform for effective aid. Fourth, my message to the private sector. To business and industry, I say: your skills, ideas and dynamism can make the difference. Partnership is the way: governments, the international community, private enterprise, philanthropic and non-governmental organizations, working together.

I have seen the power of such partnership. I have seen it in Rwanda – President Paul Kagame is here with us – where the government is setting trends in gender empowerment, service delivery, internet connectivity and green growth.

I have seen it in Nigeria, Ethiopia, and Bangladesh, Indonesia and Thailand, where the Global Strategy for Women's and Children's Health is a vivid example of development cooperation at its smartest.

I have seen how strategic partnerships can work to Scale Up Nutrition – another showcase for effective aid. I would like to highly commend again, applaud the leadership of Secretary Clinton here, with whom I have been working very hard to raise awareness of Scale Up Nutrition and the Global Strategy for Women's and Children's Health.

We are building a similar alliance to ensure Sustainable Energy for All. These examples point toward the realization of the eighth Millennium Development Goal - the global partnership for development.

We must be able to measure not only resources invested but the results: how we can deliver these results on the ground, to the people who are in need of our support. We need to know when aid is not delivered, or lost to corruption.

That is why my first principle for effective aid is accountability. And that is why I have asked the United Nations system to develop an Integrated Implementation Framework, which will enable us to monitor global commitments to the MDGs and their delivery.

My second principle is flexibility. Countries need to be able to react swiftly to shocks and changes. Aid too often comes with strings attached. Such conditionality can add to the obstacles countries already face, especially in times of crisis. We need to work in partnership so that donors and client countries are agreed on the most appropriate use of assistance.

This leads me to my third principle: ownership. Aid can be most effective when recipients have a say in where it is most needed and how it should be used. Countries that are accountable, countries that receive flexible aid, and countries that have the most ownership will be best placed to achieve the best results.

The discussions at this conference may get very detailed at times. But let us remember: aid is not only a technical matter. It is a path to building the future we want: sustainable, equitable, peaceful and just. Bear that in mind; bear in mind the people who need our solidarity. I am confident we can create a virtuous circle that will benefit us all. Ladies and gentlemen, I count on your leadership. And let us work together to make this world better for all of us.

Remarks to the General Assembly on the prevention and control of non-communicable diseases

NEW YORK, 19 SEPTEMBER 2011

This is a landmark meeting. Three out of every five people on earth die from the diseases that we gather here to address. I am guessing that each one of us has been close to someone whose life has been changed or ended too early by a non-communicable disease.

This is the second health issue ever to be addressed at a special meeting of the General Assembly. Our collaboration is more than a public health necessity. Non-communicable diseases are a threat to development. Non-communicable diseases hit the poor and vulnerable particularly hard, and drive them deeper into poverty.

More than a quarter of all people who die from non-communicable diseases succumb in the prime of their lives. The vast majority live in developing countries. Millions of families are pushed into poverty each year when one of their members have become too weak to work. Or when the costs of medicines and treatments overwhelm the family budget. Or when the main breadwinner has to stay home to care for someone else who is sick. Women and children are affected differently but significantly by non-communicable diseases and their impact on families.

The prognosis is grim. According to the World Health Organization, deaths from non-communicable diseases will increase by 17 per cent in the next decade. In Africa, that number will jump by 24 per cent. These statistics are alarming – but we know how to drive them down.

Treating non-communicable diseases can be affordable. But preventing them can cost next to nothing, and even save money. When people cycle to work instead of driving, they get exercise and the planet is spared more greenhouse gas emissions. When children are fed a nutritious diet at school, their attendance goes up and these eating habits can last a lifetime. When a woman has the access to quality screening and vaccines to prevent cervical cancer, her life can be saved. That is just one example of the simple solutions at the ready.

This is not a problem that health ministers can solve on their own. We need all partners: governments, to provide the right incentives. Individuals, to protect their own health. Civic groups, to maintain the pressure for responsible marketing. Businesses, to produce healthier, more sustainable goods.

We should encourage individuals to make the smart choices that will protect their health. Exercise, eat well, limit alcohol consumption and stop smoking. But even the healthiest individual cannot escape toxic substances in the environment. So we need to keep our air, water and land clean.

States crippled by these diseases cannot progress. Early detection is in everyone's interest. Early treatment reduces pain, cuts costs and lowers the risk of disability or death. We have to get medicine to all who need them. And those treatments need to be more affordable and accessible. I count on governments to lead this campaign.

I depend on our friends in industry to do what is right. I am a strong believer in the power of businesses to improve our world. Time and again, I have seen the private sector do extraordinary things for human well-being with its ingenuity and foresight that economic productivity depends on good health.

> **"Addressing non-communicable diseases is critical for global public health, but it will also be good for the economy; for the environment; for the global public good in the broader sense. If we come together to tackle non-communicable diseases, we can do more than heal individuals: we can safeguard our very future. "**

Precisely because I am a champion of the private sector, I must acknowledge some hard truths. There is a well-documented and shameful history of certain players in industry who ignored the science – sometimes even their own research – and put public health at risk to protect their own profits. There are many, many more industry giants which acted responsibly. That is all the more reason we must hold everyone accountable, so that the disgraceful actions of a few do not sully the reputation of the many which are doing such important work to foster our progress.

I especially call on corporations that profit from selling processed foods to children to act with the utmost integrity. I refer not only to food manufacturers, but also the media, marketing and advertising companies that play central roles in these enterprises. Those who profit from alcohol sales have to do their part to promote moderation in alcohol consumption. And we can all work to end tobacco use.

Individuals can have a say through the choices they make each day. Governments should educate people and encourage healthier options. This will be a massive effort. But I am convinced we can succeed. Success requires public-private partnerships. It requires political vision and resource mobilization.

I have seen similar success happen before. Ten years ago, the General Assembly held its first-ever meeting on a health issue. That was AIDS. Since then, we have made enormous progress. We have a long way to go, but no one can deny that political commitment from government officials saved lives. No one can minimize the contributions of industry leaders who made medicines affordable and available. No one can doubt the value of the United Nations in driving the global campaign to stop AIDS.

Non-communicable diseases are different from AIDS, but many of the same tools work in response. From visiting clinics and hospitals around the world, I know that holistic action on health works. Improving health systems improves health services. Involving all parts of government attacks all sides of a problem. And taking comprehensive action is the best way to protect against all diseases.

Addressing non-communicable diseases is critical for global public health, but it will also be good for the economy; for the environment; for the global public good in the broadest sense. If we come together to tackle non-communicable diseases, we can do more than heal individuals: we can safeguard our very future.

The Political Declaration that so many of you worked hard to draft and build consensus on is an excellent foundation. We must act together to carry out its provisions and bring non-communicable diseases into our broader global health and development agenda. We should all work to meet targets to reduce the risks. The World Health Organization's "best buys" serve as excellent guidance.

I especially challenge Member States to step up accountability for carrying out the Political Declaration. If this document remains just a set of words, we will have failed in our obligations towards future generations. But if we can give this Political Declaration meaning through multiple, concerted and tough actions, we will honour our responsibility to safeguard our shared future.

Remarks at launch of Roll Back Malaria Partnership report

NEW YORK, 13 SEPTEMBER 2011

Today we launch the Roll Back Malaria Partnership report, A Decade of Partnership and Results. It paints a picture of remarkable achievement: malaria is on the retreat across the globe.

Since the beginning of the century, malaria deaths and cases have fallen by half in more than ten countries in Africa, and in most endemic countries. Millions of pregnant women and young children in poor areas have been saved from this lethal, yet treatable, disease. Millions of children are in school instead of languishing, sick, at home. They come home to healthier parents.

None of this would have been possible without a fifteen-fold increase in international funding for malaria control – and without creating a new way of doing business.

In the late 1990s, malaria was the top cause of child mortality in Africa. Yet, few fought to change the status quo. Efforts were disjointed. Piecemeal approaches led to piecemeal results. Achievements in Africa, Asia and the Americas were undermined by drug resistance and resurgence.

> **Our joint efforts have brought cohesion and resources to malaria control and drawn hundreds of partners under its umbrella. We have saved the lives of more than one million children in sub-Saharan Africa. And we have changed the way we think about malaria control.**

Then, in 1998, a new malaria initiative emerged from the gloom. Three UN agencies – the World Health Organization, UNICEF and the UN Development Programme – joined forces with the World Bank to found the Roll Back Malaria Partnership. Ten years on, I appointed my Special Envoy for Malaria, Mr. Ray Chambers, who has further helped to bring together the private sector and all stakeholders in our common fight against malaria.

Our joint efforts have brought cohesion and resources to malaria control and drawn hundreds of partners under its umbrella. Such multi-stakeholder alliances are the wave of the future. We have saved the lives of more than one million children in sub-Saharan Africa. And we have changed the way we think about malaria control.

Combating malaria has become a global health priority. Three years ago, I called for malaria prevention and treatment programmes to be made universally available to at-risk populations by the end of 2010. This was an ambitious goal, but today, I am pleased to confirm that ten endemic countries have met their universal coverage targets for bed nets and vector control through indoor spraying. These two interventions alone have reduced child mortality in Africa by an estimated 20 per cent. This shows what can be achieved when all members of the international community join forces and align their efforts with those of developing countries.

But the work is nowhere near finished. Although the successes of recent years are remarkable, they need to be sustained and expanded, to prevent the disease from resurging. That is why our future goals are even more ambitious: near-zero deaths by 2015 and the elimination of malaria in ten additional countries.

The international community needs to go beyond business as usual, and all sectors of society will have a role to play: governments, international and non-governmental organizations, researchers and health professionals, businesses and philanthropies, celebrities and ordinary individuals.

Investing in malaria control is an investment in people, economies and nations. I am encouraged by the rapid progress made in the past few years. And I am eager to see this effort continue through 2015 and beyond.

Remarks to General Assembly High-Level Meeting on HIV/AIDS

NEW YORK, 8 JUNE 2011

Thirty years ago, AIDS was terrifying, deadly and spreading fast. Today, we have a chance to end this epidemic once and for all. The story of how we got here was written by many of you. The governments, the medical community, the private sector and, above all, the activists who struggled against AIDS in their lives and around the world.

Many of you remember the early days in the 1980s. The terrible fear of a new plague. The isolation of those infected. Some would not even shake hands with a person living with HIV. Our fellow human beings suffered not only sickness, but also discrimination or, worse, vilification.

Looking back, there is much we could have done differently. Looking ahead, there are also proud accomplishments that this General Assembly can build on. From its birth, the campaign against AIDS was much more than a battle against disease. It was a cry for human rights. It was a call for gender equality. It was a fight to end discrimination based on sexual orientation. And it was a demand for the equal treatment of all people.

In 2001, leaders in this room adopted an historic declaration. They took responsibility for controlling the epidemic. And they promised to be accountable for results. Since then, new infections have declined by 20 percent.

Five years ago, here in the General Assembly, leaders set specific targets for the global AIDS response. They pledged that every individual would get services, care and support to cope with HIV and AIDS. Since then, AIDS-related deaths fell by 20 percent.

Thirty years ago, AIDS threatened development gains in poor regions around the world. Today, HIV is on a steep decline in some of the most affected countries. Countries like Ethiopia, South Africa, Zambia and Zimbabwe. They had the largest epidemics in the world, and they have cut infection rates by one quarter. Globally, more than six million people now get treatment.

All of these advances come thanks to you and the commitments you made, first ten years ago and then again in 2006. Today, the challenge has changed. Today, we gather to end AIDS. That is our goal: an end to AIDS within the decade – zero new infections, zero stigma and zero AIDS related deaths.

But if we are to relegate AIDS to the history books, we must be bold. That means facing sensitive issues, including men who have sex with men, drug users and the sex trade. I admit that those were not subjects I was used to dealing with when I came to this job. But I have learned to say what needs to be said, because millions of lives are at stake.

I was inspired by young people, by people living with HIV and by my predecessor, Kofi Annan. He made the campaign against AIDS a top personal priority. Ten years ago last month, Secretary-General Annan met in a small conference room in Amsterdam with six leading pharmaceutical companies. At the time, the first AIDS drugs offered hope – hope for people who could afford them. The pharmaceutical companies were coming under great pressure. Non-governmental organizations were mobilizing against them, demanding universal access.

> 66 Thirty years ago, AIDS was terrifying, deadly and spreading fast. Today, we have a chance to end this epidemic once and for all. 99

Secretary-General Annan extended a hand. He asked the pharmaceutical conglomerates for help in getting AIDS medicines to all who need them. And the companies agreed. This led to the establishment of the Global Fund to fight AIDS, Tuberculosis and Malaria – a revolution that has been saving lives around the world.

I applied this model to our campaign to reduce child and maternal mortality. The Global Strategy on Women's and Children's Health is built on the same principle of partnership. And it also addresses AIDS. We also have a new global plan to eliminate HIV infections in children by 2015 and keep their mothers alive. That will bring our global strategy to life with clear, time-bound commitments, shared responsibility and leadership.

Today's historic meeting is a call to action. First, we need all partners to come together in global solidarity as never before. That is the only way to truly provide universal access to HIV prevention, treatment and care by 2015. Second, we have to lower costs and deliver better programmes. Third, we must commit to accountability. Fourth, we must ensure that our HIV responses promote the health, human rights, security and dignity of women and girls. Fifth, we must trigger a prevention revolution, harnessing the power of youth and new communications technology to reach the entire world.

If we take these five steps, we can stop AIDS. We can end the fear. We can stop the suffering and death it brings. We can get to an AIDS-free world.

Remarks on redefining sustainable development

DAVOS, 28 JANUARY 2011

For most of the last century, economic growth was fuelled by what seemed to be a certain truth: the abundance of natural resources. We mined our way to growth. We burned our way to prosperity. We believed in consumption without consequences.

Those days are gone. In the 21st century, supplies are running short and the global thermostat is running high. Climate change is also showing us that the old model is more than obsolete. It has rendered it extremely dangerous. Over time, that model is a recipe for national disaster. It is a global suicide pact.

So what do we do in this current challenging situation? How do we create growth in a resource constrained environment? How do we lift people out of poverty while protecting the planet and ecosystems that support economic growth? How do we regain the balance?

All of this requires rethinking. Here at Davos – this meeting of the mighty and the powerful, represented by some key countries – it may sound strange to speak of revolution. But that is what we need at this time. We need a revolution. Revolutionary thinking. Revolutionary action. A free market revolution for global sustainability.

It is easy to mouth the words "sustainable development", but to make it happen we have to be prepared to make major changes: in our lifestyles, our economic models, our social organization, and our political life. We have to connect the dots between climate change and what I might call here, WEF – water, energy and food.

I have asked President Halonen of Finland and President Zuma of South Africa to connect those dots as they lead our High Level Panel on Global Sustainability. I have asked them to take on the tough questions: how do we organize ourselves economically? How do we manage increasingly scarce resources? Those same questions guide our discussion here. I have asked them to bring us visionary recommendations by the end of December so they can be feed into intergovernmental processes until Rio 2012.

But as we begin, let me highlight the one resource that is scarcest of all: time. We are running out of time. Time to tackle climate change. Time to ensure sustainable, climate-resilient green growth. Time to generate a clean energy revolution.

The sustainable development agenda is the growth agenda for the 21st century. To get there, we need your participation, your initiative. We need you to step up. Spark innovation. Lead by action.

Climate change is showing us that the old model is more than obsolete. It is extremely dangerous. It is a global suicide pact. We need a free market revolution for global sustainability.

Invest in energy efficiency and renewable energy for those who need them most – your future customers. Expand clean energy access in developing countries – your markets of tomorrow.

> 66 Climate change is showing us that the old model is more than obsolete. It is extremely dangerous. It is a global suicide pact. We need a free market revolution for global sustainability. 99

Join our UN Global Compact, the largest corporate sustainability initiative in the world. Embed those sustainability principles into your strategies, your operations, your supply chain. To government leaders sitting here and elsewhere around the world, send the right signals to build the green economy.

Together, let us tear down the walls. The walls between the development agenda and the climate agenda. Between business, government, and civil society. Between global security and global sustainability. It is good business, good politics, and good for society.

In an odd way, what we are really talking about is going back to the future. The ancients saw no division between themselves and the natural world. They understood how to live in harmony with the world around them. It is time to recover that sense of living harmoniously for our economies and our societies.

Not to go back to some imagined past, but to leap confidently into the future with cutting-edge technologies, the best science and entrepreneurship has to offer, to build a safer, cleaner, greener and more prosperous world for all. There is no time to waste.

Remarks at launch of Every Woman Every Child initiative

NEW YORK, 22 SEPTEMBER 2010

We have been building towards this day for more than a year. And in some ways, for decades. It is a great pleasure to see so many global leaders here in today's audience. Today we are witnessing the kind of leadership we have long needed.

Every Woman, Every Child. This focus is overdue. Today, with the launch of the Global Strategy for Women's and Children's Health, we have an opportunity to improve the health of hundreds of millions of women and children around the world, and in so doing, to improve the lives of all people.

We know the facts. In some countries, one woman in eight dies in childbirth. In many parts of the world, women have yet to benefit from advances that made childbirth much safer nearly one hundred years ago. Millions of children die from malnutrition and diseases which we have known how to treat for decades.

These realities are simply unacceptable. The 21st century must be and will be different. We can do this by addressing the savage inequalities that affect women and children. By expanding access to basic healthcare, simple blood tests, a doctor's advice, a trained birth attendant, and immunizations. We can make the most simple, the most powerful investment for the development of our economies, our communities and our societies.

This Global Strategy for Women's and Children's Health provides a clear road map for making a fundamental difference in millions of lives. Piecemeal approaches yield piecemeal results. We need a broad partnership. We all have a role to play: governments, international organizations, business, researchers, philanthropists, health professionals, and civil society.

We must scale up our successes. We must provide the resources. Because investing in women's and children's health has a multiplier effect across the Millennium Development Goals. It is the best investment we can make.

Our strategy includes women's empowerment. Women must lead the way. Because by empowering women, we empower societies.

That is why the creation of UN Women is such an important step. And that is why I am pleased that Michelle Bachelet is here with us today.

It is time to turn the tide, time to right a historic wrong, time to deliver on the promise of health and a better future, for every woman, every child.

Remarks to "1,000 Days, Change a Life" event on child under-nutrition

NEW YORK, 21 SEPTEMBER 2010

I thank Secretary of State Clinton and Minister Martin for their initiative in organizing this meeting.

Hundreds of millions of people depend on us. Food insecurity and poor nutrition weaken the fabric of humanity.

Two years ago, the world received a harsh wake-up call. Food prices escalated and food-related instability erupted in many places. During the crisis, Prime Minister Brian Cowen and I launched the report of the Irish Government's Hunger Task Force. One year ago, Secretary of State Clinton and I co-chaired an event highlighting the importance of partnerships between governments, businesses and civil society – including farmers' organizations. And in L' Aquila, twenty-six nations agreed on the comprehensive food security initiative.

The world is moving on food security. The L' Aquila initiative, which draws on the African Union's Comprehensive Africa Agriculture Development Programme, emphasizes smallholder farmers, sustainable agriculture, the links between climate change and agriculture, and the interests of women both as farmers and as care providers. It highlights the importance of safety nets and social protection. It is a recipe for people to enjoy their right to food: long-term increases in food production, stable food supplies and prices, and universal access to essential nutrition.

We are making progress in bringing the initiative to life. Such progress gives me hope: hope that we can better coordinate agriculture, health and social protection and improve links between research and investment to achieve long-term results.

Numerous food security partnerships have been started, including the U.S. Government's Feed the Future initiative. Many countries are implementing long-term investment plans. Last year's G-20 meeting in Pittsburgh called for a Global Agriculture and Food Security Programme to help finance these partnerships. Funds were received from several sources – including Ireland and the United States – and the first five grants were awarded in June this year. Many more countries are preparing applications. Let us work to expand the pool of donors, and increase the resources that are available.

Today, we focus on two important new initiatives: the SUN Road Map for Scaling Up Nutrition, and the Thousand Day Movement, which will increase political attention to this essential element of the food security equation. I strongly support both initiatives. They can help us to make significant headway on the first Millennium Development Goal.

SUN shines the light on our most precious and vulnerable resource. Under-nourished children are more likely to get sick. They cannot concentrate in school and often earn less as adults. They pay the price throughout their lives. Poor women do not eat enough nutrient-rich foods in pregnancy, nor are such foods readily available to their new-born children. Furthermore, women who are poor can often be too busy working in the fields and markets to breastfeed or provide the care a baby needs.

SUN proposes a set of effective nutrition interventions from the start of each pregnancy until a child reaches the age of two. We call this the thousand day window of opportunity. These interventions are extremely cost-effective. They prioritize the interests of women and the importance of nutritious diets for mothers and babies.

> ❝ Food insecurity and poor nutrition weaken the fabric of humanity. If overall development policies are sensitive to the importance of the thousand day window, we can make a big difference. ❞

If overall development policies are sensitive to the importance of the thousand day window, we can make a big difference to under-nutrition. The SUN Framework has been endorsed by more than one hundred key stakeholders. It gives us a unique opportunity to bring the SUN into young lives everywhere. Today I encourage leaders to ensure that each decision they make helps reduce the risk of under-nutrition.

Secretary Clinton and Minister Martin, I thank you for your support across this agenda. Please know that I am glad to be counted as a Global Nutrition Leader.

Remarks at High-level Meeting of the General Assembly on the Millennium Development Goals

NEW YORK, 20 SEPTEMBER 2010

Welcome to the Millennium Development Goals Summit. I thank the world's leaders for being here in such impressive numbers. We are here because the fight for a more prosperous, stable and equitable world is at the heart itself of the mission of the United Nations. We are here because ten years ago, meeting here at the highest level, the international community promised to spare no effort to free the entire human race from want.

The eight Millennium Development Goals were a breakthrough. Together, we created a blueprint for ending extreme poverty. We defined achievable targets and timetables. We established a framework that all partners, even those with different views, have been able to embrace. We brought new urgency to an age-old mission.

And now, we have real results. New thinking and path-breaking public-private partnerships. Dramatic increases in school enrollment. Expanded access to clean water. Better control of disease. The spread of technology – from mobile to green. We have more development success stories than ever before. The transformative impact of the MDGs is undeniable. This is an achievement we can be proud of.

But we must protect these advances, many of which are still fragile. And the clock is ticking, with much more to do. There is more to do for the mother who watches her children go to bed hungry – a scandal played out a billion times each and every night. There is more to do for the young girl weighed down with wood or water when instead she should be in school. And more to do for the worker far from home in a city slum, watching jobs and remittances disappear amid global recession.

You all know where we stand; the gaps and the gains, what works and what does not work. The reports we have put before you are filled with statistics, analysis and recommendations – everything we need for effective policies and programmes. We have led you to the river.

So what are we asking of you today? To stay true. True to our identity as an international community built on a foundation of solidarity. True to our commitment to end the dehumanizing conditions of extreme poverty.

That means making the smart investments in infrastructure, small farmers, social services and above all in women and girls. On Wednesday I will launch a Global Strategy for Women's and Children's Health – our best chance for a multiplier effect across the goals.

Being true means supporting the vulnerable despite the economic crisis. We should not balance budgets on the backs of the poor. We must not draw back from official development assistance – a life-line of billions, for billions. It means truly fair trade and action on climate change. Deferring the tough decisions to future climate conferences and future generations only increases the costs. We need to set a course towards sustainable practices.

> ❝ None of us should be able to rest easy knowing the fear and despair that pervade the human family. Let us make this investment in a better future for all. There is no global project more worthwhile. ❞

Being true means addressing inequality, both among and within countries. Even in countries that have registered impressive gains, inequality eats away at social cohesion. And it means reconsidering conventional wisdom. Recovery from the economic crisis should not mean a return to the flawed and unjust path that got us into trouble in the first place.

Despite the obstacles, despite the scepticism, despite the fast-approaching deadline of 2015, the Millennium Development Goals are achievable. This year I visited nearly a dozen countries in Africa and saw for myself what is possible: at the Millennium Village of Mwandama in Malawi. At the Songhai community in Benin. I saw innovation, integrated projects and perseverance.

We must reward such faith with resolve of our own. By using the tools we have. By delivering the resources we need. And above all, by exercising political leadership. I urge you to make the Millennium Development Goals your own.

As our Nigerian citizen ambassador said in the short video that was screened as we were taking our seats: "We're waiting on you, world leaders". And as Mingas of Mozambique sings in the MDG song, Eight Goals for Africa: "We have the power, at this very hour."

None of us can be truly fulfilled while so many lack the basics for a life in dignity. None of us should be able to rest easy knowing the fear and despair that pervade the human family.

Let us make this investment in a better future for all. There is no global project more worthwhile. Let us send a strong message of hope, of fundamental hope. Let us keep the promise.

Remarks to the National Assembly of Cameroon

YAOUNDE, 10 JUNE 2010

Thank you for your warm welcome, and for the productive meetings we have had on a wide range of topics. Wherever I go in the world, I also try to visit lawmakers. I seek out the Parliaments of the world. Parliaments make the laws. They express the diversity of any nation.

That diversity is especially evident here in Cameroon, often referred to as "Africa in miniature" thanks to your rich ethnic, linguistic, geographical and religious diversity. It is through Parliaments that the people's voices are heard. And those voices, together, become the voice of any robust democracy.

It is a privilege to be here at this moment. This year, you celebrate fifty years of independence. Fifty years of Africa's growing presence on the international stage. We have seen it in the field of politics, peace and security. And, this month, we will see it on another field of play.

The World Cup will showcase Africa: Bafana Bafana, the host country team of South Africa. Les Fennecs from Algeria. Ivory Coast's Elephants and the Black Stars of Ghana. Nigeria's Super Eagles. And, of course, the Indomitable Lions.

Tomorrow I fly to Johannesburg for the opening game. I do not claim to be a sports expert. But I can let you in on a secret. I already know the winner of the World Cup. The real victor will be Africa.

I am so excited to be on the continent. To experience the pride. To feel the energy. To tap into the hope. To look forward together. Today, I would like to focus on the opportunities and obligations I see ahead – both the promises to Africa and the promise of Africa.

The United Nations' relationship with Cameroon is as old as the Organization itself. Cameroon joined the United Nations fifty years ago, but our bonds stretch back to 1946 and the UN Trusteeship Council. Through the years, our partnership has grown. Today, Cameroon is a generous contributor to United Nations peace operations. More than 130 of Cameroon's finest are serving as police officers from Burundi to Cote d'Ivoire, and from Sudan to Haiti. Cameroon is host to 100,000 refugees, many from the Central African Republic.

And together with Nigeria, Cameroon has provided the world with a model for the peaceful resolution of disputes. Both countries have committed to the 2002 ruling of the International Court of Justice as well as the 2006 Greentree Agreement on the settlement of their border dispute. Your leadership has shown that, with the support of the United Nations, peace and common understanding can prevail. Your significant investment in the Bakassi Peninsula is testament to your determination.

The United Nations stands ready to offer its full support as you consolidate peace and strengthen cooperation in the region.

Cameroon is also helping to show the world that the Millennium Development Goals are within reach. You have made significant progress in reducing extreme poverty. You are working to make sure every child is in primary school.

Some may call progress like this a miracle. But there is nothing miraculous about it. It is the result of one simple truth: That is, where we try, we succeed. When we don't try, we fail.

66 Africa's people need neither pity nor charity. They need only the tools to create jobs and generate incomes. 99

I saw the same today in Mbalmayo. I met women being empowered to help themselves and others, a community radio station that is helping to lift a whole community, and a water project that is providing a sound foundation for health. What I saw, today, showed what can be achieved when partners take comprehensive and coherent action when partners stand, together, against poverty, hunger and disease.

I will take these lessons to the G-20 summit in Canada in July and the MDG summit in September in New York. The message is simple. Africa can achieve the Millennium Development Goals. Africa has boundless potential. Amazing human and material wealth. One billion people, more than half of whom are under the age of thirty.

As I see it, delivering for the people of Africa is a matter of commitment. Africa's people need neither pity nor charity. They need only the tools to create jobs and generate incomes. Developed countries should make good on promises to double aid to Africa; promises made repeatedly at summit meetings of the G-8 and G-20 and at the United Nations.

There must also be more room for free trade. Africa's products should not be priced out of markets by heavy import taxes. Africa's farmers should not have to run up against unfair agricultural subsidies. Africa's governments must be empowered to scale up investments in agriculture, water, education, health and infrastructure.

At September's MDG Summit, I will call on governments to develop a results-oriented action plan, with concrete steps and timelines. As the Cameroonian proverb teaches us: "A chattering bird builds no nest." We need less talk, more action. That is why we will showcase success stories, scale them up and create partnerships that will allow us to do even more. Africa needs true partnership – partnerships where donors listen to recipients and tailor their assistance to Africa's needs.

Maternal health is the Millennium Development Goal where we have lagged furthest behind. Yet if we can succeed here, we will touch off a virtuous ripple effect through all the Goals. We need to combine the efforts of donors and recipients with private sector and civil society initiatives. This week, I announced a plan in Washington that does just that.

We know that climate change is a threat to development, a threat to stability and a particular threat to Africa. Cameroon and other members of the Lake Chad Basin Commission have voiced valid and legitimate concerns over the dramatic decrease in water levels of this vital source. Africa needs help in reducing its vulnerability.

Last year's Copenhagen climate conference marked a significant step forward in a number of areas: a goal of limiting global temperature rise to within two degrees centigrades by 2050, mitigation actions by all countries, progress on addressing deforestation and forest degradation,funding for developing countries for adaptation and mitigation.

My High-level Advisory Group on Climate Change Financing is working to mobilize new and innovative public and private funding to reach our annual $100 billion target by 2020. This funding will support mitigation and adaptation strategies in developing countries. It will help countries like Cameroon to reach the Millennium Development Goals.

I have spoken about the developed world's responsibilities in keeping the Millennium promise. But Africa, too, has a promise to keep. Sustainable development can only be built on the firm bedrock of peace and good governance. Over recent years, Africa has moved steadily from a principle of "non-interference" in one another's affairs toward a new and more modern principle of "non-indifference". We must keep and build on this momentum.

The organization of peaceful, credible and transparent elections is critical. We cannot allow the will of the people to be thwarted by electoral fraud. We cannot accept unconstitutional changes of government. We cannot permit endless manipulations of the law to preserve the privileges of those in power. We cannot turn a blind eye to corruption, nepotism and tyranny. Nor can we stay quiet when people are denied fundamental rights.

Without durable peace there will be no sustained development. Without sustained development, Africa will not attain the Millennium Development Goals. And without achieving the Millennium Development Goals, Africa will not find the promise and prosperity that its people so richly deserve.

The United Nations is your partner: as mediator, peacekeeper and peacebuilder. Only by living together as good neighbours – as individuals, as communities and as nations – can we fulfil the promise of the United Nations Charter. In this pursuit, I assure you: the United Nations will always be your ally. For peace and security, for development and human rights, the United Nations will be with you every step of the way.

Remarks to Global Forum on Migration and Development

On behalf of the United Nations and all of its Member States here, I would like to thank the Government of Greece for hosting this third Global Forum on Migration and Development.

What a fitting place for us to meet. Greece is a crossroads. One of the most beautiful words in the Greek lexicon is *philoxenia*: friendship towards strangers. For thousands of years, the sons and daughters of Greece have been venturing to all reaches of our planet. Today, Hellenes can be found almost everywhere in the world contributing in countless ways to the societies of which they are now an integral part.

Meanwhile, the economic success of Greece has transformed this country into a magnet for migrants, both returning nationals and many others as well. They, too, are becoming an integral part of your country, contributing to your economy and enriching your culture.

This dual experience of yours – as a country of both emigration and immigration – has endowed Greece with a more profound understanding of the opportunities and challenges posed by migration. Thank you for your contribution.

This is only the third Global Forum on Migration and Development, but it is already shaping the debate in important ways. Participation remains extraordinarily strong. As a result of the Forum, practices on the ground are changing. Migrants, diaspora organizations, and other civil society leaders are enriching the conversation.

Together, our goal is to harness the power of migration to reduce poverty and inequality – to help more people share in the world's prosperity - and to achieve the Millennium Development Goals. We are here to ensure that migration and development policies are founded on evidence, not fuelled by prejudice.

We meet in what I call an age of mobility. An era where people cross borders in growing numbers in pursuit of opportunity and hope for a better life. Today, the number of international migrants is greater than at anytime in history, with 214 million people living outside their country of birth. Thanks to the work of the Forum and others, there is a growing understanding about the good that such mobility can generate.

When managed well, international migration greatly improves human welfare and development. That message was at the heart of this year's UN Human Development Report. In countries of origin, migrants contribute to development by transferring remittances and transmitting new ideas and technologies. In countries of destination, migrants fill gaps in labour demand and skills to make the economy more productive.

But we have work ahead of us. Around the world, migration is often the subject of shrill debate – a wedge to provoke social tensions, drive political extremes, fan the flames of discrimination and hatred. We cannot yet say that the development potential of international migration is being fully realized. We cannot yet declare that the rights of migrants are being fully respected.

The conditions in which many migrants move and live continue to be treacherous. Human trafficking and sexual exploitation are disturbing realities. Many migrants still face high costs in migrating and lack vital information. Every year, thousands put their lives into the hands of smugglers or unlicensed recruiters. In many parts of the world, migrant workers still face appalling working conditions.

And in every part of the world, more can be done to build places where natives and newcomers join together for a common purpose; places where migrants and their families have assured access to education and health and other vital services.

Like so many of today's global challenges, migration cannot be addressed unilaterally. We must work together. United in purpose. United in action. I would like to highlight three challenges that add to the urgency for action. Three issues that underscore how and why more countries have a stake in managing migration well.

> 66 We are here to ensure that migration and development policies are founded on evidence, not fuelled by prejudice. 99

First, the economic crisis. The global recession has highlighted the vulnerability of migrants, particularly recent migrants. Unemployment rates are usually higher among migrants and foreigners. They are often concentrated in sectors hit hardest by the crisis, such as construction, manufacturing and tourism. Migrants often lack safety nets. And many cannot afford to return home, which makes them vulnerable to predatory practices.

The crisis has also soured public perceptions of migrants. They become easy scapegoats for job losses or lower wages. Yet, the facts paint a different picture. Migrants tend to complement, rather than displace, national workers. They generate additional demand. They often perform jobs that nationals do not want, even in times of economic crisis. We must work together to expand that development potential and uphold the basic human rights of all people.

There is added urgency. Remittance flows – the most tangible development benefit of migration – are being affected. By the last quarter of 2008, there were signs that flows were slowing down. The World Bank projects that remittance flows are likely to fall 7 to 10 per cent in 2009. As a result of all these developments, more countries have a stake in better managing migration flows.

The second challenge is climate change. The effects of global warming will be far-reaching. At least 10 per cent of the world population lives in low-elevation coastal zones that would be the first to suffer from rising sea levels. Forecasts of migration caused by climate change and environmental degradation vary widely.

Yet even the lower range would mean major population movements. Already, we are painfully aware of how the devastation of a modern city like New Orleans forced the evacuation of hundreds of thousands. In poor countries, such as Bangladesh, perennial floods temporarily displace millions. In Africa, expanding desertification is affecting the migratory patterns of pastoralists and prompting more people to leave rural areas. So far these movements have occurred mostly within countries. But that could very well change over time.

We are in a critical period, just weeks away from the climate change conference in Copenhagen. Negotiations have recognized that migration is a likely consequence of climate impacts. Populations will relocate due to more extreme weather including prolonged droughts, intensive storms, wildfires. In some cases, as with small island nations, whole countries are under threat. Protecting vulnerable communities must be a priority in both national and international adaptation efforts. We need action and agreement in Copenhagen. We will continue to push for the most ambitious targets and agreement possible.

Third, we must devote special attention to the most vulnerable migrants of all – victims of human trafficking, especially women and girls. Human trafficking injures, traumatizes and kills. It devastates families and threatens global security. And it involves abhorrent practices, including debt bondage, forced labour, torture, organ removal, sexual exploitation and slavery-like conditions.

Traffickers deny victims their fundamental rights, including freedom of movement and freedom from abuse as well as access to health, education and decent work. There are still many countries that are not yet parties to the UN Protocol to Prevent, Suppress and Punish Trafficking in Persons. There is still much to do to boost international cooperation in combating such heinous practices. That is why I have launched a global campaign to prevent all forms of violence against women. I ask you to join with me in making this commitment: no tolerance for trafficking in women and girls.

As we look to these challenges, we recognize that in many ways, migration is not just a journey of people – it is a journey of policy. Our destination is a global system of mobility that allows people to move in legal, safe and orderly ways, with full respect for their dignity and human rights. Together we seek a transformation of the conditions in which people move across borders, forge fulfilling livelihoods in their adopted societies and, in the process, expand their freedoms. The evolving system must respond to the new realities of our globalized world.

Too many migration policies assume migrants will behave in ways that most people do not. For instance, policies might assume that migrants would willingly go home after a short time abroad even if they lack a legal pathway to migrate again.

Policies might assume that highly skilled people would accept working abroad for long periods without their families. We must work to develop supportive policies that do not go against human aspirations, subvert our development goals or complicate inter-State relations.

This year's Human Development Report proposes a policy package that includes access to migration opportunities, better treatment of migrants and sensible measures to optimize migration's contribution to development. The package is politically feasible, responsive and adaptable to the changing nature of the global economy and the global environment.

The United Nations system is reaching out to a broad range of stakeholders. The European Commission-United Nations Joint Migration and Development Initiative, for example, is playing an important role in forging the supportive system needed to realize the benefits of migration. Many governments are working to realize their commitment to safeguard the rights of migrants.

But there is more work ahead. Let us never forget that in the end, policies and laws are really about people and values. We are here to deepen our commitment to the common values of inclusion and social acceptance, education and understanding.

Here in Athens, let us take inspiration from the ancient Greek term of *philoxenia* – and let us work together to make it a modern and global reality in every corner of our world.

Remarks to High-level meeting on food security for all

MADRID, 27 JANUARY 2009

Thank you, Prime Minister Zapatero, and the Government and people of Spain, for calling us here to Madrid to focus on the shocking problem of ever-increasing world hunger and the fragility of our food security systems.

During 2008, a chain reaction pushed up food prices so high that basic rations were beyond the reach of millions of people. By the end of the year, the total number of hungry people in our world approached an intolerable one billion.

The statistics are startling, but the stories of each household affected by hunger, and each malnourished child, are truly appalling. I saw it myself in my village when I was younger. I see it now when I travel, and it never ceases to disturb me.

Parents cutting down on the food they eat to ensure their children have enough.

Households selling their animals, land or even homes to buy food.

Mothers struggling each day to protect their children from the physical and mental scars of malnutrition.

World poverty cannot be reduced without improvements in agriculture and food systems. Most poor people are farmers. Most farm work is done by women. And those efforts contribute significantly to the domestic product of poor countries.

Farmers can produce more, but not without help – credit, seeds, fertilizers and land security.

During the past year, many of the 400 million farmers who produce food from small holdings could not respond to growing demands. They lack the inputs they needed to make the most of their land, animals and rivers. Moreover, many cannot get their produce to market. Far too many joined the ranks of the hungry.

Food prices may have come down for the time being. But the number of hungry people is set to rise again. And the prospects for smallholders remain grim.

With the spreading misery of shrinking economies, communities that were starting to emerge from poverty must wrestle instead with fewer jobs, limited access to credit, and restricted market opportunities. The increasing numbers of urban poor are being hardest hit.

Poor people are constantly being put to the test by food and nutrition insecurity, the impact of climate change, water shortages and animal diseases. We need to do far more to strengthen social protection systems that promote community resilience and prevent long-term despair and destruction.

Much good work has been done in the last year. Farmers' groups, community organizations, private enterprises and governments in many of the affected countries have worked hard, often together, to tackle the crisis.

Many nations increased their domestic programmes to ensure food security.

Donors increased their assistance as best they could. And members of the international community came together and committed to do more to help – at the high-level conference in Rome, at the African Union Assembly in Sharm el Sheikh, and at the UN General Assembly in New York.

The UN system and international financial institutions established a High Level Task Force, and committed to work together and to enable others to track our performance.

The result is an unprecedented effort to support nations and respond to the impact of the food crisis on the world's most vulnerable people.

As food prices rose and brought the number of hungry people close to one billion, we achieved the largest emergency scale-up against hunger and malnutrition in human history.

We continue to work for coherent partnerships involving the members of my High Level Task Force, governments, the private sector, civil society, and NGOs, including tens of thousands of dedicated people, many who are risking their lives under difficult and dangerous conditions.

With generous support from many nations including Saudi Arabia, we have delivered urgent food and nutrition assistance and safety net support to more than 100 million hungry people, mostly women and children, including 20 million children in school feeding programs.

We have developed robust programmes and plans to help smallholder farmers gain access to markets, credits, seeds and fertilizers. The support of the European Commission has been crucial in this regard, as was the engagement of private partners such as the Gates and Buffett foundations. Tens of millions of farmers have been helped to produce more food.

Our institutions – including FAO, WFP, IFAD and the World Bank – spared no effort to stand with those in need. Make no mistake, when funds are available, our system delivers help to where it is needed.

But Mr. Prime Minister, I understand your sense – indeed, the sense of this meeting – that we must all do more.

We worked hard to bring food assistance to those who needed it in 2008. I expect we will have to work even harder in 2009, this year of recession. In 2008, for example, we were unable to get the seeds and fertilizers to all the smallholders who needed them in two planting seasons. We must do better in 2009.

We must build on what was done last year, sustain our successes and scale up our responses, especially as the financial crisis compounds the impact of the food crisis. We must continue to meet urgent hunger and humanitarian needs by providing food and nutrition assistance and safety nets, while focusing on improving food production and smallholder agriculture. This is the twin-track approach taken in the Comprehensive Framework for Action. We should be ready to add a third track – the right to food – as a basis for analysis, action and accountability.

Mr. Prime Minister, I agree that we should reach out even more and forge a broad and inclusive movement that draws on the best available knowledge and spends money wisely, through a better coordination mechanism.

I met with members of the task force this morning. Based on their briefing and your clear messages, I have reached a number of conclusions.

First, the way forward must link actions to reduce hunger, improve food and nutrition security, broaden social protection for the vulnerable, improve agricultural production, and make trading systems work for the world's poor. We must raise the political profile of actions in all these areas, advocating for finance, action and results,

Second, we must support consultations for inclusive partnerships that help generate sustained national, regional and global level commitment for the movement against hunger, malnutrition and food insecurity. I welcome the suggestion of a Global Partnership for Agriculture and Food Security that is truly inclusive and broad based. In supporting the consultations to develop this partnership I will be guided by the views expressed by the range of stakeholder groups in this conference, and by follow-up discussions that involve countries, civil society and members of my High Level Task Force.

66 The stories of each household affected by hunger, and each malnourished child, are truly appalling. I saw it myself in my village when I was younger 99

Third, countries need easier access to external assistance for their food security and smallholder farming programmes. If we can mobilize and move funds, know-how or private investment in a more consistent and predictable way, the volume of resources will increase. But if we do not get our house in order, if we do not build a responsive consortium that serves as a viable and coordinated financial mechanism for food security, the money will not come through. Our choice is as simple as that.

We have enough institutions to ensure that needs are prioritized, that proposals are assessed and that funds are made available in a coordinated, efficient and accountable way. What we need is more effective coordination within countries in the framework of the Comprehensive Framework for Action, underpinned by significantly greater resources.

I urge all of you, and those you represent, to move forward within the spirit of the Comprehensive Framework for Action in all its aspects. I also call on you to engage with WFP, FAO, IFAD, the World Bank and others in carrying their vital work.

Mr. Prime Minister, you and the team that organized this meeting have provided a valuable forum in which to assess our progress and identify what needs to be done. Indeed, this meeting signals that there is strong collective will to support and sustain a lasting movement. I pledge that members of our High Level Task Force will do our part to make this happen.

I know you all agree that continuing hunger is a deep stain on our world. The time has come to remove it – forever. We have the wealth and know-how to do so. Let us do our utmost to keep hunger at the centre of the political lens. History will judge us on our response.

Remarks at G-20 Summit

WASHINGTON, D.C., 14 NOVEMBER 2008

I t is a great honor to participate in this crucial and historic gathering. During the last two years, we have dealt with so many crises: regional crises in Darfur or the Democratic Republic of the Congo, global challenges such as the food crisis and climate change. But we can, perhaps, all agree that this financial crisis is unique and overpowering in its immediate as well as potential impact. It has become a full-scale economic crisis, spreading across the globe. Many financial experts have diagnosed its causes. Policymakers have offered prescriptions for solving it. We talk of new banking regulations and a new global financial architecture.

All this is desirable. Yet while I welcome this debate and fully recognize the need for long-term measures, I am acutely conscious of passing time. As UN Secretary-General, my greatest concern is that today's financial crisis should not evolve into tomorrow's human crisis. We cannot allow it to become a reason for neglecting other critical issues: unacceptable levels of poverty and hunger, the food crisis, climate change. For that will only exacerbate the already fragile political and security situation in many countries that are hardest hit. I therefore come, tonight, with four messages reflecting my dialogue with member states of the United Nations.

First. We need a truly global stimulus package. The IMF projects that virtually all global growth in 2009 will come from emerging and developing economies. Large increases in public expenditures will be required in many regions of the world to counteract falling demand. The emerging green economy should be key to the stimulus plan. Eco-friendly renewable energy will drive the world's next great industrial transformation. It has the potential to create millions of jobs and spur growth. Let us therefore invest in fighting climate change.

Second. These financial rescue and assistance packages cannot stop at the borders of the richest countries. Emerging markets and other developing countries need access to liquidity. They need the oxygen of credit lines and trade financing. And we must stand against protectionism. Without open trade, this engine of growth and development could break down entirely.

Third. Some part of our global stimulus package should come from our commitments on aid. In today's environment, fulfilling the Millennium Development Goals is more than a moral imperative. It is a matter of pragmatic economic necessity. For that reason I welcome the latest IMF and World Bank initiatives.

Fourth. Inclusivity must be our watch-word on financial reform. The challenges we face can only be met through a new multilateralism: one that is fair, flexible and responsive, with leaders coming from all quarters.

The next few months will be crucial. Many of us will meet again in two weeks in Doha to review progress made in implementing the Monterrey Consensus on financing for development. Six years ago, President Bush and other leaders adopted the ambitious goals that constitute the core of the MDGs. History will judge us harshly if we fail to live up to these commitments.

I urge all nations to send their highest-level representatives to Doha with full determination to do what needs to be done. In December, our climate change negotiators meet in Poland. We have one year until Copenhagen: one year to reach an agreement that all nations can embrace.

> 66 My greatest concern is that today's financial crisis should not evolve into tomorrow's human crisis. We cannot allow it to become a reason for neglecting other critical issues: unacceptable levels of poverty and hunger, the food crisis, climate change. 99

The sooner we have a climate change agreement, the sooner we will see the green investments and green growth we so badly need. These great challenges are interrelated — the global economy, climate change and development. We need solutions to each that are solutions to all.

Remarks on sanitation and water

NEW YORK, 24 SEPTEMBER 2008

Thank you for this opportunity to speak on an issue that affects the lives of every human being in this planet. Safe drinking water and basic sanitation are intrinsic to human survival, well-being and dignity.

Infants and young children are the most vulnerable to unsafe water and poor sanitation. Each day, thousands of parents in the developing world are left to watch their children die from these wholly preventable causes. Their plight, their daily suffering, diminishes all of us and compels us to act.

The international community can say, with some pride, that since 1990, 1.6 billion people have gained access to safe drinking water, and more than 1.2 billion have gained access to improved sanitation. This is significant progress.

Yet current trends are disturbing. To meet the sanitation target by the year 2015, about 173 million people will need to gain access to sanitation each year between now and then. That will be an immense undertaking; over the past decade-and-a-half, new sanitation services reached an average of about 76 million people per year.

In sub-Saharan Africa, the situation is alarming. To meet the targets, the region will need to more than double the annual number of additional people served with drinking water, and increase by six-fold the additional number served with basic sanitation.

And now climate change has emerged as a formidable challenge to water resources. The extreme weather associated with global warming threatens to bring more frequent floods and droughts in various parts of the world. By 2025, an estimated 2.8 billion people will live in countries facing water stress or water scarcity.

“ “ We say often that water is life. Let us act like we mean it, and work together to achieve sanitation and water for all. ” ”

A world short of water will be an unstable world. Yet the worst need not happen. We know what the problems are, and what to do about them. It is not lack of knowledge or technology that is holding us back. We simply are not doing enough of what needs to be done. Three areas in particular cry out for action.

First, we need concrete steps to build up infrastructure, transfer technology and scale up good practices, especially in agriculture, so as to produce more food with less water.

Second, we need to improve the management of water resources, from public utilities to rural areas, including taking account of the dynamics of climate change.

Third, we need to increase investment. The estimated cost of closing the gap between current trends and what is needed to meet the target ranges from $10 to $18 billion per year. That is in addition to the $54 billion per year required to maintain existing water and sanitation systems.

Without a serious advance in implementing the water and sanitation agenda, there is little prospect of achieving development for all. I congratulate the organizers of this event, which has brought together so many top leaders from government, civil society and the private sector. The collective wisdom, capacities and resources of all of you will be critical in getting the world on track.

We say often that water is life. Let us act like we mean it, and work together to achieve sanitation and water for all.

Remarks at the launch of UN Cares, the UN workplace programme on HIV

NEW YORK, 6 MAY 2008

Today, we join as one UN to launch UN Cares, the workplace programme on HIV embracing the entire United Nations family. With this initiative, we commit to making available the staff, time and resources needed to meet a specific set of ten minimum standards by the end of 2011 – from training, counselling and testing to insurance coverage and access to condoms.

This launch marks a milestone in the UN response to HIV. Since the early 1990s, the impact of the virus on our work and on the communities we serve has been historic in magnitude. At the same time, our workplace, our staff and our families are profoundly affected.

Because our workplace is global and spans so many activities, cultures and conditions, the challenge is particularly great. Some parts of the UN system have put in place successful workplace programmes in response to HIV. But the approach has been fragmented, and progress has been uneven. Many UN staff members are still not well-prepared to protect themselves and their families from HIV. Others may be afraid to be tested, or uncomfortable working with colleagues living with HIV.

> ❝ Since taking office as Secretary-General, I have been committed to making the UN a model of how the workplace should respond to HIV and AIDS. ❞

Now, with UN Cares, we have a unified, system-wide programme that will provide a common framework for action and collaboration at the global, regional and national levels; offer our personnel and their families access to quality information and services; fight stigma and discrimination in the workplace; build up staff capacity, prevent duplication and save resources; work hand in hand with UN Plus, the advocacy and support network for UN staff living with HIV.

So far, fifteen entities of the UN family have pledged a total of about $1.3 million to UN Cares. Today I am delighted to announce that the Secretariat will make available $350,000 as an initial contribution through next year.

Since taking office as Secretary-General, I have been committed to making the UN a model of how the workplace should respond to HIV and AIDS. But our performance will be only as good as the commitment and contribution of every one of us. Today, I ask all colleagues to make sure they and their families know the essential facts about HIV and AIDS, protect themselves from HIV transmission, and demonstrate zero tolerance of stigma and discrimination in our workplace. I ask all managers to familiarize themselves thoroughly with the UN Cares Ten Minimum Standards, and ensure they provide the resources required to meet them – including staff, time and budget. And I ask all of you to lead by example, participating in UN Cares learning sessions and encouraging your colleagues to do the same.

You should remember that I myself participated in this learning session, including all the senior managers of the Secretariat. Please take the opportunity here today to pick up important fact sheets about the programme.

I am confident that together, we can meet the UN Cares Minimum Standards by the end of 2011, and ensure we live up to them on an ongoing basis. We can make our UN family stronger, more coherent and more responsive to the needs of all staff and their families. We can unite to show that the UN cares.

Climate Change

Address to UN conference on climate change

DURBAN, 6 DECEMBER 2011

I t is a great pleasure and privilege to be with you today.

President Zuma, we thank you – and the citizens of South Africa and particularly the citizens of Durban – for your gracious and stirring welcome.

The negotiations over the coming days will be challenging. This we know. Let us therefore determine that, in spirit, we will be as warm and generous with one another as the hospitality we have been shown.

Let me speak plainly. We must be realistic about expectations for a breakthrough in Durban. We know the reasons: grave economic troubles in many countries, abiding political differences, conflicting priorities and strategies for responding to climate change. And it may be true, as many say: the ultimate goal of a comprehensive and binding climate change agreement may be beyond our reach – for now.

Yet let me emphasize: none of these uncertainties should prevent us from making real progress here in Durban. Indeed, we can and must move forward on key issues. I am pleased that many parties have proposed creative ways forward.

Throughout human history, in any great endeavour requiring the common effort of many nations and men and women everywhere, we have learned it is only through seriousness of purpose and persistence that we ultimately carry the day.

We might liken it to riding a bicycle. You stay upright and move forward so long as you keep up the momentum. We must keep up our momentum. That is the challenge before us today. That is the imperative.

It would be difficult to overstate the gravity of this moment. Without exaggeration, we can say: the future of our planet is at stake. People's lives, the health of global economy, the very survival of some nations.

The science is clear. The World Meteorological Organisation has reported that carbon emissions are at their highest in history and rising. The Intergovernmental Panel on Climate Change tells us, unequivocally, that greenhouse gas emissions must be reduced by half by 2050 – if we are to keep the rise in global temperatures to two degrees centigrades since pre-industrial times. According to the International Energy Agency, we are nearing the point of no return, and we must pull back from the abyss.

You are the people who can bring us from the edge. The world is looking to you for leadership.

As Secretary-General, I travel widely. And everywhere, people ask me for help. They ask the United Nations for help; as nations, united.

This year, on the Pacific island of Kiribati, a young boy told me: "I am afraid to sleep at my home at night." Because his land, his island, Kiribati, is slipping beneath the waves. There are many such islands in the Pacific and elsewhere. He is afraid he will be swept away by the tide while sleeping.

> **" The future of our planet is at stake. People's lives, the health of global economy, the very survival of some nations. The science is clear. "**

In the Andes and the Alps, I have seen melting glaciers. At both of the Earth's Poles, I have seen open sea where ice once dominated the horizon. I have seen arid lands where in the sun once shone on mighty rivers and great lakes – in the Amazon, flying over Lake Chad in the African Sahel and flying over the Aral Sea on the vast steppe of Central Asia. I have met, personally, with thousands of people who have lost all to catastrophic floods and spreading deserts. And, just last month, I flew over miles and miles of devastated virgin forest and peatland in Central Kalimantan, Indonesia.

Is this the future we want? A world of out-of-control climate change and a devastating scarcity of vital resources? A world divided bitterly between rich and poor, and the vulnerable and the privileged?

Or do we want a sustainable future that fulfils the promise of the United Nations Charter?

The answer is clear, even if the exact path is not.

Yes, we all recognize the realities of our time: the economic crisis, the dictates of fiscal austerity, often difficult domestic politics.

Yet the world and its people cannot accept no for an answer in Durban. To the contrary, I say to you that now is the moment to be ambitious. This is not the first time that we have confronted the sceptics, the naysayers, and proved them wrong. In 2007, you showed leadership and came away with the Bali Roadmap. In 2009, people said Copenhagen was a failure. Yet it was not. There were significant commitments on financing for mitigation, adaptation and technology transfer.

Last year, in Cancun, you firmed up and built on these foundations. We saw international commitment to deep cuts in global greenhouse gas emissions that will hold the increase in global average temperature below two degrees Celsius from industrial times. You have shown that multilateralism can deliver.

Here in Durban, we must keep up the momentum. Let us not falter. Let us not allow our valuable work to go to waste. I expect four things from you at this conference – four incremental advances that will carry us toward the future we want.

First, we must implement what was agreed in Cancun. This means ensuring that the Adaptation Framework and its Committee, and the Technology Mechanism and its Climate Technology Centre and Network, are ready to start working as soon as possible. Assisting the most vulnerable is both an obligation and a smart investment in a sustainable future.

Second, we need tangible progress on short- and long-term financing.

On short-term, fast-track financing, $30 billion dollars has been pledged, and almost all of it has been identified in national budgets. However, recipient countries want to see greater transparency in how the funds are allocated and disbursed. The UNFCCC Secretariat has created a tool to do this. We also need prompt delivery of these funds to where they are most needed.

On longer-term financing, we need to mobilize $100 billion per annum by 2020 from governmental, private sector and innovative new sources. My High Level Advisory Group on Climate Financing, led by Prime Minister Meles and Prime Minister Stoltenberg, has shown that this is feasible – and it is essential that we stick to our commitment. In Cancun you created the Green Climate Fund. Let us launch it here in Durban. And I appeal to industrialized nations to inject sufficient initial capital to allow the fund to begin its work immediately. This will inspire confidence and generate further momentum for action.

Third: the future of the Kyoto Protocol. In the absence of a global binding climate agreement, the Kyoto Protocol is the closest we have. While Kyoto alone will not solve today's climate problem, it is a foundation to build on, with important institutions. It provides the framework that markets sorely need. Carbon pricing, carbon-trading depend on a rules-based system. It is important that we do not create a vacuum. Therefore, I urge you to carefully consider a second commitment period part of the Kyoto Protocol here in Durban.

Fourth and finally: we must not forsake our collective vision of a comprehensive, binding climate change agreement that is both effective and fair for all. Here in Durban, we can and must take concrete steps towards a more robust climate regime – steps that will carry the momentum to next year's Conference of Parties in Qatar. Time is not on our side, nor is the rest of the world waiting for us to decide.

Across the globe, governments, cities, businesses and individuals have recognized the threat of climate change. They are acting. They are choosing a lower-carbon path because they know it is good for the planet, good for them and good for us. Global investment in clean energy rose from $50 billion dollars in 2004 to $240 billion in 2010, according to one recent report.

Several UNFCCC parties have taken significant steps on mitigation – including putting a price on industrial emissions, pledging to reduce carbon intensity, committing to drastically cut greenhouse gas emissions and working to reduce deforestation. The Reducing Emissions from Deforestation and Forest Degradation Initiative programme is creating a financial value for the carbon stored in forests. Governments and the private sector are combining to create a vision for Sustainable Energy for All – a win-win-win for poverty reduction, economic growth and cutting greenhouse gas emissions.

Let us take inspiration from the progress some are making. Let us find the will to lead, despite the many difficulties. Let us prove that we not only know where we are going and how to get there, but that we are prepared to take collective action that will move us down that road. Let us make Durban a profile in political courage.

Remarks to UN Climate Change Summit

NEW YORK, 22 SEPTEMBER 2009

I am honoured to welcome you to this Summit – the largest-ever gathering of world leaders on climate change.

Your presence bears witness to the gravity of the climate challenge. It is testament to the opportunity Copenhagen offers.

Your decisions will have momentous consequences. You have the power to chart a safer, more sustainable and prosperous course for this and future generations. The power to reduce the emissions that are causing climate change; to help the most vulnerable adapt to changes that are already under way; to catalyze a new era of global green growth.

Now is your moment to act.

Greenhouse gas emissions continue to rise. We will soon reach critical thresholds. Consequences that we cannot reverse. The world's leading scientists warn that we have less than ten years to avoid the worst-case scenarios projected by the Intergovernmental Panel on Climate Change. Indeed those worst-case scenarios are becoming ever more likely. We must halt the rise in global emissions.

Earlier this month I was in the Arctic. I was alarmed by the rapid pace of change. The Arctic could be nearly ice-free by 2030. The consequences will be felt by people on every continent.

Just yesterday I met with many leaders from small island states. They were forceful and eloquent in describing how climate change is rewriting their future.

All across Africa – the most vulnerable continent – climate change threatens to roll back years of development gains.

Climate change is the pre-eminent geopolitical and economic issue of the 21st century. It rewrites the global equation for development, peace and prosperity. It will increase pressure on water, food and land; reverse years of development gains; exacerbate poverty; destabilize fragile states and topple governments.

Some say tackling climate change is too expensive. They are wrong. The opposite is true. We will pay an unacceptable price if we do not act now.

The climate negotiations are proceeding too slow. The world's glaciers are now melting faster than human progress to protect them – and us. There are now only fifteen negotiating days left until Copenhagen. Your negotiators need your direct political support and guidance to resolve core issues, to accelerate the pace of negotiations, and to strengthen the ambition of what is on offer. Instead of demanding concessions from others, let us ask how we can contribute to the greater good. A successful deal in Copenhagen will mean more prosperity, more security, more equity. It will expand the pie for all.

We need to build trust step by step. Today, I call on all the leaders of the industrialized countries in this room to take the first steps forward. If you do so, others will take bold measures of their own. I also call on leaders from developing countries to accelerate their efforts. All countries must do more – now.

66 Your decisions will have momentous consequences. You have the power to chart a safer, more sustainable and prosperous course for this and future generations. 99

Let us be clear about the signposts for success at Copenhagen and beyond.

First, a successful deal must involve all countries working toward a common, long-term goal to limit global temperature rise to safe levels consistent with science. It will include ambitious emission reduction targets from industrialized countries by 2020. It will address all major sources of greenhouse gases, including deforestation and emissions from shipping and aviation. It will also include actions by developing countries to limit the growth of their emissions while they grow sustainably. They will need substantial financial and technological support to achieve this.

Second, a successful deal must strengthen the world's ability to cope with inevitable changes. In particular, it must provide comprehensive support to the most vulnerable. They have contributed least to this crisis and are suffering first – and worst. Adaptation is a moral obligation. It is a political imperative. It is a smart investment in a more secure future. It must be given equal priority in the negotiations, though not at the expense of mitigation.

Third, a deal needs to be backed by money and the means to deliver it. Without proper financing, the solutions we discuss are empty. A deal must make available the full range of public and private resources, so developing countries can pursue low-emissions growth, as well as adapt. It must provide a framework that will unlock private investment, including through the carbon markets.

Fourth, a successful deal must include an equitable global governance structure that addresses the needs of developing countries.

The true test of leadership is to take the long view. National leaders must become global leaders to meet the needs of their own people.

Copenhagen offers a new path. It can catalyze a global economy based on low emissions growth that can strengthen sustainable development and lift billions out of poverty. Success in Copenhagen will have positive ripple effects for global cooperation on trade, energy, security and health.

Failure to reach broad agreement in Copenhagen would be morally inexcusable, economically short-sighted and politically unwise. We cannot go down this road. If we have learned anything from the crises of the past year, it is that our fates are intertwined. Climate change links us more directly and dramatically than any other issue. Now is the moment to act in common cause.

History may not offer us a better chance. I urge you to seal a deal in Copenhagen in December this year: an equitable, scientifically robust deal that strengthens sustainable development and powers green growth for every country.

The science demands it. The world economy needs it. The fate of future generations, and the hopes and livelihoods of billions today, rest, literally, with you. I count on your leadership and strong commitment.

The ice is melting
Op-ed article in The New York Times

17 SEPTEMBER 2009

Two weeks ago, I visited the Arctic. I saw the remains of a glacier that just a few years ago was a majestic mass of ice. It had collapsed. Not slowly melted - collapsed. I traveled nine hours by ship from the world's northernmost settlement to reach the polar ice rim. In just a few years, the same ship may be able to sail unimpeded all the way to the North Pole. The Arctic could be virtually ice-free by 2030. Scientists told me their sobering findings. The Arctic is our canary in the coal mine for climate impacts that will affect us all.

I was alarmed by the rapid pace of change there. Worse still, changes in the Arctic are now accelerating global warming. Thawing permafrost is releasing methane, a greenhouse gas twenty times more powerful than carbon dioxide. Melting ice in Greenland threatens to raise sea levels. Meanwhile, global greenhouse gas emissions continue to rise. I am therefore all the more convinced we must act - now.

To that end, on Sept. 22 I am convening a special summit on climate change at the United Nations for some 100 world leaders - history's largest-ever such gathering of heads of state and government. Their collective challenge: transform the climate crisis into an opportunity for safer, cleaner, sustainable green growth for all.

The key is Copenhagen, where governments will gather to negotiate a new global climate agreement in December. I will have a simple message to convey to leaders: the world needs you to actively push for a fair, effective and ambitious deal in Copenhagen. Fail to act, and we will count the cost for generations to come.

Climate change is the preeminent geopolitical issue of our time. It rewrites the global equation for development, peace and prosperity. It threatens markets, economies and development gains. It can deplete food and water supplies, provoke conflict and migration, destabilize fragile societies and even topple governments.

Hyperbole? Not according to the world's best scientists. The Intergovernmental Panel on Climate Change (IPCC) says global greenhouse gas emissions need to peak within ten years if we are to avoid unleashing powerful, natural forces that are now slipping out of our control. Ten years is within the political lifetime of many attending the summit. The climate crisis is occurring on their watch.

There is an alternative: sustainable growth based on green technologies and policies that favor low emissions over current carbon-intensive models. Many national stimulus packages devised in the wake of the global economic downturn feature a strong green component that creates jobs and positions countries to excel in the clean energy economy of the 21st century.

Change is in the air. The key lies in a global climate deal to reduce greenhouse gas emissions and limit global temperature rise to a scientifically safe level. A deal to catalyze clean energy growth. Most urgently, an agreement must protect and assist those who are most vulnerable from inevitable climate impacts.

What is needed is political will at the highest levels - presidents and prime ministers - that translates into rapid progress in the negotiating room. It requires more trust among nations, more imagination, ambition and cooperation. I expect leaders to roll up their sleeves and speak with - not past - each other. I expect them to intensify efforts to resolve the key political issues that have so far slowed global negotiations to a glacial pace. Ironically, that expression - until recently - connoted slowness. But the glaciers I saw a few weeks ago in the Arctic are melting faster than human progress to preserve them.

> ❝ Climate change is the preeminent geopolitical issue of our time. It rewrites the global equation for development, peace and prosperity. ❞

We must place the planet's long-term interests ahead of short-term political expediency. National leaders need to be global leaders who take the long view. Today's threats transcend borders. So, too, must our thinking. Copenhagen need not resolve all the details. But a successful global climate deal must involve all countries, consistent with their capabilities, working toward a common, long-term goal. Here are my benchmarks for success.

First, every country must do its utmost to reduce emissions from all major sources. Industrialized countries have to strengthen their mitigation targets, which are currently nowhere close to what the IPCC says is needed. Developing countries, too, must slow the rise in their emissions and accelerate green growth as part of their strategies to reduce poverty.

Second, a successful deal must help the most vulnerable to adapt to the inevitable impacts of climate change. This is an ethical imperative as well as a smart investment in a more stable, secure world.

Third, developing countries need funding and technology so they can move more quickly toward low-emissions growth. A deal must also unlock private investment, including through carbon markets.

Fourth, resources must be equitably managed and deployed in a way that all countries have a voice.

This year at Copenhagen, we have a powerful opportunity to get on the right side of history. It's an opportunity not only to avert disaster, but to launch a fundamental transformation of the global economy. Strong new political winds now fill our sails. Millions of citizens are mobilized. Savvy businesses are charting a cleaner energy course. We must seize this moment to act boldly on climate change.

Address on adapting to climate change

ULAANBAATAR, 27 JULY 2009

It is a great pleasure to be here with you today. Over the past two days, Mrs Ban and I, and all my colleagues, have had a wonderful visit to this beautiful country. It was indeed a special privilege to visit the Hustai National Park, to spend a night in a traditional *ger*, and to get a taste of the rich culture of Mongolia. As you may know, I was honoured to name a horse - one of the original *Takhi*. I named it Peace, *Enkhtaivan* in Mongolian, for reasons all of us understand.

Very early in my term I settled on a list of urgent priorities. At the top of that list is climate change. This is a fundamental challenge which confronts our planet and all of humanity.

When it comes to climate change, we often focus on the question of cutting green house gas emissions. This is understandable and necessary. But it is not the whole story.

Today I want to talk about how we can and must adapt to the effects of climate change.

We must get serious about adaptation and we must do so now. There is no time for delay.

The people who are bearing the brunt of the effects of climate change are those who can least afford to do so and who have done least to cause the problem. Adaptation is both a practical need and a moral imperative.

I am here in Mongolia to talk about the imperative of adaptation, not only because you face many challenges in this regard, but also because you are doing something about it.

Mongolia is already experiencing the unrelenting effects of climate change. As a landlocked country, you have long faced particular development challenges. These are today compounded by the effects of increasingly extreme weather. Expanding deserts suffocate livelihoods and a way of life. The degradation of vital pasture lands directly affects Mongolia's economy and culture. And you are not alone. You are part of the one third of the world's population – two billion people – who are potential victims of desertification.

The government has proposed new policies for better managing grasslands and pastures.

Improved weather forecasting and insurance funds for herders can help protect livelihoods. This is vital work. It is key to helping the people of Mongolia adapt to a changing climate. The United Nations, the World Bank and donor countries are working with Mongolia to assist in these efforts.

Here, as elsewhere around the globe, I have seen the human face of climate change. Already, hundreds of millions of people are facing increased hardships. Three-quarters of all disasters globally are now climate related, up from half just a decade ago.

In my travels in Africa, I have met families whose crops have been scorched by droughts.

In Haiti and Latin America, I have visited those whose homes have been destroyed by floods and storms, and I have been deeply moved by their suffering.

In a matter of years, climate change could usher in widespread chronic hunger and malnutrition across broad swathes of the developing world. Already, over one billion people go to bed hungry each night.

Imagine what will happen when rains become more erratic and droughts intensify. Imagine, for a moment, that the glaciers of the Himalaya melt. The lives and livelihoods of a billion people will change across Asia.

But we do not need to imagine. Reality is grim enough. Scientists say that by 2020, 75 to 250 million people in Africa will face growing shortages of water due to climate change.

Yields from rain-fed agriculture could fall by half in some African countries over the next ten years.

These are frightening scenarios. Even the world's richest nations are not immune. In the United States, the Energy Secretary has warned that California – the world's fifth largest economy – could see prime farm land reduced to a dustbowl, and major cities running out of water by the end of the century.

Past and present emissions are already changing the climate. And the emissions are still increasing. The adverse impacts will increase. The point is clear: the climate is changing and so, therefore, must we.

There is only one way forward. Together, we must transform our economies and embark on a lower emission, clean energy pathway. We must strengthen our ability to adapt to a changing climate. Adaptation is an essential investment in our common future. We must invest in making our communities more resilient and in reducing our vulnerability to natural disasters. And we must invest in the eco-systems that sustain us.

66 Climate change carries no passport. And no country is immune. 99

Across the globe, we see that humankind is neglecting or destroying our environment at an accelerating rate. They include the fisheries and fields that feed people and drive economies. They include the wetlands that protect us from floods, and the forests that provide fresh air, clean water and livelihoods for 1.6 billion people. We must walk a different path.

In September, I will convene a summit of all nations in New York to mobilize global action. I will press for an effective, fair and comprehensive agreement at the United Nations Climate Change Conference this December in Copenhagen.

We must seal a deal. That deal must provide a clear formula and ambitious targets for reducing greenhouse gas emissions in line with what science requires. No less important, that deal must also assist vulnerable nations adapt to climate change.

Copenhagen presents us with an historic opportunity. We have a chance to preserve our planet and build a safer, cleaner, more prosperous and sustainable future for all.

66 Past and present emissions are already changing the climate. The adverse impacts will increase. The climate is changing and so, therefore, must we 99

Scientists warn these climate impacts will increase in the decades to come. The good news is we are far from helpless in preparing for these consequences. That is why it is absolutely crucial that the world agree on a comprehensive framework for adaptation at Copenhagen.

In our work, we must be guided by the principles of equity and transparency, and involve all in the decisions that affect us all. Pledges must be paid, and words translated into deeds. Lives are on the line. Fidelity to these principles and concrete action are needed to build trust between developing and industrialized countries. Trust is the essential cornerstone of a Copenhagen agreement.

Adapting to climate change requires practical action on several fronts.

First, we need more detailed scientific data on climate impacts, particularly at the regional and national levels. This will enable us to target scarce resources where they can do the most good. The upcoming World Climate Conference in Geneva in August will focus needed attention on this issue.

Second, developing countries need resources to adapt to the deadly increase in floods, droughts, and storms. Billions in public financing will be required. There must be new money, not just re-packaged official development assistance. The most vulnerable countries need immediate support. Lives are on the line. I urge developed countries to contribute to transitional funding arrangements and to other mechanisms for providing urgent support. Funding needs to be governed in ways that address the needs of developing countries, while ensuring efficiency and accountability.

Admittedly, these costs are not insignificant. Let us remember, however, that the sums we invest today will pale in comparison with the costs of inaction. Huge sums are being spent to blunt the financial crisis. If we can bail out banks, certainly we can find the funds to protect millions if not billions of people and their means of survival.

Third, we need to green our development efforts so that climate resilience, sustainability and low-carbon growth become the foundations of future prosperity. We need to make resources go further and last longer in a world with greater climate volatility. This was the recommendation of a group of prominent experts commissioned by the Swedish government earlier this year.

Fourth, we should reduce disaster risks wherever possible. Disaster risk reduction is our first line of defense against the impacts of climate change. In Bangladesh, Cuba, Vietnam and elsewhere, it has proven to be among the most cost-effective investments the world can make. Prevention is always cheaper than cure. Many of the most effective risk reduction tools are about mobilizing people, not expensive technology. For example, planting mangrove trees on unprotected coastlines. Community education and evacuation plans. Thousands of lives have been saved in just these ways.

We will all need to adapt. Ultimately we will all benefit from adaptation. Climate change carries no passport. And no country is immune. In our inter-connected world, a disaster that is local in origin can quickly become regional or even global in impact.

Disaster. Disease. Displacement. Destitution. Adaptation is an essential investment in our common future. At the September climate change summit in New York, I will call on world leaders to recognize this fact. As we have seen here in Mongolia, the human family directly depends on the health of our global home. When we live in harmony with nature we all benefit. Only by working together can we hope to seal the deal for a safer, healthier, more prosperous future for ourselves and for generations to come.

Address to UN conference on climate change

BALI, 12 DECEMBER 2007

L et me thank the Government and people of Indonesia for hosting us, and all of you for being here.

Before I speak to the reason we all came here today, to address climate change, let me say a word about the outrageous attacks perpetrated against the UN and innocent civilians yesterday in Algiers. These cowardly attacks cannot be justified under any circumstances. The sacrifice of UN officials – who serve the highest ideals of humanity – and innocent civilians who died alongside them, cannot and will not be forgotten. The perpetrators of these crimes cannot escape the strongest possible condemnation of the entire international community.

As we convene here in Bali the eyes of the world are upon us. This is a historic moment, long in the making. Decades of careful study by the planet's leading scientists. Years of heated argument among the world's policy makers. Countless media stories debating the linkage between observed natural disasters and global warming.

Now, finally, we are gathered together in Bali to address the defining challenge of our age. We gather because the time for equivocation is over. The science is clear. Climate change is happening. The impact is real. The time to act is now.

The latest report of the Intergovernmental Panel on Climate Change tells us that, unless we act, there will be serious consequences: rising sea levels; more frequent and less predictable floods and severe droughts; famine around the world, particularly in Africa and Central Asia; and the loss of up to a third of our plant and animal species.

They emphasize that the costs of inaction – in ecological, human and financial terms – far exceed the costs of action now.

But the scientists also stress a silver lining: that we can still address the problem, in ways that are both affordable and promote prosperity. By being creative, we can reduce greenhouse gas emissions while promoting economic growth.

In this sense, climate change is as much an opportunity as it is a threat. It is our chance to usher in a new age of green economics and truly sustainable development. New economies can and must grow with reduced carbon intensity even as they create new jobs and alleviate poverty.

This shift toward a greener future is in its infancy and needs urgent nurturing. The multilateral agreement that will emerge from the UNFCCC negotiations needs to make the necessary changes possible. We must ensure an incentive structure for countries, businesses, and individuals. There is no trade-off between fighting climate change and pursuing development. In the long run, we can prosper only by doing both.

Already, there is an emerging consensus on the building blocks of a climate agreement, including adaptation, mitigation, technology and financing. It must also be comprehensive and involve all nations, developed and developing: our atmosphere cannot tell the difference between emissions from an Asian factory, the exhaust from a North American SUV, or deforestation in South America or Africa. And it must be fair, reflecting the principle of common but differentiated responsibilities.

> 66 We are gathered together in Bali to address the defining challenge of our age. We gather because the time for equivocation is over. The science is clear. Climate change is happening. The impact is real. 99

The issue of equity is crucial. Climate change affects us all, but it does not affect us all equally. Those who are least able to cope are being hit hardest. Those who have done the least to cause the problem bear the gravest consequences.

We have an ethical obligation to right this injustice. We have a duty to protect the most vulnerable.

That is why any agreement should look to developed countries to continue taking the lead on curbing emissions. And developing nations need to be given incentives to limit the growth of their emissions. Together, we can spur a new era of green economics, an era of truly sustainable development based on clean technology and a low-emission economy.

But we must also take action on the immediate challenges. It is critical that we follow through on existing commitments and ensure the resilience of populations that are or will be the hardest hit by climate change impacts.

What the world expects from Bali – from all of you – is an agreement to launch negotiations towards a comprehensive climate change agreement. You need to set an agenda; a roadmap to a more secure climate future, coupled with a tight timeline that produces a deal by 2009. The date is crucial not only to ensure continuity after 2012, when the first commitment period of the Kyoto Protocol expires, but equally, to address the desperate urgency of the situation itself.

I am encouraged by progress in the negotiation on both the Convention and the Kyoto Protocol. The implementation and enhancement of agreements on adaptation, deforestation, and technology will be important both now and in the period after 2012.

I also note with satisfaction the movements within Annex I countries toward the enactment of serious climate mitigation measures. I recognize the actions in non-Annex I countries through new national climate plans, policies and measures for sustainable development. I welcome these actions and urge that, as indicated in statements made during these negotiations, they pursue their expressed intentions to do still more.

Reaching a comprehensive climate agreement will not be easy. Having the right tools for such an agreement will help us to implement it in a cost-effective way. And the United Nations will assist you in every way possible. We stand ready to deliver on the mandates that you have already entrusted us, to support you throughout the negotiating period, and to help implement the agreements reached.

Every UN agency, fund and programme is committed. We are determined to be a part of the answer to climate change. Indeed, as the summary paper distributed to all delegations explains, the Chief Executives of the UN system have already begun to define a joint UN contribution on this issue.

As this work progresses, we will continue to provide a credible, coherent scientific foundation for understanding what is happening to our planet and how we might best address it. We will continue to expand support for global, regional and national action on climate change, drawing on the agenda you set. And we will lead by example, by moving towards carbon neutrality throughout the UN System.

You have come here with a clear charge. At the High Level Event on Climate Change in New York in September, world leaders called for a breakthrough in Bali. This is your chance to live up to what the leaders have been calling for. If we leave Bali without such a breakthrough, we will not only have failed our leaders, but also those who look to us to find solutions, namely, the peoples of this world.

This is the moral challenge of our generation. Not only are the eyes of the world upon us. More important, succeeding generations depend on us. We cannot rob our children of their future.

We are all part of the problem of global warming. Let us all be part of the solution that begins in Bali. Let us turn the climate crisis into a climate compact.

Remarks during visit to Antarctica

ANTARCTICA, 09 NOVEMBER 2007

I am here today to observe the impact of global warming. To see for myself and learn all I can. We joke among ourselves that we are on an eco-tour, although I am not here as a tourist, but as a messenger of early warning.

What we saw today was extraordinarily beautiful. These dramatic landscapes are rare and wonderful, but they are deeply disturbing as well. We can clearly see this world changing. The ice is melting far faster than we think.

All this may be gone, and not in the distant future, unless we act, together, now.

Look about us. We have seen it with our own eyes. Antarctica is on the verge of a catastrophe – a catastrophe for the world. The glaciers here on King George Island have shrunk by 10 per cent. Some in Admiralty Bay have retreated by twenty-five kilometres. You know how the Larsen B ice sheet collapsed several years ago and disappeared within weeks. It was the size of Rhode Island, eighty-seven kilometres.

> " These dramatic landscapes are rare and wonderful, but they are deeply disturbing as well. We can clearly see this world changing. The ice is melting far faster than we think. All this may be gone, and not in the distant future, unless we act, together. "

What alarms me is not the melting snow and glaciers, alone. It is that the Larsen phenomenon could repeat itself on a vastly greater scale. Scientists here have told me that the entire Western Antarctic Ice Shelf — the WAIS — is at risk. It is all floating ice, one fifth of the entire continent. If it broke up, sea levels could rise by 6 metres or eighteen feet. Think of that. And it could happen quickly, almost overnight in geological terms.

This is not scare-mongering. I am not trying to frighten you. According to recent studies, 138 tons of ice are now being lost every year, mostly from the Western Ice Shelf.

You know, also, that deep blue water absorbs more heat than sea covered with ice. The sea ice around Antarctica is vanishing too.

There are other deeply worrying signs. The penguin population of Chabrier Rock, a main breeding ground, has declined by 57 per cent in the last twenty-five years. It is the same elsewhere. What will happen to the annual march of the penguins in the future? Will there even be one?

Grass is growing for the first time ever here on King George Island — including a grass used on American golf courses. It rains increasingly often in the summer rather than snows.

These things should alarm us all. Antarctica is a natural lab that helps us understand what is happening to our world. We must save this precious earth, including all that is here. It is a natural wonder, but above all, it is our common home.

It is here where our work, together, comes into focus. We see Antarctica's beauty, the danger global warming represents, and the urgency that we do something about it. I am determined that we shall.

Peace and Security

Remarks to international conference on Afghanistan

TOKYO, 8 JULY 2012

I would like to express my deep appreciation to the Government of Japan for its commitment to peace in Afghanistan and for generously hosting this event. I also commend the Government of Afghanistan for defining its vision for the Transformation Decade.

This is the third international conference on Afghanistan in just three months. It is aimed at defining and solidifying the engagement between Afghanistan and its partners in support of the country's self-reliance. In Chicago last May, commitments for the future of the Afghan security forces were secured. In Kabul last month, we saw pledges to regional support and agreement on measures to strengthen cooperation to address common threats and achieve common goals. Today, we focus on another issue of great importance: Afghanistan's development and governance priorities and its efforts to achieve the Millennium Development Goals.

Under the leadership of President Karzai and his Government, real progress has been made on the path to security and broad-based development. But these gains remain fragile. Failure to invest in governance, justice, human rights, employment and social development could negate the investments and sacrifices that have been made over the past ten years. We must also not forget Afghanistan's humanitarian needs and its refugees.

I would also like to reiterate what I said at the NATO Summit in Chicago in May: we must do more for the country's women and children – including girls' education and women's participation in the country's political life.

We are at a critical moment in Afghanistan's history. We are in transition from reliance on the aid that has enabled the country's institutions to take root, to a normalized relationship of a sovereign, functioning Afghanistan with its people and with its international partners.

But let us be clear: transition must not translate into short-term measures only. We should give the people of Afghanistan the long-term prospect of a better future, and ease their worries that Afghanistan may be abandoned.

We are all aware of serious concerns regarding Afghan delivery and accountability on governance commitments. These must be addressed in the interest of the Afghan people and also to maintain donor confidence.

But we must be fully conscious that Afghanistan's institutions are still in their nascent stages. The very programmes which offer the best hope for the sustainability of Afghan institutions should not be held hostage to complex pre-conditions. Donors should live up to the commitments they have made to provide predictable assistance in a way that genuinely strengthens national ownership and capacity.

At the same time, it is of course Afghanistan itself that bears the primary responsibility to live up to its obligations to better serve its people, in line with the commitments made in Bonn, Kabul and London. I therefore welcome the Tokyo Mutual Accountability Framework. This should give confidence to Afghans and donors that the commitments they have made to each other – and will make today – will be monitored and honored. That includes ensuring that development assistance follows aid effectiveness principles.

> ❝ We are at a critical moment. We are in transition from reliance on aid to a sovereign, functioning Afghanistan. But transition must not translate into short-term measures only. We should give the people of Afghanistan the long-term prospect of a better future, and ease their worries that Afghanistan may be abandoned. ❞

The United Nations has been engaged in Afghanistan for many decades, well before the attention the country has received over the past decade. As we look ahead, let us have reasonable expectations of what the United Nations can and cannot achieve. In close coordination with the major stakeholders and within the limits of our limited resources, we will do our utmost to help the Afghans fill the gaps that may arise as transition deepens.

That means strong support, throughout the Transformation Decade, for the country's economic and social development, for building its institutional capacity, for basic services and social protection, for jobs, justice and the rule of law.

We must all continue to stand with the people of Afghanistan in their quest for security, stability and prosperity. An Afghanistan at peace with itself would at long last respond to its peoples' hopes of better lives for themselves and their children. And an Afghanistan living in harmony with its neighbours, near and far, would make a tremendous contribution to regional and international peace and security. These are the important stakes involved, well known to all of us.

In closing, allow me to recognize the contributions of so many Member States, troop contributing countries, donors, NATO and others. Let me also commend the work of my Special Representative, Jan Kubis, and his UNAMA team. Let us work together, at this conference and beyond, so that Afghanistan can gain the path it seeks. Thank you very much for your leadership.

Remarks to Action Group on Syria

GENEVA, 30 JUNE 2012

L et me begin by thanking the Joint Special Envoy, Mr. Kofi Annan, for bringing us together. We fully support his efforts to bring peace to Syria, and I commend his persistence and tenacity. I would also like to thank all of you for being here today. Our responsibility is clear: to act. This is the Action Group on Syria. We must act to end the killing. We must act to help the people of Syria realize their legitimate political, social and economic aspirations for change and a better future.

The crisis in Syria grows worse by the day. Neither side is making any effective effort to abide by their commitments under Mr. Annan's six-point plan. Government forces continue to use heavy weapons against civilian populations. The armed opposition is intensifying their attacks. Every day brings another hundred deaths, according to our best estimates. Since March, approximately 15,000 people have died. Another month of inaction would translate to another 3,000 dead.

The UN observer mission remains in place, ready to resume its work if the security situation improves. Yet we must be realistic about the risks and limitations that confront these brave UN men and women. That is why, next week, I will submit a proposal for reconfiguring the mission to the Security Council. Meanwhile, UN-SMIS continues to maintain direct contact with the parties wherever possible. The mission is also trying to facilitate humanitarian access, recently with some modest success.

As many as 1.5 million people need assistance. In areas where fighting has been most intense, we see growing scarcities of food and water. Hospitals and health facilities have regularly been raided and shelled; sometimes they have been used as a base for military operations or detention centres. The numbers of displaced people has more than tripled since April. UNHCR supports more than 90,000 refugees in Iraq, Jordan, Lebanon and Turkey, according to our official count. The actual number of unregistered refugees, of course, is far higher.

It is our collective responsibility to not let guns triumph over diplomacy and dialogue. The international community must remain united in pursuit of a peaceful solution. I ask all around this table to exert their maximum influence. All stakeholders in Syria and beyond must be convinced that violence will only breed more violence. To fail in this would be catastrophic for Syria and the region. We have seen a preview of what may come in Al Qubeir and El Houla, described in grim detail in the Commission of Inquiry report submitted earlier this week to the Human Rights Council. We must make every effort not to further militarize the situation.

This vicious circle of killing, this quickening descent into prospective chaos, must be stopped before it is too late.

Time is no one's friend. As I see it, this is the critical moment; possibly a last chance to shift from conflict to dialogue, and to set the stage for a transition that can end the violence. We all accept that Syria's future is for Syrians to decide. Our duty, here today, is to help set that transition in motion; to strongly and unambiguously push the parties toward dialogue and a sustainable agreement on their common future.

❝ It is our collective responsibility to not let guns triumph over diplomacy and dialogue. ❞

Expectations for this meeting are extremely high. I strongly hope we will be able to agree on measures to advance the six-point plan, in particular a cessation of violence. Beyond that, we should agree on concrete guidelines and principles for an inclusive political transition that meets the aspirations of the Syrian people.

The question before us is how best to bring about change, what should a new Syria look like, and how can we, as outsiders, help to develop a plan for peace and political progress that all Syrians, of every ethnicity and affiliation, can embrace. I believe we all recognize this basic reality. The current situation, the status quo is unacceptable. It cannot go on.

Our unity is essential. If we, here today, can agree on the ground rules for charting a way ahead, I am confident that we will depart from Geneva with a new optimism. The Syrian people are suffering. Every day we are witness to gross and grotesque violations of human rights. It is time for us to act, with unity and determination.

Address to the Union Assembly of Myanmar

NYAPYIDAW, 30 APRIL 2012

What a privilege it is for me to take part in this extraordinary session of the Union Assembly. And what an honour to be the first outside guest to address this august assembly.

I believe deeply in the potential of this great land. Above all, I believe in the future of the great people of Myanmar. That is why, as Secretary-General of the United Nations, I have sought always to help Myanmar open once again to the wider world. We have worked for constructive engagement. We have worked publicly and we have worked privately to help advance peace, democracy and development and mobilize international support.

This is my third visit as UN Secretary-General. In 2008, I came in the wake of Cyclone Nargis. In those difficult days, the United Nations helped bring international aid. Even then, amid so much hardship, we sensed the potential for dramatic change. I returned once again, in 2009, and spoke frankly, as a friend, about the need for dialogue and reconciliation; about the importance of pursuing peace, development and human rights as different faces of the same future – a future held dear by all the people of Myanmar.

Today, I return to a new Myanmar; a Myanmar that is making history. The dramatic changes sweeping Myanmar have inspired the world. And we know that your ambitions for the future reach higher still. I have no doubt that Myanmar will quickly regain its place as a respected and responsible member of the international community. I have no doubt that Myanmar will quickly catch up with its Asian neighbours and our fast-changing world. And I have no doubt that Myanmar has within it a vast potential to become a 21st century model for peace, democracy and prosperity.

I am here to urge you to stay on that path. And I call on the international community to walk with you. I am here to tell the people of Myanmar: you can count on the United Nations. You can count on me, as Secretary-General. Together, we will help Myanmar build a new and better future for all its people.

And I am here to say, and to say clearly: the road before you is exciting. But it will not always be easy. Eventual success will rest largely with this Assembly. This Parliament can transform people's aspirations for democracy and a better life into concrete change.

The perils and pitfalls are many. There is no single formula for success. In this Golden Land, blessed with great human and natural resources, the teachings of Buddha have offered guidance through the ages. Your sages have long known the *iddhipadas*, the basic rules of success: *chanda*, diligence and will; *citta*, right intent and attitude; *viriya*, perseverance in action; *vimamsa* or *panna*, wisdom. These transcendent values remain your moral compass. In our wider multicultural world, they are a source of inspiration for us all.

Let me share with you how I believe these four principles can guide our work together.

First, will: political will and leadership. I commend President Thein Sein for his vision, leadership and courage to put Myanmar on the path of change. I salute Daw Aung San Suu Kyi, the National League for Democracy and others for joining the political process and participating in the recent elections. For many years, you displayed resilience and fortitude that for generations have distinguished the Myanmar people.

We know that Myanmar can meet the challenges of reconciliation, democracy and development. But it will take your full determination and your common leadership and partnership.

The path of change is still fragile and uncertain, but it is indeed too narrow to turn back. The regional and global economies are growing; so, too, are the expectations of people – especially young people. Let us work together to meet all of these challenges by summoning the political will to make lasting change. Elections and open government are the keystones of democracy. But they must be matched with a healthy and vibrant political climate.

This leads me to the second principle, the need for a positive attitude in the face of differences. President Thein Sein and Daw Aung San Suu Kyi have demonstrated the confidence and statesmanship needed to look beyond politics to the longer and larger interests of the nation.

It is not surprising for there to be differences among parties – differences both big and small, as we now see regarding the oath-taking of newly elected members of the Parliament. I am confident that you will resolve these issues by keeping the focus on the longer term interests of the country – and the immediate needs of the people who look to your leadership and results. In a country as complex and diverse as Myanmar, there must be unity of purpose. Confrontation and repression were tried, and they failed.

President Thein Sein speaks of the need to mobilize the "strong force" of a "new political generation for a mature democracy". Across Myanmar society, the generational shift now taking place – including within the *Tatmadaw*, the armed forces – requires more understanding, more solidarity and more cooperation from all. The reform agenda gives you a broad framework for addressing different policy priorities – from development to the rule of law, from peace and stability to human rights.

This Parliament is at the very center of your country's democratic transition. It is here that representatives from various ethnicities, religions, and institutional backgrounds come together. It is here that different parties will need to join hands to write an inclusive and forward-looking national agenda for change.

Under the chairmanship of Speakers U Khin Aung Myint and U Shwe Mann, the parliamentary framework offers a new space to do this. For Parliament to become the wellspring of democracy, however, it must be fed from many sources. The waters of genuine participatory development must come together in this place.

Above all, that means listening to people. It means providing citizens with the political space to take part in national politics at all levels: women; young people; the rural poor; ethnic and religious communities; media and civil society. All have a role in building a new Myanmar.

> **❝ The dramatic changes sweeping Myanmar have inspired the world. The road before you is exciting. But it will not always be easy. ❞**

This brings me to the third principle: perseverance in action. There is no substitute for action. But action cannot deliver desired results without perseverance. For the people of Myanmar, expectations are very high. They expect this Parliament to not only advance reform, but to accelerate the pace of change. That will require drawing on the final principle: wisdom.

True leadership is grounded in wisdom. Each country must walk the path of progress in ways that best suit the needs and aspirations of its people. For Myanmar, wisdom means parties making the most of what they have. It means not getting locked into rigid dogma or inflexible ideological positions. Wisdom means flexibility in accommodating competing demands in a way that allows all to move forward.

There are important milestones ahead. By 2014, Myanmar's chairmanship of ASEAN will raise expectations and responsibilities that come with regional leadership. By 2015, national elections will take place.

At this critical moment, both Myanmar and the international community must work together. We must do so in the name of the people of Myanmar. Those yearning for change. Those braving great risks. Those never willing to give up on their dream for democracy, their thirst for change. Now we must match our actions with their ambitions.

There may be differences in pace and approach, but everyone is a partner in this effort. That is why, today, I want to outline a four-point agenda for action to advance national reconciliation and the democratic transition at this historic moment.

First, ordinary people must see quickly the dividends of democratic transition in their daily lives. The recent decision to increase investments in health and education is a good start. More action is needed across the socio-economic spectrum. That means a focus on job creation and lifting millions out of rural poverty. These are priorities of the people of Myanmar. They must also be for this Parliament. I welcome action taken so far by the international community. But more needs to be done. Today, I urge the international community to go even further in lifting, suspending or easing trade restrictions and other sanctions.

Second, Myanmar needs a substantial increase in international development assistance as well as foreign direct investment. Today, Myanmar receives a small percentage of per capita development assistance compared to other neighboring countries. The best way for the international community to support reform is to invest in it.

At the same time, this Parliament must continue to create conditions to ensure greater aid effectiveness. Learning from the experiences of its neighbours, Myanmar must look for ways to develop its natural resources while supporting its emerging manufacturing and services industries, enhancing governance in both the public and private sectors, and preserving the precious landscape and ecology of the country.

Let us work for policies that balance equitable development, so that all communities and regions can share in the benefits of growth. Now is the time for the people of Myanmar to share in the economic dynamism of this region.

Third, more action is needed to advance a fully national reconciliation process. This requires progress on a number of difficult issues. Among them: resettlement of displaced communities, security guarantees for various ethnic and political groups and the release of all political prisoners.

The positive momentum has to be maintained through steady progress towards lasting peace that is anchored in equality and justice. That is the way to build trust and restore confidence among the government and the country's diverse ethnic, political and religious groups.

I commend the progress made by the Government and ethnic groups in achieving ceasefires, and encourage both sides to rapidly reconcile all outstanding issues. Meanwhile, the situation in Kachin State is inconsistent with the successful conclusion of ceasefire agreements with all other major groups. The Kachin people should no longer be denied the opportunity that a ceasefire and a political agreement can bring for peace and development. Let me acknowledge the humanitarian access that now we have in Kachin. That access must continue. Success in national reconciliation will hinge on how these issues are discussed in Parliament and within the newly elected state and regional parliaments.

Fourth, a new discourse is needed to develop an inclusive democratic culture based on the rule of law and respect for human rights, especially those of free association and free speech. There must be safeguards for civil society and protections for the rights of ethnic minorities. The establishment of a new National Human Rights Commission is only a start.

Priority must be placed on nationally inclusive human rights norms along with the rights of self-expression of ethnic groups. This will have to be the essential basis for the emergence of an authentic national democratic unity. This parliament must be the arena where all the people's diverse voices can be heard and join together to advance your nation's agendas.

Everywhere in the world, governments have learned they cannot do the job alone. Progress takes partnership. The United Nations stands ready to help in every way we can. I welcome Myanmar's desire for guidance and advice from the United Nations and other multilateral institutions.

Initiatives by the UN Global Compact, the Economic and Social Commission for Asia and the Pacific (ESCAP), and the UN Office of Drugs and Crime show how partnerships can multiply national efforts. Similarly, the UNDP must begin a normal country programme for Myanmar.

I am pleased to announce a new partnership by the UN to support Myanmar's first population and housing census in thirty years – a process with far-reaching implications for the country's development.

As our United Nations team in Myanmar continues its mission, including the delivery of humanitarian aid, I will make sure that our unique services are at your disposal. These include expertise in peace-building, rule of law, electoral assistance, anti-corruption and democratic practices. Closer partnership between Myanmar and the United Nations is natural.

Myanmar, after all, has an important place in the history of our Organization. You are not only a founding member of the United Nations, but also an early contributor to our peacekeeping operations. Today, let us renew and strengthen our partnership for the years to come.

As Secretary-General, I follow in the footsteps of a great son of this nation, U Thant. He constantly reminded the world to overcome violence, to rise above ego, and to look to our common humanity. He believed in our mutual obligations to one another and stressed the need, as he said, "to understand each other and to develop a spirit of One World."

Today, the world needs Myanmar's contribution to help address the global challenges of our time. Answering that call is in your hands, and I thank you very much for your leadership. *Kyae zoo tin bar tae.*

Remarks to Herzliya Conference

HERZLIYA, ISRAEL, 2 FEBRUARY 2012

What a pleasure to be in Israel - my fourth visit as UN Secretary-General. And what an honour to address this distinguished gathering of the annual Herzliya Conference.

Your chosen theme this year is apt: "In the Eye of Storms: Israel and the Middle East." The storms of the Arab Spring are indeed sweeping the region. Change keeps coming, with blinding and often bewildering speed.

Some in Israel, and elsewhere, view these events with concern. One year later, they say that the Arab Spring has failed, that these dramatic transformations have moved the Middle East backward, not forward. Others fear new governments will emerge that are unfriendly to Israel. Understandably, they point to the conflict in Syria, to the emergence of Islamist-oriented leadership in some governments, to critical issues concerning Iran

Yet to speak frankly among good friends, I would have to say that it pains me to hear such complaints. I am Secretary-General of the United Nations, an organization dedicated to promoting democracy, human rights and the worth of the individual. These principles are deeply embedded in the UN Charter and the Universal Declaration of Human Rights. We have worked to advance these ideals for many, many years. It is hard not to view the dramatic events of the past year as a fulfilment of our most noble aspirations.

Cast your eye over this new landscape, so profoundly different from a year ago. We see a newly democratizing Egypt and Tunisia. A newly liberated Libya rebuilding itself on basic principles of democracy and the rule of law. Everywhere, people are expressing a fundamental human yearning, the universal hunger for dignity, freedom and human rights. Young people have been in the vanguard. As have women, standing for their rights against those who would deny them.

Surely, no one in the modern world would conclude that a repressive regime that grants no rights to its people, or seeks to limit them, is somehow preferable to a democracy. We should welcome this historic, this inevitable evolution. We should not perpetuate the fallacy that the Arab world is not ready for democracy.

Two decades ago, a previous generation rebelled against tyranny in Eastern Europe. The international community was quick to help. Today, the international community should step up once again. We should help these new Arab governments as they try to respond to the needs and aspirations of their citizens.

The road to democracy is not easy. It has to be shaped and formed in a true democratic spirit. This is a once-in-a-generation opportunity. And I have put helping nations in transition at the very top of my priorities for my second term as Secretary-General. Israel, the United Nations and the entire international community should unite in this effort.

As I see it, there is no eye in this sea of geopolitical storms. There is no untouched safe haven, no island of calm. We all recognize that Israel has special security concerns. That is why as Secretary-General I have spoken out, loudly and repeatedly, against anti-Semitism and anti-Israel hate-speech. Again and again, I have condemned those who would deny the Holocaust. I have stood firm against terrorist attacks and defended Israel strongly in world bodies where it has been singled out.

And that is why, tonight, I say that Israel's future is not in isolation. Israel's place is in this larger world, firmly anchored in a newly democratic Middle East. Ultimately, the best way to survive and thrive amid change is to embrace it, and help shape it. This brings me to the question of peace and Israel's responsibility to achieve it.

The United Nations helped bring the State of Israel into this world. It did so in the name of peace, not war. Yet the Israeli-Palestinian conflict is entering its seventh decade. The current peace process began in Madrid more than 20 years ago. It raised high hopes - but delivered two decades of delay, mistrust and missed opportunities. A succession of failed talks created a climate of mistrust. So-called "rejectionists" gained strength. Many have come to question the very basis of the peace process - land for peace.

❝ There is no eye in this sea of geopolitical storms. There is no untouched safe haven, no island of calm. Israel's future is not in isolation. Israel's place is in this larger world, firmly anchored in a newly democratic Middle East. ❞

And yet we have come close. Civil society initiatives have shown that the gaps can be bridged, that differences are not beyond the ability of people of good will to resolve. And recent years have brought another welcome and positive development – the emergence of a credible Palestinian partner, serving its people and, I suggest, challenging Israel to rethink some of its assumptions. In some ways, the Palestinian Authority is ahead of the regional curve. In the West Bank, it is building the institutions for a functioning democracy and a future Palestinian state. Yesterday, I once again visited Ramallah. Every time I go, I am impressed by the pace of progress. I was also struck by the professionalism of the security forces, as well as the broader sense of economic and social progress. The creation of functioning and well-governed Palestinian institutions is clearly a strategic Israeli interest.

Yet these advances are at risk. Why? Because the politics is not keeping pace with developments on the ground. Negotiations have bogged down. We see too many pointless provocations. Israel continues to erect settlements, some in the most sensitive areas for any future peace. Meeting with Palestinians in the West Bank yesterday, I heard their deep frustration. The international community's position is well-known: these settlements are illegal. I strongly agree.

For Palestinians, the borders of a future state based on the 1967 lines, with agreed swaps of territory, are the essence of its viability. It is not surprising, therefore, that growing numbers of Palestinians see what is happening elsewhere in the region and are coming to support popular, non-violent action - a Palestinian Spring, some call it. They can also be expected to take their case for statehood to the United Nations and its various funds and programmes, as they have already with UNESCO. All of us here today understand Israel's very real security concerns. I saw for myself the terrible effects of the rocket attacks out of Gaza at Sapir College, only three kilometres from the border.

We must work together to stop the smuggling of weapons into Gaza. We must strengthen the institutions of mutual security in the West Bank, and we must promote a culture of tolerance and mutual acceptance in both Israel and the occupied Palestinian Territory. And clearly, we must condemn all acts of violence. We must speak clearly for Israel's right to exist, always bearing in mind that a negotiated peace must rest on accepted principles of self-determination in their own democratic states.

In these circumstances, Israel must think carefully about how to empower those on the other side who wish for peace. Now is the moment for a demonstration of good will by both sides. There is much Israel can do.

By opening Gaza to construction materials, for example, Israel would give ordinary Gazans a chance for a normal life. For people to live normal lives, they have to have schools, decent housing and health care. There has to be an economy, with jobs and a free flow of commerce. Palestinian poverty is not Israel's friend.

Our highest priority must be to return to negotiations - not merely procedural talks, but genuine and substantive negotiations to resolve the core issues. And when those talks begin, both sides should understand the profound costs if they lead nowhere, particularly in terms of public alienation.

As you know, Israeli and Palestinian representatives are meeting in Jordan. That is why I travelled to Amman earlier this week. I commended King Abdullah for his stewardship, and I told him that I would do anything possible to push the negotiations forward. That is also why I have visited Israel and the occupied Palestinian Territory. I have used this occasion to urge both the Israeli and Palestinian leadership to act constructively and refrain from provocations.

Prime Minister Netanyahu and President Abbas each re-affirmed their commitment to a negotiated solution. I told each, as well, that this is their moment. This is the moment to try to rebuild the confidence and momentum that has so sadly - and often so needlessly - been lost.

The road is not easy, but every step counts. Confidence demands that Palestinians and Israelis are able to live normal lives. It demands that both sides accept that each has a legitimate narrative and legitimate needs, and that neither demonize the other. A radicalization of societies would hurt Israel and Palestine alike. Negotiations will go nowhere without a shared sense of urgency and a genuine determination to succeed.

The Palestinians must engage, seriously, on security. Israel must engage, seriously, on territory. The elements of peace are what they have long been: an end of the 1967 occupation, a just resolution of all core issues including security, borders, Jerusalem and refugees, and the creation of a Palestinian state living side-by-side in peace with a secure Israel.

I have spoken frankly, today, because I believe that time is running out and because I am a true friend of Israel. If this chance is not seized, future conferences here at Herzliya will face even more difficult questions and challenges. The world is ready to help ensure Israel's security, just as it is ready to help Palestinians to establish a new nation - so long overdue.

You have my personal commitment as Secretary-General to spare no effort to help Israelis and Palestinians arrive at a new and brighter future - and to place at the centre of this profoundly changing region an historic peace whose benefits will be felt in every corner of the world.

Address to High-level Meeting on Reform and Transitions to Democracy

BEIRUT, 15 JANUARY 2012

Prime Minister Mikati, thank you for joining us for this important gathering, held under the auspices of ESCWA and also the Government of Lebanon. And our great thanks again to Rima Khalaf and the four regional commissions for bringing us together.

The remarkable events of the past year transformed the region and changed the world. It was a story written by people – but the story has just begun. Those who believe in a future of freedom and dignity must now come together and help the people of the region and their leaders to write the next chapters. That is why we are here today.

Six centuries ago, the famous Arab philosopher, Ibn Khaldun, offered a clear warning to those in power. Leaders can lead only with the will of the people. Those who wield power by force or coercion bring about their own downfall, he said. Sooner or later, they are abandoned by their people. That in a nutshell is the history of 2011 and it may go on this year and on.

From the very beginning of the last year's revolutions, from Tunisia through Egypt and beyond, I called on leaders to listen to their people, listen to the genuine aspirations of their people, what do they need and what are their voices. Some did, and benefitted. Some did not, and today they are reaping the whirlwind. And today, I say again to President Assad of Syria: stop the violence. Stop killing your own people. The path of repression is a dead end.

The lessons of the past year are eloquent and clear: the winds of change will not cease to blow. The flame ignited in Tunisia will not be dimmed. Let us remember, as well: none of these great changes began with a call for a regime change.

First and foremost, people wanted dignity. They want an end to corruption. They want a say in their future. They want jobs and justice, a fair share of political power. They want their human rights.

For too long, Arabs stood on the sidelines. They watched as others threw off tyranny – in Europe, Asia and Africa. They asked: why not us? Why so little democracy in a part of the world so rich in human potential? Now their time has come. Now your time has come.

The old way, the old order, is crumbling one-man rule and the perpetuation of family dynasties, monopolies of wealth and power, the silencing of the media, the deprivation of fundamental freedoms that are the birthright of men, women and children on this planet. To all of this, the people say: enough! Enough is enough.

This is cause to celebrate, and much more. The spontaneous, homegrown and non-violent movements are a credit to the Arab people. They are also rebuke to those, Arab and non-Arab alike, who claimed this part of the world is not ready for democracy. But it has been hard. The cost in human suffering and loss of life has been so large. These great changes also come at a time of global economic difficulty. In fact, in many cases they compounded the effects. Commerce has been hurt. Unemployment is rising. So is the cost of fuel and food. Families everywhere are struggling.

Meanwhile, old elites remain entrenched, the levers of coercion remain in their hands. Long-term hope coexists with short-term worry. We have reached a sober moment.

> 66 For too long, Arabs stood on the sidelines. They watched as others threw off tyranny – in Europe, Asia and Africa. They asked: why not us? Why so little democracy in a part of the world so rich in human potential? Now their time has come. 99

Democracy is not easy. It takes time and effort to build. It does not come into being with one or two elections. Yet there is no going back. I see four prerequisites for success:

First, reform must be real and genuine. Too often, changes are cosmetic. They give the appearance of democracy without substance, without a shift of real power to the people.

The people do not seek authoritarianism with a human face. People want meaningful changes in security services and armed forces. These should serve the people, not keep them down. They want a virtuous circle of rights and opportunity under the rule of law, a vibrant civil society and an enterprising private sector, backed by efficient and accountable state institutions.

Second, inclusive dialogue is crucial. Diversity is a strength. We must oppose those who exploit ethnic or social differences for political gain.

It is sometimes said that authoritarian regimes, whatever else their faults, at least kept a lid on sectarian conflict. This is a cruel canard. Yet it could be equally mistaken to assume that all of the new regimes now emerging will automatically uphold universal human rights. We must work together to promote pluralism and protect the rights of minorities and the vulnerable. The new regimes must not elevate certain religious or ethnic communities at the expense of others.

Third, women must be at the centre of the region's future. Women stood in the streets and squares demanding changes. They now have a right to sit at the table, real influence in decision-making and governance. Protection from violence, intimidation and abuse is a fundamental matter of human dignity and equality. Sexual violence, discrimination, violence against women are not acceptable.

More, they are universal rights they are not, as some may claim, values that are imposed from outside. The deficit in women's empowerment has held back the Arab region for too long. Change is not merely necessary, it is essential, and there must be changes. There can be no democracy worthy of the name without women.

Fourth, we must heed the voices of the young. Arab countries need to create 50 million new jobs within the next decade to absorb young entrants to the workforce. This profound demographic pressure drove the Arab Spring. Faced with bleak prospects and unresponsive governments, young Arabs acted on their own to reclaim their future. They have not finished the job.

Let us recognize that dignity and justice are threatened not only by authoritarian rule, but also by conflict. The Israeli occupation of Arab and Palestinian territories must end. So must violence against civilians. Settlements, new and old, are illegal. They work against the emergence of a viable Palestinian state. A two-State solution is long overdue. The status quo offers only the guarantee of future conflict. We must all do our part to break the impasse and secure a lasting peace.

Much depends on us. Much depends upon you. There can be no economic recovery and development without international support. And we all have much to offer in these delicate political transitions. Now is the moment to share best practices and lessons learned during similar transitions elsewhere. We thank the leaders from Asia, Africa, Europe and Latin America who are here to do just that.

We must also move beyond the assumptions that have traditionally governed relationships between Arab countries and their partners. Among these is the dangerous idea that security is somehow more important than human rights. This has had the effect of keeping non-democratic states in power – with little to show for either security or people's well-being or human rights.

The United Nations also has a responsibility to update its approach to the region. Our Arab Human Development Reports broke new ground in frankly diagnosing the region's problems, deficits in democracy, knowledge, women's empowerment and human security. But those reports were not fully integrated into our work. Looking to the future, we know that business as usual, business as it has always been done, will no longer suffice.

As I begin my second term as Secretary-General of the United Nations, I want to emphasize that the United Nations will be always here for you and with you. We are firmly committed to help Arab countries through this transition, by every means. Our assistance mission in Libya (UNSMIL) is supporting the interim authorities in three key priorities: elections, transitional justice and public security. In

Tunisia, our engagement focuses on electoral assistance, the empowerment of civil society and protection of human rights.

A UN mediator has been at the heart of negotiations in Yemen. I call again on President Saleh to abide by the terms of the agreement he has signed. UN Women is active in Egypt and Tunisia. The UN Democracy Fund is helping to strengthen civil society. The Department of Political Affairs of the United Nations and UNDP are working together to support free and fair elections. This is just a small sample of what we at the United Nations are doing. The UN system is fully engaged, the UN and its staff are dedicated to your future.

Let me close by noting this important anniversary: on January 14, yesterday, one year ago, Tunisia's president-for-life, Zine El Abidene Ben Ali, stepped down in the face of the popular uprising against him. A few months later, I went to Tunisia and met the family of the man who set these events in motion, Mohamed Bouazizi. His mother when I met her, in tears, told me of her son's anger at being unable to care for his family, his anger at being robbed of his worth as a human being. She said, "I will not be sad anymore - I will just be proud." This is what she told me.

Since then I have travelled widely elsewhere in the region. In Cairo I met with the leaders of the revolution in Tahrir Square. In Tripoli, I stood in a warehouse where Muamar Qadaffi executed his political opponents. And I have met or spoken with Arab leaders of every country, at UN headquarters in New York, in their own capitals, or by telephone at summits around the world.

In all this, I have come to one inescapable conclusion: there cannot be a gulf between rulers and the ruled. The wider the gap, the greater the certainty of social unhappiness, even of conflict. This is true throughout the world, not just in Arab world.

Let us listen to our people. Let us live by cherished principle of mutual respect and tolerance for difference. At this moment of history, let us work together to build prosperous and open societies throughout the Arab world, founded in fairness, justice and opportunity for all.

Let us work together to make this better for all regardless of religion, regardless of sex, regardless of ethnicity, poor and rich, small and big. That is the priority of United Nations. And I count on your support, and let us work together, and join together toward that goal.

Remarks to the Security Council on Somalia

NEW YORK, 13 DECEMBER 2011

I am pleased to attend this meeting on Somalia and to have this opportunity to share with you my perspectives on the situation, based on recent developments and on my own visit last Friday.

Since I took office, Somalia has been a priority. A few years ago, people tended to think of Somalia only as a place of famine or bloodshed. Often, when I spoke about Somalia, people wanted to change the subject. I wanted to change the way we see Somalia.

We finally face a moment of fresh opportunities. We must seize it. That is why the President of General Assembly and I travelled to Mogadishu on December 9th. It was the first visit by a UN Secretary-General in over eighteen years.

That my visit was even possible is a sign of improved security and the investment that the United Nations has made in supporting the African Union Mission in Somalia. All city districts are now effectively under the control of the Transitional Federal Government with the support of AMISOM. I congratulated the brave TFG and AMISOM soldiers and extended my condolences to the families of the fallen soldiers and the Governments of Somalia, Burundi and Uganda.

The AMISOM Force Commander, Major General Fred Mugashi of Uganda, explained the difficult circumstances they face, and the need for adequate military assets to fight an asymmetric terrorist war.

In an urban environment, we must secure gains and extend them beyond Mogadishu. That requires AMISOM to deploy at its full strength of 12,000 troops. It also demands the necessary force enablers, including air assets, like helicopters, and military engineering capabilities.

During my visit I announced that the UN Political Office for Somalia will relocate to Mogadishu in January, next year. That will begin with my Special Representative, Mr. Mahiga and his core team and expand gradually as more resources become available. I have also asked the UN country team to work more closely with UNPOS to support the TFG's efforts in governance, recovery, development and capacity building.

For all of this to be possible, we must expedite arrangements for protecting UN and AMISOM civilian personnel. I also renew my appeal for supporting the UN's Recovery and Stabilization Plan.

In Mogadishu, we were welcomed by President Sheikh Sharif Sheikh Ahmed, Prime Minister Abdiweli Mohamed Ali, Speaker Sharif Hassan Sheikh Aden and others. They thanked the United Nations and urged continued assistance. The leadership has heeded the Security Council's call to work together.

Nonetheless, despite some progress, important deadlines have been missed. I asked the leadership to intensify efforts to implement the Roadmap. I made clear that the transition must end in August 2012. In particular, I urged them to accelerate constitutional and parliamentary reforms – which do not require financial resources, but political will. I echoed the Council's call that continued international assistance rests on continued reform. I encouraged them to build trust by ensuring accountability and transparency. I warmly welcomed the active engagement of civil society and the Somali diaspora.

> ❝ Often, when I spoke about Somalia, people wanted to change the subject. I wanted to change the way we see Somalia. ❞

President Sharif assured me of his Government's commitment to a broadly inclusive implementation of the Roadmap. He cited the upcoming meeting on the constitution-making process as an important step.

Beyond Mogadishu, the Islamist insurgents in Somalia are retreating under mounting pressure from the Government forces and their militia allies, backed by Kenyan and Ethiopian forces. This represents a unique opportunity to help stabilize the country at large.

The UN is helping the African Union and the Intergovernmental Authority on Development to develop coherent military planning in the country. We must ensure that the military strategy is aligned with political objectives. As more territory is liberated, the TFG must strengthen its outreach to the local population and form new regional entities in line with the Transitional Federal Charter. On the military front, we must not exclude the incorporation of new forces and the expansion of AMISOM. We are undertaking a joint assessment on the ground and will revert to this Council with a proposal.

In the meantime, I echo the African Union and AMISOM troop contributors and ask you to reconsider the financial and logistical arrangements for supporting AMISOM operations in the next phase. We must also boost our efforts to safeguard civilians and the safety of the relief supply route. I have urged the Government of Kenya, AMISOM and the TFG to uphold the right of civilians, refugees and Somalis asylum-seekers.

Prior to my visit, I met with President Mwai Kibaki of Kenya in Nairobi. I expressed my gratitude for his leadership and asked for his continued generosity and support to those fleeing Somalia. I also visited the Dadaab refugee complex in Kenya. It now hosts almost half a million Somali refugees – including more than 190,000 people fleeing famine and insecurity in the past year. I met one family that had lost two children during their hard journey. I was deeply moved and saddened by their suffering. I assured all parties of our strong commitment to ending the transition so these refugees can return home and rebuild their lives.

Generous donor contributions and concerted relief efforts have saved hundreds of thousands of lives. Parts of southern Somalia have been lifted out of famine. However, millions are still in crisis. To add to the suffering, on 28 November, Al-Shabaab occupied the compounds of sixteen organizations operating in areas under its control in South-Central Somalia. I condemn these actions and once again call on all parties to immediately allow unimpeded humanitarian access and to refrain from actions which threaten the safety of Somalis and those assisting them.

Recent developments and our work in Somalia are detailed in the report before you. I renew my thanks to my Special Representative, Mr. Mahiga, and to all our colleagues and partners who serve in such difficult and dangerous circumstances. I look forward to attending the high level meeting on Somalia that Prime Minister Cameron intends to organize in London early next year. This is a crucial moment for the international community. We must seize this moment for the people of Somalia and the stability of the region.

Remarks at UN Memorial Cemetery in Korea

Today we honour the 2,300 fallen heroes from eleven countries who found their final rest in this quiet and sacred place. As Secretary-General of the United Nations, as a Korean and above all as a citizen of our world I pay my deepest respects to the 2,300 fallen heroes. More than half a century ago, they stood against communist aggression. They fought and died so that we could be here today, living in larger freedom. We shall never forget them.

This is the only United Nations cemetery in the world. And I am the first United Nations Secretary-General to visit these hallowed grounds. It is a deep and profoundly moving privilege to be here with you. As a Korean, you are my countrymen; my brothers and sisters. To the veterans among you, especially, I offer the thanks and best wishes of a grateful world and a United Nations that is indebted to your service and your sacrifice. I also thank the citizens of Busan, who come each day to lay wreaths of remembrance. You will always be in my thoughts.

This place has special meaning for me, personally. As a young boy, I watched the United Nations-blue flag fly. I knew many of the soldiers who defended my country. They were brave and they were kind. You remember, then, that Korea was on the verge of collapse. It was the courage of soldiers from sixteen peace-loving nations and the support of five others who saved Korea from tyranny and helped to bring us to where we are today.

> 66 **This place has special meaning for me. As a young boy, I watched the United Nations blue flag fly. I knew many of the soldiers who defended my country. They were brave and they were kind.** 99

Now, as Secretary-General of the United Nations, I am pleased to see this sacred place has become a beautiful monument to the brave UN soldiers who gave their lives for a noble ideal: the vision of collective security enshrined in the UN Charter.

This United Nations Memorial Cemetery is proof that countries and peoples of all cultures, faiths and geographies can unite to fight for universal principles: freedom, justice, democracy.

To the families of those who rest here, to their descendants and my fellow countrymen, I say: thank you on behalf of the grateful people of the Republic of Korea. Thank you on behalf of the United Nations.

Let me conclude with a wise and ancient saying: "What you give, you shall receive." During the war, this port of Busan was the gateway for UN troops to Korea. Today, Busan is where Korea sends forth its own peacekeepers into the world. More recently, I am grateful that the Korean Government has chosen to send a peacekeeping contribution to the new nation of South Sudan. And so we come full circle, past to present. What an inspiration.

Today, we remember those who fell in freedom's name, and we remember the families and communities that still suffer from the war's grim legacy. Let us recommit ourselves to reuniting this Peninsula so that all Koreans can live in peace and prosperity for generations to come. I will leave all the more determined to carry forward the cause of peace for which these heroes gave their lives.

Remarks at Press Conference

TRIPOLI, 2 NOVEMBER 2011

It is a great honour for me to be visiting at this historic time in Libya – a liberated and new Libya, together with the President of the General Assembly of the United Nations. We are here together to send our strong support and admiration and respect for all your heroic struggles to achieve democracy and freedom.

I salute the brave people of Libya. You have paid a heavy price for freedom. To the families of those who died in liberating your country, please accept my deepest condolences and sympathy. To the many thousand people who have been wounded, I wish you all a speedy recovery and happiness. Your injuries are a testament to your courage and determination.

I have just had a good and very productive meeting with Chairman Jalil of the National Transitional Council and the new Prime Minister, Abdulrahim el-Keib. This meeting, together with the two leaders and all the members of the National Transitional Council was very productive and useful for us to know how we can, how the United Nations can help the Libyan people in overcoming all the challenges lying ahead after this liberation.

All expressed a clear commitment to building a democratic Libya, grounded in respect for human rights and the dignity of every woman, man and child. The new Libya aspires to be a nation free from fear, free from injustice and free from the oppression of the past. The United Nations will be your partner in turning those hopes to reality.

> " The new Libya aspires to be a nation free from fear, free from injustice and free from the oppression of the past. The United Nations will be your partner in turning those hopes to reality. "

The path to democracy is not easy. Building a state with effective and accountable institutions takes time. But the Libyan people have shown that they have the skills, resources, determination and will to rise to these challenges.

In my remarks to the National Transitional Council, I said frankly that there is no magic formula, no one size that fits all. But there is at least one common denominator in any solid democracy - that is inclusiveness and dialogue. As Libya moves forward, it is critical that you find consensus on major issues, that you remain united. That, in turn, will require a great deal of pragmatism and compromise, especially during this very important initial phase.

We spoke at length about public security and the need to secure the arsenals of the previous regime, particularly stocks of shoulder-fired missiles and chemical and biological weapons. And we recognized the centrality of human rights and the rule of law. Issues of transnational justice must be resolved with wisdom and restraint. It is important to hold perpetrators of human rights crimes to account, as well as to promote national reconciliation.

Women and young people helped win the revolution. They deserve to participate fully in the decisions and emerging institutions that will shape their future. The role of civil society and non-governmental organizations is key. Very shortly, I will have a meeting with a number of their representatives of civil society. The United Nations stands ready to support the Libyan people in all the areas we discussed: elections, a new constitution, human rights, public security and the control of weapons.

Libyans inspired the world in throwing off tyranny. In building a future of peace and dignity for all, I am confident that you will inspire the world once again. Let me repeat: the United Nations is here to help – we are ready to provide all necessary technical assistance an logistics in every way we can, in any way you choose. That is why we have come to Tripoli. And today, I say to you from the heart: *Mabrouk Libya al-Hurra. Shukran jazeelan.*

Remarks at ceremony marking the independence of South Sudan

JUBA, 9 JULY 2011

On behalf of the United Nations, on behalf of the international community, I greet the eight million citizens of the Republic of South Sudan, and on this great and momentous occasion, I send all of you our very best wishes for a peaceful, prosperous and happy future as the newest nation in Africa and as the newest nation on earth!

Today, we witness history. The birth of this new nation marks the culmination of a long struggle. A struggle that saw terrible violence, a struggle that destroyed so many lives, for so many years. Today, we open a new chapter: a day when the people of South Sudan claim the freedom and dignity that are their birthright. I commend you both for having come so far. Both of you have made difficult decisions and compromises. Seeing both of you here today testifies to your common commitment to peace and partnership.

We gather in celebration, but we are mindful of the enormous challenges ahead: deep poverty, lack of basic infrastructure and institutions of government, political insecurity. And yet, at the same time, we must not underestimate South Sudan's remarkable potential. Its resilient and talented people, abundant natural resources, huge areas of arable land, and the great Nile running through it. With these assets, South Sudan could grow into a prosperous, productive nation capable of meeting the needs of its people.

But it cannot do so alone. Alone, South Sudan cannot meet the challenges it faces nor realize its potential. Doing so will require partnership, a full and on-going engagement with the international community and, most especially, its own neighbours. That is why we are here today, because we are committed to helping South Sudan shape its future.

As we look toward that future, we must acknowledge the past. As the South separates from the North, we must recognize the ties that continue to bind them: ties of culture, politics and economics. Though the North and South Sudanese people now belong to different countries, they will continue to live side by side. Trade will continue across their common border. Nomadic groups will continue their seasonal migrations. The waters of the Nile will continue to flow from South to North. A viable South will need a viable North. And vice versa.

Today is therefore a day for the North and the South to reaffirm their common heritage and mutual interdependence. It is an opportunity to renew their commitment to building peaceful and productive relations and to face their common future as partners. With this in mind, let us remember that key aspects of the peace process have not been completed.

The referendum in Abyei has yet to take place. The voices of the people of Southern Kordofan and Blue Nile have not yet been heard in popular consultations. And in recent weeks we have seen new violence and human suffering, inflamed by potentially dangerous rhetoric. So, today, let this be a moment for North and South to declare, unequivocally, that they remain committed to addressing the unfinished business of the Comprehensive Peace Agreement. Let differences be resolved around the negotiating table. Let us accept that sovereignty is both a right and a great responsibility.

> **" To the people of South Sudan, we offer a solemn pledge: as you work to build your country as you strive for peace and prosperity, we will work with you, partners for peace and prosperity. "**

South Sudan's success will be measured by how well it serves its citizens. The basic rights of a modern, democratic state must be guaranteed: free expression, full political rights for all, including women and young people, inclusive institutions of government that can provide stability and opportunity South Sudan is wonderfully diverse. It should find strength in that diversity.

In closing, I would like to say that this is an important day for the United Nations, as well. We have been engaged in the quest for peace in Sudan for many years, through peacekeeping and diplomacy, through humanitarian assistance and development. The African Union, international NGOs, individual Member States and many others have been strong and close partners. We gratefully acknowledge their role in accompanying the Sudanese, from the North and South, along this bumpy road, recognizing in particular the contribution of the African Union high-level panel under the chairmanship of President Thabo Mbeki.

Together, we welcome the Republic of South Sudan to the community of nations. Together, we affirm our commitment to helping it meet its many responsibilities as a nation. Today, a new United Nations mission begins its work. Our mandate: to help South Sudan establish effective institutions of governance and deliver on the high hopes of its people.

The presence of so many world leaders in itself confirms the engagement and good will of the international community. Congratulations to all who made this great day possible.

And to the people of South Sudan, we offer a solemn pledge: as you work to build your country, as you strive for peace and prosperity, we will work with you, partners for peace and prosperity.

Shukran wa mobruk le intum nas ta junub Sudan! Thank you and congratulations to the people of South Sudan!

Address to the Sofia Platform

I am very much honoured to be among you – leaders, great thinkers, activists from across Europe and around the world.

Twenty years ago, when revolution swept Eastern Europe, I was a career diplomat, stationed in Washington. But my heart was in Prague, Berlin, Budapest, Warsaw and Sofia - cheering you from afar.

I remember how powerful my emotions were, for in a small way this was my story as well. As a university student, long ago, I was one of tens of thousands of students who went into the streets, shouting for greater freedom, liberty and democracy. I believe I was one of many small seeds, planted in those days that grew to allow Koreans to realize the democracy and economic prosperity that they enjoy today. I relived these emotions, watching the great changes in the Arab world.

In recent weeks, I have visited the region – Tunisia, Egypt several times, and elsewhere. All was in flux. What once was down is up; what was up is down. Everywhere I found the euphoria of the new, the enthusiasm of fresh possibilities. "Welcome to a new Egypt," I was told in Cairo – not once, but again and again. In Tunis, it was the same: "Welcome to a free Tunisia," people said. Everyone spoke the new language of democracy, openness, freedom and human rights.

I went to listen to the new voices that emerged with these once-in-a-generation events. But more, I went to show solidarity and offer a helping hand. The revolutions in Tunisia and Egypt represent one of the greatest opportunities to advance democracy and human rights in a generation. Yet we all know: success cannot be assumed. It will require the strong support of the entire international community.

That is why you are here. And rightly so, you are looking for ways to apply the lessons learned from the European experience of 1989 to the here and now. You have experience and good advice to offer: how to build democracy, how to enhance good governance, how to support civil society, dismantle a police state and establish the rule of law.

Yet despite all the hopeful similarities, let us also remember the differences. For one, the revolutions of twenty years ago were more or less assured a happy ending. There was a more or less certain destination – a "return to Europe" for nations long cut off behind the Iron Curtain. Within eleven months of the fall of the Berlin Wall, the former East Germany joined the Federal Republic – with immediate benefits.

Other nations could look forward to joining the European Union – some sooner, some later, but all with high expectations of social and economic advancement. Meanwhile, foreign investment flowed in.

A second important difference: the revolutions of 1989 were more or less "velvet." They were largely free of bloodshed. None of this is so with the Arab revolutions. No guardian angels hover in the wings. The ultimate destination is far from clear. The possibilities are far more open, even dangerous.

Look at Bahrain. Yemen. Syria. Rather than negotiating, rather than listening to their people's legitimate aspirations for change, these governments are responding with force.

Just before coming to Sofia, I spoke with President al-Assad of Syria. This was my third call to him, and a lengthy one. We were arguing. "Why do you keep calling me?" he said. I told him that, as Secretary-General, I do not interfere with internal politics. But when it comes to fundamental human rights, when there is a clear violation of those rights, I will speak out. Stop the violence now, I told him. I advised him, strongly, to do what I have advised all other leaders in the region: listen to your people, really listen to what they are asking. Hear their aspirations. Make bold reforms. Change before it is too late.

> 66 Today, we are moving decisively towards a new age of sovereignty as responsibility, an era where those who commit crimes against humanity and violate the human rights of their people will be held accountable. 99

In Libya, the situation is worse. Yet in response, the international community has been united, and not only united, but swift, very bold and very decisive. Not at any time in the past, in fact, have we seen such decisiveness in common purpose.

And in taking this strong stand, we have stood against the shadow of the past. In Rwanda, so many years ago, UN peacekeepers were on the ground. We had ample warning of what was to happen. And yet we did not act. The peacekeepers were constrained by too narrow a mandate. And so, 800,000 innocent people perished. In Bosnia, during the war, we also had peacekeepers. We created safe havens. How the gods must laugh at that phrase, in the aftermath of Srebrenica where thousands of people were murdered. Today, we have learned a lesson, I believe. World leaders have resolved that, never again, would there be another Rwanda, another Srebrenica. Today, we are acting. In Libya, Security Council resolutions 1970 and 1973 authorize us to take "all necessary measures" to protect Libyan civilians from harm. That is why NATO is enforcing a no-fly zone and why military operations are targeting heavy weaponry that the Libyan government has used to lay siege to cities.

We are working for a political solution. My Special Envoy has travelled to Libya six times in recent weeks, to Tripoli and to Benghazi and meeting all sides. But these political efforts underscore a basic truth: the Libyan people must be free to determine their future. That is the only lasting path to peace.

We are being tested elsewhere, as well. Late last year, the incumbent president of Cote d'Ivoire was defeated in fair elections but then refused to step down. He defied repeated calls from the international community – the Economic Community of West African States, the African Union, the UN Security Council itself. He exploited ethnic tensions to retain power, imported mercenaries and used heavy weapons on civilians. One million people have been displaced - a thriving economy was brought to a standstill.

Throughout, the international community stood firm on principle: that in a democracy, people have the right to choose their leaders. Last month, the man who broke this democratic trust was finally ousted. A duly-elected new president has taken office, determined to bring peace, promote reconciliation, rebuild his country and restore normal life. We cannot call this victory. Too many people have died; too much damage has been done. Yet let me emphasize nonetheless: this was a milestone. The international community stood firm on a fundamental principle, and it did not back down.

What is happening in Libya, Côte d'Ivoire and elsewhere is an historic precedent, a watershed in the emerging doctrine of the responsibility to protect. Never again, world leaders resolved in 2005 after the tragedies in Rwanda and Srebrenica. They enunciated this new doctrine: the responsibility to protect. Today, the age of impunity is dead. Today, we are moving decisively towards a new age of sovereignty as responsibility, an era where those who commit crimes against humanity and violate the human rights of their people will be held accountable. More broadly, we can expect that in the future the Security Council will increasingly place civilian protection at the center of the UN's peace and security agenda.

Let me be clear on another point, as well: at no time has the UN exceeded its Security Council mandates. In Côte d'Ivoire, UN forces undertook a limited military operation whose sole purpose was to protect innocent people. The only targets of armed action were the heavy weapons used by the former regime to attack civilians and our own headquarters and peacekeepers. We are observing the same discipline, and the same principles in Libya.

I understand that not everyone may agree on these issues. Even some of my own advisers have come to me, in recent months, telling me that the United Nations should always be neutral. This is wrong, I say. It is a mistaken understanding of the UN's responsibilities and obligations under the Charter. Yes, it is true: the UN should be impartial. But neutral – how can the UN be neutral in the face of gross violations of human rights? How can the UN stay silent, not act, in the face of basic challenges to its core values? In these matters, the United Nations must be strong. It must be firm and unyielding in defense of our most fundamental principles.

Let me close by quoting President Zhelev, who could not be here today: without the principles laid down in the United Nations Charter and the Universal Declaration of Human Rights, he has said, the 1989 velvet revolutions would never have been. These principles embodied the promise of social progress, a higher standard of living through individual choice and free enterprise and, most importantly, justice, dignity and freedom under the rule of law.

So it is today, in a different time and place. It is up to us to help. It is up to us to stand with the region's people. That is why we are here, together, in Sofia. To show solidarity. To offer a hand to those in need. To stand for fundamental principles – all in the name of our common humanity.

Remarks to civil society groups

L et me begin by saying what an honor it is to be here with you today. Profound and dramatic changes are sweeping the Arab world. And you, the brave people of Tunisia, have led the way. You are the vanguard of the most epic events of the new century – the revolutions of 2011.

The history of human progress is a history of struggle. That struggle may be moral. It may be physical. It may be both, as it was here. No change, great or small, comes without demand – the voice of the people speaking as one. Your demand for freedom, dignity and social justice has echoed throughout the world.

Earlier today, I had a chance to visit the Qasbah: the streets where you gathered by the thousands; the streets where you chanted the words of the poet Abu al-Qasim al-Shabi: "If, one day, a people desire to live, then fate will answer their call."

Fate has answered your call. The chains of injustice have been broken. And yet we know: the way ahead will be hard. That is why I have come. I wanted to be here with you, where it all began, to express my solidarity and to offer help.

For decades, the United Nations has been your partner. Today, in a new Tunisia, I hope we can prove ourselves an even better partner. And so I have instructed our entire UN team to engage not only with the new government but also the whole of civil society. That includes you.

Let us remember: the victory of the Tunisian people – a testament to the power of the many – began with the courage of one; the lone act of self-sacrifice by an ordinary young man put in motion an extraordinary chain of events. Mohamed Bouazizi's story is as tragic as it is inspiring.

He died in despair; not for lack of a job or livelihood, however modest. No, the real violation was the affront to Mohamed Bouazizi's sense of human dignity. That was the real crime, against him and so many others: the daily indignities, the crushing of a people's potential, his own aspirations and spirit. "No more," he said.

His cry resonated so widely that Tunisia, and the rest of the Arab world, will never be the same. We must not forget the essential meaning of Mohamed Bouazizi's death. It reminds us of something essential – a moral absolute: individuals matter. Individual choices, individual commitment, individual worth, individual leadership. And that is why we have gathered this afternoon. Because your leadership matters – each and every one of you, working together in common cause for a better future for all.

And you are showing a new way of leadership: a leadership based not on personalities but values and high principle. You have shown that the role of government is to work for the people, not exploit them. Your campaign for change has only begun. There are grave risks, as we see elsewhere.

As you chart the future, however, you enjoy important advantages. Tunisia has long been a crossroads for trade, culture and ideas. You draw strength and wisdom from many traditions, over many centuries. You embrace universal values, live in harmony and a spirit of tolerance and mutual respect.

Already, you have a map for the way forward. Most important, you have chosen this path through peaceful consensus. A democratic transition is well under way – toward a nation of the people, by the people and for the people.

In July, you will elect a constitutional assembly charged with drafting a new constitution founded on universal human rights, the rule of law, and political and social pluralism. You are putting in place other essential building blocks of a free and prosperous society: representative political parties and guarantees of free and fair elections; a reformed security sector and independent judiciary that will guarantee human rights and not infringe on them. A free and open media. Social justice and equal opportunity – for women and men, in cities and the countryside, on the coast and in the south.

Keeping Tunisia on this progressive path requires an active and engaged civil society. Governments can only be held accountable by a vigilant people.

> ❝ No change, great or small, comes without demand— the voice of the people speaking as one. Your demand for freedom, dignity and social justice has echoed throughout the world. ❞

Through decades of repression, you kept a dream alive: the fundamental principle that freedom of association, freedom of speech and freedom of opportunity are inalienable human rights. Now, your day has come. Now, you will help to promote civic education. You will speak out against corruption and abuse of power. You will press for good governance and reform that is concrete, not cosmetic. You will fight for women's rights and full participation in your country's politics and society. You are the voice of the people. That is your role. That is your sacred duty, hallowed by all you have fought for and those whose blood was shed.

The United Nations stands ready to help. Our expertise covers the spectrum of challenges before you: supporting elections. Building transparent and trustworthy institutions. Reducing inequality. Advancing inclusive development and creating jobs. We have helped many countries through difficult transitions. Your own countryman, Hedi Annabi – the head of our UN mission in Haiti, who died in last year's earthquake – dedicated his life to helping Haitians find the dignity and freedoms that you seek today. Our people, our lessons learned, our best practices, our technical assistance: all this is at your disposal, should you wish.

Let me close by saying that your future is yours alone. In the evolution of democratic transition, there is no single way, no one set of rules. That said, successful transitions share common aspects. In my discussions today with ministers of the interim government, I stressed the importance of compromise, accommodation and consensus-building. I welcomed the steps being taken to prepare for elections to a constitutional assembly and others that will follow.

In tandem, it will be essential to hold open and inclusive discussions with the widest range of social organizations – a national dialogue that includes political parties and civil society groups.

It is also essential that election authorities have the public's confidence, that political candidates compete on equal footing, that all eligible voters are enfranchised, and that there are credible mechanisms for fairly and quickly resolving disputes.

At the request of the interim authorities, the United Nations will soon deploy a team of experts to advise on these issues. I urge you to fully engage in the election process. By mobilizing volunteers and sending election observers throughout the country, you can enhance the transparency and legitimacy of the vote and ensure the election of an inclusive Constituent Assembly.

Your leadership, your commitment, can make Tunisia a model for the Arab world and all those who seek a new beginning. The region needs a prosperous, democratic Tunisia. And the world needs a prosperous, democratic region – a region whose rulers listen to their people; where human rights are respected and justice is served; where national wealth and human capital are invested in education, science and better living standards for all; where girls can dream; where conflict gives way to peace.

This history is yours to write. You sang its opening verses in the street, resounding around the world: show us how to turn the dark of night into a guiding light; show us how to grow a jasmine from a wounded heart; show us how to turn our hearts into flowers for our homeland, and a healing kiss for every wound.

Listening to the people: a changing Arab World and the United Nations

CAIRO, 21 MARCH 2011

Thank you for your warm welcome. I am very impressed and overwhelmed by such a warm, wholehearted welcome.

This is a very vibrant, democratic society. Everybody has freedom of expression. I have been urging and stressing that everybody should have freedom of expression and freedom of assembly. This is what I have been urging the authorities to allow.

During my time here I have experienced a different kind of welcome. I have seen many people demonstrating near the Prime Minister's office. I was a little bit alarmed that they were welcoming me again, but I realized that they were welcoming your Prime Minister.

It is a great honour and pleasure for me to visit Egypt. This is a very historic and exciting and dramatic time of change. For that, I feel a sense of responsibility: how can the United Nations do more to help you and your people – the young, women and civil society – so that they can express their own will to the Government leaders so that the Government leaders can reflect their wishes and challenges in national policies. That is the main purpose of my coming.

Another purpose of my coming is to demonstrate my firm solidarity, the firm solidarity of the United Nations and the international community. You have received many other international leaders here, and I am one of them, but I convey the message of the United Nations to all of you, wishing you a more democratic, prosperous, more stable society of Egypt.

Egypt has been playing a very important role in this region, and your progress – fuller democracy, fuller participatory democracy – will have a significant impact on countries across the region. And even beyond this region. While you are building your democracy and prosperous society, you should also keep in mind that what you are doing will have a very important meaning to other parts of the world.

We have seen such situations in many places in this area, starting from Tunisia, Egypt, Bahrain, Yemen and elsewhere. The most serious is taking place in Libya. The Security Council has taken a very decisive and historic decision by adopting two resolutions under Chapter VII of the United Nations Charter – 1970 and 1973 – authorizing all Member States of the United Nations to use "all necessary measures" including the declaration of a no-fly zone.

Decisive action has already been taken. The main purpose of this action is to protect civilians, to save lives from indiscriminate attacks. Using airplanes, helicopters, tanks – this is totally unacceptable. This is a violation of international human rights law, international humanitarian law.

I would like to discuss with you today this very important situation, how we can work together to bring peace and stability and to bring fuller democracy, fundamental rights, and the fundamental principles of human rights.

You have changed, you have just entered into a new world from an old one. When one age ends, another begins. When the soul of a nation and a people, long asleep, awakens and finds its voice. You, today, are that voice, the voice of change, the voice and face of Egypt's future.

Friends and admirers of your great country cheer you on, sharing in your pride and the promise that Egypt is once again on the move. Those who gathered on Tahrir Square inspired the world with a call for unity and change. It was above all a moral call, sounding with exquisite clarity. And you answered – from every corner of Egypt, from around the world. *Kullena masreyeen.* Today, we are all Egyptians.

I have come to Cairo to demonstrate solidarity, but more importantly to listen, to listen to your aspirations, to listen to your concerns. What do you expect of the United Nations? How can the international community help you? The process toward democracy is Egyptian-owned, Egyptian-led. Nobody can interfere in your future. Nobody can interfere in your domestic political affairs.

I am here to offer a helping hand. The United Nations has an accumulated experience and know-how, in the electoral process, constitution drafting, and promoting and helping in establishing rule of law and promoting human rights. These are all what I am going to discuss with you.

Your victory came down to something older and far more deeply human. It came down to courage. The courage to stand for justice. To demand your rights and reclaim your dignity. To come together in the name of the Egyptian people to build a better future for all. Young and old, women and men, Muslims and Copts, from the Delta to the upper Nile. And they changed Egypt. Let us honour them.

At this moment, I ask you to please join me in a moment of silence for those who lost their lives in the name of freedom and human rights, in Egypt and elsewhere in the Arab world. May their sacrifices not be in vain.

There is no going back. Yesterday and today, I met with the Supreme Council of the Armed Forces, as well as your new Prime Minister and other senior officials. All Egyptians look to them to discharge their responsibilities to the nation.

I commended the Council for their public commitment to a democratic transition. But I also asked them to listen to the many voices of society in charting the course ahead. I urged them to lift the state of emergency well before elections. I emphasized the importance of fair and transparent elections, according to a mutually

agreed road-map. I stressed the need for a transparent and inclusive national dialogue that spans the full spectrum of Egyptian society.

Your ancestors built the wonders of the ancient world. We look to you, today,
to inspire us once more, to build a modern-day pyramid of democracy in the heart
of the Arab world.

This weekend, you took an important step. Millions of Egyptians turned out to
vote in Saturday's referendum - many of you for the first time. Now you must lay a
firm foundation, including free and fair elections and a new constitution, grounded in universal human rights, the rule of law and political and political and social
pluralism.

**❝❝ I have come to Cairo to demonstrate solidarity,
but more importantly to listen, to listen to your
aspirations, to listen to your concerns. This process
toward democracy is Egyptian owned, Egyptian led.
Nobody can interfere in your future. ❞❞**

I am confident that you will quickly put in place other essential building blocks.
Free and vibrant political parties. A fully inclusive Constituent Assembly. New programmes for social equity and inclusive economic growth. A renewed emphasis on
quality education. Open space for the civil society groups driving change. Equal
rights for women and minorities. Full freedom of religion, media and assembly.

In all this, the United Nations can be your partner. For a decade, we called attention to the problems. The United Nations' Arab Human Development Reports
warned of the pressures building toward explosion. Since 2002 we have been pre-
senting these recommendations through our reports.

We have been a reliable development partner. We have worked to create jobs,
reduce food insecurity and save children from dying of preventable diseases. We
have sought to advance girls' education and promote gender equity and women's
empowerment. On gender equality and empowerment, I have emphasized to the
leadership that this is a vital moment, now, before it is too late, you must do more to
improve women's empowerment and social status.

Yet clearly, we, too, must do a better job of listening and speaking out – in Egypt
and elsewhere in the region. That is my pledge to today to you. My message is that
the United Nations is your United Nations. We are as excited as you about the prospect of new space opening up, a new era of responsive, effective governance.

Your future is yours, and yours alone, but the United Nations stands ready to
help in every way possible. We have vast experience in assisting countries through
delicate transitions. In Europe, Latin America, the Middle East, Africa and Asia we
have helped to organize free and fair elections and build transparent civic institu-

tions. This knowledge, these experiences, may prove useful. Our people are ready to work with you if needed and if asked.

Already, I am urging the international community to provide ambitious economic and financial assistance to Egypt. I am concerned that rising food prices will make it even more difficult for ordinary Egyptians to feed their families. I want all Egyptians to have medical care and a decent education. These are not luxuries. They are human rights. And they are rights that must be fully shared by those who have been disenfranchised for too long: women and young people.

> ❝ There is a different reality. A future of education and invention, of freedom and good governance, of the empowerment of women and opportunities for young people. ❞

For too long, Egypt's young men and women have searched in vain for opportunities to exercise their talents and pursue their dreams. Some have coined a name for this stage of life: "waithood." Not quite adulthood, but rather a kind of limbo where young people spend their days in long unemployment lines: Waiting for a job, waiting to earn enough to marry and have a family, waiting to own a home, waiting for life to begin.

There is a different reality. A future of education and invention, of freedom and good governance, of the empowerment of women and opportunities for young people. I believe the people of Egypt and the region can create this future for themselves. It is a future that we can help create together. No more waiting for tomorrow, particularly for young people!

Let me close by saying: your success is not for you alone. Egypt is a model. If you succeed here, the rest of the Arab world can hope. Yes, the wind of change is sweeping in this part of the world. From Tunisia and Egypt to Bahrain, Yemen and beyond.

Egypt was fortunate that change came without greater violence. This is a great tribute to your country and its people. The situation in Libya stands in stark contrast. The UN Security Council directed Member States to "take all necessary measures" to protect civilians and save lives, including the declaration of a no-fly zone. On Saturday, in Paris, I met with world leaders to coordinate our plans for immediate and effective action. We will continue to do our utmost to end hostilities and find a political solution. We put special emphasis on providing humanitarian aid to those in need. Please know: we take particular pride in the United Nations' role in helping tens of thousands of Egyptians return safely home.

My hope is that an Egypt, reborn, can help produce a Middle East, reborn: a Middle East with dignity and justice for all, a Middle East that is prosperous and at peace. The road ahead will be hard. My own country, the Republic of Korea, also experienced a long and difficult transition. After decades of military rule, it evolved into what it is today: a robust democracy and one of the strongest and biggest economies in the world.

There, too, at that time, students initiated the protests that set Korea on its current path. I remember well. I was a student of the University. I was there, together with many students, shouting and yearning for democracy. We came together in great numbers, which gave us strength.

You began writing a new chapter of your nation's history. I urge you to keep fighting – peacefully, without violence, but with passion and commitment for change. Work with others – your fellow students, your family, your neighbours, your community and your nation's minority groups. Listen to others, including those you disagree with.

Remember that nothing great is built without cooperation, compromise and common cause. Remember the call: *Kullena masreyeen*. This is Egypt's moment.

The Cyril Foster Lecture: human protection and the 21st century United Nations

OXFORD, 2 FEBRUARY 2011

I am honoured to have this opportunity after my distinguished predecessors, as fourth United Nations Secretary-General to speak before you in this very esteemed and one of the oldest universities. It is an honour to be part of the Oxford community, if only for a day.

Few universities have produced so much scholarship on the United Nations, or so many dedicated international civil servants. Among those have been the late Marrack Goulding, the legendary Brian Urquhart, Kieran Prendergast and John Holmes, with whom I have worked when he served as UN Under-Secretary-General for Humanitarian Affairs our Special Envoys Prime Minister Tony Blair and former U.S. President Bill Clinton.

My talk tonight has long been advertised as one devoted to the subject of human protection. And indeed, I will speak to you at length on that very important challenge.

But of course, our attention continues to be riveted on the events unfolding in Egypt. So let me say in just a few words how I assess the situation in Egypt. In fact, this afternoon I had a very good discussion in a bilateral meeting with Prime Minister David Cameron and again we discussed at length this situation. I have been closely following the reports from Egypt.

The protests reflect the great frustration of the Egyptian people about the lack of change over the past few decades. This discontent calls for bold reforms, not repression. The United Nations has been warning about the democracy deficit and other challenges in the Arab world through successive Human Development Reports dating back to 2002.

I am concerned at the growing violence in Egypt. I once again urge all sides to exercise restraint. I condemn any attack against peaceful protest. Such acts are unacceptable. It is important at this important juncture to ensure an orderly and peaceful transition. I urge all parties to engage in such a process without delay, with full respect for human rights, in particular the freedoms of expression, association and information. We should not underestimate the danger of instability across the Middle East. The United Nations stands ready to support reform efforts aimed at meeting the people's aspirations.

The Cyril Foster lecture has become a rite of passage at the United Nations. Three of my distinguished predecessors have made the pilgrimage - Javier Pérez de Cuéllar, Boutros Boutros-Ghali and Kofi Annan. Secretaries-General are often better advised to listen than to lecture. Yet there are times when we should use our "bully pulpit" to address the peoples' concerns, particularly when it comes to this important pillar of the United Nations: human rights.

That is why I would like to talk to you tonight about human protection and the UN. In addressing this very broad topic, let me begin with a few distinctions.

Human protection is a subset of the more encompassing concept of human security. The latter reminds us that the security of "we the peoples" matters every bit as much as the security of states. Human protection addresses more immediate threats to the survival of individuals and groups.

Even with these distinctions, I will have to be selective in citing examples of our human protection endeavours. I do so without diminishing what the broad UN family achieves on a daily basis in protecting people.

Indeed almost all our major initiatives, from climate change to food security, from the activities of the World Health Organization to UNICEF, are concerned with human security in the fullest sense. As I will argue, the founders of the United Nations understood that sovereignty confers responsibility, a responsibility to ensure protection of human beings from want, from war, and from repression. When that responsibility is not discharged, the international community is morally obliged to consider its duty to act in the service of human protection. This evening, I will concentrate on those issues related to human protection that have been developed under my watch.

Cyril Foster was a simple man, an ordinary man, by his own modest account. Yet he possessed an extraordinary faith in humanity's capacity to promote peace, prevent war and better the human condition.

The United Nations was born of just such an aspiration. Sixty-five years after the Member States first assembled in Westminster, we are still striving "to save succeeding generations from the scourge of war."

I was born during the last part of Second World War. As a child, I witnessed the ravages of the Korean War and the promise of peace. I learned about hunger, poverty and displacement in the ultimate classroom, personal experience. While everybody was studying in a classroom I had to study outside, under a tree. When it rained we had to wait until it turned sunny to resume class under the tree.

Against all odds, the United Nations came to our rescue. It fed my family and my people it helped rebuild our country. And it has given us hope. It continues to offer hope to our troubled peninsula. That quest, like many others, remains unfulfilled. Korea is still divided.

But I often wonder how many children, in similar straits, ask the same questions today that I did more than sixty years ago: Is the world listening? Will help arrive in time? Who will be there for me and my family? This is exactly the experience I am having these days as Secretary-General of the United Nations.

I am just back from Africa. At least in the past five times when I travelled to Africa or many other developing countries, I met many young people and children and helpless people, who are very poor and very sick, who try get help, and hope, from me and from the United Nations. So the United Nations is still a beacon of hope for millions of children. So I feel very much humbled whenever I meet them. I wonder, what can I do, how can I bring a sense of hope to them?

The task of human protection is neither simple nor easy. We do not always succeed. But we must keep trying to make a difference. That is our individual and collective responsibility. People like myself, as Secretary-General, and the leaders of the world have a moral and political responsibility to protect populations. Indeed, the struggle to fulfill the Charter's promise of protection demands the best that this and other world-class universities have to offer.

The world and its conflicts have changed significantly since the founding of the United Nations. And as the world has changed, so too must its institutions. The most enduring bend without breaking. They adjust to changing circumstances and opportunities, trimming their sails in shifting winds, knowing that the quickest route to their destination is rarely a straight line. Their pace varies, but never their guiding principles.

The challenges facing us have changed, but our core responsibility to maintain international peace and security has not. Slowly but surely, sometimes by trial and error, we have learned to use the instruments available under the Charter in new ways, adapting to evolving circumstances.

Through this evolution, the need to operationalize a concept of human protection has emerged. Gaining momentum, it is reshaping our work. It is entrenched in our operational practice. It is finding expression in the development of doctrine and in new international legal institutions. It is reflected in bolder Security Council resolutions and progressively broader mandates, and in the General Assembly's continuing consideration of the concept of Responsibility to Protect.

This evening, I will focus on three areas.

First, I will address human protection in the context of conflict and complex emergencies where the UN serves as a firefighter. We are now trying to change this, by trying to prevent the fire in the first place. This encompasses our initiatives in peacekeeping and emergency interventions in the context of disaster relief. I will also deal here with peacebuilding and peace consolidation.

Second, I will deal with prevention, so that fires do not happen in the first place. And third, human protection and the development of legal institutions promoting accountability.

First, let us look first at peacekeeping, one of our core tools for human protection. At the turn of the century, the Brahimi Report called on the UN to retool itself operationally. It identified gaps in the practice and policy of UN peacekeeping, including the need to devote resources to conflict prevention.

The search for an improved UN response to conflict has continued unabated since then, including the recent New Horizon review of practice and policy. The expansion of peacekeeping operations throughout the world we are now considering what the optimal size of the UN Peacekeeping should be. That is the concept we call New Horizon and about which I have reported to the Security Council.

Peacekeepers have been entrusted with growing responsibilities not only to keep armies at bay, but to protect civilians who are prey to militias and other combatants. This, in itself, involved very different methods of work, rules of engagement and capacities.

For example, protecting civilians necessarily implies mobility and, in difficult terrain, that means air mobility. As we repeatedly pointed out in Sudan, if we do not have helicopters, we are only able to field a static force. We would not have been able to assist with the referendum in Southern Sudan, transporting ballots and other necessities in a region the size of Eastern Europe. If we are not properly equipped, that would radically undermine our capacity to protect civilians.

Acting by consensus, the Security Council has repeatedly placed civilian protection at the operational centre of the United Nations' peace and security agenda.

Darfur is just one recent example where the Council stressed this objective. Securing the required resources and troops has consumed much of my energy. I have been begging leaders to make resources available to us. That experience underscores what can happen when Member States fail to provide the resources necessary to carry out the Council's mandates.

> **66 The task of human protection is neither simple nor easy. We do not always succeed. But we must keep trying to make a difference. That is our individual and collective responsibility. 99**

Today, more than 120,000 soldiers, police and civilians serve under the United Nations flag in fifteen theatres around the world. Support services have dramatically improved by the reorganizations undertaken at the beginning of my term. More and more frequently, peacekeepers are subject to contradictory pressures within countries. They often face perilous challenges that strain the very credibility of the mission.

For example, our mandate may provide for civilian protection yet a host government may interpret its terms differently, as we have seen recently in Sudan, Chad, and the Democratic Republic of Congo.

Today, we face another challenge in Côte d'Ivoire, where the former leader clings to power despite the united demand of the international community and the democratic will of the people. This is just an unacceptable. I arrived this morning from the African Union Summit. I am pleased to report that the United Nations has taken a strong and unequivocal stand, in step with the African Union and the Economic Community of West African States. The rule of law, human rights and the future of democracy are at stake, as well as the integrity of the African Union and to some extent that of the United Nations.

Our mandate encompasses both guaranteeing the electoral process and protecting recently elected officials and vulnerable populations throughout the country. It is a task that must be performed in the face of direct attacks, harassment and provocation. The final chapter of this saga has yet to be written, but this we know: the growing international solidarity on protection principles gives us better tools and better chances than ever before.

Our experience has taught us that to keep the peace in volatile situations, we have to build the peace at the same time. Countries that have recently come out of conflict are the most vulnerable to suffering new ones. So the 2005 World Summit established the Peacebuilding Commission and its Support Office. They are helping us to address peacemaking, peacekeeping and peacebuilding as simultaneous and mutually reinforcing undertakings.

Protection is more than standing guard over vulnerable communities. We have learned this most painfully in trying to combat unimaginable sexual violence in armed conflict, most notably in the Democratic Republic of the Congo. This has been of great concern to me personally.

Undoubtedly, the UN needs to perform its protection duties more effectively. Our peacekeepers are upgrading their methods of patrolling and systems of communication to cover vulnerable communities more adequately in the most difficult terrain.

Again, the United Nations has been the subject of criticism. We have been asked why, when you have more than 10,000 soldiers, you are not able to protect women and girls from sexual violence? But we are talking about sometimes vast lands where there is not much transportation, not much communications. This is quite a challenge. Of course, we strengthen our patrol, we try to establish communications with the village community leaders. But it is quite difficult but we have been trying to keep all these situations from happening.

The authority of the state, I believe is the most important, and the institution with highest responsibility. Through the rule of law, through strengthening their institutional capacity, they have to carry out their primary responsibility. But we have seen in many countries, because of the weak institutional capacity, they cannot address all these very appalling situations. That is why I established the Office of Rule of Law and Security Institutions to help rebuild legal institutions and train police, prison and judicial officers in countries recovering from conflict. Without security sector reform, sustainable peace is often elusive.

At the United Nations, we need to bolster our capacities as well. We are monitoring, reporting and combating the recruitment and exploitation of children in armed conflict. On sexual violence, I have appointed, last year, a Special Representative who is devoted to and focusing in preventing, stopping this Sexual Violence in Armed Conflict by employing training, advocacy, sanctions and sometimes naming and shaming to combat sexual violence and the impunity that allows it.

There is a very important Security Council resolution, 1325, which was adopted eleven years ago. The Security Council called for the empowerment of women as a crucial protection tool. Our newest agency – UN Women, headed by former President of Chile Michelle Bachelet – will help sharpen this important element of peacekeeping and peacebuilding.

Human protection, "fire fighting," also extends to our responses to natural and manmade disasters. As well-established UN principles underscore, the safety and access of humanitarian actors responding to vulnerable communities must be assured. In conflict or disaster settings, the guarantee of humanitarian access serves to limit the political manipulation of hunger and disease.

In 2008, for example, when Myanmar was hit by Cyclone Nargis, because of these authorities just closing their borders to international humanitarian assistance, I was compelled to press Myanmar authorities to respect the principle of humanitarian access. This served the human protection imperatives even if it fell outside a strict application of the Responsibility to Protect.

Let me make this distinction clear: To me, there is a moral imperative to help a child trapped in a collapsed building in Port au Prince or to assist women and children fleeing conflict. Let me draw your attention to the Central Emergency Relief Fund, abbreviated as CERF. This was created by John Holmes as Under-Secretary-General in the United Nations, which helps speed our initial response to disasters.

When people are dying from earthquakes we have no time to lose. This CERF is the best, most effective, efficient way of delivering aid. Within twenty-four hours – or a maximum of forty-eight hours –urgent first aid assistance can be dispatched to the disaster areas. This, I believe, is one of the most successful mechanisms the UN introduced five years ago. Remember, we relied on CERF for our early response in Myanmar, Haiti, and Pakistan, to name just a few.

A core challenge for human protection is assisting those displaced by natural and manmade disasters. Our refugee agencies are helping 34 million people a day, every day. The United Nations is feeding 100 million people a day. We are working to improve protection efforts to keep the vulnerable from double jeopardy.

The best form of protection is prevention. Prevention saves lives as well as resources. When you have to deploy 10,000 soldiers, it costs billions of dollars. But if you can prevent through mediation or preventive diplomacy, you may do it, even with a few million dollars.

Prevention is not a one-off affair. Article 34 of the Charter authorizes the Security Council to investigate any situation that might lead to a dispute or threat to international peace and security. Fact-finding and mediation should not wait for conflicts to erupt.

Our renewed focus on prevention is a recognition that all conflicts are ultimately political. So we have strengthened the UN's capacities for preventive diplomacy and mediation, and to support viable peace processes that produce durable agreements. In 2010 alone, last year, we supported thirty-four different mediation, facilitation and dialogue efforts. The persistent work of UN envoys helped to ease the situation in Kyrgyzstan and Guinea and keep the transition to democracy.

We are adapting our doctrines, capacities and training, working with our partners and regional organizations. We have a group of mediation experts who are on standby, who can be deployed within seventy-two hours to any place around the world. That is why we have established a Mediation Support Unit within the Department of Political Affairs.

Nowhere is prevention needed more than during elections, especially in societies divided by or recovering from conflict. We have already experienced many such unfortunate tragedies and violence because of elections. Elections are a democratic system. It can be a rallying force, it can be a force of unity and solidarity, but sometimes it can also be a source of division and violence.

66 Accountability is now an indispensable element of the framework of protection. It is a frontal challenge to impunity. And it also serves as a powerful deterrent against potential perpetrators. 99

There will be at least twenty elections in Africa this year alone. We have seen still issues pending in Côte d'Ivoire. Properly managed, transparent elections can ease tensions and build transparent and accountable institutions. But they also entail risks.

Sudan is a case in point. We have been pleased to assist the successful conduct of the referendum in Sudan. Engagement by the United Nations and its regional partners was a key element in that referendum's success – a process that could have gone dangerously wrong.

This was also the case in Guinea, where our regional office continuously engaged the parties when the election process threatened to break down.

These situation-specific efforts have been reinforced by more generic and thematic ones. They include our efforts to limit small arms, light weapons and anti-personnel mines, as well as to eliminate nuclear weapons.

What is true for preventing manmade threats, such as armed conflict, is also true for natural disasters. The UN is looking to enhance its ability to respond immediately to disasters and to assist countries at disaster preparedness.

I have fully backed this campaign. By having good preparedness against disaster, we can save a lot of human lives. Consider two cyclones in Bangladesh, sixteen years apart: the first killed 150,000 people in Bangladesh. After sixteen years, with all these preparations, the number of dead was just over 4,000. That is a huge, huge difference. The difference was a considered investment in disaster risk reduction. Had Myanmar been able to do the same as Bangladesh for Cyclone Nargis, a storm of similar force, many of the 191,000 who died might still be alive today.

A proper treatment of the centrality of human rights as one of the United Nations' three pillars would require maybe a separate, long lecture. But tonight let me simply say that human rights are an essential component of human protection.

The last decade of the twentieth century saw unprecedented progress in international law, humanitarian law and the establishment of international legal institutions. There also was increased acceptance of international norms by Member States, at least in principle. These steps led to important human protection advances in the Outcome Document of the 2005 World Summit. The Heads of State and Government embraced a responsibility to protect. You might have heard of R2P, the responsibility to protect – protecting populations by preventing genocide, war crimes, crimes against humanity and ethnic cleansing.

The Responsibility to Protect has undergone further doctrinal elaboration and institutional expression over the last five years. When I was campaigning to become Secretary-General, I pledged that if and when I was elected as Secretary-General, I would do my best to operationalize it. This is what I have been doing for that last four years. There are some states that are still feeling uncomfortable and who have skepticism of the concept of R2P, whether this is going to be used as a tool by the big powers to interfere in their domestic politics.

However, my doctrine envisages that our efforts to prevent these awful crimes rest on three pillars: first, state responsibility; second, international responsibility to help states to succeed and third, timely and decisive response should national authorities manifestly fail to protect, including under Chapter VII, if the Security Council deems such steps necessary.

I am working with my two Special Advisors to prevent genocide and to promote the Responsibility to Protect. Both in dangerous situations and among UN Member States as a whole, it has been standard operating procedure at the world body to take these perspectives into account in times of crisis.

This summer, the General Assembly is again going to address the regional and subregional aspects of my strategy. A similar effort is under way with respect to elaborating the concept of Human Security. These parallel efforts help expand common ground for placing human protection at the centre of the UN's doctrine and operational activities.

Alongside the development of norms and rules has come legal enforcement through the tribunals established by the United Nations to ensure accountability for gross human rights violations as we have seen in Rwanda and the former Yugoslavia. This trend towards accountability, albeit in hybrid institutions, can be seen in places like Cambodia and Sierra Leone, as well as with the Special Tribunal on Lebanon.

We have welcomed the parallel establishment of the International Criminal Court, a signal advance in the age-old struggle to overcome impunity. Accountability is now an indispensable element of the framework of protection. It is a frontal challenge to impunity. And it also serves as a powerful deterrent against potential perpetrators.

As Secretary-General, I have insisted on standards of accountability, especially as they relate to conduct during conflict. This applies to our inquiry regarding the violent end to Sri Lanka's long internal war, and to the commission of inquiry in the case of the Middle East, most recently the flotilla case. We have also seen resistance to accountability efforts in Sudan and Kenya.

It is essential that we stand firm in support of the Special Tribunal in Lebanon in the name of accountability. I have been stressing that the Special Tribunal for Lebanon, being part of the international justice system, should not be the subject of political interference. The Tribunal's prosecutor and judges are independent professionals.

Here I want to note in particular the vital role of civil society in advancing contemporary standards of justice and accountability. Our valued partners have called national governments to account and mobilized international action. I think civil society, they can be the eyes, they can be the watchers, how governments are implementing all these principles of justice and accountability.

Has the Security Council gone too far in its insistence on human protection? I think not. Critics should recall that the emphasis on human protection is the legacy of tragic events and high aspirations of the last century. They are grounded in the UN's founding principles and purposes.

Article 2(7) of the Charter clearly contemplates that essentially domestic matters are the responsibility of the state, this will not preclude intervention when needed by the United Nations under Chapter VII. The drafting committee in San Francisco underscored that if fundamental freedoms and rights are "grievously outraged so as to create conditions which threaten peace or to obstruct the application of the provisions of the Charter, then they cease to be the sole concern of each state."

For some time, international protections for populations in situations of internal, transnational, or international conflict have grown. It has been almost a century and a half since the founding of the International Committee of the Red Cross and the subsequent agreement on the first Geneva Convention on the treatment of combatants. The subsequent Conventions of 1949, and the Additional Protocols of 1977, extended legal protections to civilians affected by conflict, including by conflicts of a non-international character.

And so we must ask: where do we go now, from here? Recently, I set out five core challenges to the Security Council on the Protection of Civilians in Armed Conflict:

The first is enhancing compliance with international law. Second is engaging with non-State armed groups and rebel movements to seek their compliance on critical protection issues. Third: enhancing protection through more effective and better resourced peacekeeping and other relevant missions. Fourth, improving humanitarian access. And fifth: ensuring accountability for violations.

Beyond the immediate protection agenda, the United Nations is addressing the creeping vulnerabilities. They also put populations at risk and weaken societies, and also plant the seeds of violence and conflict: water scarcity, food insecurity, corruption, transnational crimes, the effects of climate change. Climate change and water scarcity could become the source of very serious regional conflict. So it is not surprising that these human security issues are finding their way onto our peacebuilding agenda, and specifically that of the Peacebuilding Commission.

It has also become clear that in line with our more complex mandates, we need to help governments and civil society to deliver tangible peace dividends in post-conflict situations and to help them rebuild their capacity to govern. Peace will not last unless people see real benefits in real time: safety, justice, jobs, education and prospects for a better future. In general, our peace engagements are very often places with limited infrastructure. Such countries are highly vulnerable, for example, to epidemics, diseases, and infant mortality.

This means that an effective emergency civilian surge may be just as important as the deployment of peacekeeping troops. Improving our civilian capacities is key to effective delivery at an early stage and we have a major project underway to see how we can do this better.

And clearly, the 21st century United Nations must continue to focus, sharpen, and extend its work. In this regard, global power shifts have brought new voices, new partners and new opportunities. We are identifying synergies across the United Nations system, with the World Bank and other multilateral institutions.

In these efforts, we are finding ready partners in regional organizations, national governments and local actors. Chapter VIII of the United Nations Charter provides a ready framework for deeper and closer, more innovative collaboration with regional organizations, such as the African Union, where we are working together from Sudan to Côte d'Ivoire, from Guinea to Somalia.

As the Secretary-General, I am often amazed by the foresight of the drafters of the United Nations Charter. At a time when there was not a single regional organization, the drafters had the foresight that one day the United Nations would have to work closely with regional organizations. So this is quite a visionary vision.

We are also promoting cross-cultural dialogue in situations of potential conflict through the UN's Alliance of Civilizations, and warning against rising intolerance and the politics of polarization.

The United Nations was created to be an agent of change, not just an object of change. It has made history, even as it evolved with it. From its inception, the UN has been an incubator of ideas, a builder of norms, and an arbiter of standards. It remains so today. Through its actions, as well as its words, the world body has helped transform the global agenda by embracing human protection as an essential component.

This evening, I have set out a big agenda with you. So we must ask ourselves: have our strategies and our operational practice on the ground kept pace with the ever-increasing demand for human protection? We must concede that on many occasions, our words are ahead of our deeds. But I am convinced this is a challenge we can meet. Momentum is on our side.

What is required is a shared responsibility. But this cannot be done alone, without the help of governments or the help of business communities, generous philanthropists, NGOs and students like yourselves. This is a shared responsibility. Together, we can answer the cry of that child I mentioned before, trapped under the rubble of an earthquake, and people caught in the crossfire and those who are wondering: Can the world hear my call? Who will help me and my family?

This brings us full circle. The UN recognizes that human protection stands at the centre of both its purposes and principles. As Dag Hammarskjöld said, the Secretary-General can be partisan in one case only, and that is precisely in the defense of the UN's own purposes and principles.

Whenever I see all these great challenges, global and local, I cannot but be humbled by how I can address these challenges as the Secretary-General. The words of the framers of the UN Charter still ring true today. "The Secretary-General, more than anyone else, will stand for the United Nations as a whole. In the eyes of the world, he must embody the principles and ideals of the Charter."

That is why human protection will remain a hallmark of my administration, continuously striving to make our deeds match our words. "We the peoples" expect and deserve nothing less.

Remarks at High-level Meeting on Côte d'Ivoire

ADDIS ABABA, 29 JANUARY 2011

Thank you for your participation in this timely and important meeting. We face a complex and volatile situation.

Yet the goals that the Economic Community of West African States, the African Union and the UN share in Côte d'Ivoire are clear. We seek to help bring an end to a decade of crisis and avert a tragic return to civil war. We seek to protect civilians from ongoing violence, and ensure respect for the human rights and democratically-expressed will of the people.

I am greatly encouraged by yesterday's action by the African Union Peace and Security Council reaffirming the firm stands taken by ECOWAS and the African Union, and reiterating strong support for the work of the United Nations. I commend the Council for demanding the immediate removal of the siege on the Golf Hotel and an end to all violence and abuses against the civilian population. I welcome the decision to establish a high-level panel to find a political resolution to the crisis. Let me be very clear about the United Nations' role, because I have been very much troubled and concerned by misrepresentations of the role of the United Nations.

When then-President Gbagbo's term in office expired in 2005, the Ivorian parties agreed that elections were central to the process of restoring normality to their country. The framework was essentially provided by the 2005 Pretoria Agreements under the auspices of President Mbeki, and the 2007 Ouagadougou Agreement under the auspices of President Compaoré.

With the Ouagadougou Political Agreement and its supplementary texts, the Ivorian parties assumed full ownership of implementation of the peace process. The certification mandate of the United Nations was created voluntarily by the Ivorians themselves to guarantee the credibility of the elections. Throughout the three-year process, the Ivorian parties set the pace, determined the timelines and devised solutions to numerous obstacles. Nothing was imposed on the parties: not by the UN, nor by the African Union, ECOWAS or any other partner.

On 5 August 2010, then-President Gbagbo signed a decree setting 31 October 2010 as the election date, indicating his satisfaction with progress made on reunification and security issues. My Special Representative and his colleagues monitored the electoral process in a meticulous, objective and independent manner. They analyzed tally sheets from the more than 20,000 polling stations around the country, and on this basis carefully arrived at the certification determination. Let us remember that the arrangements and certification procedures for the run-off election were identical to those for the first round which had been praised by then-President Gbagbo.

Our first duty is to the people of Côte d'Ivoire. We have an obligation to remain firm and unified, and to signal to Africa's peoples that our commitment to our principles is real. We must preserve our unified position, act together, and stand firm against Mr. Gbagbo's attempt to hang on to power through the use of force.

I am deeply concerned about the hostile actions ordered by Mr. Gbagbo against UN peacekeepers. I must stress that the peacekeepers have a clear mandate from the Peace Agreements signed by then-President Gbagbo himself and other Ivorian leaders to protect President Ouattara and Prime Minister Soro. Regrettably, since 16 December, regular and irregular forces loyal to Mr. Gbagbo have obstructed movement of our peacekeepers, cut their fuel and other vital life support supplies, used live fire against them and blockaded the Golf Hotel.

> 66 Our first duty is to the people of Côte d'Ivoire. We have an obligation to remain firm and unified, and to signal to Africa's peoples that our commitment to our principles is real. 99

I am also deeply concerned about the deteriorating human rights and humanitarian situation. Since mid-December, violence has claimed more than 260 lives. More than 30,000 Ivorians have fled to neighbouring countries which could result in regional instability, and more than 17,000 have been displaced internally, with more on the move. UNHCR and other UN agencies are doing a lot to help and address humanitarian needs. Mass graves have also been reported, and UN human rights staff have been blocked from accessing these areas.

The State broadcasting service is being used as a weapon, disseminating hate messages and inciting violence. We need not look far into the past for lessons about the consequences of such actions. We must heed those lessons. All those responsible for grave acts against the Ivorian people and UN peacekeepers must be brought to justice and held responsible for their crimes.

Allow me here to express my profound admiration and support to UNOCI (United Nations Operation in Côte d'Ivoire) troops and staff working under extremely difficult and dangerous condition – and my deep gratitude to all those Member States who have contributed troops.

The positions we take today will have an impact not only on our credibility, but also on other democratic transitions and elections in divided societies. The solutions we seek must therefore be grounded in principle and promote our shared values. Above all, we must not let the Ivorian people down; we cannot allow their democratically-expressed will to be foiled.

As we look ahead, I believe there are five principles that must guide our work and your work, including that of the High-level Panel.

First, the imperative to focus on the future, not on the past. Reopening the results of the election would be a grave injustice and set an unfortunate precedent.

Second, a peaceful and honorable exit of Mr. Gbago and urging President Ouattara to form a national unity government.

Third, concrete action to remove the siege on the Golf Hotel and other obstructions to the vital work of the United Nations on the ground.

Fourth, full support for the legitimate government to effectively address social and economic challenges, promote reconciliation, and uphold human rights and justice.

Fifth, in view of the United Nations' unique role in Côte d'Ivoire, the Panel should work in close coordination with the UN in all aspects and every stage of the process. In this regard, the UN is prepared to provide a senior official to work with the team of experts that will support the Panel.

You have my personal commitment that the United Nations will work hand-in-hand with you in this crucial period and beyond. I look forward to our work together. Thank you for your leadership, commitment and resolve.

Remarks to the Parliament of Kyrgyzstan

BISHKEK, 3 APRIL 2010

alamatsizby Urmattu Myrza Janna iymdar. Greetings, ladies and gentlemen. The world knows Kyrgyzstan for the warmth of your freedom-loving people, the richness of your culture, the beauty of your ancient lands. It is a pleasure and a great honour to be here for the first time, to see and experience all this for myself.

From the epic tale of the Manas to the legendary Silk Road, you have enriched civilization with centuries of history, philosophy and exchange. Now this ancient crossroads of cultures and ideas is nearing a milestone – one that showcases your past and present, your nation's youth and vigor.

Next year marks the twentieth anniversary of independence. The United Nations has been honored to partner with you from the beginning. Despite the challenging circumstances of your early days, you immediately set ambitious goals worthy of the proud history and independent spirit of Kyrgyzstan.

I cannot put it better than the Preamble of your Constitution: "[…] guided by the ancestors' precepts to live in unity (and) peace […] to confirm our adherence to human rights and freedoms […] to establish ourselves […] as a free and democratic civil society." Your aspirations echo our common United Nations Charter.

I have come to Kyrgyzstan to offer the full support of the United Nations in realizing these universal values. I carry with me a clear message: Central Asia is central to our world. It is a player on the global stage. Your goals, your hopes, your challenges and your responses to them will help shape not only a stronger region, but a better world.

Your role is critical. As parliamentarians, you have a high responsibility for building consensus, framing new policies, building social institutions and laws, promoting democracy and political freedoms, advancing progress and social well-being. Here in Kyrgyzstan, the *Jogorku Kenesh*, the Parliament, has helped lead the way, to develop an independent state, build a market economy and take care of people's concerns, and build democratic society and institutions. The United Nations has been proud to work with you.

As parliamentarians, you also engage with diverse constituencies and listen to disparate voices: independent political parties, local associations and non-governmental organizations, women's groups and human rights associations, media organizations.

Everywhere I go, I also seek different views. It widens my understanding, helps me appreciate diversity and culture, equips me to develop fresh responses and solutions. Robust civil society, tolerance for diversity and media freedom – all are fundamental to modernization. They are essential to civil harmony and growth, prosperity, opportunity.

We live today in a new world, very different from that of two decades ago. I call this an era of renewed multilateralism, an era that rewards progress on the universal values embedded in the United Nations Charter. Justice. Tolerance. Dignity. Equality. All of this requires vigorous regional cooperation. And I encourage the nations of Central Asia to work together more closely.

> ❝ All of us who believe in the United Nations understand that security has many dimensions. It starts with people. Respect for the rights of all people. For the UN, the protection of human rights is a bedrock principle if a country is to prosper. ❞

Today, I would like to highlight three common goals for the future.

First, reducing extreme poverty. The Millennium Development Goals are the world's blueprint for reducing poverty, hunger and disease, for improving education and the environment, for establishing time-lines and benchmarks for success. A decade has passed since our world leaders, including that of Kyrgyzstan, committed to these goals. The deadline is now just over five years away. The clock is ticking.

Globally, we have made progress: on fighting malaria, polio, and other diseases; on enrolling more children in schools, especially girls. Kyrgyzstan has made significant headway. But the path is hard, and the global financial crisis has made it harder. Unemployment is rising. Remittances have declined. Food insecurity has grown. Corruption persists.

That is why the UN developed a Global Jobs Pact: more jobs for decent pay, in decent working conditions. It is why we created the new Global Impact Vulnerability Alert System – to better understand what is really happening to the poorest and the most vulnerable people around the world. And it is why I will convene a special United Nations Summit meeting focusing on the Millennium Development Goals. I look forward to strong participation from Kyrgyzstan, as well as the entire region. I was assured by President Bakiev that he would attend this Summit in September in New York.

The world can benefit from your experiences and ideas. As one landlocked country, as one of the developing countries, you have to share your challenges and concerns with the world.

And we must focus on specific areas for action such as maternal and child health. Most experts see one sure route to advancing on every one of the goals, that is by empowering women. When we invest in women and girls, families are stronger. Societies are more stable. Economies thrive. Countries move closer to peace.

Yet women around the world continue to face discrimination and abuse. As many as 70 percent of women can expect to experience some form of violence in their lifetime.

That is why I have started a global campaign called Unite to End Violence Against Women. President Bakiev has signed and committed himself to this campaign. I thank him and ask each Parliamentarian, particularly men parliamentarians, to join this campaign.

I have created a Network of Men Leaders because I believe that to end violence against women, men must change. I have asked Desmond Tutu, some Prime Ministers and very distinguished world leaders to join in this Network of Men Leaders. I have recently appointed a very distinguished woman leader to work as a Special Representative of the Secretary-General to fight against violence against women. Last month, it launched in Kyrgyzstan. Others have joined as well – business leaders, universities, artists, young people. Let us pledge, together, to end violence against women. No exceptions. No excuses. No delay.

The second challenge, both global and regional, is to leave our children a cleaner, greener world. Emissions continue to rise. Climate change is accelerating. Accelerating much much faster than you realize. Glaciers are melting. It is caused by human actions. These are the facts.

That is why, from the moment I took office, I have urged leaders to make climate change a top priority of the international community. Governments have agreed to keep the rise in global temperature to two degrees Celsius. But every year's delay costs billions. We need to cut emissions more rapidly. We need to help vulnerable countries adapt. We need to build on last December's Copenhagen Accord.

And the governments of Central Asia need to help push the negotiations toward a comprehensive, legally binding treaty in Mexico this year. People in Central Asia know the danger of climate change, of neglect of the environment, not by reading about it, but by suffering from it. Here in Central Asia, it is also time to act. Growing pressure on resources – water, in particular – underscores the need for quality management and cooperation.

I encourage Kyrgyzstan, and your neighbors, to build on the momentum and understanding achieved last year at the summit of the International Fund for Saving the Aral Sea. The Presidents of Central Asia pledged to work together on this crucial but sensitive issue. You are exploring ways to invest in high-efficiency water management systems, to provide for both energy and agricultural needs, to advance better land management. I see a big opportunity here, and I offer my help and the help of the United Nations, to reduce tensions, to build consensus, to engage in conversation among the leaders of the five Central Asian nations.

The United Nations is also working with you to address the remnants and risks of uranium and toxic metal wastes. Kyrgyzstan has played a leading role in searching for solutions. I also want to recognize your global leadership in highlighting the unique challenges of mountain ecosystems and in helping to establish the International Day of Mountains.

The third and final challenge, again both regional and global, is to reinforce peace, security and human rights. Afghanistan concerns us all – and I thank you for your leadership. If we are to see a stable and democratic Afghanistan, we need your engagement. Without your help and cooperation, the plague of instability and drug-trafficking will never disappear from this region.

I also applaud this region for leading the way on issues of nuclear security. The Central Asia Nuclear Weapons Free Zone entered into force last year. You have contributed to the gathering of global momentum for non-proliferation and disarmament. We have important opportunities for global progress in the weeks ahead including the review of the Nuclear Non Proliferation Treaty in May, at UN Headquarters in New York. I welcome the agreement between the Russian Federation and the United States for a fresh start toward a safer world.

66 A robust civil society, grounded in democratic principles and the rule of law, is the way of the future and the foundation of prosperity and progress. 99

I also salute Kyrgyzstan for being the first country in this region to contribute police and military officers for United Nations peacekeeping operations. You have sent your people to Sudan, Darfur, Liberia and Timor-Leste. I thank you very much for your contribution.

All of us who believe in the United Nations understand that security has many dimensions. It starts with people. Respect for the rights of all people. For the UN, the protection of human rights is a bedrock principle if a country is to prosper. Quite frankly, ladies and gentlemen, recent events have been troubling, including the last few days. I repeat: all human rights must be protected, including free speech and freedom of the media.

I thank Kyrgyzstan for hosting the Central Asia Office of the UN High Commissioner for Human Rights here in Bishkek, and I ask for your full support. Like all 192 Member States of the United Nations, Kyrgyzstan will undergo a Universal Periodic Review by the Human Rights Council next month. This takes your full commitment. I look forward to a vigorous discussion of these fundamental principles.

I also commend Kyrgyzstan for signing the Rome Statute of the International Criminal Court and encourage your Government to favourably consider ratifying the Statute as soon as possible. This will help reinforce the global commitment to ending impunity for genocide and other serious international crimes.

These universal values are fundamental to building the dynamic, competitive, modern, forward-looking, democratic society you are seeking. Robust civil society, grounded in democratic principles and the rule of law, is the way of the future and the foundation of prosperity and progress. This understanding is at the heart of your Constitution and our United Nations Charter. Let us pledge together to deepen those values.

On all of these issues, the United Nations stands ready to assist. I encourage you to support the UN Centre for Preventive Diplomacy for Central Asia, established soon after I became Secretary-General.

I have seen that Kyrgyzstan is a land of majestic peaks and magnificent vistas. I have learned that the Kyrgyz people possess a questing spirit, always looking to the next mountain, always with an eye on the farthest horizon.

In describing the Kyrgyz hero of the Manas, your national epic poem put it like this: "He will build roads where none exist". Centuries ago, your ancestors traveled and traded along the Silk Road. Two decades ago, your generation embarked on another historic road – the road of independence, democracy, dignity, opportunity for all the people of Kyrgyzstan.

This is the 21st century road that you travel today. And this I pledge as Secretary-General of the United Nations: the United Nations will accompany you every step of the way. Thank you. *Chong Rahmat.*

Remarks to Security Council on organized crime

NEW YORK, 24 FEBRUARY 2010

I thank the French presidency for putting this important issue on the agenda of the Security Council. Transnational issues, including drug trafficking and organized crime, are increasingly on the Council's agenda. This reflects the seriousness of the threat. Indeed, drug trafficking and organized crime affect almost all aspects of the UN's work: development, security, the environment, and the rule of law.

But seen from a different perspective, this also means that all our work, in every sphere, can reduce the risk and impact of transnational threats. That is why our response must be global and integrated, both within the UN family, and as a family of nations.

First, the global response: Member States have united to fight pandemics, poverty, climate change and terrorism. We can and must do the same to counter organized crime.

Already, Member States have worked together on a number of important initiatives. These include the General Assembly's efforts against drugs, the Kimberly process against blood diamonds, and the UN Global Initiative to Fight Human Trafficking.

> ❝ We cannot fight fire with fire. The criminals use ruthless and exploitative methods which we can never contemplate. Human rights must always be at the forefront of efforts to control crime. ❞

But there is so much more to be done against emerging threats like cyber-crime, money-laundering, environmental crime, and the dumping of hazardous waste. The Crime Prevention Congress to be held in April in Salvador, Brazil, offers an opportunity to explore how we can strengthen the legal and operational means to fight them. This year is also the tenth anniversary of the UN Convention against Transnational Organized Crime. I urge you to sharpen this powerful instrument at the Conference of Parties in October. One of the most important improvements would be the establishment of a monitoring mechanism.

In this work, we should not only focus on what we are battling against. We must never lose sight of what we are fighting for: that is, justice and the rule of law.

We can not fight fire with fire. The criminals use ruthless and exploitative methods which we can never contemplate. Human rights must always be at the forefront of efforts to control crime.

My second keyword today is integration. Integration is essential at many levels. Nationally, agencies must pull together to fight all aspects of crime. Regionally, states must share information and carry out joint operations. This is not always easy. Lack of capacity and lack of trust often cause problems.

Lack of capacity can be overcome. We have seen this in West Africa, where vulnerability to drugs and crime is being reduced thanks to the work of the Economic Community of West African States in support of the Praia Process. The West Africa Coast Initiative involving the UN Office on Drugs and Crime, the Department of Peacekeeping Operations, and the Department of Political Affairs is also a good example of the "one UN" approach. I urge you to support similar regional initiatives, like the Santo Domingo Pact launched here at the United Nations today, which has the same aims for Central America and the Caribbean.

As for building trust: experience shows that tackling common threats can build confidence and good neighbourly relations between countries that may otherwise have their differences. Initiatives to share information on the drug trade in West Asia, Central Asia and the Gulf are among the examples where this has happened.

With transnational threats, States have no choice but to work together. We are all affected – whether as countries of supply, trafficking or demand. Therefore we have a shared responsibility to act. I welcome the Security Council's Presidential statement of 8 December 2009, in which you called for the issue of drug trafficking and organized crime to be mainstreamed into the UN's work throughout the conflict cycle.

The UN Office on Drugs and Crime continues to carry out important work in providing the evidence on these transnational threats, and the technical assistance with which to respond. Transnational networks create vectors of violence that blaze trails of death and destruction through some of the world's most vulnerable regions. Crime prevention is conflict prevention: together they build safer and healthier societies. Criminal justice should figure more prominently in UN peacebuilding and peace-keeping.

Finally, there is a need for timely action. The Council's most recent Presidential statement also recommended that I provide more information on transnational threats. I will work more closely with all relevant parts of the UN system to bring impending threats to your attention. In return, I urge you to ensure that early warning is followed up by early action.

Together, let us prevent drug trafficking and organized crime from threatening international peace and security and all our hard-won work, across our agenda.

Remarks to diplomatic missions, non-governmental organizations and UN agencies

YANGON, 4 JULY 2009

This is my second visit to Myanmar in just over a year. Both visits have been at critical times for the country's future. My first visit was in the aftermath of Cyclone Nargis. This devastating natural disaster, which took so many lives and created so much hardship, touched hearts across the globe. In Myanmar's moment of need, the world responded generously.

I want to personally thank everyone here today for your remarkable contributions to the relief and recovery effort. You have saved lives, rejuvenated communities and made it possible for many thousands of people to reclaim their livelihoods. You have helped Myanmar to overcome adversity. It is important that this work continues.

I felt the tragedy of Cyclone Nargis deeply – as a fellow Asian and as Secretary-General.

I am Asia's second Secretary-General. The first was Myanmar's U Thant. I revere his memory. I also recall his wise words. U Thant said: "The worth of the individual human being is the most unique and precious of all our assets and must be the beginning and end of all our efforts. Governments, systems, ideologies and institutions come and go, but humanity remains."

This is why I have returned. As Secretary-General, I attach the highest importance to helping the people of this country to achieve their legitimate aspirations. The United Nations works for people – their rights, their well-being, their dignity. It is not an option. It is our responsibility. I have come to show the unequivocal shared commitment of the United Nations to the people of Myanmar.

I am here today to say: Myanmar, you are not alone. We want to work with you for a united, peaceful, prosperous, democratic and modern Myanmar. We want to help you rise from poverty. We want to work with you so your country can take its place as a respected and responsible member of the international community. We want to help you achieve national reconciliation, durable peace and sustainable development. But, let me emphasize: neither peace nor development can thrive without democracy and respect for human rights. Myanmar is no exception.

The challenges are many. But they are not insurmountable. We know from experience that securing Myanmar's peaceful, democratic and prosperous future is a complex process. None of Myanmar's challenges can be solved on their own. Peace, development and human rights are closely inter-related. Failure to address them with equal attention will risk undermining the prospects for democracy, durable peace and prosperity. However, we also know that where there is a genuine will for dialogue and reconciliation, all obstacles can be overcome.

The question today is this: how much longer can Myanmar afford to wait for national reconciliation, democratic transition and full respect for human rights? The cost of delay will be counted in wasted lives, lost opportunities and prolonged isolation from the international community.

> ❝ The region and the world are changing fast. Myanmar only stands to gain from engagement – and from embarking on its own change. ❞

Let me be clear: all the people of Myanmar must work in the national interest. I said this yesterday when I met with representatives of Myanmar's registered political parties and with those armed groups that have chosen to observe a cease-fire. I encouraged them respectively to honour their commitments to the democratic process and peace.

Nonetheless, the primary responsibility lies with the Government to move the country towards its stated goals of national reconciliation and democracy. Failure to do so will prevent the people of Myanmar from realizing their full potential. Failure to do so will deny the people of Myanmar their right to live in dignity and to pursue better standards of life in larger freedom.

These principles lie at the core of the United Nations Charter, whose opening words are "We the peoples". The founding Constitution of independent Myanmar echoes these noble words. We must work together to ensure that Myanmar's future embodies these principles too. With this in mind, I bring three messages.

First, respect for human dignity is the precondition for peace and development everywhere. Myanmar was one of the first United Nations Member States to adopt the Universal Declaration of Human Rights. It subscribed early on to the consensus that respect for human rights and fundamental freedoms is indispensable to political, economic and social progress. Unfortunately, that commitment has not been matched in deed.

Myanmar's human rights record remains a matter of grave concern. The Government has articulated its goals as stability, national reconciliation and democracy. The upcoming election –the first in twenty years – must be inclusive, participatory and transparent if it is to be credible and legitimate. Myanmar's way forward must be rooted in respect for human rights

This is why I say that all political prisoners, including Daw Aung San Suu Kyi, should be released without delay. When I met Senior General Than Shwe yesterday and today, I asked and pressed as hard as I could to visit Ms. Suu Kyi. I am deeply disappointed that he refused. I believe the government of Myanmar has missed a unique opportunity to show its commitment to a new era of political openness. It was a setback to the international community's efforts to reach hands to Myanmar's needs.

Allowing a visit to Daw Aung San Suu Kyi would have been an important symbol of the government's willingness to embark on the kind of meaningful engagement that will be essential if the elections in 2010 are to be seen as credible. Daw Aung San Suu Kyi must be allowed to participate in the political process without further delay.

Indeed, all the citizens of Myanmar must be given the opportunity to contribute fully to the future of this country. National reconciliation cannot be complete without the free and active participation of all who seek to contribute. The country must embark on a process of genuine dialogue that includes all concerned parties, all ethnic groups and all minorities. People must be free to debate and to engage in political dialogue, and they must have free access to the information that will help them participate meaningfully in the democratic process.

Any transition is difficult. Myanmar has already undergone transitions from sovereign kingdom, to occupied colony, and now independent State. This history carries a twin legacy of armed conflict and political deadlock, including recent painful events: the repression of demonstrators in 1988, the cancellation of the 1990 election results, and the clampdown on peaceful dissent that continues to this day.

At the same time, there have been some positive efforts that should be recognized. Although still fragile, the cease-fire agreements between the Government and armed groups have reduced the level of conflict. The United Nations has wide-ranging experience in making such gains irreversible.

Sovereignty, territorial integrity and national unity are legitimate concerns for any government. We contend that opening and broadening the political space is the best way to ensure that each group and each individual becomes part of the greater collective project. The military, all political parties, ethnic minority groups, civil society, and indeed every son and daughter of Myanmar has a role to play in this country's transition. Only mutual compromise, respect and understanding can lay the foundations for durable peace, national reconciliation and democracy.

My second message is on addressing the humanitarian needs of Myanmar's people. I am glad I have been able to return to see the progress made in the Irrawaddy Delta. The loss of some 130,000 people was tragic, but the rebuilding I saw today was impressive. The tragedy showed the resilience of the people of Myanmar. It also demonstrated that people throughout the world care deeply about Myanmar and its people.

Above all, the response to Cyclone Nargis proved the value of engagement over isolation. The unprecedented cooperation between Myanmar, the United Nations and ASEAN through the Tripartite Core Group, with the support of the donor community, has demonstrated that humanitarian imperatives and the principles of sovereignty do not conflict. Humanitarian assistance – in Myanmar as elsewhere – should never be held hostage to political considerations. We can and must work together to ensure access to humanitarian and development assistance to all those in Myanmar who need it.

This brings me to my third message. It is time for Myanmar to unleash its economic potential. Myanmar sits in the middle of Asia's economic miracle. Harnessing Myanmar to the rapid advances taking place around it is the surest way to raise living standards. I welcome the Government's policy of opening up to outside trade and investment, and its efforts to achieve the Millennium Development Goals, control HIV, combat human trafficking and curtail opium production.

But the reality is that millions continue to live in poverty. Standards of living in Myanmar remain among the lowest in Asia. The people of Myanmar need jobs, they need food security and they need access to health care. We must work to ensure that the people of Myanmar can benefit from and contribute to the regional and global economy. We must recognize that the region and the world have much to gain from a stable, prosperous and democratic Myanmar. We must work together for that goal.

The Government of Myanmar must seize the moment. It must take advantage of the opportunities that the international community is prepared to offer to the people of Myanmar.

I came here as a friend. My duty is to uphold the ideals and principles of the United Nations Charter. My role is to encourage all of you – the Government, political parties, ethnic groups, civil society – to move forward together as one people and one nation. Nothing is insurmountable or impossible when the people's interest is placed above divisions.

The region and the world are changing fast. Myanmar only stands to gain from engagement – and from embarking on its own change. The Government of Myanmar has repeatedly stated that cooperation with the United Nations is the cornerstone of the country's foreign policy. We ask it to match deeds with words.

The more Myanmar works in partnership with the United Nations to respond to its people's needs and aspirations, the more it affirms its sovereignty. Similarly it is incumbent on the international community as whole to work together to help Myanmar meet our shared goals: a united, peaceful, prosperous and democratic future, with full respect for the human rights of all the country's people. *Kyae zoo tin bar tae.*

Remarks to the press

It is particularly significant for me as Secretary-General of the United Nations to stand in front of this bombed site of the United Nations compound. I am just appalled. I am not able to describe how I am feeling, having seen this site of the bombing of the United Nations compound.

Everyone is smelling the bombing still. It is still burning. It is an outrageous and totally unacceptable attack against the United Nations. I have protested many times, and am today protesting in the strongest terms and condemning it. I have asked for a full investigation and to make those responsible accountable.

I have come to Gaza to see for myself the extent of the damage caused by the past three weeks of fighting and to demonstrate my solidarity with the population of Gaza, as well as to assure you of the United Nations' and the international community's full support to help you overcome these difficult times.

I will try to mobilize all humanitarian resources, and I am going to dispatch a humanitarian needs assessment team on Thursday –the day after tomorrow –led by UNSCO (Office of the United Nations Special Coordinator for the Middle East Peace Process) Director, Special Representative Robert Serry, and my Humanitarian Coordinator, John Holmes, to lead this mission.

> " We need to restore a basic respect for civilians. Where civilians have been killed, there has to be a thorough investigation, full explanations and accountability. "

I have also come to Gaza to express my deepest admiration and solidarity with the staff of the United Nations – the United Nations Relief and Works Agency and UNSCO – for their bravery; for their dedicated commitment to help you, the population of Gaza, during the past three weeks. I commend their leadership and their commitment.

I have seen only a fraction of the damage. This is shocking and alarming. These are heartbreaking scenes. I am deeply grieved by what I have seen here today.

To the people of Gaza I have this to say: I have seen only a fraction of the destruction and suffering caused to this tiny and crowded place by more than three weeks of heavy bombardment, shelling and street fighting on top of months and years of economic deprivation.

I will do all I can, as Secretary-General of the United Nations, to help in this time of need. I have condemned from the outbreak of this conflict the excessive use of force by the Israeli forces in Gaza. I view the rocket attacks into Israel as completely unacceptable. We need to restore a basic respect for civilians. Where civilians have been killed, there has to be a thorough investigation, full explanations and, where it is required, accountability.

International humanitarian law must be upheld and respected by all. I am very worried by the potential long-term impact of the recent crisis on this entire society, and particularly young children. I am sobered by the extent of the damage, and of relief and recovery challenges ahead. I promise the United Nations will do all we can.

I also want to make an appeal to the Palestinian people. We need Palestinian unity. Without unity we cannot succeed in achieving Palestinian self-determination.

Palestinian unity is the framework for international agreements to be restored, for crossings to be opened, for the whole world to help you build Gaza, for elections, for political negotiations with Israel. I appeal to Fatah, Hamas, to all Palestinian factions, to reunite within the framework of the legitimate Palestinian Authority. The United Nations will work together with a united Palestinian Government encompassing Gaza and the West Bank.

To the staff of the United Nations, you have my deepest respect and thanks for your hard work. You have performed heroically. I know this is easy to say, but it is very difficult to act. Without you, many more people would have died. Without you, the suffering of thousands upon thousands of innocent people would have been much greater. To the world, I have this to say: the repeated violence felt by Palestinians and Israelis is a mark of collective political failure.

A genuine effort was made in 2008, but it was not enough. We all must do more. I will be speaking to many world leaders about what I have seen, including to the new President of the United States. As Secretary-General of the United Nations, I will uphold the need for an end of occupation, a just and lasting resolution of the refugee issue, and the creation of a Palestinian state in accordance with international law and resolutions of the Security Council. I believe a massive and united international effort is required to help Palestinians achieve statehood and Israel and Palestine to live side by side in peace and security. I am more determined than ever to see this achieved.

Thank you very much. *Shukran Jazeelan.*

Remarks at symposium on supporting victims of terrorism

NEW YORK, 9 SEPTEMBER 2008

Today is a historic day for the United Nations. We come together with common and unwavering purpose: the support of victims of terrorism. We are honored and humbled to have as our guests individuals who bear directly the scars, physically and mentally, from unspeakable acts of terrorism and experts who have attempted to understand and help victims.

Some of you have been injured or disabled in terror attacks, your wounds a daily reminder of the viciousness of terrorism. Some of you have been kidnapped and held captive, deprived of a most fundamental human right: your freedom. Some of you have lost loved ones – sisters, brothers, mothers, fathers, daughters and sons, whose lives have been ended by senseless and indiscriminate murder.

Most of you have been haunted by images and memories too horrific to live with and struggled with ears deaf and indifferent to your plight. All of you have dedicated your lives to denouncing the evil of terrorism, to making the voice of the victims heard, and to supporting others who have suffered.

You have come all the way to New York to bear witness to one of the great scourges of our time. From many different countries, religions, and ethnicities, you demonstrate that terrorism does not discriminate among victims. In your diversity, you stand for hundreds of thousands around the world who have suffered loss and injury from terrorism.

Together, we remember and pay tribute to all those who have been victims of terrorism in far too many places. Let us remember Bali, Beslan, and Bombay. Let us remember Algiers, Baghdad, and Casablanca. Let us remember Kabul, Riyadh and Nairobi. Let us remember London, New York, San Vincente, and Madrid. Let us remember Istanbul, Islamabad, Jerusalem, and Dar-es-Salaam.

The list keeps growing longer, bringing with it greater pain and grief that cascades mercilessly through families, communities and nations. Each act reminds us that terrorism is global. It can affect anyone, anywhere. It targets all ethnic groups, religions, nationalities, and civilizations. It attacks humanity itself.

It is for the sake of humanity that we must create a global forum for your voice and listen to you, the victims. Your stories of how terrorism has affected your lives are our strongest argument why it can never be justified. By giving a human face to the painful consequences of terrorism, you help build a global culture against it. You are the real heroes in the global struggle against terrorism. You humble the world by your strength and courage.

You deserve support and solidarity. You deserve social recognition, respect and dignity. You deserve to have your needs addressed. You deserve to have your human rights defended. And you deserve justice.

Like many of you, I have witnessed the aftermath of terror. I was serving at the United Nations in New York at the time of the terrorist attacks of 11 September 2001. My heart went out to the victims of that grim day who, like me, were New Yorkers going about their lives.

Six years later, in December last year, I was profoundly shocked when I visited the grounds of the UN compound in Algiers, which had been ripped apart by a terrorist bomb blast. I met with survivors and with the families of the victims – encounters that left me deeply moved.

I had seen the devastation from a distance in New York but in Algiers, I walked through the rubble of this tragedy. I looked into the faces of the children whose parents had lost their lives while serving the United Nations. And I caught a glimpse, for the first time, of the reality that many of you here live with every day – of what it means to be a victim of terrorism. I lost members of my UN family that day.

> **" By giving a human face to the painful consequences of terrorism, you help build a global culture against it. "**

Since that time, I feel each loss more deeply. And the United Nations family has lost too many of our staff to terrorist attacks not only in Algiers but elsewhere. Just last week, I attended a ceremony in Geneva commemorating the heinous attack five years ago at the UN Headquarters in Baghdad, in which we lost some of our best and bravest staff. Twenty-two people were killed and over 150 wounded. I met with some 300 survivors, victims, and their families. And I was overwhelmed with grief at how fresh the wounds still are five years after the attack.

Today, it fills me with pride that we are convening at the United Nations to show solidarity with victims of terrorism, and to find better ways to support them. I am heartened by the overwhelming interest. It is a testament to the great importance we are attaching to supporting victims of terrorism.

I am equally encouraged by the high level of expertise here today. We are joined by a number of eminent terrorism experts. But we are also joined by experts whose focus of work is on violence and conflict situations. It is time to expand the small community that works on terrorism and see whether new insights can be brought to bear by those with experience in studying conflict and violence. And we will hear from Member States who have responded to terrorist attacks by developing assistance programmes.

I look forward to an open dialogue, in which we all share our experiences and practices. We have so much to learn from each other. In this way, we can strengthen the international community's solidarity with victims, and improve our under-standing of their needs and how governments, the UN and civil society can better support them.

That is the fundamental purpose of this meeting.

The United Nations Global Counter-Terrorism Strategy, unanimously adopted by all UN Member States in 2006, called on us to stop the dehumanization of vic-tims of terrorism in all its forms and manifestations.

In the Strategy, Member States committed themselves to consolidating nation-al systems of assistance that would promote the needs of victims of terrorism and their families and facilitate the normalization of their lives; they pledged to promote international solidarity in support of victims of terrorism; and they promised to promote and protect the rights of victims of terrorism.

Today, we must strive to give practical meaning to these commitments. Let us embark then on this journey together, in mutual respect and determination.

Remarks at international meeting on the Middle East

Today, we bear witness to a new beginning of the Middle East peace process. I am very pleased and moved to be a part of this historic meeting.

After years of failed hopes and terrible suffering, I commend Prime Minister Olmert and President Abbas for re-dedicating Israel and the Palestine Liberation Organization to resolving the conflict between them. They know the risks and sacrifices involved, and also know that there is no alternative to peace.

Let me thank and congratulate our hosts, President Bush and Secretary Rice, and, most importantly, President Abbas and Prime Minister Olmert. Their leadership and commitment has made this new beginning possible. The engagement of the United States has always been crucial to the peace process, and it remains so today.

I also want to thank the many members of the Arab League who are here today. Five years ago, the Arab countries made a historic strategic commitment to peace. Earlier this year, they renewed the Arab Peace Initiative. Their presence today shows their determination to participate actively in the search for peace in the region.

I pledge the full support of the United Nations family for the renewed effort. For sixty years, the Organization has provided the broad parameters for peace, first in the partition plan, and then in Security Council resolutions 242, 338, 1397 and 1515. Today, the UN has few higher priorities than seeing this conflict resolved.

The Palestinians have been deprived of their fundamental right to self-determination for sixty years. Their society has been increasingly fragmented – territorially, by settlements, land expropriation and the barrier; socially and economically, by closure; and politically, between Gaza and the West Bank. They have begun to fear that the dream of statehood may slip beyond their grasp.

We must reverse this growing sense of despair, and build a process that begins to change the lives of Palestinians, and secures their independence and freedom. The process must end the occupation and create an independent and viable State of Palestine, at peace with itself and its neighbours.

For its part, Israel faces genuine security challenges. The Israeli people have sought security and freedom from threat for sixty years. But this has proven elusive. Recently, they have felt anew the threat of attack, and their very right to exist has been questioned. Some have started believing that territorial withdrawal only brings new acts of terrorism.

We must reverse this loss of faith, and build a process that delivers on the vital interests of Israelis: a Palestinian State that is a true partner, secure and recognized borders, and a permanent end to the conflict.

The Middle East as a whole craves peace too. An Israeli-Palestinian peace, and indeed a comprehensive peace between Israel and its neighbours, would be the surest way to stabilize the region and stem the appeal of violence and rejectionism.

Success depends not on what we say today, but on what we do tomorrow. There will be a steering committee and the Quartet will have its own role, complementary to a trilateral monitoring mechanism. To successfully implement the Road Map, we must abandon piecemeal approaches, and address all aspects of the conflict.

> **66 The Palestinians have been deprived of their fundamental right to self-determination for sixty years. We must reverse this growing sense of despair. The Israeli people have sought security and freedom from threat for sixty years. But this has proven elusive. We must reverse this loss of faith. 99**

First, final status negotiations need to begin in earnest, and address all the issues: Jerusalem, refugees, borders, settlements, security and water. The broad outlines of solutions to these issues are clear. There is no reason they cannot be resolved in 2008.

Second, we must help the Palestinian Authority to rebuild, reform and perform. I commend Prime Minister Fayyad and his Government for the responsible reform plan it has developed, and the actions on security it has already taken. This must continue – and I hope a wide range of donors will step forward with political and financial support at Paris and beyond.

Third, the situation on the ground must improve, rapidly and visibly. Without implementing long-standing commitments under the Road Map and the Agreement on Movement and Access, the diplomatic process cannot succeed. Progress requires parallel actions and clear monitoring.

The Quartet will continue to provide international leadership and support for these efforts. I thank the Quartet Representative, Mr. Tony Blair, for the clear vision and intense focus he has brought to ensure that these three tracks are advanced together and reinforce each other.

The people of Gaza have suffered more than anyone else from conflict and poverty. We must reach out to them. Humanitarian aid is no substitute for a functioning economy. The time has come for concrete initiatives to ease their suffering, and replace despair with hope.

We will also have to work politically to restore the unity of Gaza and the West Bank under the legitimate Palestinian Authority. This will be vital if a peace agreement is to be sustainable.

Let us also hope that today's meeting heralds an easing of regional tensions, and opens the door to exploring possibilities for comprehensive peace. I am committed to a peace between Israel and all its Arab neighbours, including Lebanon and Syria.

Above all, today marks a beginning, not an end. I know that different expectations exist. But I ask you all to approach this effort with flexibility, patience and resolve. Let us base expectations on a realistic assessment and take responsibility for the things we each can do, without losing faith. As we re-embark together on this quest, there can be no second thoughts, no half-measures, no going back. This time, come what may, let us see it through.

Disarmament

Remarks at Summit on the Safe and Innovative Use of Nuclear Energy

KIEV, 19 APRIL 2011

I thank President Yanukovych for his vision in organizing this conference long before issues of nuclear safety made it back to the world's front pages.

Twenty-five years ago, the explosion at Chernobyl cast a radioactive cloud over Europe and a shadow around the world. At this moment, the tragedy at Japan's Fukushima Daiichi nuclear power plant continues to unfold.

Together, these accidents raise popular fears and disturbing questions. The disaster at Chernobyl offers one set of lessons. The disaster in Japan offers another, vastly more complex.

As we are painfully learning once again, nuclear accidents respect no borders. They pose direct threats to human health and the environment. They cause economic disruptions, affecting everything from agricultural production to trade and global services.

This is a moment for deep reflection: how do we ensure both the peaceful uses of nuclear energy and maximum safety? We need a global rethink on this fundamental question.

Because the consequences are catastrophic, safety must be paramount. Because the consequences are transnational, they must be debated globally.

Today, let me offer five concrete steps to enhance nuclear safety for our future.

First, it is time for a top to bottom review of current nuclear safety standards, both at the national and international levels.

Today, the primary responsibility for ensuring the safety of nuclear installations lies with national governments. I strongly urge States to consider lessons learned and adopt appropriate measures to apply the highest possible safety standards. This includes safety precautions, staff training, a reliable quality assurance system, and independent regulatory oversight. It also means greater transparency if there is to be public trust.

I am encouraged that many governments are reassessing their national policies and regulations. Last week's review meeting of the Convention on Nuclear Safety in Vienna also produced many useful suggestions. I strongly urge those States that have not acceded to the Convention on Nuclear Safety to do so without delay.

That leads me to my second point: we must strengthen support for the International Atomic Energy Agency on the challenge of nuclear safety.

I want to once again commend the IAEA and Director-General Amano for the rapid response to events in Japan. The Joint Radiation Emergency Plan went into action just hours after the earthquake and tsunami. I also convened a high-level meeting with the heads of the relevant international organizations to assess the implications of the nuclear crisis. We have shared information and expertise, participated in global monitoring and helped reassure a concerned global public.

> " By joining forces, we can make sure that the tragedies of Chernobyl and Fukushima are a thing of the past, not a harbinger of the future. "

The time has come to strengthen the capacity of the IAEA in the further development and universal application of the highest possible nuclear safety standards. The IAEA Ministerial Conference on Nuclear Safety in June in Vienna will serve as an important forum in this regard. As a follow-up, I also will consider convening a high-level meeting on strengthening the international nuclear safety regime when world leaders gather in New York this September. We need international standards for construction, agreed guarantees of public safety, full transparency and information-sharing among nations.

Third, we must put a sharper focus on the new nexus between natural disasters and nuclear safety. The challenge of climate change is bringing with it greater extremes of weather. Nuclear power plants must be prepared to withstand everything from earthquakes to tsunamis, from fires to floods.

According to the IAEA, sixty-four new reactors are under construction. Today, 443 are operating in twenty-nine countries worldwide, some located in areas of seismic activity. This requires us to place new importance on disaster preparedness, in rich and poor nations alike. Japan, after all, is among the best prepared and most technically advanced nuclear energy powers. What are the implications for countries that are less ready for the worst? That is why I will make sure that disaster preparedness for nuclear accidents is included in the themes of the Third Session of the Global Platform for Disaster Risk Reduction in Geneva next month.

Fourth, we must undertake a renewed cost-benefit analysis of nuclear energy. The right to the peaceful use of nuclear energy is enshrined in the Nuclear Non-Proliferation Treaty. Nuclear power will likely continue to be an important resource for many nations and can be a part of a low-carbon-emission energy mix; but it has to become credibly safe, and globally so. Again, it is time to pause and rethink our approach. For this reason, I will launch a UN system-wide study on the implications of the accident at Fukushima. I will ask the relevant UN agencies and specialized organizations to undertake this task.

> ❝ **Nuclear power plants must be prepared to withstand everything from earthquakes to tsunamis, from fires to floods.** ❞

Fifth and finally, we need to build a stronger connection between nuclear safety and nuclear security. Though nuclear safety and nuclear security are distinct issues, boosting one can bolster the other. At a time when terrorists and others are seeking nuclear materials and technology, stringent safety systems at nuclear power plants will reinforce efforts to strengthen nuclear security. A nuclear power plant that is safer for its community is also one that is more secure for our world. Addressing this challenge requires the active cooperation of the nuclear industry. As I proposed at the Nuclear Security Summit in Washington last year, a broad-based partnership is essential to building a better framework for nuclear safety and security. Such an approach is critical in the run-up to the 2012 Seoul Nuclear Security Summit.

These are five practical steps we can take to reassure the global public and better prepare our people and our planet for the energy challenges of the 21st century. By joining forces, we can make sure that the tragedies of Chernobyl and Fukushima are a thing of the past, not a harbinger of the future. Thank you for coming together in that noble cause.

Remarks to the Conference on Disarmament

GENEVA, 26 JANUARY 2011

I t is a great pleasure to address the Conference on Disarmament. Thank you for welcoming me for the third time since I took office.

I am here to express my confidence in the great potential of this body to play a catalytic role in advancing the disarmament agenda.

But I am also here to make a fresh appeal to you to live up to that potential and to meet the expectations of the international community.

In the past several years, we have built important momentum: hard-won momentum on which we can and must build. The next few years will be critical. We can push forward on nuclear non-proliferation and disarmament, or risk sliding back.

This is why disarmament and non-proliferation are among my top priorities for the year ahead. As I told the General Assembly two weeks ago, if we are to build on the current momentum, we need even more concrete action than we have achieved to date.

It is my sincere hope that such action will again emanate from the Conference on Disarmament. The world's multilateral disarmament machinery should deliver more and more quickly. I call on you to become a first harbinger of hope for 2011 in the field of disarmament.

The Conference on Disarmament is the undisputed home of international arms control efforts. From its inception, the Conference has had a unique function. As the world's single multilateral disarmament negotiating forum, it has produced landmark treaties that have promoted international security while demonstrating that multilateral collaboration can serve the global and national interest alike.

However, the Conference's record of achievement has been overshadowed by inertia that has now lasted for more than a decade. The very credibility of this body is at risk. Continued inaction will only endanger its future as a multilateral negotiating forum.

There was a brief glimmer of hope almost two years ago, when the sense of crisis led the Conference to adopt a programme of work by consensus under the Algerian presidency.

Coming so soon after I last addressed you, this apparent break in the deadlock was very encouraging. It seemed like a real breakthrough, and there was great expectation that the Conference, at long last, would fulfil its mandate and begin negotiations.

Unfortunately, the programme of work for your 2009 session was not implemented, and the Conference ended its 2010 session without starting substantive work. This has been deeply disappointing. Indeed, there appears to be a disconnect between the Conference on Disarmament and the recent positive developments in the field of disarmament and non-proliferation.

On the one hand, States have made welcome progress on a variety of matters that have a direct impact on the global security environment. They have taken steps to strengthen nuclear security, with more expected. The States parties to the Treaty on the Non-Proliferation of Nuclear Weapons had a successful review conference in 2010 – the first in ten years. Important bilateral efforts are coming to fruition, as we have seen with the new Strategic Arms Reduction Treaty (START).

> 66 The Conference's record of achievement has been overshadowed by inertia that has now lasted for more than a decade. The very credibility of this body is at risk. The longer it persists, the graver the nuclear threat. 99

But on the other hand, the Conference on Disarmament has played little or no role in these advances. Where States and civil society initiatives are on the move, this body has remained stagnant.

Because of the impasse, I decided to convene, this past September, a high-level meeting on revitalizing the work of the Conference and taking forward multilateral disarmament negotiations. The Non-Proliferation Treaty Review Conference also invited me to convene such a meeting. You are all aware that at that meeting, many foreign ministers and other high-level political leaders expressed their deep concern about the inability of the Conference on Disarmament to overcome its differences, and joined me in urging it to start substantive work in 2011. The participants in the meeting were also unanimous in stressing that limited membership of the Conference on Disarmament is a privilege. So is the consensus rule. Members of the Conference must accept that this privilege comes with responsibility.

The message was clear. This should not be another year of business as usual. Just one or two countries must not be able to block the process indefinitely. Moreover, we must not risk pushing States to resort to alternative arrangements outside the Conference on Disarmament.

The future of the Conference on Disarmament is in your hands. It is for you, the members, to decide whether it will live up to the expectations of the international community or face the consequences.

At the September meeting I also noted that the programme of work adopted by consensus in 2009 remains the most common denominator. Therefore, I suggest, once again, that early in your 2011 session, the Conference adopt this programme of work or any other similar subsequent proposal that the Conference can agree by consensus.

In this regard, I welcome the joint statement last week in Washington, D.C. by the Presidents of China and the United States reaffirming their support for the early commencement of negotiations on a fissile material cut-off treaty in the Conference on Disarmament.

The continued deadlock has ominous implications for international security. The longer it persists, the graver the nuclear threat - from existing arsenals, from the proliferation of such weapons, and from their possible acquisition by terrorists.

The Conference on Disarmament must find a way to continue its invaluable work. It must focus on promoting global goals that are fully universal in scope. It must do its part to advance the rule of law in the field of disarmament. It must not let one lost decade for the Conference turn into a second.

For my part, I have asked my Advisory Board on Disarmament Matters to undertake a thorough review of the issues raised at the high-level meeting, including the possible establishment of a High-level Panel of Eminent Persons with a special focus on the functioning of the Conference on Disarmament. I will keep you updated on this matter.

The world is waiting for one bold step by the Conference. But it requires collective action from you, the members of the Conference. Multilateral efforts continue to show their immense value in addressing a wide variety of global challenges and threats. The Conference on Disarmament and the world's multilateral disarmament machinery should keep pace. I call on you to put aside your differences. Let us serve the global interest. Let us build a safer world.

With respect to the Fissile Material Treaty, it is clear that within the Conference on Disarmament, there is almost universal support for negotiations on such a treaty. While many Members continue to hope that formal negotiations will take place in the Conference, a number of Members have recently suggested that alternative arrangements should be explored.

As a first step, I am wondering whether you could commence an informal process before you agree on formal negotiations on the Fissile Material Treaty within the Conference on Disarmament. It could simply be a basic process to educate each other and build trust, which will inform and facilitate the formal process once the Conference adopts its work programme.

Before concluding, I would like to express my profound gratitude to Mr. Sergei Ordzhonikidze, my personal representative to the Conference on Disarmament, who will soon be leaving the Organization. I hold highest respect for the professionalism and dedication he brought to the critical period in which he has served.

Please accept my best wishes for the success of your work.

Remarks at
Peace Memorial Ceremony

HIROSHIMA, 6 AUGUST 2010

We are here, on hallowed ground, to see, to feel, to absorb and reflect. I am honoured to be the first UN Secretary-General to take part in this Peace Memorial Ceremony on the sixty-fifth anniversary of this tragic day. And I am deeply moved.

When the atomic bombs fell on Hiroshima and Nagasaki, I was one year old. Only later in life, could I begin to understand the full dimension of all that happened here. As a young boy, I lived through the Korean War. One of my earliest memories is marching along a muddy road into the mountains, my village burning behind me. All those lives lost, families destroyed – so much sadness. Ever since, I have devoted my life to peace. It has brought me here today.

Watakushiwa sekai heiwa no tameni Hiroshima ni mairimashita.

We gather to pay our solemn respects to those who perished, sixty-five years ago, and to the many more whose lives forever changed. Life is short, but memory is long.

For many of you, that day endures, as vivid as the white light that seared the sky, as dark as the black rains that followed. To you, I offer a message of hope. To all of you, I offer my message of peace. A more peaceful world can be ours. You are helping to make it happen. You, the survivors, who inspired us with your courage and fortitude. You, the next generations, the young generation, striving for a better day.

Together, you have made Hiroshima an epicentre of peace. Together, we are on a journey from ground zero to Global Zero; a world free of weapons of mass destruction. That is the only sane path to a safer world. For as long as nuclear weapons exist, we will live under a nuclear shadow.

And that is why I have made nuclear disarmament and non-proliferation a top priority for the United Nations – and put forward a five-point plan.

Our moment has come. Everywhere, we find new friends and allies. We see new leadership from the most powerful nations. We see new engagement in the UN Security Council. We see new energy from civil society. Russia and the United States have a new START treaty. We made important progress at the Nuclear Security Summit in Washington last April, which we will build upon in Korea.

We must keep up the momentum. In September, I will convene a high-level meeting in support of the work of the Conference on Disarmament at the United Nations. We will push for negotiations towards nuclear disarmament; a Comprehensive Nuclear Test Ban Treaty; a Fissile Material Cut-Off Treaty; disarmament education in our schools – including translating the testimonies of the survivors in the world's major languages. We must teach an elemental truth: that status and prestige belong not to those who possess nuclear weapons, but to those who reject them.

> 66 Together, we are on a journey from ground zero to Global Zero; a world free of weapons of mass destruction. For as long as nuclear weapons exist, we will live under a nuclear shadow. 99

Sixty-five years ago, the fires of hell descended upon this place. Today, one fire burns, here in this Peace Park. That is the Flame of Peace – a flame that will remain lit until nuclear weapons are no more. Together, let us work for that day, in our lifetime, in the lifetimes of the survivors. Together, let us put out the last fire of Hiroshima. Let us replace that flame with the light of hope. Let us realize our dream of a world free of nuclear weapons so that our children and all succeeding generations can live in freedom, security and peace.

Thank you.

Domo arigato gozaimasu.

Remarks to International Conference for a Nuclear- Free, Peaceful, Just and Sustainable World

NEW YORK, 1 MAY 2010

Reading the list of organizations and individuals with us this evening, I want to say what an honour it is to be here. I know of your hard work and dedication. I know how much you have sacrificed in standing for your principles and beliefs. I know how much courage it takes to speak out, to protest, to carry the banner of this most noble human aspiration: world peace. And so, most of all, I am here tonight to thank you.

Let me begin by saying how humbling it is to speak to you in this famous place, Riverside Church. It was here that Martin Luther King Junior spoke against the war in Vietnam. Nelson Mandela spoke here on his first visit to the United States after being freed from prison.

Standing with you, looking out, I can see what they saw: a sea of committed women and men, who come from all corners to move the world. It reminds us that what matters most in life is not so much the message from the bully pulpit, but rather the movement from the pews. From people like you. And so I say: keep it up.

Our shared vision is within reach: a nuclear-free world. On the eve of the Nuclear Non-Proliferation Treaty review conference, beginning on Monday, we know the world is watching. Let it heed our call. Disarm now!

From my first day in office, I have made nuclear disarmament a top priority. Perhaps, in part, this deep personal commitment comes from my experience as a boy in Korea, growing up after the war. My school was rubble. There were no walls. We studied in the open air.

The United Nations rebuilt my country. I was lucky enough to receive a good education. But more than that, I learned about peace, solidarity and, above all, the power of community action. These values are not abstract principles to me. I owe my life to them. I try to embody them in all my work.

Just a few weeks ago, I travelled to Ground Zero – the former test site at Semipalatinsk, in Kazakhstan, where the Soviet Union detonated more than 450 nuclear explosions. It was strangely beautiful. The great green steppe reached as far as the eye could see. But of course, the eye does not immediately see the scope of the devastation. Vast areas where people still cannot go. Poisoned lakes and rivers. High rates of cancer and birth defects. After independence, in 1991, Kazakhstan closed the site and banished nuclear weapons from its territory. Today, Semipalatinsk is a powerful symbol of hope. It is a new Ground Zero for disarmament, the birth place of the Central Asian nuclear-weapon-free zone.

In August, I will travel to another Ground Zero – Mayor Akiba's proud city of Hiroshima. There, I will repeat our call for a nuclear free-world. The people of Hiroshima and Nagasaki and especially the *hibakusha*, the survivors, know too well the horror of nuclear war. It must never be repeated.

Yet sixty-five years later, the world still lives under a nuclear shadow. How long must we wait to rid ourselves of this threat? How long will we keep passing the problem to succeeding generations?

We here tonight know that it is time to end this senseless cycle. We know that nuclear disarmament is not a distant, unattainable dream. It is an urgent necessity, here and now. We are determined to achieve it.

We have come close in the past. Twenty-four years ago, in Reykjavik, Ronald Reagan and Mikhail Gorbachev came within a hair's breadth of agreeing to eliminate nuclear weapons. It was a dramatic reminder of how far we can go – as long as we have the vision and the will.

❝ Nuclear disarmament is not a distant, unattainable dream. It is an urgent necessity, here and now. ❞

Today's generation of nuclear negotiators must take a lesson from Reykjavik: be bold. Think big, for it yields big results. And that is why, again, we need people like you. People who understand that the world is over-armed and that peace is under funded. People who understand that the time for change is now.

The Non-Proliferation Treaty entered into force forty years ago. Ever since, it has been the foundation of the non-proliferation regime and our efforts for nuclear disarmament. It is one of the seminal agreements of the 20th century. Let us not forget. In 1963, experts predicted that there could be as many as twenty-five nuclear powers by the end of the last century. It did not happen, in large part because the Non-Proliferation Treaty guided the world in the right direction.

Today, we have reason for renewed optimism. Global public opinion is swinging our way. Governments are looking at the issue with fresh eyes. Consider just the most recent events.

Leading by example, the United States announced a review of its nuclear posture, foreswearing the use of nuclear weapons against non-nuclear states, so long as they are in compliance with the Non-Proliferation Treaty. In Prague, President Obama and President Medvedev signed a new START treaty, accompanied by serious cuts in arsenals. In Washington, the leaders of forty-seven nations united in their efforts to keep nuclear weapons and materials out of the hands of terrorists. And on Monday, we hope to open a new chapter in the life of the Nuclear Non-Proliferation Treaty.

In 2005, when leaders gathered for the last review of the Non-Proliferation Treaty, the outcome did not match expectations. In plainer English, it failed – utterly. We cannot afford to fail again. After all, there are more than 25,000 nuclear weapons in the world's arsenals. Nuclear terrorism remains a real and present danger. There has been no progress in establishing a nuclear-weapon-free zone in the Middle East. The nuclear programs of Iran and the Democratic People's Republic of Korea are of serious concern to global efforts to curb nuclear proliferation.

To deal with these and other issues, I have set out my own five-point action plan, and I thank you for your encouraging response. I especially welcome your support for the idea of concluding a Nuclear Weapon Convention. Article VI of the Non-Proliferation Treaty requires the Parties to pursue negotiations on a treaty on general and complete disarmament under international control. These negotiations are long overdue. Next week, I will call on all countries, and most particularly the nuclear-weapon states, to fulfil this obligation.

We should not have unrealistic expectations for the conference. But neither can we afford to lower our sights. What I see on the horizon is a world free of nuclear weapons. What I see before me are the people who will help make it happen. Please keep up your good work. Sound the alarm, keep up the pressure. Ask your leaders what they are doing personally to eliminate the nuclear menace. Above all, continue to be the voice of conscience.

We will rid the world of nuclear weapons. And when we do, it will be because of people like you. The world owes you its gratitude.

Remarks at Semipalatinsk Test Site

KURCHATOV, KAZAKHSTAN, 6 APRIL 2010

I have just flown over Ground Zero. Standing on Ground Zero just two kilometres from the real site of nuclear tests is a very sobering experience for me.

More than 450 nuclear bombs were tested here with a terrible effect on people and nature. They have totally destroyed our environment. Poisoned earth, rivers and lakes, children suffering from cancer, birth defects.

In 1991, soon after the independence of Kazakhstan, President Nazarbayev took extraordinary leadership by closing the Semipalatinsk Nuclear Test Site and banished all nuclear weapons. It was a visionary step, a true declaration of independence.

Today, this site stands as a symbol of disarmament and hope for the future. The Treaty on a Nuclear-Weapon-Free Zone in Central Asia was signed here. Now we have a good reason to believe that the promise of Semipalatinsk – the abolition of nuclear weapons – will become reality.

In just two days from now, President Dimitri Medvedev and President Barack Obama will sign a successor treaty to the START – that is really a fresh START. Today, President Obama has announced the nuclear posture review, that is an important initiative. To lead by example, the United States would renounce the development of new nuclear weapons. And for the first time, the United States explicitly committed not to use nuclear weapons against any non-nuclear nations that are in compliance with the Nuclear Non-Proliferation Treaty, even if the United States were attacked.

> **❝ Today, this site stands as a symbol of disarmament and hope for the future. I will spare no efforts to realize, together with the whole international community, a world free of nuclear weapons. ❞**

I cannot think of a more fitting, even poignant place to hear this news. All these developments will add significant momentum to the forthcoming Non-Proliferation Treaty Review Conference at the United Nations in May. At next week's nuclear security summit, which will be held in Washington, I will urge the leaders of the Russian Federation and the United States, and other nuclear states leaders, to abandon all nuclear weapons.

To realize a world free of nuclear weapons is a top priority of the United Nations and the most ardent aspiration of human beings. Here today in Semipalatinsk, I call on all nuclear weapons states to follow the lead of Kazakhstan. For inspiration, they can look to Kazakhstan. Kazakhstan has led by example. You encouraged the United Nations General Assembly to establish August 29 as the International Day Against Nuclear Tests. And you are working to help people experiencing the adverse effects of nuclear testing.

> **❝ To realize a world free of nuclear weapons is a top priority of the United Nations and the most ardent aspiration of human beings. ❞**

As Secretary-General, I will spare no efforts to realize, together with the whole international community, a world free of nuclear weapons. As you may know, on October 24, 2008, I introduced my five-point plan for nuclear disarmament. The United Nations is working in Semipalatinsk to restore the area, to improve the health of the people and to provide an environment for economic growth.

Again, I urge all the leaders of the world, particularly nuclear weapon states, to work together with the United Nations to realize the aspiration and dream of a world free of nuclear weapons.

Address to the East-West Institute

NEW YORK, 24 OCTOBER 2008

I t is a great pleasure to welcome you all to the United Nations. I salute the East-West Institute and its partner non-governmental groups for organizing this event on weapons of mass destruction and disarmament.

This is one of the gravest challenges facing international peace and security. So I thank the East-West Institute for its timely and important new global initiative to build consensus. Under the leadership of George Russell and Martti Ahtisaari, the East-West Institute is challenging each of us to rethink our international security priorities in order to get things moving again. You know, as we do, that we need specific actions, not just words. As your slogan so aptly puts it, you are a "think and do tank".

One of my priorities as Secretary-General is to promote global goods and remedies to challenges that do not respect borders. A world free of nuclear weapons would be a global public good of the highest order, and will be the focus of my remarks today. I will speak mainly about nuclear weapons because of their unique dangers and the lack of any treaty outlawing them. But we must also work for a world free of all weapons of mass destruction.

Some of my interest in this subject stems from my own personal experience. As I come from the Republic of Korea, my country has suffered the ravages of conventional war and faced threats from nuclear weapons and other weapons of mass destruction. But of course, such threats are not unique to my country.

Today, there is support throughout the world for the view that nuclear weapons should never again be used because of their indiscriminate effects, their impact on the environment and their profound implications for regional and global security. Some call this the nuclear taboo.

Yet nuclear disarmament has remained only an aspiration, rather than a reality. This forces us to ask whether a taboo merely on the use of such weapons is sufficient.

States make the key decisions in this field. But the United Nations has important roles to play. We provide a central forum where states can agree on norms to serve their common interests. We analyse, educate and advocate in the pursuit of agreed goals.

Moreover, we have pursued general and complete disarmament for so long that it has become part of the Organization's very identity. Disarmament and the regulation of armaments are found in the Charter. The very first resolution adopted by the General Assembly, in London in 1946, called for eliminating "weapons adaptable to mass destruction". These goals have been supported by every Secretary-General. They have been the subject of hundreds of General Assembly resolutions, and have been endorsed repeatedly by all our Member States.

And for good reason. Nuclear weapons produce horrific, indiscriminate effects. Even when not used, they pose great risks. Accidents could happen any time. The manufacture of nuclear weapons can harm public health and the environment. And of course, terrorists could acquire nuclear weapons or nuclear material.

Most states have chosen to forgo the nuclear option, and have complied with their commitments under the Nuclear Non-Proliferation Treaty. Yet some states view possession of such weapons as a status symbol. And some states view nuclear weapons as offering the ultimate deterrent of nuclear attack, which largely accounts for the estimated 26,000 that still exist.

Unfortunately, the doctrine of nuclear deterrence has proven to be contagious. This has made non-proliferation more difficult, which in turn raises new risks that nuclear weapons will be used.

The world remains concerned about nuclear activities in the Democratic People's Republic of Korea and in Iran. There is widespread support for efforts to address these concerns by peaceful means through dialogue.

There are also concerns that a nuclear renaissance could soon take place, with nuclear energy being seen as a clean, emission-free alternative at a time of intensifying efforts to combat climate change. The main worry is that this will lead to the production and use of more nuclear materials that must be protected against proliferation and terrorist threats.

The obstacles to disarmament are formidable. But the costs and risks of its alternatives never get the attention they deserve. Consider the tremendous opportunity cost of huge military budgets. Consider the vast resources that are consumed by the endless pursuit of military superiority.

According to the Stockholm International Peace Research Institute, global military expenditures last year exceeded $1.3 trillion. Ten years ago, the Brookings Institution published a study that estimated the total costs of nuclear weapons in just one country, the United States, to be over $5.8 trillion, including future cleanup costs. By any definition, this has been a huge investment of financial and technical resources that could have had many other productive uses.

Concerns over such costs and the inherent dangers of nuclear weapons have led to a global outpouring of ideas to breathe new life into the cause of nuclear disarmament. We have seen the Weapons of Mass Destruction Commission led by Hans Blix, the New Agenda Coalition and Norway's seven-nation initiative. Australia and Japan have just launched the International Commission on Nuclear Non-Proliferation and Disarmament. Civil society groups and nuclear-weapon states have also made proposals.

There is also the Hoover plan. I am pleased to note the presence here today of some of that effort's authors. Dr. Kissinger, Mr. Kampelman: allow me to thank you for your commitment and for the great wisdom you have brought to this effort.

Such initiatives deserve greater support. As the world faces crises in the economic and environmental arenas, there is growing awareness of the fragility of our planet and the need for global solutions to global challenges. This changing consciousness can also help us revitalize the international disarmament agenda.

> 66 The obstacles to disarmament are formidable. But the costs and risks of its alternatives never get the attention they deserve. 99

In that spirit, I hereby offer a five-point proposal.

First, I urge all Non-Proliferation Treaty parties, in particular the nuclear-weapon-states, to fulfil their obligation under the treaty to undertake negotiations on effective measures leading to nuclear disarmament.

They could pursue this goal by agreement on a framework of separate, mutually reinforcing instruments. Or they could consider negotiating a nuclear-weapons convention, backed by a strong system of verification, as has long been proposed at the United Nations. Upon the request of Costa Rica and Malaysia, I have circulated to all UN member states a draft of such a convention, which offers a good point of departure.

The nuclear powers should actively engage with other states on this issue at the Conference on Disarmament in Geneva, the world's single multilateral disarmament negotiating forum. The world would also welcome a resumption of bilateral negotiations between the United States and the Russian Federation aimed at deep and verifiable reductions of their respective arsenals.

Governments should also invest more in verification research and development. The United Kingdom's proposal to host a conference of nuclear-weapon states on verification is a concrete step in the right direction.

Second, the Security Council's permanent members should commence discussions, perhaps within its Military Staff Committee, on security issues in the nuclear disarmament process. They could unambiguously assure non-nuclear-weapon states that they will not be the subject of the use or threat of use of nuclear weapons. The Council could also convene a summit on nuclear disarmament. States that are not part of the Non-Proliferation Treaty should freeze their own nuclear-weapon capabilities and make their own disarmament commitments.

My third initiative relates to the rule of law. Unilateral moratoria on nuclear tests and the production of fissile materials can go only so far. We need new efforts to bring the Comprehensive Nuclear-Test-Ban Treaty into force, and for the Conference on Disarmament to begin negotiations on a fissile material treaty immediately, without preconditions. I support the entry into force of the Central Asian and African nuclear-weapon-free zone treaties. I encourage the nuclear-weapon states to ratify all the protocols to the nuclear-weapon-free zone treaties. I strongly support efforts to establish such a zone in the Middle East. And I urge all Non-Proliferation Treaty parties to conclude their safeguards agreements with the IAEA, and to voluntarily adopt the strengthened safeguards under the Additional Protocol. We should never forget that the nuclear fuel cycle is more than an issue involving energy or non-proliferation; its fate will also shape prospects for disarmament.

My fourth proposal concerns accountability and transparency. The nuclear-weapon states often circulate descriptions of what they are doing to pursue these goals, yet these accounts seldom reach the public. I invite the nuclear-weapon states to send such material to the UN Secretariat, and to encourage its wider dissemination. The nuclear powers could also expand the amount of information they publish about the size of their arsenals, stocks of fissile material and specific disarmament achievements. The lack of an authoritative estimate of the total number of nuclear weapons testifies to the need for greater transparency.

Fifth and finally, a number of complementary measures are needed. These include the elimination of other types of weapons of mass destruction; new efforts against weapons of mass destruction terrorism; limits on the production and trade in conventional arms; and new weapons bans, including of missiles and space weapons. The General Assembly could also take up the recommendation of the Blix Commission for a "World Summit on disarmament, non-proliferation and terrorist use of weapons of mass destruction".

Some doubt that the problem of weapons of mass destruction terrorism can ever be solved. But if there is real, verified progress in disarmament, the ability to eliminate this threat will grow exponentially. It will be much easier to encourage governments to tighten relevant controls if a basic, global taboo exists on the very possession of certain types of weapons. As we progressively eliminate the world's deadliest weapons and their components, we will make it harder to execute terrorist attacks with weapons of mass destruction. And if our efforts also manage to address the social, economic, cultural, and political conditions that aggravate terrorist threats, so much the better.

At the United Nations in 1961, President Kennedy said, "Let us call a truce to terror. Let us invoke the blessings of peace. And as we build an international capacity to keep peace, let us join in dismantling the national capacity to wage war."

The keys to world peace have been in our collective hands all along. They are found in the UN Charter and in our own endless capacity for political will. The proposals I have offered today seek a fresh start not just on disarmament, but to strengthen our system of international peace and security.

We must all be grateful for the contributions that many of the participants at this meeting have already made in this great cause. When disarmament advances, the world advances. That is why it has such strong support at the United Nations. And that is why you can count on my full support in the vital work that lies ahead.

Humanitarian
Action

Welcoming America inspired my public service
Op-ed article in USA Today

22 AUGUST 2012

As Secretary-General of the United Nations, I have more stamps in my passport than I can count, but there is none that I treasure as much as the first one. "United States of America," it said. The date: August 1962. I was a wide-eyed eighteen-year-old from a rural village in war-shattered Korea. The American Red Cross had invited me to join 112 teenagers from forty-two countries to travel across the United States visiting Red Cross chapters, meet each other and learn the value of service. It was an incredible privilege.

As soon as I stepped off the plane, I was overwhelmed by the warmth of the people. The wealth and plenty was a cultural shock to a very poor boy from devastated Korea. But what moved me most was the spirit of helping others I witnessed from small-town America to the capital.

We met President John F. Kennedy in the Rose Garden. He noted that we came from countries where the governments may not get along, but people do. He said he placed great hopes in us. It was at that moment that I resolved to embark on a life of public service. That journey, which began fifty years ago, continues to this day at the United Nations.

Half a century later, the importance of reaching out across boundaries to help others is more critical than ever. In this digital age, where people can connect with a click, everyone has the potential to make a difference.

Earlier this month, I had the opportunity to meet Beyoncé Knowles. She is well-known as a singer, actress and all-around superstar, but I met a global humanitarian lending her spotlight to the work of the United Nations. Her song, "I Was Here," is dedicated to World Humanitarian Day, an occasion to pay tribute to those who have given their lives for the cause and to support those who carry out vital life-saving work around the world.

This year, we launched a campaign for people to take action. Across generations and continents, they replied with initiatives to help those in need. Thanks to the immense power of social media, these acts of service were shared globally, inspiring countless others to carry out their own good deeds. It was a clear reminder of the lesson I first learned fifty years ago and still live by today: engaging in the world is the best path to a better future. Individual acts of service may seem small, but each reverberates far beyond the people who are directly affected, generating a momentum that builds to protect our world.

> ❝ As secretary-general of the United Nations, I have more stamps in my passport than I can count, but there is none that I treasure as much as the first one. "United States of America," it said. The date: August 1962. ❞

At a time when extremists are exploiting national, racial and religious differences in new deadly ways, we must never forget the importance of our common humanity. The United Nations is addressing global challenges such as insecurity, injustice and inequality. We succeed to the extent that this spirit of human solidarity is understood and practiced by governments and peoples. And we depend on our partners, such as the International Red Cross and Red Crescent movement, which share our common values and brave danger to uphold them.

In many cases, the Red Cross is the last hope in the most hazardous, conflict-stricken areas where even UN humanitarian workers cannot travel. Today, the United Nations and the Syrian Arab Red Crescent are working together to bring aid to the suffering people of Syria. In crisis spots around the world, we work together to save lives, protect human rights and promote dignity.

My own fifty-year journey will come full circle this month as that original international group of Red Cross student leaders gathers together for a reunion. With all the changes we have experienced, President Kennedy's words to us remain as true as when we first heard them: "There are no national boundaries; there is only a question of whether we can extend a helping hand."

Pakistan needs our help, now
Op-ed article in The New York Times

18 AUGUST 2010

Standing under leaden skies in Pakistan last Sunday, I saw a sea of suffering. Flood waters have washed away thousands of towns and villages. Roads, bridges and homes in every province of the country have been destroyed. From the sky, I saw thousands of acres of prime farmland – the bread and butter of the Pakistani economy – swallowed up by the rising tides. On the ground, I met terrified people, living in daily fear that they could not feed their children or protect them from the next wave of crisis: the spread of diarrhea, hepatitis, malaria and, most deadly, cholera.

The sheer scale of the disaster almost defies comprehension. Around the country, an estimated 15 to 20 million people have been affected. That is more than the entire population hit by the Indian Ocean tsunami and Kashmir earthquake in 2005, the 2007 Cyclone Nargis and this year's earthquake in Haiti combined. An area as big as Italy and larger than more than half the countries in the world – some 160,000 square kilometers, or 62,000 square miles – is under water.

Why has the world been slow to grasp the dimensions of this calamity? Perhaps because this is no made-for-TV disaster, with sudden impact and dramatic rescues. An earthquake may claim tens of thousands of lives in an instant; in a tsunami, whole cities and their populations vanish in a flash.

By contrast, this is a slow motion catastrophe – one that builds over time. And it is far from over. The monsoon rains could continue for weeks. Even as waters recede from some areas, new floods are affecting others, particularly in the south. And, of course, we know this is happening in one of the most challenged regions of the world – a place where stability and prosperity is profoundly in the world's interest. For all of these reasons, the floods of August are far more than a disaster for Pakistan alone. Indeed, they represent one of the greatest tests of global solidarity in our time.

That is why the United Nations has issued an emergency appeal for $460 million. That amounts to less than $1 a day per person to keep six million people alive for the next three months – including 3.5 million children. International aid commitments are growing by the day. Less than a week after the appeal was launched, we are halfway there. And yet, the scale of the response is insufficient for the scale of this disaster.

On Thursday, the United Nations General Assembly will meet to intensify our collective efforts. If we act now, a second wave of deaths caused by waterborne diseases can still be prevented. It is not easy to mount relief operations in such difficult and sometimes perilous places. But I have seen it happen around the world, from the most remote and dangerous parts of Africa to Haiti's shattered cities. And I saw it in Pakistan this week.

> ❝ An earthquake may claim tens of thousands of lives in an instant; in a tsunami, whole cities and their populations vanish in a flash. By contrast, this is a slow motion catastrophe – one that builds over time. And it is far from over. ❞

A host of UN agencies, international aid groups such as the Red Cross/Red Crescent and other nongovernmental organizations have been supporting the government of Pakistan's response to the emergency. Using trucks, helicopters and even mules to transport food around the country and reach those cut off from help, we have provided one-month food rations to nearly one million people. Roughly that many now have emergency shelter, and more are receiving clean water every day. Cholera kits, anti-snake venom doses, surgical supply kits and oral dehydration salts are saving growing numbers of lives.

This is a start, but it needs a massive boost. Six million people are short of food; 14 million need emergency health care, with a special focus on children and pregnant women. And as the waters recede, we must move quickly to help people build back their country and pick up the pieces of their lives.

The World Bank has estimated crop damage to be at least $1 billion. Farmers will need seeds, fertilizers and tools to replant, lest next year's harvest be lost along with this one. Already, we are seeing price spikes for food in Pakistan's major cities. In the longer term, the huge damage to infrastructure must be repaired, from schools and hospitals to irrigation canals, communications and transport links. The United Nations will be part of all this, too.

In the media, we hear some talk of fatigue – suggestions that governments are reluctant to cope with yet another disaster, that they hesitate to contribute more to this part of the world. In fact, the evidence is otherwise. Donors are giving to Pakistan, and that is encouraging. If anyone should be fatigued, it is the ordinary people I met in Pakistan – women, children and small farmers, tired of troubles, conflict and economic hard times and who have now lost everything.

Yet instead of fatigue, I saw determination, resilience and hope – hope and the expectation that they are not alone in their darkest hour of need. We simply cannot stand by and let this natural disaster turn into a man-made catastrophe. Let us stand with the people of Pakistan every step of the long and difficult road ahead.

Remarks to Haiti reconstruction and donors conference

NEW YORK, 31 MARCH 2010

Good morning, and welcome to the United Nations on this important occasion. We greatly appreciate your participation and count on your generous support.

We come together, today, in solidarity with Haiti and its people – these resilient, courageous people, who have suffered so much, and who now deserve our help. President Préval rightly speaks of this critical moment as a "rendezvous with history." It is the moment we come together in a global compact to build a new Haiti; a Haiti transformed.

For weeks, experts have been assessing the needs and costs of the January 12 disaster. In tandem, President Préval, Prime Minister Bellerive and their government have worked out the blueprint for a national strategic plan, a plan to guide Haiti's recovery and reconstruction. He will present that vision in a moment. And I am sure you will agree that it deserves our full and generous support. As a plan for action, it is concrete, specific and, above all, ambitious.

Our goal is not just to rebuild. It is to build back better. Again to quote the President, it is a plan to create a new Haiti. A Haiti where the majority of people no longer live in deep poverty, where they can go to school and enjoy better health, where they have better options than going without jobs or leaving the country altogether.

Under this plan, a new Interim Haiti Recovery Commission will channel $3.9 billion into specific programmes and projects during the next eighteen months. Over the next ten years, Haiti's reconstruction needs will total an estimated $11.5 billion. Clearly, this assistance must be well-invested and well-coordinated. In parallel with reconstruction, it must provide for continuing emergency relief: food, sanitation, health care and, most urgently at this moment, shelter.

You are all aware how difficult the situation is right now. The rainy season is fast approaching. Some camps for displaced persons are at risk of flooding. Health and sanitation issues are growing more serious. We are also very concerned about the security situation in some of the camps, especially for women and children. I therefore appeal for further support for the Revised Humanitarian Appeal for $1.4 billion, currently only 50 percent funded.

As we move from emergency aid to long-term reconstruction, let us recognize that we cannot accept business as usual. What we envision, today, is wholesale national renewal, a sweeping exercise in nation-building on a scale and scope not seen in generations. In partnership with the United Nations, Haiti's leaders are committing to a new social contract with the people.

That means fully democratic government; sound economic and social policies that address extreme poverty and deep-rooted disparities of wealth; human rights for all guaranteed by an independent judiciary and a vigilant civil society; programs that empower women as heads of households, as business leaders, as political decision-makers.

❝ Our goal is not to rebuild. It is to build back better – to create a new Haiti. ❞

This new partnership rests on principles of good governance, transparency, mutual accountability. Accountability between the government and the governed, between the private and public sectors, between Haiti and the international community. It requires fresh approaches to old problems. Among them: investments that create jobs, modeled on the UN's own cash-for-work programmes, as well as incentives for people to relocate from Port au Prince to cities and villages elsewhere in the country.

Today, you will rise in solidarity with Haiti. By the end of this day, I am confident we will truly have helped Haiti along the road to a new and better future.

Do not wait for disaster
Op-ed article in The Daily Star

19 MARCH 2010

No country can afford to ignore the lessons of the earthquakes in Chile and Haiti. We cannot stop such disasters from happening. But we can dramatically reduce their impact, if the right disaster risk reduction measures are taken in advance.

A week ago I visited Chile's earthquake zone and saw how countless lives were saved because Chile's leaders had learned the lessons of the past and heeded the warnings of crises to come. Because stringent earthquake building codes were enforced, much worse casualties were prevented. Training and equipping first responders ahead of time meant help was there within minutes of the tremor. Embracing the spirit that governments have a responsibility for future challenges as well as current ones did more to prevent human casualties than any relief effort could.

Deaths were in the hundreds in Chile, despite the magnitude of the earthquake, at 8.8 on the Richter Scale, the fifth largest since records began. In Haiti, a less intense earthquake caused hundreds of thousands of deaths. Haiti had non-existent or un-enforced building codes, and very poor preparedness.

The lessons are universally applicable. No country is immune from disaster, be it earthquakes or floods, storms or heat waves. More and more intense natural disasters are affecting all five continents, we believe as a result of climate change. Many of the world's poorest people live in high-risk densely populated cities in flood or earthquake zones, or both.

The culture of disaster risk reduction must spread. I am encouraged that we already have a head start in this regard. The Hyogo Framework for Action, a ten-year plan to make the world safer from disasters triggered by natural hazards, was adopted by 168 governments in 2005. Hyogo gives national authorities a blueprint to assess and reduce risks through planning, training, and better public education. For example, making sure that schools, hospitals, and other key public infrastructure meet certain safety standards. Based on the Hyogo Framework, the UN has made disaster risk reduction a priority. I have appointed a Special Representative for implementation of the Hyogo Framework of Action. Last year I launched the first global assessment report on disaster risk reduction in Bahrain.

There has been progress. Bangladesh lost more than 500,000 people during Cyclone Bhola in 1970. It subsequently built 2,500 cyclone shelters on elevated concrete platforms and trained more than 32,000 volunteers to help in evacuations. When Cyclone Sidr struck in 2007 with an enormous sea surge, the death toll was less than 4,000. Cyclone Nargis, a similar event in unprepared Myanmar in May

2008, cost 140,000 lives. Cuba weathered four hurricanes in 2008. It sustained $9 billion of physical damage but very few lives were lost.

The evidence is overwhelming. Yet the lessons of these disasters are forgotten with depressing speed. Many governments have failed to follow through on the practical measures Hyogo proposes.

66 Some states argue that they cannot afford to embrace the prevention model. I say no country can afford to ignore it. 99

Some states argue that they cannot afford to embrace the prevention model. I say no country can afford to ignore it. We know prevention actually saves governments money in the long run. When China spent $3.15 billion on reducing the impact of floods between 1960 and 2000, it averted losses estimated at about $12 billion. Similar savings have been recorded in Brazil, India, Vietnam and elsewhere.

Everyone has a role to play. Governments, central and local, have to do what it takes to make communities able to cope with both continuing challenges and sudden shocks.

In flood and earthquake-prone areas, the solution is to enact and enforce building regulations. For flood prone areas, it is to move or improve squatter settlements, restore natural coastal barriers such as mangrove swamps, provide more suitable land and better infrastructure for the urban poor and install effective early warning systems.

These measures will keep many thousands of people alive who may otherwise perish. The UN is ready to help governments build preparedness at the country and regional levels. Donor nations need to fund disaster risk reduction and preparedness measures. Adaptation to climate change in particular means investing in systems for disaster reduction, preparedness and management.

The Chile and Haiti earthquakes showed us once again why action *before* disasters makes all the difference. To prevent natural hazards turning into disasters, we must all act sooner and act smarter.

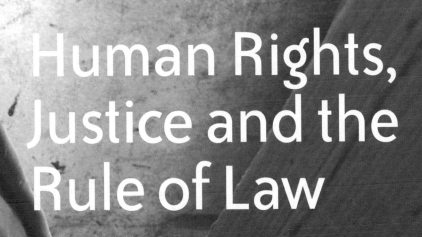

Human Rights, Justice and the Rule of Law

Remarks to High-level meeting of the General Assembly on the Rule of Law

NEW YORK, 24 SEPTEMBER 2012

The rule of law is like the law of gravity. It holds our world and societies together, replacing chaos with order; it roots us to common values; it grounds us to the common good.

But unlike the rule of gravity, the rule of law does not just happen. It requires the sustained and concerted efforts of true leaders.

This High-level meeting marks the first time that leaders of governments, ministers of justice, attorneys-general and partners from civil society have gathered in this Hall to focus solely on strengthening justice for the world's people.

It is a long time coming. But it is also the result of decades of United Nations work for the rule of law – and it coincides with a growing, global grassroots movement for justice, accountability and an end to impunity.

We know that when we strengthen the rule of law, we reinforce all three pillars of the United Nations: peace, development and human rights.

Justice is not an abstract concept. It is the voter ID in the hands of a citizen, the entrepreneur's legitimate contract, the badge of a trusted police officer and the birth certificate that lets a girl be counted. Widows who are denied their inheritance, human rights defenders who suffer retributions and victims of sexual abuse: they all need the rule of law to obtain the justice they deserve.

The Charter of the United Nations – the Constitution of the international community – provides indispensable tools to deepen the rule of law: the universal standard-setting power of the General Assembly, the enforcement power of the Security Council, the judicial power of the International Court of Justice.

The wider body of international law developed at the United Nations gives the international community a basis to cooperate and peacefully resolve conflicts, and the means to ensure that there is no relapse of fighting. And with the development of accountability mechanisms, no war criminal should ever find safe harbour in the modern world.

The rule of law is also fundamental to development and achieving the Millennium Development Goals. Today's discussion should strengthen our resolve to ensure that the post-2015 international development agenda takes full account of the rule of law.

I am proud that the United Nations is promoting the rule of law in more than 150 countries. I am grateful for the many voluntary pledges being made today. I thank the governments that have made the commitments. But I ask for concrete action in five specific areas.

> **" Strengthening the rule of law is for every country and is in everyone's interest. It is as essential within countries as it is among the family of nations. "**

First, I call on all States to commit to the equal application of the law at both the national and international levels. There should be no selectivity in applying resolutions, decisions and laws. We cannot allow political self-interest to undermine justice.

Second, I call on Heads of State and Government to uphold the highest standards of the rule of law in their decision making at all times. The rule of law must be the foundation for every government action.

Third, I call on all Heads of State and Government to accept the jurisdiction of the International Court of Justice.

Fourth, I urge Member States to support peace by strengthening UN initiatives in the field of the rule of law: training police, improving corrections and enhancing the judiciary in fragile and conflict-torn countries around the world.

Fifth, and fundamentally, I urge you to adopt the solemn declaration that is before you to make the most of this truly historic occasion to commit to respect for international law and justice and to an international order based on the rule of law.

Civil society plays a crucial role in holding leaders to account, and I urge you to keep pushing for action in all of these action areas to give the rule of law the place it deserves.

It is not enough to disperse our rule of law activities across the United Nations agenda. They deserve a central place in the structure of our work. I count on you to help forge a new, structured approach to strengthening the rule of law and delivering justice so we can achieve peace, development and human rights.

Strengthening the rule of law is for every country and is in everyone's interest. It is as essential within countries as it is among the family of nations. Today's meeting is a milestone – but it is not an end in itself. Our challenge now is to follow up, generate momentum and continue to give a high profile to this essential foundation for a better future.

Remarks at Memorial Centre

I stand here with profound sadness and loss. There is perhaps no other place in the world more difficult, more painful, than here for the United Nations Secretary-General to visit. Srebrenica was a great crime of our time.

I have just met a number of ladies whose family members have been killed. I would like to express my deepest respect to the families and to the victims. I am here to tell you all: we grieve with you. The world is grieving with you.

I know nothing can ease such pain, an empty heart. No one can replace a father's warmth, a child's smile, and a grandparent's embrace. I know many mothers are still burying their sons in their hearts. I pay again my deepest respect.

> **❝ I stand here with profound sadness and loss. There is perhaps nowhere in the world more difficult, more painful, than here for the United Nations Secretary-General to visit. ❞**

Standing here and having seen endless rows of tombstones, the names on the wall, I cannot remember them all: Amir, Fikret, Hamdija, on and on – more than 8,000. Srebrenica is hallowed ground for the families of the victims and also the family of nations. We must learn from the lessons of Srebrenica. The United Nations is doing, and will continue to do, all that we can to ensure that Srebrenica will not happen anytime, anywhere, to anyone.

The international community failed to provide the necessary protection to many people who were killed at the time when they needed our support. The leaders of the world in 2005 finally came up with the principle of the "Responsibility to Protect" civilians. In some places, like in Libya, in Cote d'Ivoire, we were able to apply this, but in many other places we are still not able to fully protect civilians.

We have to do all that we can to protect civilians, to prevent and to stop bloodshed, particularly in Syria now. When we learn from the lessons of Srebrenica, we have to do all that we can. The international community must be united to prevent any further bloodshed in Syria because I do not want to see any of my successors, after twenty years, visiting Syria, apologizing for what we could have done today to protect the civilians in Syria and which we are not doing now.

Standing in this place before all the victims, I pledge again, I appeal to you all: let us honour them with our memories and let us do them justice with our actions. Never Srebrenica, nowhere and to no one. My deepest respect to all the victims and families and my admiration to the people of Bosnia and Herzegovina. *Hvala.*

Message to Human Rights Council on discrimination based on sexual orientation or gender identity

GENEVA, 7 MARCH 2012

I am pleased to address this historic Human Rights Council session. Some say sexual orientation and gender identity is a sensitive subject. I understand: like many of my generation, I did not grow up talking about these issues.

But I learned to speak out because lives are at stake, and because it is our duty, under the United Nations Charter and the Universal Declaration of Human Rights, to protect the rights of everyone, everywhere.

The High Commissioner's report documents disturbing abuses in all regions.

We see a pattern of violence and discrimination directed at people just because they are gay, lesbian, bisexual or transgender.

There is widespread bias at jobs, schools and hospitals. And appalling violent attacks, including sexual assault. People have been imprisoned, tortured, even killed.

This is a monumental tragedy for those affected, and a stain on our collective conscience. It is also a violation of international law. You, as members of the Human Rights Council, must respond.

To those who are lesbian, gay, bisexual or transgender, let me say: you are not alone. Your struggle for an end to violence and discrimination is a shared struggle. Any attack on you is an attack on the universal values the United Nations and I have sworn to defend and uphold. Today, I stand with you and I call upon all countries and people to stand with you, too.

A historic shift is under way. More States see the gravity of the problem. We need constructive actions. The High Commissioner's report points the way. We must tackle the violence, decriminalize consensual same-sex relationships, ban discrimination and educate the public. We also need regular reporting to verify that violations are genuinely being addressed.

I count on this Council and all people of conscience to make this happen. The time has come.

Address to Stanley Foundation conference on the Responsibility to Protect

NEW YORK, 18 JANUARY 2012

It is a great honour and pleasure for me to participate in this very important gathering and addressing this very esteemed group of experts and supporters of Responsibility to Protect. I just started my second term as Secretary-General and I know that when I was elected as Secretary-General for the second time, all of you have supported me, and I thank you very much.

This Responsibility to Protect initiative has given me the opportunity of raising my voice and profile, and I thank you for such an opportunity. Even though I have met only briefly some of the participants, I know many of you in person. I am sorry that I am not able to greet you in person this time but I wish you all the best in the New Year.

Today we mark the first decade of the Responsibility to Protect. There will be many more, for we can now say with confidence that this fundamental principle of human protection is here to stay.

We salute the foresight of Gareth Evans, Mohamed Sahnoun and the distinguished members of their Commission, and of course my predecessor Kofi Annan. They pointed the way.

And we thank again Mr. Gregorian of the Carnegie Corporation, Mr. Lowenkron of the MacArthur Foundation and Mr. Stanley of the Stanley Foundation, with whom I have been regularly discussing this matter, for co-sponsoring this special day. We count on your continuing support and partnership.

While I already knew that this concept was introduced by our distinguished colleagues, former Foreign Minister Gareth Evans and Dr. Robert Stanley, today I have come to appreciate that with this humanitarian principle, we are really talking about saving human lives. The United Nations is heavily engaged and committed to saving lives – human lives – from natural disasters. Dr. Gregorian was one those who championed the UN humanitarian mechanism of an emergency response fund. He may not have been fully aware of this, but the CERF is now saving thousands and thousands of lives. We are grateful for the kindness and foresight of Dr. Gareth Evans, Mohamed Sahnoun, and Dr. Gregorian. Now we are more actively and efficiently working to save lives in natural disasters. That said, we are here today to discuss how we can save lives in man-made disasters.

In 2011, history took a turn for the better. The Responsibility to Protect came of age; the principle was tested as never before. The results were uneven but, at the end of the day, tens of thousands of lives were saved.

We gave hope to people long oppressed. In Libya, Côte d'Ivoire, South Sudan, Yemen and Syria, by our words and actions, we demonstrated that human protection is a defining purpose of the United Nations in the 21st century.

We also learned important lessons.

For one, we have learned that this Organization cannot stand on the sidelines when challenged to take preventive action. Where there is a clear and present danger, we may need to define the field: cautiously but proactively.

We have also learned that delivering on the Responsibility to Protect requires partnership and common purpose. We get the best results when global and regional institutions push in the same direction.

> **" Prevention does not mean looking the other way in times of crisis, vainly hoping that things will get better. Prevention means proactive, decisive and early action to stop violence before it begins. "**

In 2011, we stood firm for democracy in Côte d'Ivoire. Yet, we could not have succeeded without the leadership and partnership of the African Union and the Economic Community of West African States, ECOWAS. I would like to recognize the presence of Mr. Abdul Ilah al-Khatib, who worked as the United Nations Special Envoy to Libya. I thank you very much for your contribution.

That in turn set the stage for Libya, where Mr. Al-Khatib has been travelling and negotiating with the then Libyan authorities. When Muammar Gaddafi threatened to kill his people "like rats," the Arab League and Organization of Islamic Cooperation called on the international community to act. Thus the Security Council could find the unity to do so.

We learned lessons about our own limitations, as well. Consider the recent violence in South Sudan. We saw it coming weeks ahead. Yet we were not able to stop it - unfortunately. Nor was the government which, like other governments, has primary responsibility for protecting its citizens. The reason was painfully simple: we were denied the use of necessary resources, in particular helicopters that would have given us mobility to bring all the UN Peacekeepers where there are no roads, except by air mobility. At this critical moment, I was left to beg for replacements from neighboring countries and missions. With limited resources, we tried our best.

So, a key challenge in putting the Responsibility to Protect into practice is this: how do we do our job, how do we deliver on Security Council mandates, when the very members of the Council do not give us the support we need.

All these issues are enormously complex. That is why I have asked my Special Adviser, Ed Luck, to lead a system-wide assessment of how the UN can best employ the tools given to us under the Charter - and specifically Chapters VI, VII and VIII.

I know you will want to discuss all these matters in depth, especially the aspects that are dominating the news. Before we do so, however, let me speak to an issue that I believe has not received sufficient attention. That is the importance of prevention.

Today, I ask you to join me in making 2012 the Year of Prevention. This is going to be one of what I consider the five generational opportunities of the United Nations for the coming five years. The 2005 World Summit called for assisting States under stress before crises and conflicts break out.

Prevention does not mean looking the other way in times of crisis, vainly hoping that things will get better. We have done that too often. Nor can it be just a brief pause while Chapter VII enforcement measures are being prepared. Prevention means proactive, decisive and early action to stop violence before it begins.

My recent report on preventive diplomacy sets forth the ways and means by which we are strengthening our capacities for mediation, fact-finding and peaceful settlement. We need to sharpen our tools for preventing atrocities as well.

Over the last year or two, we have seen encouraging successes. In Kenya, Kyrgyzstan and Guinea, the United Nations helped prevent, or at least limit, what we might call atrocity crimes. There, as elsewhere, we learned an important fact: that the key to preventing genocide, war crimes, ethnic cleansing and other crimes against humanity lies within each society. These crimes occur far less often in places where civil society is robust, where tolerance is practiced, and where diversity is celebrated. Political figures cannot incite mass violence for their own ends where the rights of minorities and the rule of law are respected.

That is why, during my second term as Secretary-General, the UN will redouble its efforts at training, education and capacity-building on human rights, humanitarian law and democratic values and practices. We will undertake development and peacebuilding in ways that reduce tensions among groups and strengthen institutional barriers to sectarian violence.

Too often, we have seen how one round of violence ignites the next. For societies under stress, early warning may come too late to prevent the outbreak of mass violence. Such situations call for a dynamic assessment of how such stresses are developing over time, and how the international community can help.

It means little, however, to get the assessment right if it is not followed by targeted, measured and determined action. That action can take – and has taken – many forms. For instance, we have been quick to respond to incitement in Kenya, Côte d'Ivoire, Libya and elsewhere. Because outbreaks of mass violence are rarely spontaneous, we generally have the time and opportunity to remind government and opposition leaders that they could be held accountable by the International Criminal Court (ICC) or other tribunals.

One of my greatest satisfactions as Secretary-General has been to help advance the powers of these courts – and to see how effective a deterrent the ICC, in particular, has become. If we are going to be serious about prevention, then we need to develop more innovative ways to use the under-utilized tools of Chapter VI.

Truth can be a powerful weapon against those who try to hide or rationalize their criminality. It is the first step toward accountability. I welcome, therefore, the Human Rights Council's growing use of commissions of inquiry, as in Syria and Libya. The Security Council can make more use of its own missions and its power to investigate under Article 34 if the Charter to look into situations before they escalate. Fact-finding by the United Nations and regional and sub-regional arrangements should focus more intently on preventing atrocity crimes. In some cases, these efforts could be usefully supplemented by the deployment of unarmed observers from global and regional organizations, civil society and national police units. The Arab League observer mission in Syria has encountered serious difficulties. The United Nations is helping with training and capacity-building, but clearly the situation calls for more than a small, circumscribed presence.

> 66 Our chief failing as an international community has been the reluctance to act in the face of serious threats. The result, too often, has been a loss of lives and credibility that haunt us ever after. Let us not let the pendulum swing back to the past. 99

Used in measured and targeted ways, peacekeepers can help prevent atrocities as well as armed conflict. The African Union did so in Burundi, as did our own blue helmets in the Former Yugoslav Republic of Macedonia.

When national leaders want to protect their populations, there are ample consent-based tools under Chapters VI and VIII to assist them. In Rwanda, Kenya and Kyrgyzstan, local groups were able to reach across sectarian lines to defuse tensions in some communities despite rising violence around them. Civil society could be critical to avoiding an escalation of violence in Syria and South Sudan. We need to give such groups our support and encouragement.

Let me close by returning to some current challenges.

I have listened carefully to those who have raised concerns about how some Security Council mandates were carried out last year. And I agree: at times, the execution of our collective responsibilities was not always perfect. In Côte d'Ivoire and Libya, some innocent lives were lost in the name of the Responsibility to Protect. That is why the use of force is never our first choice. Many more lives were saved, however. We all agree on the need for responsibility while protecting. In that spirit, I very much welcome the Brazilian initiative to open a dialogue on these matters.

Yet let us also remember: historically, our chief failing as an international community has been the reluctance to act in the face of serious threats. The result, too often, has been a loss of lives and credibility that haunts us ever after. Let us not let the pendulum swing back to the past. Let us not make the best the enemy of the good.

A final point: we have been discussing, today, how to prepare ourselves for the next test of our common humanity. We need not look far. That test is here – in Syria. Since the uprising began, I have spoken out, forcefully and directly. I did so again just days ago in Lebanon at a conference on reform and democracy in the Arab world. Stop the violence, I told President Assad. The path of repression is a dead end. Listen to your people, I said repeatedly. Listen to your people's genuine aspirations. I told him this publicly and privately in conversations. Change now, act boldly and make decisive reforms before it is too late, before more innocents die.

Even as I make these calls, however, I am mindful of the complexities of the situation. At a time when unity is required, the Security Council is deeply divided. Efforts by regional friends and organizations such as the Arab League are very welcome, but so far they have not borne fruit. I am also acutely aware of the need to preserve my own diplomatic space for the crucial moment when the UN's good offices may be needed.

Such is the nature of the Responsibility to Protect. It can be a minefield of nuance, political calculation and competing national interests. The result too often is hesitation or inaction. This we cannot afford.

We must not forget how remarkably far we have come in so short time. The world has embraced the Responsibility to Protect - not because it is easy, but because it is right. We therefore have a moral responsibility to push ahead. Together, let us work, with optimism and determination, to make the Responsibility to Protect a living reality for the peoples of the world.

Remarks at Space for Memory and for the protection and defense of human rights

BUENOS AIRES, 13 JUNE 2011

uenas tardes. This is really a very moving and sad experience for me, to have seen the torture rooms where many thousands of people were arrested, tortured and disappeared, without leaving any messages, any clues to their loving family members.

The stories which I heard from the Mothers of the Plaza of the Mayo where really saddening, and I heard the story of a man who was arrested and tortured in those dark rooms.

Words are sometimes inadequate to the occasion, and this is one of those moments.

As the Secretary-General of the United Nations, I have been to many places of such dark history. I was at the detention centre of the Khmer Rouge in Cambodia, and I visited the memorial to the Rwandan genocide memorial. In the past, the international community has experienced terrible human rights violations, massacres and genocides, including Srebrenica in the former Yugoslavia. And now this grim place, Ground Zero in Argentina's Dirty War.

To speak very personally, I am very humbled, very sad, and deeply moved. It is one thing to read of the terrible events, but it is another to see it for myself. Let me say, also, that it is an honor for me to be here today with all of you, with some of those who suffered so much, who endured with such courage and inner strength.

The *Abuelas and Madres de Plaza de Mayo* – the Mothers of the Plaza de Mayo – waged a long struggle in the name of our common humanity. I highly praise your courage and the courage of those who have fought against dictators. They stood on principles of justice and decency and dignity, and demanded answers from dictators. In doing so, they sent a message to the world that decency, justice and law can prevail, even in the darkest times.

In that spirit, in this symbolic place, let us send a message of hope and encouragement to many people whose human rights, whose basic fundamental rights, are still being abused and oppressed, not only in Argentina but everywhere in the world.

You have repealed laws that protected the guilty. You have built strong and enduring democratic institutions. And I again highly praise the leadership of former President Dr. Nestor Kirchner and incumbent President Cristina Fernandez for their strong commitment and belief in human rights, in protecting human life and promoting human rights. You have shown that there can be no safe refuge for those who commit crimes against humanity.

In this world, there is no safe place now for any perpetrators who violate international human rights laws and international humanitarian laws. They must be held responsible; they must be brought to justice. This has been a fundamental principle and my strong commitment as Secretary-General of the United Nations.

> " The *Abuelas and Madres de Plaza de Mayo* – the Mothers of the Plaza de Mayo – demanded answers from dictators. In doing so, they sent a message to the world that decency, justice and law can prevail, even in the darkest times. "

Here in Argentina, and around the world, we can clearly say the age of impunity is dead. The age of impunity is gone and a new era of accountability has arrived, an era where justice, sooner or later, will be done.

Argentina today is dedicated to truth, the truth about what happened here decades ago. The truth about who gave the orders, who carried out the crimes, and who knew about these crimes. Perhaps those people could have prevented them, but stayed silent.

They were cowards.

The people of Argentina deserve the full truth. For Argentina, as for other societies experiencing such tragedies, the path to healing and reconciliation begins with truth, with restoring historical memory.

That is why I am here today, with humility, to encourage your authorities to continue to investigate, prosecute and sanction those responsible. Witnesses must be protected. So must judges, prosecutors and all those involved in the ongoing trials.

In closing, let us pay tribute to all those courageous citizens, mothers, particularly, and their families who won this victory against lawlessness and dictatorship. Let us remember the victims and, in their honor, remind ourselves of our own sacred duty.

One of the cardinal missions of the United Nations is to shine the light of human rights everywhere. There are still many dark places where people's human rights are abused. That is my strong commitment as Secretary-General; that is why I am here. I express my full support and my full sympathy to those family members who have lost their loved ones and my strong commitment and encouragement to all of you.

As the Universal Declaration of Human Rights declares: "Recognition of the inherent dignity, and of the equal and inalienable rights of all members of the human family, is the foundation of freedom, justice and peace in the world." That remains our mission, here and everywhere.

Let us do our best to make this world better for all, where everybody's human rights and well-being are protected and promoted.

Address to Review Conference of the International Criminal Court
An age of accountability

KAMPALA, 31 MAY 2010

L et me begin by thanking President Museveni and the people of Uganda for organizing this historic gathering. Thank you, as well, for the warmth of your welcome. I am sure I speak for all in saying that we felt among friends as soon as we landed at Entebbe.

Twelve years ago, world leaders gathered in Rome to establish the International Criminal Court (ICC). Few could have believed, then, that this court would spring so vigorously into life, fully operational, investigating, and trying war crimes and crimes against humanity across a broadening geography of countries. Seldom since the founding of the United Nations itself has such a resounding blow been struck for peace, justice and human rights.

Today, we come together for this first Review Conference of the Rome Statute. It is a chance not only to take stock of our progress, but to build for the future. More, it is an occasion to strengthen our collective determination that crimes against humanity cannot go unpunished, the better to deter them in the future.

I see this as a landmark in the history of international criminal justice. The old era of impunity is over. In its place, slowly but surely, we are witnessing the birth of a new age of accountability.

It began, many decades ago, with the Nuremberg and Tokyo tribunals. It gained strength with the international criminal tribunals for Rwanda and the former Yugoslavia, as well as the so-called hybrid tribunals in Sierra Leone, Cambodia and Lebanon. Now we have the ICC, permanent, increasingly powerful, casting a long shadow. There is no going back.

In this new age of accountability, those who commit the worst of human crimes will be held responsible. Whether they are rank-and-file foot soldiers or military commanders, whether they are lowly civil servants following orders, or top political leaders, they will be held accountable.

Hear the roster of names for those who have already been called to justice: General Ante Gotovina. Jean-Paul Akayesu, a city mayor. Chea Nuaon and Radovan Karadzic, prominent political leaders. Jean Kambanda, a Prime Minister. Slobodan Milosevic and Charles Taylor, heads of state.

Not long ago, this would have been unimaginable. Today, it is the way of the future. We are here in Kampala to build on this success, to help build this court into all that it can be and all that it must be. Let us do so by recognizing certain realities.

First, if the ICC is to have the reach it should possess, if it is to become an effective deterrent as well as an avenue of justice, it must have universal support. Only then will perpetrators have no place to hide. I congratulate Bangladesh for ratifying the Rome Statute and becoming its 111th State Party. And I again urge all States that have not yet done so to become a party to the Rome Statute.

Second, this court breaks new ground on the rights of victims, including the right of compensation. Rightly, it holds that justice is not only retributive, but restorative as well.

Third, the ICC remains a court of last resort. It exercises jurisdiction only where national courts do not (or cannot) act themselves. This is important: where a State is unwilling to genuinely investigate and prosecute perpetrators, the Court can get involved. No government or justice system that is complicit in international crimes can any longer shield the perpetrators from justice.

---

66 **The old era of impunity is over. In its place, slowly but surely, we are witnessing the birth of a new Age of Accountability.** 99

Your debates over the coming week are likely to be wide ranging and intense. The issues are so difficult and often controversial that there are few easy answers.

Perhaps the most contentious challenge you face is the balance between peace and justice. Yet frankly, I see it as a false choice. In today's conflicts, civilians have become the chief victims. Women, children and the elderly are deliberately targeted. Armies or militias rape, maim, kill and devastate towns, villages, crops, cattle and water sources, all as a strategy of war. The more shocking the crime, the more effective it is as a weapon.

Any victim would understandably yearn to stop such horrors, even at the cost of granting immunity to those who have wronged them.

But this is a false peace. This is a truce at gunpoint, without dignity, justice or hope for a better future. Yes, it may be true: demanding criminal accountability, at the wrong time, can discourage warring parties from sitting down at the negotiating table. Yes, it may even perpetuate bloodshed. Even so, one thing is clear: the time has passed when we might speak of peace versus justice, or think of them as somehow opposed to each other.

Between war and peace must first come something else: reconciliation, forgiveness, a mending of the social fabric. These are the hand-maidens of peace and justice. We have no choice but to pursue them both, hand in hand.

In recent years, international criminal justice has emerged as a powerful voice against the epidemic of violence against women. In 1998, for the first time in international criminal law, the Rwanda Tribunal gave us a definition of rape as a crime against humanity. The Special Court for Sierra Leone convicted three members of the Revolutionary United Front for sexual enslavement. Right now, at the ICC, alleged perpetrators of rape and sexual slavery in the Democratic Republic of the Congo face war crimes charges. This jurisprudence sends a strong and necessary signal. It is up to you to make sure that the message continues to be heard.

Indeed, it is time to turn up the volume. Executing the mandate given to me by the Security Council, I recently appointed Ms. Margot Wallström as my Special Representative on Sexual Violence in Conflict. She is a forceful advocate, and I count on her to use her position to the fullest. I urge the court to continue treating this issue as one of its top priorities.

We have all heard at least one criticism of this court: that it is selective; that African nations are too frequently the focus of its work; that grave crimes elsewhere escape such scrutiny. As I see it, however, these criticisms are both unfair and inaccurate. As a matter of factual accuracy, yes. All of the on-going cases before the court relate to Africa. That said, most of these situations were referred to the Prosecutor by the governments concerned. Correctly, they see the court as a help to them, not a threat.

In the case of Darfur, I might add, the referral was a decision of the Security Council. Only with regard to the situation in Kenya did the Prosecutor take the initiative to request an authorization from the Court to formally investigate. The merits of each case warrant no less. The Court is meant to follow the evidence.

> **" In this new age of accountability, those who commit the worst of human crimes will be held responsible. Whether they are rank-and-file foot soldiers or military commanders, lowly civil servants following orders, or top political leaders, they will be held accountable. "**

There is a broader point, as well: in all these cases, African society is cheering. To them, the court is where we all should be, firmly on the side of the victims. The presence today of so many African NGOs is a clear expression of support for the ICC by Africa's people and civil society.

Let me close on a note of high praise. We are here, today, largely because of the immense contribution of civil society. These globally minded civic action organizations were among the originators of the very idea of a permanent international criminal court. Many joined in a common cause, the Coalition for the ICC, and campaigned far and wide in the run-up to Rome. Ever since, they have been instrumental in promoting the ICC and pushing world leaders to embrace it. That this court exists is a testament to their vision, their tenacity and determination, their sense of justice and humanity. Many are here today, coming to Kampala from all corners of the earth. To them I say: thank you. None of us would be here without you.

The decisions you take this week will be felt around the world, wherever there is injustice, wherever people live in fear. Let us remember the mothers of Srebrenica, the orphans of Sierra Leone, the killing fields of Cambodia and Rwanda. So many terrible names, so many haunted places. Long ago, we said: never again. That is why this court exists. That is why we are here. That is what we have all worked so hard to achieve.

The Rome Statute represents the best that is in us, our most noble instinct: the instinct for peace and justice. We pay tribute to my predecessor, Kofi Annan, for speaking so often and so strongly for the court's creation. We applaud all those who have signed the Rome Statute, and we welcome those who have not yet done so but are with us today. In this regard, let us especially welcome the United States and the new sprit of re-engagement under President Barack Obama.

In 1998, we made Rome a by-word for international criminal justice. Let us now write Kampala in that illustrious history, as well. Let it be known as the place where the international community, coming together in concert, closed the door on the era of impunity and, acting in concert, ushered in the new age of accountability.

Remarks to the press following address to the Parliament of Malawi

LILONGWE, 29 MAY 2010

I just had the honour to be the first guest to address the newly built Parliament. This Parliament is magnificent and a fitting monument to a modern democracy. I was particularly pleased to see that the proportion of women representatives is growing. Women are the backbone of any society. As we know, the backbone starts at the head.

My speech to parliament focused on Africa's development challenges, in particular, the Millennium Development Goals. I had a simple message. We can and we will achieve the Millennium Development Goals.

The reason for my optimism is right here in Malawi. In a few short years Malawi has gone from famine to feast, from food deficit to surplus, from a food importing country to a food exporting country. There is nothing miraculous about it.

It is the result of one simple truth: where we try, we succeed. Where we do not try, we fail. It is a message that Malawi can proudly proclaim across the world. It is a message that I will take with me to the G-20 and the Millennium Development Goals Summit meeting in September. And, I hope, ladies and gentlemen, it is a message you too can spread around the world. The role of the media is crucially important in sending this message around the world.

> **"It is unfortunate that laws that criminalize people on the basis of their sexual orientation or gender entity still exist in some countries. Penal codes criminalizing homosexuality should be reformed."**

In my speech to the Parliament I laid out four elements for success.

First, many promises have been made by the developed world. Now Africa needs the implementation of these promises.

Second, unleashing Africa's potential is a job for all: donor nations, African governments, the private sector and civil society. Africa's people may be poor, but the continent is rich in resources and potential.

Third, the fight against poverty, hunger and disease must be coordinated. We cannot pick and choose. That is why I am going to Mwandama tomorrow morning to see how effective integrated, holistic development is done on the ground.

The fourth element for success is leadership. Africa too has a responsibility to deliver on development, on good governance and on human rights.

This is a responsibility for governments and for the African Union. In that regard, it is unfortunate that laws that criminalize people on the basis of their sexual orientation or gender entity still exists in some countries. Penal codes criminalizing homosexuality should be reformed.

This is what I have asked this Parliament. For this reason, I am very happy to report that in our discussions today, President Mutharika announced officially that he would pardon two young men recently convicted of homosexuality and sentenced to fourteen years of prison. This was a very courageous decision and I applaud the leadership of President Mutharika. I am confident that Malawi will take appropriate steps to update these laws in a way that lives up to international standards.

Malawi should be known throughout the world for its successes in combating poverty and hunger and leading the Millennium Development Goals campaign. This is what I told Parliament today.

Remarks to the Third Forum of the Alliance of Civilizations

RIO DE JANEIRO, 28 MAY 2010

B*om Dia.* President Lula, my deepest thanks to you and the Brazilian people for your hospitality and warm welcome. *Muito obrigado.*

To the original co-sponsors of the Alliance of Civilizations – Spain and Turkey – thank you for your consistent support. I thank High Representative Sampaio for his dedication.

I also commend the Custodian of the Two Holy Mosques, King Abdullah, for his interfaith initiative, including his call to live an authentic faith that emphasizes dialogue and cooperation.

We meet at a unique moment. Times are changing. Power is shifting. Brazil is rising. I speak not just of the economy of Brazil, but the story of Brazil. This is a melting pot of cultures, peoples and traditions. All pulling as one, especially during World Cup season! There is no better place for the Alliance of Civilizations to meet and take its work forward.

On the surface, it may appear that I come from a different world. Growing up, my homeland of Korea was one of the most homogenous places on earth. But I was raised in the wake of the Korean war. The international community rebuilt my country. From an early age, I saw the power of cultures uniting in common cause. I saw solidarity in action. I am not merely a witness: I am a product of it. This is not just my history; it is an essential part of who I am.

That is why this Forum means so much to me. And that is why I know the Alliance of Civilizations matters to the world. From the beginning, we all knew the Alliance could not be business as usual. The work could not be left to beautifully written reports stuck in the United Nations library. We understood the Alliance must be action-oriented. It must reach far and wide.

Since 2005, the Alliance of Civilizations has been doing just that. With your support, the Alliance is bringing together journalists from around the globe to confront prejudice and misunderstanding – including the first-of-its-kind joint reporting from Israel and the Arab world. You are expanding dialogue for young people of different ethnicities in Burundi, promoting mediation and conflict resolution in South Asia, mentoring in immigrant neighborhoods in Europe, and providing jobs for young people throughout the Middle East and North Africa. At the same time, the Alliance is widening its own network of partners and community of friends. We are pleased to welcome the one-hundredth member, the United States of America.

All this is impressive. But it is only a start. The Alliance is a process, a work in progress. In communities where symbols of religious minorities are seen as something to oppose or fear, we need continued engagement. In places where people are screened out of opportunity because of race, faith or even their name, we have more work to do. But the mission of the Alliance must go deeper still. I would like to briefly point to three reasons why.

First, and fundamentally, because your mission is among the most important of the 21st century. Three quarters of the major conflicts in the world today have a cultural dimension. You are seeking to defuse those tensions by finding answers to some of the most urgent issues of our day: how do we build inclusive societies? How can we strengthen education and empower women? How do we drown out the siren songs that divert young people to extremism? In short, how do we build communities rooted in convivencia – living together in peace, based on trust and mutual respect?

> ❝ We live in a world where, too often, division sells. It wins votes. It gets ratings. It is much easier to blame others than to think for oneself. And yet wherever I go, I have found something else – a growing realization that we are in this together. ❞

That leads me to the second reason for deepening our work – because the process of building inclusive societies must itself be inclusive. It takes each and every one of us. After all, peace and reconciliation cannot be imposed. They are seeds, planted by people, nurtured by communities. Day, after day, after day.

The Alliance cultivates through outreach, through understanding, through education. And we know that education is more than learning. Sometimes it is also unlearning. We must let go of the stereotypes of the monolithic "other". We must put an end to labels that do more to divide than define.

The third reason to deepen our work: globalization. Globalization can both connect and alienate. We have access to more information, ideas and technology. And yet, fears and hatred are just a mouse click away. The gains of globalization are more visible – but so, too, is the feeling among many that those benefits are out of reach.

In many places around the world, such fears cause people to retreat – away from globalization into an extreme localization. One that sends the message: "Our way is best". Or worse, "There is no other way but my way". This creates tension and instability. Tackling this, too, is the work of the Alliance.

As we expand all of our efforts, we must do even more to reach out, to listen and to learn from young people. Tomorrow, I will go to Africa. 70 percent of Africans are under the age of thirty. Half the world's population is under twenty-five, the vast majority in the developing world. We need to tap this great potential. They need to see a world of hope and possibility, of quality education and decent work.

Yesterday I met with young people in the Babilonia favela here in Rio de Janeiro. One young woman said: "When I go to wealthy areas, they see what I am, not who I am." But she showed all of us. The young people I met had such passion and commitment to work against discrimination and for a better life. I learn from you. You learn from me. We grow together. That was their message. That is our message

I am not naive about the challenge. There is unease in our world. Tensions, rooted in fear. Fear, driven by ignorance. We live in a world where, too often, division sells. It wins votes. It gets ratings. It is much easier to blame others than to think for oneself.

And yet wherever I go, I have found something else – a growing realization that we are in this together. A sharper awareness that my child's future depends on your child's future. A greater understanding that we are a single global family with many members and no monoliths.

We are not there yet. The journey is long. But I take strength from the Brazilian proverb: goodwill makes the road shorter. Your goodwill and your good works are making all our roads shorter.

I can see on the horizon a world that understands that, together, we are better. I can hear shouting replaced with listening. I can feel a force committed to making it happen. Governments, civil society, the private sector, the faith community, young people. You - and all this Alliance represents.

A global social movement. An Alliance of Humanity. Regardless of religious tradition, we have a common faith: a faith in our shared future. Let us harness our common humanity and make a better world.

Remarks at Holocaust Remembrance Day ceremony at Park East Synagogue

NEW YORK, 24 JANUARY 2009

To all, I wish you *Shabat Shalom*.

Today we mark the International Day of Commemoration honoring victims of the Holocaust. This is a most important and solemn occasion.

As you know, my friend, the late Tom Lantos, died shortly after last year's observance. Some of you may have met him when he came to this Synagogue. He was dear to me, as he was to you. He made an extraordinary journey from a Nazi labor camp to the halls of Congress. He became a leading champion of truth and justice. Like those of you who also lived through the Holocaust, he was never defeated by the unspeakable horrors that he survived.

I can only imagine what he endured. Yet I, too, have witnessed man's inhumanity to man. I have seen it as Secretary-General, traveling in places torn by war. And I saw it as a six-year old boy fleeing to the mountains to escape fighting in my own country. The UN helped South Korea to recover. Like Tom Lantos, like many of you, I came to believe in the transformative power of the United Nations.

Today, the UN is on the cusp of a great transition. Never have global challenges been so large. Climate change, terrorism, the global financial crisis - these troubles transcend borders. They affect all countries, rich and poor. They will be overcome only when all countries come together in response. That's why we have a United Nations.

Yes, the UN has its imperfections. It is not perfect. Because of this, from day one since I took office, I have pushed to change it. I have insisted on a new culture of transparency and accountability. I have worked to make the UN more efficient, effective, modern. In short, we have tried to make it a better instrument to serve mankind.

We are here to mark the Holocaust. Like you, the United Nations is determined to tell its timeless lessons. Precisely two years ago, the UN General Assembly adopted a resolution condemning, without reservation, any denial of the Holocaust. I quote: "Ignoring the historical fact of those terrible events increases the risk they will be repeated."

With you, I stand in saying: never again. Never. When I paid tribute to Holocaust victims at Yad Vashem, I wrote in the book there, "Never again. Never."

Memory speaks. That is why it must be preserved and passed to future generations. Our Holocaust Outreach Program sponsors exhibits, workshops and panel discussions. The aim: to confront deniers, or those who would minimize the importance of the Holocaust. When President Ahmadinejad of Iran declared that Israel should disappear, or be wiped off the map, I strongly condemned his remarks - twice.

We at the United Nations stand for human rights. We stand for democracy and the rule of law. By working for economic and social development, we build the foundations for peace.

We have a new instrument in our hands. It is called the Responsibility to Protect – the idea that every nation has a legal obligation to protect its people from genocide, war crimes, ethnic cleansing and crimes against humanity. Where nations fall short, the international community has the right to take collective action. Yes, it is difficult in practice. But I assure you: this is a major advance in safeguarding mankind from crimes against humanity.

> " As we remember the victims of the Holocaust, let us reaffirm our faith in the dignity of humankind and our extraordinary resilience – our moral strength – even amid history's darkest chapters. "

Today is not simply a time for remembering. The Holocaust has lessons for us, here and now. Let us heed them.

My job can sometimes be terribly painful. I see unbelievable hardship, the worst human suffering. You are familiar with the grim catalogue of names and places: the Democratic Republic of the Congo, Darfur, Somalia and, of course, the Middle East.

I am just back from the region. I went to push for a cease-fire. More, I went in search of a lasting peace. The recurring violence between Palestinians and Israelis is a mark of collective political failure – by both sides and by the international community. I saw first-hand what most people saw on television. I met a child and his parents in Sderot, southern Israel, traumatized by falling rockets. Never for one moment have I forgotten that a million people in southern Israel live in a daily state of terror and fear. In Gaza, I saw the most appalling devastation. I saw the UN compound, still burning. I said to all I met, on both sides: this must stop. I left the region more determined than ever to work toward a world where two States, Israel and Palestine, live side by side in peace and security. War can never be an answer. We need to strengthen the forces of peaceful coexistence and dialogue.

No one sees this more clearly than your own Rabbi Schneier. He has devoted his life to overcoming hatred and intolerance. You all know him as the founder and president of the Appeal for Conscience Foundation. What you may not know, and what I am very grateful to him for, is his pioneering work for the UN's Alliance of Civilizations.

He knows first-hand that no one man or nation has all the answers. He knows the sacred value of tolerance. He has survived the greatest trials that life can hurl at a man or a woman and emerged not only with his humanity and spirit intact but stronger. He survived the Holocaust. Like others among you, he never lost sight of man's essential humanity, our capacity for good, our inherent dignity.

So, let us be frank. We must recognize the limits of power and goodwill. We here know that we can never entirely rid the world of its tyrants and its intolerance. We cannot turn all extremists to the path of reason and light. We can only stand against them and raise our voices in the name of our common humanity.

Tom Lantos was fond of saying that even the littlest actions, the smallest of our daily deeds, can do much to leave this earth better, less evil, less selfish, less monstrous than we found it. And he stressed that doing these things, even in a modest way, gives you the energy to keep moving forward. On this day of days, that seems to me to be good advice.

As we remember the victims of the Holocaust, let us reaffirm our faith in the dignity of humankind and our extraordinary resilience – our moral strength – even amid history's darkest chapters.

Address to forum on responsible sovereignty

BERLIN, 15 JULY 2008

I t is an honour to be with you. I commend the organizers – Managing Global Insecurity and the Bertelsmann Foundation – for convening this forum on responsible sovereignty, one of the defining challenges of the 21st century.

How fitting it is that we address these matters in Berlin, where the 20th century
learned such hard lessons about the dangers of unbridled and irresponsible sovereignty. Today, Germany stands as a model of the responsible sovereign, at home and
abroad. Indeed, the leading role that a united Germany now plays in the United Nations speaks to the curative properties of the principles of human rights, tolerance,
and the rule of law for which the world body proudly stands.

This evening, I would like to address one of the more powerful but less understood ideas of our times: the Responsibility to Protect, or R2P for short. Now that
the concept has received the ultimate UN accolade, a distinctive acronym, we need
a common understanding of what the Responsibility to Protect is and, just as importantly, of what it is not.

Responsibility to Protect is not a new code for humanitarian intervention.
Rather, it is built on a more positive and affirmative concept of sovereignty as responsibility – a concept developed by my Special Adviser for the Prevention of
Genocide, Francis Deng, and his colleagues at the Brookings Institution more than
a decade ago. The Responsibility to Protect should be also distinguished from its
conceptual cousin, human security. The latter, which is broader, posits that policy
should take into account the security of people, not just of States, across the whole
range of possible threats.

The concept of responsibility to protect is more firmly anchored in current international law than the two related concepts. It was adopted by the 2005 World
Summit – the largest gathering of Heads of State and Government the world has
seen – and was subsequently endorsed by both the General Assembly and Security
Council. It rests on three pillars.

First, Governments unanimously affirmed the primary and continuing legal
obligations of States to protect their populations – whether citizens or not – from
genocide, war crimes, ethnic cleansing, and crimes against humanity, and from
their incitement. They declared – and this is the bedrock of the Responsibility to
Protect – that "we accept that responsibility and will act in accordance with it."

The second, more innovative pillar speaks to the UN's institutional strengths
and comparative advantages. The Summit underscored the commitment of the international community to assist States in meeting these obligations. Our goal is to
help States succeed, not just to react once they have failed to meet their prevention

and protection obligations. It would be neither sound morality, nor wise policy, to limit the world's options to watching the slaughter of innocents or to sending the marines. The magnitude of these four crimes and violations demands early, preventive steps – and these steps should require neither unanimity in the Security Council, nor pictures of unfolding atrocities that shock the conscience of the world.

The third pillar is much discussed, but generally understood too narrowly. It is Member States' acceptance of their responsibility to respond in a timely and decisive manner, in accordance with the UN Charter, to help protect populations from the four listed crimes and violations. The response could involve any of the whole range of UN tools, whether pacific measures under Chapter VI of the Charter, coercive ones under Chapter VII, and/or collaboration with regional and sub-regional arrangements under Chapter VIII. The key lies in an early and flexible response, tailored to the specific needs of each situation.

Our conception of the Responsibility to Protect, then, is narrow but deep. Its scope is narrow, focused solely on the four crimes and violations agreed by the world leaders in 2005. Extending the principle to cover other calamities, such as HIV/AIDS, climate change, or response to natural disasters, would undermine the 2005 consensus and stretch the concept beyond recognition or operational utility.

At the same time, our response should be deep, utilizing the whole prevention and protection tool kit available to the UN system, to its regional, sub-regional and civil society partners, and, not least, to the Member States themselves. As the Summit urged, we need to enhance UN early warning mechanisms, integrating the system's multiple channels of information and assessment. We need to strengthen the capacities of States to resist taking the path to genocide, war crimes, ethnic cleansing, and crimes against humanity.

In this context, capacity-building could cover a range of areas – from development, good governance and human rights to gender equality, the rule of law, and security sector reform. Our goal is not to add a new layer of bureaucracy, or to re-label existing UN programmes; it is to incorporate the responsibility to protect as a perspective into ongoing efforts.

This actually happened for the first time earlier this year, following the elections in Kenya. The combined efforts of the African Union, influential Member States, the UN, and my esteemed predecessor, Kofi Annan, were instrumental in curbing the post-election violence.

As the 2005 Summit recognized, there are times when persuasion and peaceful measures fall short. Allow me to quote in part from the Summit Outcome Document: when "national authorities are manifestly failing to protect their populations" from the four crimes and violations, Governments "are prepared to take collective action, in a timely and decisive manner, through the Security Council, in accordance with the Charter, including Chapter VII, on a case-by-case basis and in cooperation with relevant regional and sub-regional organizations as appropriate."

Caveats aside, this declaration could have profound implications. If Member States can indeed summon the will to act collectively in some cases like this, then others may be deterred from inciting or committing such atrocities. Likewise, if UN rules, procedures, and practices are developed in line with this bold declaration, then there is less likelihood of Responsibility to Protect principles being used to justify extra-legal interventions for other purposes.

In other words, the responsibility to protect does not alter the legal obligation of Member States to refrain from the use of force except in conformity with the Charter. Rather, it reinforces this obligation. By bolstering UN prevention, protection, response, and rebuilding mechanisms, the Responsibility to Protect seeks to enhance the rule of law and expand multilateral options.

> 66 Today, the responsibility to protect is a concept, not yet a policy; an aspiration, not yet a reality. Curbing mass atrocities will be neither easy nor quick. 99

Finally, let me clear up two more misconceptions, and then say a word about how we are proceeding in the effort to turn promise into practice, words into deeds. Some contend that the responsibility to protect is a western or northern invention, being imposed on the global south. Nothing could be further from the truth. It was the first two African Secretaries-General of the United Nations – Boutros Boutros-Ghali and Kofi Annan – who first explored evolving notions of sovereignty and humanitarian intervention. And the African Union has been explicit: in the year 2000, five years before the Summit declaration, the African Union asserted "the right of the Union to intervene in a Member State pursuant to a decision of the Assembly in respect of grave circumstances, namely: war crimes, genocide, and crimes against humanity".

Equally incorrect is the assumption that the responsibility to protect is in contradiction to sovereignty. Properly understood, the Responsibility to Protect is an ally of sovereignty, not an adversary. Strong States protect their people, while weak ones are either unwilling or unable to do so. Protection was one of the core purposes of the formation of States and the Westphalian system. By helping States meet one of their core responsibilities, the Responsibility to Protect seeks to strengthen sovereignty, not weaken it.

Friends, the task is considerable. As a first step, I have asked my Special Adviser, Edward C. Luck, to work on the conceptual, institutional, and political dimensions of the Responsibility to Protect. He is consulting widely, including at productive meetings here in Berlin and recently in Brussels, as well as in the developing world. He and Francis Deng are my two professors. They will share an office on genocide prevention and responsibility to protect, helping the UN to speak and act as one.

Late this year, I will report to the General Assembly on our proposed approach to Responsibility to Protect and the challenges posed by the Summit Outcome Document. I will do so in full confidence that Member States are united in their support of the goals and purposes of the responsibility to protect.

My personal commitment is deep and enduring. I voiced it even when I was still only a candidate for this office, and I have kept voicing it since. Let me be clear: just as I am aware of the controversy and doubts the concept of the responsibility to protect have created, so do I know the public expectations and enthusiasm it has generated.

Today, the responsibility to protect is a concept, not yet a policy; an aspiration, not yet a reality. Curbing mass atrocities will be neither easy nor quick. There is no certain blueprint for getting the job done. We are all novices in this field.

But I do know that the UN was built on ideas, ideals, and aspirations, not on quick fixes, sure things or cynical calculations. This has both inspired and, occasionally, frustrated "we the peoples" of the world. But the world's people have, nevertheless, kept their faith in the institution, because it never tires of trying to accomplish the impossible. So be it with Responsibility to Protect, which speaks to the things that are most noble and most enduring in the human condition. We will not always succeed in this cardinal enterprise, and we are taking but the first steps in a long journey. But our first responsibility is to try. I invite you to join me in this common endeavor, and I will welcome your suggestions and your criticisms along the way

Remarks to the Human Rights Council

GENEVA, 3 MARCH 2008

I am honoured to be with you at the start of this seventh session. This is a pivotal year in the cause of human rights around the world, as we seek to strengthen the work of this Council while marking the sixtieth anniversary of the Universal Declaration of Human Rights.

Over the past six decades, the international human rights enterprise has made remarkable, even triumphant, strides.

We have also learnt that to make human rights a reality for all – to implement and enforce these rights where it matters – we need clear commitments, and we need clear accountability for those commitments. Such accountability depends on the collective efforts of international organizations and governments, as well as civil society. It requires appropriate checks and balances and relentless scrutiny, so as to prevent or correct abuses and negligence. It is a duty of the highest order for each individual State, and the *raison d'être* of the Human Rights Council.

Almost two years have now passed since this Council was inaugurated. You have clearly set its direction on the right track in establishing your mechanisms and procedures.

The question for the Council, however, is whether you are fully meeting the high expectations which the international community has of you. What are those expectations? Most fundamentally, and in line with the very core jurisprudence of human rights, they are that this Council will recognize and promote the universal application of human rights values and that it will do so without favour, without selectivity, without being impacted by any political machinations around the world.

If you meet this benchmark, you can count on my fullest support and defence in the face of criticisms and attacks, wherever they may come from.

Essential to the proper functioning of the Council's machinery is the system of independent Special Procedures – your vanguard mechanisms for early detection of problematic human rights situations and sustained protection.

The Universal Periodic Review, on which you are about to embark, was conceived to prompt, support, and expand the promotion and protection of human rights on the ground. This is a historic undertaking, with significant consequences for people around the globe. It must help ensure that assessments are fair, that review processes and methods are transparent, and, crucially, that nations are accountable for progress, stagnation or regression in the implementation of human rights standards.

No country, however powerful, should escape scrutiny of its record, commitments and actions on human rights. The Review must reaffirm that just as human rights are universal, so is our collective respect for them and our commitment to them. It must help prevent the distrust that surrounded the work of the Commission on Human Rights in its final years.

But the Universal Periodic Review is only one of your tools. Throughout the year, in your regular and special sessions, you must remain vigilant and proactive – by sounding early warnings, by pushing for implementation, by insisting on accountability. You must respond to crises as they build up or unfold, and address situations of concern that are neglected or forgotten by the international community.

Let us be clear: implementing international obligations entails difficult, focussed, sustained and often thankless work. But it is not hopeless. We now have wide and increasing acceptance of human rights standards. We have expanding jurisprudence of international, regional and national mechanisms. We have evidence that human rights are actionable at all levels.

" No country, however powerful, should escape scrutiny of its record, commitments and actions on human rights. "

The Office of the High Commissioner for Human Rights, with all the authority of my office behind it, has for many years played a crucial role in advancing the cause of human rights worldwide, and continues to do so.

Together, you can build on the synergies that come from your mutually reinforcing but independent and distinct mandates. I look to you to proceed on this collaborative path, as laid out in the General Assembly resolution which led to the creation of this Council.

You also have my personal commitment. To underscore it, I have mobilized the entire UN family in our campaign for the sixtieth anniversary of the Universal Declaration of Human Rights. With concrete initiatives and result-oriented advocacy, this effort will bring us closer to the goal of fully integrating human rights in all aspects of the work of the United Nations. In this way, we can advance the original vision of the Declaration: one indivisible set of rights, inalienable to all humankind.

Ultimately, the work to uphold human rights rests on integrating human rights obligations into national legislation and policy, and using these to prevent and punish violations. But the Human Rights Council is responsible for securing such an outcome. Your power lies in persuading rather than compelling, in cooperating rather than imposing mandatory measures. Your power stems from credibility, not force. Your power gathers strength and resonance from the respect you enjoy among nations around the world. Your power must be exercised at all times, in the face of all threats to human rights, wherever they occur.

Your institution-building phase is now nearly over. For the Human Rights Council to fulfil its true promise, you must create an environment of trust. You must foster a climate where best practices thrive. You must spur greater account-ability for action on human rights. That was certainly the hope of the framers of this Council, it was the conviction of the world's governments when they united behind it, and it was the spirit in which our predecessors drafted the Universal Declaration of Human Rights. I trust you will live up to their expectations. It is an outcome in which all humankind has a stake.

Remarks to the press at Rwanda Genocide Memorial

KIGALI, 29 JANUARY 2008

I t is impossible to pass through these halls and not be affected – indeed, shaken to the core – by what the Rwandan people have endured. This genocide here will haunt the United Nations, and the international community, for generations to come.

I am here today to honour the victims – more than 800 thousand innocent people who lost their lives. I am here to express our solidarity to the survivors. May their courage and resilience serve as an inspiration to all of us.

But this Memorial is not simply a register of atrocities. It is also a repository of hope. It is a call to never forget, and today I say loud and clear: never again.

This memorial is also a call to justice. Justice will not heal all wounds, but putting an end to impunity can ensure that our cry of never again will become an enduring reality: not only in Rwanda, but for our common humanity.

The tragic events of 1994 shook our conscience. But the 1994 genocide has led to a significant rethinking of how the United Nations operates in peacekeeping, in conflict prevention and in how we protect innocent people from such atrocities.

The United Nations has learnt profound lessons from the tragedy of Rwanda. We have created the position of Special Adviser for the Prevention of genocide. We have established an Advisory Committee on Genocide Prevention. And Member States have agreed in principle to the responsibility to protect: to act collectively, through the Security Council, when a population is threatened with genocide, ethnic cleansing, or crimes against humanity. Our challenge now is to give real meaning to the concept, by taking steps to make it operational. I will spare no effort in working with Member States to make this happen.

And I am determined to work for human rights everywhere – to uphold them, protect them, defend them, ensure that they are a living reality. It is particularly important as this year marks the sixtieth anniversary of the Universal Declaration of Human Rights.

This memorial was built so all of us may learn and remember the worst that humankind can do. Let us resolve to build a global architecture to uphold the best humankind can do. I will do all I can to advance that mission.

Morakoze shani.

The survivors of the Genocide – those orphaned and family members left destitute – continue to suffer and deserve our sympathy and support. I will continue to urge for generous international support for them, and as a token gesture, I will contribute $10,000 of my own to the *Fonds d'assistance aux rescapés du génocide* established by the Rwandan Government.

The Empowerment of Women and Youth

Remarks to Vienna Community
Empowering people in a changing world

VIENNA, 16 FEBRUARY 2012

I t is a great honour for me to be amongst such an influential and informed audience today. *Vielen Dank für diese Ehre. Es ist wunderbar, wieder in Wien zu sein.* There are many words to describe this very beautiful city of Vienna – historic, glorious, dazzling, dynamic. All fit – especially here in the magnificent Hofburg Palace.

But the first word that comes to mind when I think of Vienna is "home". My home, and home of the United Nations. *Ich bin in Wien zu hause.*

I am at home here for many good reasons. Personally, because I spent a couple of unforgettable years in Vienna as an ambassador. It is good to see so many familiar faces and old friends here today. And professionally, because Vienna is a pillar of the United Nations – and an epicentre for global action. You are one of four UN headquarters worldwide. Excluding UN headquarters in New York you are one of three largest UN presences and headquarters worldwide. You host the International Atomic Energy Agency, the UN Office on Drugs and Crime, the UN Industrial Development Organization, and the Preparatory Commission for the Comprehensive Test-Ban Treaty Organization where I served as Chairman a long time ago.

But perhaps most of all, I am at home in Vienna because of your commitment to multilateralism, your ethic of engagement. So it is fitting that we gather here today to talk about empowering people in our changing world.

The national leaders here are working hard to empower your people. But as Secretary-General of the United Nations, I am working to empower all the people around the world. We have 7 billion people. There are billions of underprivileged, marginalized, jobless, hopeless, frustrated people. To empower all these people, particularly women and children and youth – is a top priority and concern for the United Nations.

The time is right for us to discuss this matter. This is a period of global transition.

Economic shocks around the world. Shifts in power and new poles of global growth. The rising threat of climate change. And, of course, a revolution of people-powered change.

Think back at the events and images of the past year. The dramatic transformation which we have observed and witnessed in the Arab world and North Africa. Tahrir Square and the fight for democracy throughout the Arab world. Occupy Wall Street, *los indignados* in Puerta del Sol, protests in Greece.

What was the common thread? Look at the faces in the crowd. They were overwhelmingly women and young people. Women demanding equal opportunity and participation – decision-making participation. Young people worried about their future, fed up with corruption, and speaking out for dignity and decent jobs. Their power and activism turned the tide of history.

Throughout these events, we called on leaders to listen to their people. Listen very carefully what their aspirations, what their challenges are. Some heard – and benefitted. Some never did. Still we are seeing this kind of situation in Syria. And maybe somewhere else.

From the very beginning, I talked with President Assad by telephone and urged him to change before it was too late. Take a bold and decisive moment before it is too late. Instead, he declared war on his own people.

Lack of access has prevented the United Nations, the international community and humanitarian workers from knowing the full toll; yet credible reports indicate at least more than 5,400 people were killed as of last year. We have not been able to have credible information about how many more people have been killed between 1 January and today.

Every day those numbers rise. We see neighbourhoods shelled by tanks. Hospitals used as torture centres. Children as young as ten years old jailed and abused. We see almost certain crimes against humanity.

We cannot predict the future in Syria. We do know this, however: the longer we debate, the more people will die. I commend the efforts of the League of Arab States to find a political solution. During recent days, I have been meeting and speaking with many world leaders; among them today I will meet with the Russian and French Foreign Ministers, and of course the Austrian Foreign Minister and others. Once again, I urge the international community to speak in one voice in a coherent way: stop the violence. Stop the bloodshed.

There is a broader lesson here, beyond Syria. This is very serious, but we have to look at the broader perspective. I believe that every institution and every leader, everywhere, must ask that same question: are we listening? Are we doing enough, fast enough?

I am convinced that we must act now. We face a once-in-a-generation opportunity to empower people in our changing world.

Last month, I briefed the General Assembly on a five-action agenda for the future. I outlined five imperatives for the next five years as Secretary-General.

Sustainable development is at the top of the list. This is critical to empowering people – to eradicating poverty, lifting billions of people from poverty, generating decent jobs, expanding education, and protecting our fragile planet from this ever-warming temperature.

Today, I want to focus on providing women and young people with a greater say in their own destiny and a greater stake in their own dignity. This is fundamental to our entire agenda and crucial to everything we do. I want to talk about this with you – an esteemed audience in all seasons of life.

All of us – women and men, the young and what I might call the "formerly young", have a profound interest in getting this right. Half the world is women – and half the world is under twenty-five years of age. One out of five people are between the ages of fifteen and twenty-four. Nearly 90 per cent of them live in developing countries; nearly one billion live in Asia and Africa. In places like Gaza, three out of four people are under the age of twenty-five. In Iraq, one-quarter of the population was born since the start of the war in 2003 alone.

Some demographers call this a "youth bulge". I am not a big fan of that term. I do not see the largest-ever generation of young people as a "bulge." It is a dividend. It is not a threat; it is an opportunity. To seize it, we must face a new generation of empowerment challenges.

Let us start with empowering women. Around the world, women educate the children; they are the key to healthy families; they are increasingly the entrepreneurs. Wherever I travel, I urge leaders to put more women in genuine decision making roles. More women in the Cabinet. More women in legislatures. More women leading universities. More women on corporate boards. I am very happy to see Dr. Barbara Prammer here, as President of the National Council.

There are very few women speakers, and women leaders. I am counting how many women Ambassadors there are to the United Nations, how many women Heads of State or Heads of Government there are in the world, how many Foreign Ministers are Women. They are 15 to 25 per cent at most. There are nine countries in the world where not a single woman is sitting in the national assembly. I am challenging these nine country leaders, and I think some of them have come up with action plans, quota systems or special measures.

I think that we are making progress. Studies have found that Fortune 500 companies with the highest number of women on the governing boards were far more profitable than those with the fewest number. Today, many look to the world of social media. The majority of those who use it are women – and the Chief Operating Officer of Facebook is a woman. Yet many are asking: Why are there no women on the corporate board of Facebook, Twitter or other young, dynamic companies? I believe that is a fair question.

In my visits around the globe, I always make the case for greater women's representation in Parliaments – including in the Arab world. Some suggest quotas or other action agendas. Then they ask me, why are you focusing on women in national assemblies? We have women Cabinet ministers, women Ambassadors. They are important. But they are appointed. We want women who can really represent the voice of the people, who are elected by the people. The more women we have in the national assemblies, the more women we have in decision-making positions, the better.

There is plenty of evidence that shows how such temporary measures can make a permanent difference. We must not miss this opportunity to write women's rights more deeply into the constitutional and legal framework in the Arab region and beyond. We are also putting women at the core of our efforts to strengthen equality and growth while protecting our planet. Women hold the key to sustainable development. You will hear more about this as we approach the Rio+20 United Nations Conference on Sustainable Development.

> ❝ One out of five people are between the ages of fifteen and twenty-four. Some demographers call this a "youth bulge". I am not a big fan of that term. I do not see the largest-ever generation of young people as a 'bulge.' It is a dividend. ❞

I am committed to doing much more. This morning I emphasized the importance of the Rio+20 Conference on Sustainable Development to President Fischer. I am asking all world leaders to be present at the highest level.

This includes deepening our work to combat violence against women - and expanding women's participation in peacebuilding efforts.

And within the United Nations, I will keep leading by example. I have often been confronted with the question how many senior women we have in the United Nations. In my first five years as Secretary-General, I have nearly doubled the number of women in senior UN positions, at the rank of Assistant Secretary-General and Under-Secretary-General. Our top humanitarian official, high commissioner for human rights, our top development official, our head of management, our top doctor, top lawyer, even our top cop, all are women.

You see a lot of women in the United Nations. This is what I have changed in my first five years. You need to have political will. And we have the largest number of women in UN history – five and counting – leading UN peacekeeping missions and managing thousands of soldiers in the field. From Timor-Leste to South Sudan. From Central Africa to Cyprus to Burundi. When I became Secretary-General, I realized that before I came, during the past sixty-two years, there had been only two women heads of mission. In five years, I have appointed five more, and nine more deputy heads are waiting in line. And at New York headquarters, we have the new UN Women – as you know very well, this is headed by the former President of Chile, Michelle Bachelet.

I am also keenly aware that we have much more to do to empower women within the United Nations. I am determined to keep building on our record. We should focus more, as we have been doing on women, on young people. Window dressing will not do it. Neither will politically expedient band-aids.

Let me tell you what I mean. Not long ago, a Head of State called on the United Nations to establish an International Year on Youth. He claimed he wanted young people to make their voices heard. The bad news is that the leader was President Ben Ali of Tunisia. The good news is, it worked!

A few months into the International Year of Youth, he heard the voice of his country's young people. The protests all started by Mohamed Bouazizi, a young, jobless, frustrated and troubled young person, whose plight encapsulated the burning aspirations of young people. What happened to President Ben Ali? He was forced to leave office because he listened too late. But, once again, we are reminded that we all have an obligation to listen. That is what I do.

I try to meet with young people wherever I go. Those exchanges are some of the toughest, most candid, spirited discussions that I have. Young people everywhere talk about jobs. They want the dignity that comes from decent work. Economic hard times and austerity measures are making it more difficult. The global economic crisis is a global jobs crisis. And youth are hardest hit. Unemployment rates for young people are at record levels – two, three, sometimes even six times the rate for adults.

But joblessness is only part of the story. Many who are working are stuck in low-wage, dead-end work. Many others are finding that their degrees are not always a ticket to jobs. After years of study, they learn a new lesson: their schooling has not equipped them with the tools for today's job market. This must change.

Young people also tell me that they not only want jobs, but also the opportunity to create jobs. So we must do more on entrepreneurship. Austria has much to teach us. You are tackling youth unemployment, just as you are working to address the new requirements of an aging workforce. I am told by President Fischer that Austria has the lowest rate of unemployment in Europe. I congratulate you for that. The Austrian apprenticeship model is the kind of initiative that young people say they would like to see in their own countries. Now is the time to step up our efforts.

Last year, as you know very well, the world's population crossed 7 billion. In five years, it will be 7.5 billion. The world will need 600 million new jobs over the next decade. Without urgent measures to stem the rising tide of youth unemployment, we risk creating a lost generation of wasted opportunities and squandered potential. That is why I pledge that the United Nations will go deeper in identifying the best practices and helping countries deliver on education, skills, training, and job growth for young people.

Still, there are almost 70 million people, 67 million young people, who are out of school, even primary education. That is the second pillar of the Millennium Development Goals, providing primary education to all children.

Economic empowerment and political empowerment go hand-in-hand. Technology, education and awareness are combining to give young people a voice like never before. And they are using it. They are standing up for rights and against dis-crimination based on gender, race and sexual orientation. They are leading the way for sustainable solutions and green development. They are putting inequality on the global agenda.

Our job is to help them build the future they want. Above all, young people have told me they want a seat at the table. They want a real voice in shaping the policies that shape their future. The priorities of young people should be just as prominent in our halls as they are on the streets and squares. They should be just as present in our meeting space as they are in cyberspace.

I am determined to bring the United Nations closer to people and make it more relevant to young people. They are still marginalized and underprivileged. That is one reason we will expand the UN Volunteer Programme. Today, the aver-age age of UN Volunteers is thirty-seven; we will open the doors for young people and are looking for support.

> **❝ I urge leaders to put more women in genuine decision making roles. More women in the Cabinet. More women in legislatures. More women leading universities. More women on corporate boards. ❞**

But that is just the beginning. We must put a special focus where the challeng-es of empowering women and empowering youth come together – and that is in the lives of young women. Young women are potential engines of economic ad-vancement. They are drivers of democratic reform. Yet, far too often a combina-tion of obstacles, including discrimination, social pressure, early marriage, hold them back. These forces set in motion a chain of unequal opportunities that last a lifetime.

Young women must have the tools to participate fully in economic life and to have their voices heard in decision-making at all levels. We have been working to address all these areas at the United Nations. But I am not satisfied. Too often our work has been piecemeal, scattered. The whole is not greater than the sum of the parts. There is a coordination gap. It must be bridged.

That is why I will appoint the first-ever United Nations Special Adviser on Youth. We need a top-to-bottom review so our programmes and policies are work-ing *with* and *for* young people. We need to mobilize coalitions for action. We need to pull the system together so that is pulling for youth. I will ask my Special Advis-er to do just that. We have a choice. Young people can be embraced as partners in shaping their societies, or they can be excluded and left to simmer in frustration and despair.

Let us recognize that addressing the needs and hopes of the world's women and young people is not simply an act of solidarity, it is an act of necessity. We don't have a moment to lose. We have the world to gain.

Here in this beautiful palace, in the Redoutensäle, there is a painting. It covers the length of the entire ceiling - 400 square metres. And in it, the artist included the words of the esteemed Viennese poet, Karl Kraus, and his work Jugend (Youth). An older man reflects on life and the rejuvenating spirit of youth:

"Da schon die Blätter falb, will ich nicht säumen, innen und außerhalb Frühling zu träumen."

"Even as the leaves change, I do not want to miss, inside and outside, dreaming of spring."

We all hold on to our youth. We remember with both sadness and sweetness the moment when the doors of the future opened before us. This is what carries us. This is what rejuvenates us. Let us pass that dream to all the world's youth and women.

Let us hear their voices and let us act in the spirit of spring. We will do much more than empower people. We will empower societies. And we will change our world for good. Let us shape the future we want, let us work together to make this world better for all.

Remarks to the Global Colloquium of University Presidents

Empowering women to change the world

PHILADELPHIA, 4 APRIL 2011

t is a great pleasure to be here, to be invited to talk about one of my top priorities, one of the UN's top priorities.

Let me start by expressing my appreciation to President Amy Gutmann for her contributions and leadership in addressing some of the most delicate challenges of our time - both in her individual capacity and as President of this important institution.

Over the past six years, the Global Colloquium of University Presidents has helped the United Nations generate momentum for change on key global challenges - from migration to climate change, from academic freedom to the role of science in improving the human condition.

At last year's colloquium at Yale, President Gutmann and I talked briefly about what the topic of this year's gathering should be. It was a short conversation because the answer was so obvious to us both that we decided on the spot that this year we would focus on empowering women to change the world.

Indeed, gender equality and women's empowerment are fundamental to the very identity of the United Nations. And universities can play a significant role in advancing this crucial agenda.

Last year the General Assembly agreed to create UN Women - four UN women's organizations merged into one strong entity - designed to deliver on behalf of the world's women.

Last month we hosted the official launch of UN Women in the General Assembly Hall and welcomed its dynamic new head, Michelle Bachelet, the former President of Chile.

We are fortunate indeed to have such a global leader. Tomorrow, Ms. Bachelet will talk to you about her vision for UN Women.

Today I would like to talk more generally about why we need this organization and how your universities - and the world of education in general - can contribute to its success.

We live in exciting times. Worrying, yes. Volatile, yes. But steeped in possibility.

We have only to scan the news headlines to appreciate the scale of the changes sweeping the world.

In Côte d'Ivoire, the international community stood firm for democracy. Late last year, the incumbent president was defeated in free and fair elections, then refused to step down. Women marched in peace to ask him to go. Seven were killed. A million people have been displaced. A thriving economy brought to a standstill. Throughout, the international community has stood firm and steadily increased the pressure. Our peacekeepers are risking their lives to protect civilians throughout the dramatic chapter that is playing out as we speak. Securing a democratic outcome has been costly but is essential.

Africa alone will see sixteen presidential elections in the coming year and six more in 2012. It has been vital for the international community to insist on this fundamental principle.

We see even more dramatic events in North Africa and the Middle East.

Two weeks ago I visited Egypt and Tunisia: two countries where the actions of ordinary men and women have lit a torch throughout a region – a shining light of hope.

Hope of change, of release from years of oppression, stagnation, and neglect of their legitimate aspirations for a better life.

These events have come suddenly, but they should be no surprise. For the past decade, the United Nations Arab Human Development Reports have warned of pressures building to explosion. Now, across the region, people are taking inspiration from each other and calling for change.

From the beginning, I have asked their leaders to listen to the voices of their people. This is something I repeat in every meeting, every phone call I make with leaders throughout the region and beyond. They must engage in genuine dialogue: a national dialogue that respects the hopes and demands of their people, men, and women.

I never fail to discuss with leaders how they can increase gender equality and do more for women's empowerment, women's equal rights. The people who came in their thousands to Tahrir Square in Cairo and, before that, to Bouazizi Square in Tunis – renamed in honour of the vegetable seller whose suicide sparked the protests – were from all walks of life, men, and women.

In conversation after conversation in Cairo and Tunis, women told me that they stood shoulder-to-shoulder with men - standing up for change, for rights, for opportunity.

They expect to take their share in making the revolution succeed, having their fair share of power, making decisions, making policy. I told them that women represent half the population, they hold up half the sky, and should have their fair share in making the decisions that affects their lives and their countries.

I met with many representatives of change in Egypt and Tunisia. Women were always among them. Not always in equal numbers. But always outspoken and eloquent in defence of their aspirations and their rights. To me, this is one of the most significant aspects of what we are seeing in the people's movements in North Africa and the Middle East.

But, as we saw when women and girls marched to Tahrir Square on the 8th of March, and were met with insults and violence from men, there is still a wide gulf between aspiration and reality. This is why we need UN Women. And this is why we need the engagement of all sectors of society – governments, the business sector, communities and individuals, and you, the world of academia.

> ❝ Inequality and discrimination do not only occur in someone else's country or culture. Women and girls experience them everywhere. All the time. ❞

This year marks one hundred years since the first anniversary of International Women's Day. Women's rights have come a long way in the past century – through determined advocacy, practical action, and enlightened policy making. And let me be clear, most of what has been gained has been thanks to the efforts of women themselves.

But, in too many countries and too many societies, women are still second-class citizens, denied fundamental rights, deprived of legitimate opportunity. Too many women, in too many countries, have no other role beyond marrying and producing children at a young age, then taking care of those families.

Although the gender gap in education is closing, far too many girls are still denied schooling, leave prematurely, or complete school with few skills and fewer opportunities. Two-thirds of illiterate adults are female.

In the area of decision-making, we see more women, in more countries, taking their rightful seat in parliament. Yet fewer than 10 per cent of countries have female heads of state or government. In just twenty-eight countries are there more than 30 per cent of women in parliament. Worldwide, on average, only one in six of cabinet ministers is a woman.

And even where women are prominent in politics, they are still severely under-represented at the highest levels of business and industry. Furthermore, in the home and at school, in the workplace and in the community, being female still means being vulnerable. Women and girls continue to endure unacceptable discrimination and violence, often at the hand of intimate partners or relatives. That is why I launched my UNiTE to End Violence Against Women campaign, along with its Network of Men Leaders. And it is why I have appointed a Special Representative on Sexual Violence in Conflict. We are working to end impunity and change mindsets.

But, ladies and gentlemen, as one of the young people I met in Egypt said: "Change came from within and must keep coming from within." Inequality and discrimination do not only occur in someone else's country or culture. Women and girls experience them everywhere. All the time. Even at your universities. It is our job to change that.

When I became Secretary-General there was a lot I needed to learn, and there were things I needed to change in myself and in the organization. This process is still happening. I have increased the number of women in senior leadership posts by more than 40 per cent. One third of my senior management group is now female, including our chief humanitarian coordinator; the head of the UN Development Programme; my legal counsel; and the UN's head of management.

Women are in charge of the World Health Organization and field support for our peacekeepers. My top cop, who runs our international police operation, is a woman.

The heads of our economic commissions in Asia, Latin America and the Arab world are women too. And, of course, the new head of UN Women is a role model to women around the world.

My challenge now is to see the same kind of representation of women throughout middle management. You have a similar challenge. Gender stereotypes and barriers are common throughout academia. In Europe female graduates outnumber men, except in fields such as engineering or technology. Here in the United States, women graduate from Ph.D programmes in roughly the same numbers as men. Yet less than 30 per cent of tenured faculty are female.

There must be reasons for this. Is it because women find it harder to juggle the competing and legitimate demands of pursuing a career and raising a family? Is it because of unspoken prejudices about what women can or should do?

Universities play an important role. They can provide the training in critical thinking that a functional democracy needs. They provide a foundation for the economic and medical research that is so essential to society's well-being. And they supply graduates to the workforce.

So it is essential that this issue of women's rights and women's representation is reflected in your curricula, your appointments, your practices, and your partnerships.

Why, for instance, do your female graduates here in the United States earn less than 75 per cent of their male colleagues?

The actress Geena Davis made a simple eloquent point last month at the launch of UN Women. She said: "If girls can see it, they can be it." Our job is to give girls and young women the inspiration and the tools to be what we know they can be.

For example, in Liberia, we sent an all-female police unit from India. There was an immediate practical benefit - women felt safer and they felt more empowered to complain about the abuse they were enduring. But there was another, unanticipated, consequence. Liberian women queued up to join their own police service. Because they saw it, they knew they could be it.

So, ladies and gentlemen, this is one way you can help us make UN Women a success. You can use your power and partnerships to promote women's empowerment at home.

We know that working for gender equality and women's empowerment is the right thing to do. But often that is not enough. We need to be able to show how it is the smart thing to do. For example, only thirteen of the 500 largest corporations in the world have a female Chief Executive Officer. That is a sad statistic, but is it significant to shareholders? What if they were told that the Fortune 500 companies with the most women on their boards were 53 per cent more profitable than those with the fewest women board members?

The second area where I would like to appeal for your support is in the field of research. As academics, you understand the value of research, and well-constructed arguments. It also lies at the core of much of our work. United Nations reports are cited worldwide. One of them is our report on the World's Women, produced every five years at the request of the 1995 Fourth World Conference on Women. It looks at population patterns, health, education, women in the workplace, women's role in power and decision making, the environment, and women's share of the burden of poverty.

Last year's report lamented the lack of available statistics for many countries, and the fact that many statistics are not comparable because concepts, definitions, methods and the quality of the data vary from country to country. I believe universities can play an important role in changing this story – in helping to generate the data and in building the bridge from information to policy.

Indeed, universities can play a central role in promoting all the UN's goals. This is why I established the UN Academic Impact initiative last year. Today, it has nearly six hundred members from a hundred countries, including universities and other institutions of higher education and research. From this Colloquium, I know that New York University is a member, and I encourage all here to join. Each year, participating organizations undertake an activity that contributes to a UN objective - such as improving access to education, empowering women, or working to improve women's and children's health.

This is another top priority for me, and for UN Women. Too many women still die giving birth to new life. Too many children die from preventable illnesses. Last year, the Millennium Development Goals summit focused attention on the goals on which we are farthest behind: women's and children's health. I was especially encouraged to see Member States, private companies and the philanthropic community pledge $40 billion in support of my global strategy to improve the health of women and children over the next four years. This is important for two reasons:

First, because action on MDGs 4 and 5 – maternal and children's health – has a multiplier effect on all the other MDGs, including poverty reduction, education, gender equality, HIV/AIDS, and environmental sustainability.

Second, because the strategy embodies a new business model. Where once we might have stopped at the creation of a normative and strategic framework, today we are going further. We are facilitating partnerships between actors that have not traditionally worked together. And we are re-shaping UN operations on the ground so that the $40 billion becomes a reality. I urge you to join this effort.

Let me close by returning to where I began. I think it is no coincidence that the revolutionary fervour sweeping North Africa and the Middle East began in Tunisia, and that women played such a role. It was the first country in the Arab world to give women the right to vote. Girls grow up literate. They see women well-represented in professions and parliament. As a result, they have a strong understanding of their fundamental rights.

But, as one woman told me, the status of women is still held back by discrimination, even if it is not held up by law. Her story is not unique. We can find it in every country and every institution represented in this room. But it can change. We can change. But it will take work, just as it will take much work to translate the hopes of the young people I met in North Africa into reality.

The revolutions in Tunisia and Egypt represent one of the greatest opportunities to advance democracy and human rights in a generation. Properly handled, they can become a model for similar transformations across the Arab world and beyond.

But let me say three things, loud and clear.

First, change cannot be resisted forever. Nor should it. To paraphrase John F. Kennedy: "Those who make peaceful change impossible make violent change inevitable". History is not on the side of leaders who insist on clinging to power against the will of their people.

Second, the changes we are seeing must respect the fundamental rights and aspirations of women.

Third, the long-term success of these changes cannot be taken for granted. They need the strong backing of the international community.

If these revolutions are to produce real change for the region, and if our new UN entity for women is to produce real change for women, they need the committed and coordinated support of us all.

As I say, again and again, wherever I go, when I meet women young and old: Now is your moment. Seize it!

Remarks to ministerial meeting of the Security Council on resolution 1325

NEW YORK, 25 SEPTEMBER 2010

Welcome to this conference and thank you all for being here today. I thank the Permanent Mission of Canada for taking the lead in organizing this event.

In a month, we will mark the tenth anniversary of Security Council resolution 1325. This landmark resolution raised awareness of the unique and grave issues that women and girls face during and after conflict. It has undoubtedly increased international commitment to address the issue.

We can point to some successes. In countries like Afghanistan and Burundi, we have supported women's participation in post-war constitutional reform. In others, like Timor Leste and Sierra Leone, we have helped to raise the proportion of women in the security forces.

> ❝ We must put women at the front and centre of peace processes – in negotiation and mediation, post-conflict governance and reconstruction. Women's issues are not an add-on. They must be an integral part of all our thinking on peace and security. ❞

But this tenth anniversary is a sombre occasion. Our achievements over the past decade have not met our own expectations. Women are still excluded from peace processes. The security sector in most countries is still dominated by men. When conflicts end, and international aid begins to come in, it is still not geared to the needs of girls and women. And – most tragically and strikingly – women and girls still suffer gender-based violence, including systematic sexual attacks, in and around armed conflict.

The international community is still failing to protect the most vulnerable – as we saw recently in the Democratic Republic of the Congo. The results of this violence, for the victims and their communities, are devastating, and can last for years or decades. And those who carry out these war crimes still generally go unpunished.

This issue is of such grave concern and urgency that the Security Council has passed two further resolutions on it, and I have appointed a Special Representative on Sexual Violence in Conflict, Ms. Margot Wallström, to make sure that it gets consistent high-level attention.

How, then, can we turn the corner? As the tenth anniversary approaches, we must move beyond rhetoric. I suggest some concrete commitments.

- Above all, we must end the brutal and blatant violations of the bodies of women and girls during armed conflict and its aftermath.
- We must put women at the front and centre of peace processes – in negotiation and mediation, post-conflict governance and reconstruction.
- We must create and implement the right laws, so that those who carry out such crimes are brought to justice.
- We must develop national action plans to implement resolution 1325. So far, only nineteen countries have done this.
- We must review progress against reliable indicators.

But all these commitments will not make the difference we need without increased resources. Civil society groups cannot plan and implement their programmes when funding is not enough, or is unreliable because of donors' shifting priorities. I urge those with the power to mobilize resources for this work to do so.

For my part, I will make sure that the United Nations system takes a more coherent, comprehensive and measurable approach to implementing resolution 1325. And I will continue to work for women's empowerment, through all the means at the UN's disposal. The newly-created UN Women, under the leadership of Michelle Bachelet, will bring women's perspectives into all our work.

Women's issues are not an add-on. They must be an integral part of all our thinking on peace and security. Women are not only the victims of war. They must play a key role in bringing peace.

Launch of the UNiTE Network of Men Leaders To End Violence Against Women

NEW YORK, 24 NOVEMBER 2009

Today we mark the International Day for the Elimination of Violence Against Women.

One year ago, I launched my Campaign "UNiTE to End Violence against Women." Our Campaign is helping to galvanize action across the UN system. More than five million people have signed the Say No to Violence Against Women initiative under the Unite campaign. The UN's Stop Rape Now initiative is bringing people together to declare that rape as a tactic of war will not be tolerated. Alliances and partnerships are being built with broad networks of civil society and faith-based organizations. The entire UN system is striving to work as one.

In launching this campaign, I acted not only as the Secretary-General of the United Nations, but as a son, a husband, a father, a grandfather. I called on governments, women's organizations, faith-based groups, young people, the private sector, artists, the media, the entire UN system and all individuals to join forces.

> **66 Violence against women and girls will not be eradicated until all of us - men and boys - refuse to tolerate it. 99**

Together, we must raise public awareness and boost political will and resources to prevent and address all forms of violence against women and girls.

Some 70 percent of women experience in their lifetime some form of physical or sexual violence from men – the majority from husbands, intimate partners or someone they know. This is unacceptable.

All of us here know that unless we change our attitudes and behaviour, violence against women will continue. We must act together. We must build on the efforts of so many women and women's organizations who have worked tirelessly to address this epidemic. We must continue to widen the circle of engagement. After all, just as women's rights are human rights, women's issues are people's issues.

That is why today I am launching a dedicated Network of Men Leaders. This Network will consist of men – young and old – who have pledged to work to end violence against women and girls. These men will add their voices to the growing global chorus for action. Each has pledged to take concrete steps in his community of influence and create partnerships with women to end this violence.

As I launch this Network, I call on men and boys everywhere to join us. Break the silence. When you witness violence against women and girls, do not sit back. Act. Advocate. Unite to change the practices and attitudes that incite, perpetrate and condone this violence.

Violence against women and girls will not be eradicated until all of us – men and boys – refuse to tolerate it. Together let us make that pledge.

There are many positive examples of men taking action. Judges whose decisions paved the way to fight abuse in the workplace. Organizations that have begun networks of men who counsel male perpetrators of violence. National leaders who have publicly committed to leading the movement of men to break their silence. The White Ribbon Campaign whose members pledge never to commit or condone violence.

The list is growing, but it is not long enough. Everyone can do something.

For my part, I commit to doing everything in my power to ensure the success of this fight. Within and outside the United Nations, I will continue to use my Campaign to highlight the issues.

Today, I ask you to join us in your own unique way. I thank all of you for taking part. Through this Network, let us, once and for all, end violence against women and girls.

Remarks on UNiTE to End Violence Against Women

NEW YORK, 5 MARCH 2009

One year ago, I launched a campaign calling on people and governments the world over to unite to end violence against women and girls. We called it "UNiTE to End Violence against Women". And unite we must.

It is sometimes said that women are weavers and men are too often warriors. Women bear and care for our children. In much of the world they plant the crops that feed us. They weave the fabric of our societies.

Violence against women is thus an attack on all of us, on the foundation of our civilization. It destroys health and perpetuates poverty. It strikes against equality and empowerment. It contributes to the spread of HIV/AIDS and other diseases.

❝❝ Violence against women cannot be tolerated, in any form, in any context, in any circumstance, by any political leader or by any government. ❞❞

Worldwide, one in five women suffer rape or attempted rape. In some countries, as many as one in three women are beaten, forced into sex or otherwise abused. This is alarming and shocking. This must stop.

As you know, I have just returned from the Democratic Republic of Congo. There I visited the HealAfrica hospital in Goma. As you know too, sexual violence and abuse is prevalent throughout the country. I met a young woman there, in the hospital. She was just eighteen years old. Fleeing the fighting that destroyed her village, she was raped by four soldiers at gunpoint. Doctors at the hospital can repair her wounds. But can even doctors heal her soul?

She suffers not only from physical injury; she also bears the curse of stigma. She has been ostracized from her village and her family, from a false sense of shame. I was shocked by what she told me. I was saddened almost beyond expression. I was also very, very angry.

These women need medical care. They need to be accepted back into their communities and families. Above all they need to be able to live free of fear.

I spoke forcefully about this when I met President Kabila. I spoke to the commander of the Congolese forces in the eastern Democratic Republic of the Congo, as well as with the governor and the local authorities.

I spoke about it to everyone I met, and I will keep speaking out against such unspeakable atrocities.

When I was meeting President Kabila, I told him that the fact that 80 per cent of sexual violence was perpetuated by the other armed groups of rebels was not an excuse. As a leader of the country – a sovereign leader of a sovereign country – wherever sexual violence may happen, then he must be responsible.

Violence against women is an abomination. It stands against everything in the United Nations Charter. The consequences of violence go beyond the visible and immediate. Death, injury, medical costs and lost employment are but the tip of an iceberg. The impact on women and girls, their families, their communities and their societies in terms of shattered lives and livelihoods is beyond calculation.

Far too often, these crimes go unpunished. Perpetrators walk free. No country, no culture, no woman, young or old, is immune from these injustices.

Women have been speaking out against violence, and supporting each other in opposing it, for a long time. Often they have found a voice through the work of the United Nations system.

Increasingly, men are speaking out. Global examples include the White Ribbon Campaign and the V-Day Campaign's "V-Men" counterpart. In many countries, at workshops and community meetings, men are teaching other men that there is another way: that real men don't hit women, let alone rape them. That real men respect women.

Allow me to tell a brief story from a gender workshop in a rural community in South Africa. An older man, a leader of the community, who had sat quietly through the proceedings, raised his hand to speak. The facilitator's heart sank, because she did not know what he would say. She knew this man, this leader, had the power to sink the workshop. Older men are, normally in Africa, deeply respected in rural communities. The facilitator worried that the man was going to deliver a lecture on how it was against African culture to think of men and women as equals. That giving women power could divide families.

"Yesterday, when I got home", the man began, "I called my sons. I called my wife. And I explained what we are doing in this workshop." He told his children that things had to change now. No longer could their mother come home tired from a long day of work and be expected to cook, clean and wash the dishes. From now on, he told his children, "You have to start cleaning and tidying the house. You have to start the dinner, so when your mother comes home she can see that we have all helped." As for the man himself, he said, "I will wash the dishes."

This is the moment of change. The point of the workshop was that we are not born knowing what it means to be a man. We learn it from the people around us. And because it is something society has decided on, it can also be changed by society.

In closing, let me speak bluntly. We must unite. Violence against women cannot be tolerated, in any form, in any context, in any circumstance, by any political leader or by any government. The time to change is now. Only by standing together and speaking out can we make a difference. On this International Women's Day, let us resolve to do that.

Remarks to the General Assembly on gender equality and the empowerment of women

NEW YORK, 6 MARCH 2007

I am honoured to be with you for this debate on a crucial subject, two days before International Women's Day.

Achieving gender equality and empowering women is a goal in itself. It is also a condition for building healthier, better educated, more peaceful and more prosperous societies.

When women are fully empowered and engaged, all of society benefits. Only in this way can we successfully take on the enormous challenges confronting our world – from conflict resolution and peacebuilding to fighting AIDS and reaching all the other Millennium Development Goals.

There are countless studies that tell us that this is so. Leaders at the 2005 World Summit declared that gender equality and human rights for all are essential to advancing development, peace and security.

But while we have in place global goals and commitments on gender equality and women's empowerment, we still have far to go in implementing them fully – from school enrolment to women's economic independence and representation in decision-making bodies.

In almost all countries, women continue to be under-represented in decision-making positions. Women's work continues to be undervalued, underpaid, or not paid at all. Out of more than 100 million children who are not in school, the majority are girls. Out of more than 800 million adults who cannot read, the majority are women.

Worst of all, violence against women and girls continues unabated in every continent, country and culture. It takes a devastating toll on women's lives, on their families, and on society as a whole. Most societies prohibit such violence – yet the reality is that too often, it is covered up or tacitly condoned.

Changing this requires all of us – women and men – to work for enduring change in values and attitudes. That means transforming relations between women and men, at all levels of society. It means working in partnership – Governments, international organizations, civil society and the private sector. It means men assuming their responsibility. It means ensuring that women and girls enjoy their full rights, and take up their rightful place in society.

It means moving forward on several fronts at once:
- Ensuring that men take on a greater role in household and family care;
- Challenging traditions and customs, stereotypes and harmful practices, that stand in the way of women and girls;
- Ensuring that women have access to education and healthcare, property and land;
- Investing in infrastructure to reduce time burdens for women and girls;
- Promoting human rights and security, including freedom from violence;
- Integrating gender issues into the follow-up to UN resolutions and decisions – including the work of recently established bodies such as the Peacebuilding Commission and the Human Rights Council.

> **Achieving gender equality and empowering women is a goal in itself. It is also a condition for building healthier, better educated, more peaceful and more prosperous societies.**

For my part, as you know, I have made gender balance a fundamental consideration in shaping my senior management team, which of course includes Dr. Asha-Rose Migiro as my very able Deputy Secretary-General.

I pledge to work for a collaborative and coordinated approach to gender perspectives – one that involves and engages the entire UN system in supporting Member States' work for gender equality and the empowerment of women.

On that score, I know you have been studying proposals to strengthen the UN's gender architecture, as presented by the High-level Panel on United Nations System-wide Coherence. I hope you will consider the possibility of replacing several current structures with one dynamic UN entity, focused on gender equality and women's empowerment. Such an entity should mobilize forces of change at the global level, and inspire enhanced results at the country level.

Excellencies, distinguished delegates, I look forward to working with all of you in the years ahead, in this cause that embraces all humankind.

Glossary of abbreviations and acronyms

AMISOM	African Union Mission in Somalia
ASEAN	Association of Southeast Asian Nations
AU	African Union
CARICOM	Caribbean Community
CERF	Central Emergency Response Fund
ECOWAS	Economic Community of West African States
ESCAP	Economic and Social Commission for Asia and the Pacific
ESCWA	Economic and Social Commission for Western Asia
FAO	Food and Agriculture Organization of the United Nations
g7+	Group of fragile and conflict-affected countries
G-8	Group of Eight, a forum of eight of the largest world's economies
G-20	Group of Twenty, a forum of twenty major economies
IAEA	International Atomic Energy Agency
ICC	International Criminal Court
IFAD	International Fund for Agricultural Development
IMF	International Monetary Fund
IPCC	Intergovernmental Panel on Climate Change
MDGs	Millennium Development Goals
MINUSTAH	United Nations Stabilization Mission in Haiti
NATO	North Atlantic Treaty Organisation
NGO/NGOs	Non-Governmental Organization(s)
OECD	Organisation for Economic Co-operation and Development
P5+1	Permanent members of the United Nations Security Council (China, France, Russia, the United Kingdom and United States) plus Germany; grouping formed for diplomatic efforts related to Iran's nuclear programme

R2P	Responsibility to Protect
Rio+20	United Nations Conference on Sustainable Development, Rio de Janeiro, 2012
SDGs	Sustainable Development Goals
START	Strategic Arms Reduction Treaty
SUN	Scaling Up Nutrition initiative
TFG	Transitional Federal Government (Somalia)
UN	United Nations
UNAIDS	Joint United Nations Programme on HIV/AIDS
UNAMA	United Nations Assistance Mission in Afghanistan
UNCA	United Nations Correspondents Association
UNDP	United Nations Development Programme
UNESCO	United Nations Educational, Scientific and Cultural Organization
UNFCCC	United Nations Framework Convention on Climate Change
UNHCR	Office of the United Nations High Commissioner for Refugees
UNICEF	United Nations Children's Fund
UNIFIL	United Nations Interim Force in Lebanon
UNRWA	United Nations Relief and Works Agency for Palestine Refugees in the Near East
UNSCO	Office of the United Nations Special Coordinator for the Middle East Peace Process
UNSMIL	United Nations Support Mission in Libya
UNSMIS	United Nations Supervision Mission in Syria
WFP	World Food Programme

Credits

Photos

Cover	UN Photo/Helena Mulkerns. Afghanistan Observes 2007 International Peace Day. Photo digitally manipulated
pp. iv-v	UN Photo/Eskinder Debebe. Secretary-General Addresses Press Conference
p. vi	UN Photo/Mark Garten. Secretary-General Makes Condolence Calls after Mazar-i-Sharif Attack
pp. 1	UN Photo/Mark Garten. General Debate of the 66th General Assembly Session
pp. 46-47	UN Photo/Mark Garten. Unexploded Ordnance Destroyed by UN Demining Battalion in Lebanon
p.133	UN Photo/Mark Garten. Mother and Child at Community Clinic in Rural Bangladesh
pp. 134-135	UN Photo/Evan Schneider. Bantantinti Village, Senegal Mission
pp. 178-179	UN Photo/Mark Garten. View of Polar Ice Rim
pp. 198-199	UN Photo/Stuart Price. African Union Troops in Kismayo, South Somalia
p. 271	UN Photo/Albert Gonzalez Farran. UNAMID peacekeeper in Abu Shouk camp for Internally Displaced Persons (North Darfur)
pp. 272-273	UN Photo/Evan Schneider. Tanzania Mission
p. 291	UN Photo/Stuart Price. Djiboutian contingent of the African Union Mission in Somalia, Civilians in Belet Weyen
pp. 292-293	UN Photo/Mark Garten United Nations Relief Food Arrives in Lebanese Town
pp. 302-303	UN Photo/Tim Page. Afghanistan Holds Presidential and Provincial Council Elections
pp. 336-337	UN Photo/Evan Schneider. Women in Rural Senegalese Community Attend Classes
p. 359	UN Photo/Albert Gonzalez Farran. UNAMID opens new schools and a clinic in Kuma Garadayat, North Darfur

Design   Guido Caroti